# WHO OWNS SCOTLAND

## ANDY WIGHTMAN

CANONGATE

First published in the United Kingdom in 1996 by
Canongate Books, 14 High Street,
Edinburgh EH1 1TE

© Andy Wightman, 1996

Andy Wightman has asserted his right
under the Copyright, Designs and Patents Act, 1988
to be identified as the author of this work

Maps created by Mega Ram,
Portree, Isle of Skye
© Crown copyright

Design by James Hutcheson

A CIP catalogue record for this book
is available from the British Library

ISBN 0 86241 585 3

Typeset by Palimpsest Book Production Limited,
Polmont, Stirlingshire
Printed by Butler and Tanner, Frome.

This book is dedicated
to Cathy
and

to the memory of John McEwen
1887–1992

# Contents

| | | |
|---|---|---|
| | List of Tables and Boxes | viii |
| | Foreword | ix |
| | Preface | xi |
| | Acknowledgements | xii |
| | Abbreviations | xv |
| | Introduction | 1 |

## SECTION I

| | | |
|---|---|---|
| 1 | The Development of Feudalism | 5 |
| 2 | Landownership in Scotland Today | 12 |

## SECTION II

| | | |
|---|---|---|
| 3 | Who Owns Scotland | 19 |
| 4 | Availability of Information | 21 |
| 5 | The Research Process | 26 |
| 6 | The Tables and Maps | 29 |
| 7 | The Pattern and the People | 142 |
| 8 | Agriculture | 169 |
| 9 | The Sporting Estate | 171 |
| 10 | Forestry | 174 |
| 11 | Crofting | 179 |
| 12 | The Conservation Landowners | 182 |
| | Conclusions | 186 |

## SECTION III

| | | |
|---|---|---|
| 13 | International Comparisons | 189 |
| 14 | Land Reform and the Landownership Debate | 192 |
| 15 | Debunking the Myths | 197 |
| 16 | Opportunities for Change | 202 |
| 17 | Towards a Land Reform Agenda | 204 |
| | Conclusions | 216 |
| | References | 219 |
| | Appendix 1 A Cadastral Land Register | 225 |
| | Appendix 2 Multiple Proprietors | 227 |
| | Appendix 3 Directors of Companies | 231 |
| | Appendix 4 SOAEFD Holdings | 234 |
| | Appendix 5 SNH Holdings | 236 |
| | Appendix 6 MoD Holdings | 237 |

# List of Tables and Boxes

## Tables

| | | |
|---|---|---|
| 1. | How Scotland is owned 1995 | 157 |
| 2. | Distribution of Landholdings by size class 1970 and 1995 | 158 |
| 3. | Concentration of Land Ownership in Scotland 1970 and 1995 | 158 |
| 4. | Analysis of Acreage Covered by Estates Larger than 5000 Acres in 12 Largest Counties 1995 | 159 |
| 5. | Top 100 non-public Landowners in Scotland 1970–1995 | 160 |
| 6. | Top 20 Aristocratic Landowners in Scotland 1995 | 162 |
| 7. | Principal Not for Profit Landowners in Scotland 1995 | 162 |
| 8. | Extent of Forestry Commission Estate in Scotland 1970–1995 | 163 |
| 9. | The 25 largest overseas landowners in Scotland 1995 | 164 |
| 10. | 10 Top Investment Landowners in Scotland 1995 | 165 |
| 11. | Company and Trust Ownership (Estates Larger than 5000 acres) 1995 | 165 |
| 12. | Scottish Landowners' Federation membership 1975 | 165 |
| 13. | Scottish Landowners' Federation membership 1994 | 166 |
| 14. | Scottish Landowners' Federation membership by county 1994 | 167 |
| 15. | The 30 Wealthiest Landowners in Scotland 1996 | 168 |
| 16. | Top Forestry Investors in Scotland 1995 | 177 |
| 17. | Top 20 Forestry Grant Recipients 1993 | 178 |
| 18. | Conservation landowners in Scotland 1995 | 186 |

## Boxes

| | | |
|---|---|---|
| 1. | A Characterisation of Scottish Landownership | 145 |
| 2. | Danish Interest in Scottish Land | 148 |
| 3. | The Strange Case of Mar Lodge | 184 |

# Foreword

THIS IS A most remarkable and very timely book. It is remarkable in the thoroughness of its research, the scope of its recommendations and the breadth of its vision. It is timely in that its appearance coincides with a growing conviction, right across Scotland, that action both can and must be taken to reform the means by which our country regulates and controls the ownership of land.

As Andy Wightman comments, we have long been in the habit in Scotland of bemoaning the more obvious excesses of our current landownership system. Newspaper libraries bulge with condemnatory articles about the way in which this or that community has had its prospects blighted as a result of finding its entire future dependent on the whims of the crook, the charlatan or the speculator who has become its laird. And as each new scandal comes along, there is never any lack of politicians, local or national, to denounce its perpetrators and to declare that such a thing must never be permitted to happen again.

But it has happened again. And it will happen again. And again. And again. It will go on happening, in fact, until Scots, nationally and collectively, set the ownership of land on a new legislative basis.

This book makes a major contribution to ensuring that reform is achieved. Andy Wightman sets out more comprehensively than has ever been done before some of the basic facts about the ownership of Scotland. He contrasts our arcane and archaic land laws with the quite different legal structures which other European democracies long ago put in place to deal with land, its ownership, its occupation and its use. He demonstrates that altering the means by which we inject public money into rural areas will be every bit as vital a component of an overall reform process as altering the laws which govern the sale and purchase of estates. And he is all the time both cool and even-handed in his approach to a subject which has tended to generate more emotion than rational thought.

A wide variety of individuals and organisations have legitimate interests in the Scottish countryside. And it is by no means the least impressive characteristic of Andy Wightman's book that it is never one-sided in its advocacy of change. The book is critical of private landlords, certainly. But it is critical, too, of state bureaucracies, such as the Forestry Commission and the Scottish Office Agriculture, Environment and Fisheries Department, whose performance as landowners has so often been so disappointingly unenlightened and unimaginative. If Andy Wightman is properly suspicious of the notion that the state is automatically to be preferred to the private owner, he does not identify unreservedly with any other single group. He questions the wisdom of permitting environmental organisations to buy up more and more of the Scottish countryside. And while he welcomes the prospect of crofting communities taking over the ownership of crofting estates, he comments – correctly – that crofters have been notably reluctant to tackle manifest crofting abuses such as absentee tenancy.

In the months preceding this book's publication, government – particularly in the person of Mr Michael Forsyth, the Secretary of State for Scotland – has, for the first time in many years, indicated an interest in bringing about changes in Scotland's landownership structure. Mr Forsyth has made clear that he is prepared to transfer state-owned crofting estates to their crofter occupants. He has also made clear – and this is more significant because of the much higher capital values involved – that he is prepared to transfer at least one substantial block of Forestry Commission land, at Laggan, to a community group. These are welcome and significant initiatives. But they represent no more than the first steps along the road which this book maps out – a road along which we are going to have to travel quite some distance if we are to capitalise on the huge opportunities now available to the Scottish countryside.

It is important to remember, in this connection, that rural communities do not consist exclusively – and certainly will not so consist in the future – of farmers, foresters, crofters and other land-users of that kind. Such people, for obvious reasons, will always be important in the countryside. But when the owners of sporting estates, for example, react to Andy Wightman's book – as some of them, no doubt, will react – by saying that there is no economically viable alternative to such estates, it is important that we tell them categorically and bluntly that they are wrong.

I live on Skye which is wholly rural and which has had, for 10 or 15 years now, one of Britain's fastest-growing populations – in percentage terms at any rate. This population growth – like the very similar population growth which has affected much of the West Highland mainland and other islands such as Mull – is a result of the fact that more and more people simply wish to live, work and do business in rural areas. It is with repopulation of this sort, not with a wholly anachronistic reliance on blood sports, that the future of rural Scotland lies.

We have it in our power today to ensure that our rural areas – for far too long associated with depopulation and decay – become central to our nation's future. And we will have carefully to balance many interests – agricultural, environmental and all the rest – as we move forward. But we will certainly have to start by undertaking the comprehensive land reforms which – alone in Europe – we have so far dodged, shirked and evaded.

Andy Wightman has shown us what is wrong and made a series of perfectly feasible suggestions as to how we might begin to put things right. His book will be much debated. But it will also, I hope, be a stimulus to action – not least on the part of Scotland's politicians who, in the end, are the only people able to enact the reforms which are so desperately overdue.

*James Hunter*

# Preface

IT IS LUDICROUS that as we approach the close of the twentieth century, we know less today about the pattern of landownership in Scotland than we did 100 years ago, the last time an official survey was conducted. Continuing ignorance can only lead to ill-informed opinion and ineffective government. Amazed and frustrated at the lack of information on the fundamental question of who owns Scotland, I decided to write this book.

The purpose of the book is threefold. Firstly it is to provide a comprehensive, accurate and up to date account of the pattern of landownership in Scotland – who owns Scotland. Secondly it is to review how we got here in the first place and to analyse many of the issues surrounding landownership, some of which tend to be poorly understood. Its final purpose is to provide a critique of the current system and pattern of landownership in Scotland and outline an agenda for land reform.

It is thus a contribution to stimulating and informing interest in a subject which lies at the very heart of how the people of Scotland relate to their country and how they will enter the next millennium – as a society with a firm grip over its future or as a society drifting past the kind of opportunities that could transform the lives of everyone fortunate enough to live in a country of immense potential.

# Acknowledgements

THIS BOOK HAS only been made possible by the generosity of many people.

I am indebted to many friends and colleagues for their support and encouragement during the evolution of this book. I am particularly grateful in this respect to Graham Boyd and Robin Callander for their advice, hospitality and encouragement over the past year, as well as to many others including Jim Hunter, Frank Rennie, Drennan Watson and Adam Watson for stimulating and sustaining my interest in the subject.

Gratitude is also due to The Konrad Zweig Trust for its critical financial support at the outset without which the project would probably not have got off the ground.

The information on who owns Scotland was obtained from a wide range of sources. For some areas of Scotland, research and analysis had already been carried out and I am particularly grateful to Ralph Pickering in Dumfries, Brian Smith in Shetland and John Campbell from Skye for the comprehensive information provided for the south west of Scotland, for Shetland and for Skye.

I would also like to thank the many people employed by government agencies and private estates who gave me time and help in strict confidence. They cannot be named due to the likely adverse reaction of their employers but they know who they are.

Public agencies which were helpful in providing information include the Red Deer Commission, the Forestry Commission, the Ministry of Defence, Scottish Natural Heritage and the Scottish Office Agriculture, Environment and Fisheries Department. Thanks are also due to staff of various local authorities in Scotland who kindly supplied information on their landholdings, in particular Borders Regional Council, Ettrick and Lauderdale District Council, Grampian Regional Council, Lothian Regional Council, Tayside Regional Council and Strathclyde Regional Council.

Tayside Regional Council and Borders Regional Council also very kindly donated copies of their 1994 valuation rolls saving me much time and effort.

I am grateful to staff at the Crown Estate, National Trust for Scotland, Royal Society for the Protection of Birds and Scottish Wildlife Trust for the provision of information on their landholdings.

I would also like to thank the staff of the National Libraries of Scotland, the Scottish Records Office and the Registers of Scotland for their high standards of service. I am particularly grateful to the Keeper of the Registers of Scotland for access to the Register of Sasines and to his staff for the courteous and positive way in which they helped.

Over the course of researching the book, I was fortunate to receive the help and advice of many informative and enthusiastic individuals including:

Robin Ade, Bob Aitken, Neal Ascherson, Eric Baird, Iain Brodie, Kevin Cahill, Professor Tony Carty, Reay Clarke, Eoin Cox, Andrew Currie, John Digney, Geoffrey Dunlop, Bill Fernie, Hugh Fife, Dr Michael Foxley, Simon Fraser, Peter Gibb, Rob Gibson, Rosemary Green, Ron Greer, George Gunn, Shirley-Anne Hardy, Raymond

Henderson, George Holden, Andy Inglis, Alyne Jones, Alastair Lavery, Alan Law, Alistair Lawson, Mark Leishman, Mairi MacArthur, Norman MacAskill, Calum Macdonald MP, Patricia & Angus Macdonald, Bob McGowan, Professor Bryan MacGregor, Margot MacGregor, Duncan MacInnes, Alastair McIntosh, Alistair MacIver, John Mackay, John Kenneth Mackay, Robert McLennan, Kenneth Macleod, Angus MacLeod of Fyffe Contractors in Stornoway, Donald MacLeod, Dr George Macleod, Maxwell MacLeod, Neil MacKenzie, Rennie McOwan, Isobel, Madeline & Pat MacPhail, Allan MacRae, Kathleen Marshall, Dr Sandy Mather, Stewart Murray, Alaistar Nicolson, Alasdair Nicholson, Jane O'Donovan, John Parrot, Simon Pepper, Bernard & Emma Planterose, Derek Pretswell, Frank Rennie, Ian Richardson, Lesley Riddoch, Bill Ritchie, Graeme Robertson, John Rogerson, Roger Sandilands, Alastair Scott, Michael Scott, Ian Sillars, John Campbell Smith, Jean Stevenson, Tom Strang, Alec Sutherland, Kenny Taylor, Andrew Thompson, Camilla Toulmin, Roy Turnbull, Adam Watson, Graham White, Brian Wilson and Brian Wilson MP.

Particular acknowledgement is given to the many landowners and land agents who happily responded to my enquiries and in some cases provided much additional help. I am grateful for the time they took to edit maps and clarify ownership details. Their cooperation was sought and obtained in the interests of publishing accurate information. Their collaboration should not in any way be interpreted by them or anyone else as an endorsement of views expressed in this book. I hope they will, having read the book, still support the primary purpose to which their help has been put, namely the publication of accurate information on who owns Scotland.

Ralph Abel Smith; David Allingham; John R. Anderson; William Anderson, Managed Estates; R.G. Angus; Trustees of Sir Ralph H. Anstruther; J.K.O. Arbuthnott; Duke of Atholl; Lord Balgonie; John Ballantyne; E. Bates, Forglen Estate (Hong Kong) Ltd; George Bell; J.S. Blackett, Invercauld Estates; Blair Wilson & Co; Judy Bowser; J. & Mrs M.H. Brims; Graham Brown; Duke of Buccleuch & Michael Clarke, Buccleuch Estates Ltd; David Buchan; Burnett & Reid; Earl of Cadogan; Robert Campbell; Donald & Mrs M. Carmichael; Sir James A. Cayzer; Keith Chalmers-Watson; M.J. Chapman, Moray Estates Development Company; Sir Charles R. Connell; James R. Cordiner; John Davies; Jean Denham; Andrew Dingwall-Fordyce; Robin Dixon, Scottish Woodlands Ltd; William Drummond Moray; Mary Dudgeon; Trustees of Sir George Duff-Dunbar; Sir Archibald R. Dunbar of Northfield; Ileene & Neil Duncan; Sir Archibald B.C. Edmonstone Bt; Anthony Elvy; Captain C.A. Farquharson; Peter Ferguson; Alexander Fergusson; Duke of Fife & David Finlay; Mrs Filmer-Sankey; J.R. Fleming, Douglas & Angus Estates; Robert Fleming; Sir Andrew G. Forbes-Leith Bt; A.W. Gilby; R.R. Gledson, Wemyss and March Estates; Sir William Gladstone; Andrew Gordon; D.S. Gordon; L.A. & P.M. Gordon-Duff; C.A.H. Gow, Southesk Estate; Heather Gray; H.I.T. Gunn; Earl of Haddo; William Halliday; Helen B. Hamilton; D.F. Harbottle, Faccombe Estates Ltd; P.A. Hardie & the Marquis of Lothian; Jill Hardy; Andrew Harmsworth; Captain John Hay of Delagatie; Herbst Peat & Energy Scotland; Richard I. Holman-Baird; Andrew Howard, The MacRobert Trust; Edward C.M. Humphrey; George Hunter & Sir A.R.J. Buchanan-Jardine; Thomas Innes of Learney; Henry & Hazel Irvine-Fortescue; Francis Irving; Brian Ivory; D.R.M. James Duff; Jenners Ltd; L.H. Johnson; Alasdair Laing; B.C.G. Laughton; Cluttons; Earl of Leven; Captain Kenneth

Lumsden of Banchory; Robin Malcolm; Earl of Mansfield; Charles Marsham, C.A. Matheson, Sale & Partners; Angus C. Macalister of Glenbarr; Archibald D. McDiarmid; Sam & Evelyn Macdonald; J.I.H. Macdonald-Buchanan; A.H. Macdonald Lockhart; Alpin F. Macgregor of Cardney; Jamie McGrigor; John Mackenzie of Gairloch; Alan McLean; Sir Fitzroy Maclean; Catherine & John MacPherson; A.C.S. & E.M.S. Macphie; J.H.J. McQueen; N.N. Mellish, Bute Estates Ltd; Trustees of W.N. Graham Menzies; R.P.W. Millar; Michael Milligan, Smith Milligan; Susan Milton; Clarence G.S. Munro; Donald Munro, Skibo Ltd; Roderick H.W. Munro; James Murray Usher; Messrs W. & R. Palmer; Emma Paterson; Gillian Pattinson; Roy P. Petrie; Major General C.A. Ramsay; Paul Ramsay; Richard Ratcliffe; J.H. Richmond-Watson; G.A. Robertson, Cawdor Estates; Joylon & S.W. Robinson; John Rose-Miller; D. Rothwell, Hoddom & Kinmount Estates; Ian de Sales la Terriere; Lady Saltoun; Andrew Salveson; Ewen Scobie; John & Wendy Scott; M.C. Scott; Robert W.L. Scott, Abercorn Estates; Earl of Southesk; H. Shaw-Stewart; J.M. Sinclair; I.J. Spencer Thomas; J.T.K. Short, Luss Estates Company; E. Geraldine P. Simpson; Calum Sinclair; Bartholomew E.E. Smith; J.M. Smith, Dupplin Estate; David M.A. Smythe; D.A. Stancioff; Gordon Stewart; Robert Steuart Fothringham; J.D. Stormonth-Darling; Sir Iain Tennant; Sarah Troughton; Roy Tylden-Wright; Richard Tyser; Frank J. Usher of Dunglass; Peter Voy, Assynt Estates; C.D.R. Whittle, R.&R. Urquhart WS; Major William Warde-Aldam; Bill Williams, Williamston Estates Ltd; Dr Catherine Wills; John Wilson; Mrs Robert Wolrige Gordon of Esslemont; Angela Yeoman.

I am very grateful to Jamie, Hugh, Neville, Sheila and all the staff at Canongate Books for their faith, encouragement and support. It was a pleasure to work with a revitalised publisher with such a catholic interest in Scottish publishing. Thanks also to George McKechnie, Harry Reid and Ian Wilson at *The Herald* for their support.

Finally this book would have been impossible to complete without the freedom to spend most of 1995 working on it. My greatest debt is to Cathy to whom this book is dedicated for her love, tolerance and support.

# *Abbreviations*

Abbreviations commonly used in the text include:

| | |
|---|---|
| CAP | Common Agricultural Policy |
| CEC | Crown Estate Commissioners |
| EU | European Union |
| FC | Forestry Commission |
| HIDB | Highlands and Islands Development Board |
| JMT | John Muir Trust |
| LVT | Land Value Taxation |
| MoD | Ministry of Defence |
| NCC | Nature Conservancy Council |
| NTS | National Trust for Scotland |
| RDC | Red Deer Commission |
| RICS | Royal Institution of Chartered Surveyors |
| RSPB | Royal Society for the Protection of Birds |
| SCU | Scottish Crofters Union |
| SLF | Scottish Landowners' Federation |
| SNH | Scottish Natural Heritage |
| SNP | Scottish National Party |
| SOAEFD | Scottish Office Agriculture, Environment and Fisheries Department |
| SRO | Scottish Records Office |
| SWT | Scottish Wildlife Trust |
| WWF | World Wide Fund for Nature |

Throughout the book county names are abbreviated (Inverness-shire to Inverness for example) where they clearly refer to the county. In some places the full county name is used to avoid any confusion with the town of the same name. Further abbreviations are used in Appendix 2 as follows:

| | | | | |
|---|---|---|---|---|
| AB | Aberdeenshire | | DN | Dunbartonshire |
| AN | Angus | | EL | East Lothian |
| AR | Argyllshire | | FI | Fife |
| AY | Ayrshire | | IN | Inverness-shire |
| BA | Banffshire | | KC | Kincardineshire |
| BE | Berwickshire | | KR | Kinross-shire |
| BU | Bute | | KK | Kirkcudbrightshire |
| CA | Caithness | | LA | Lanarkshire |
| CL | Clackmannanshire | | MI | Midlothian |
| DM | Dumfriesshire | | MO | Moray |

| | | | | |
|---|---|---|---|---|
| NA | Nairnshire | | SE | Selkirkshire |
| OR | Orkney | | SH | Shetland |
| PB | Peeblesshire | | ST | Stirlingshire |
| PR | Perthshire | | SU | Sutherland |
| RE | Renfrewshire | | WL | West Lothian |
| RO | Ross & Cromarty | | WI | Wigtownshire |
| RX | Roxburghshire | | | |

Throughout the book all areas are stated in acres.

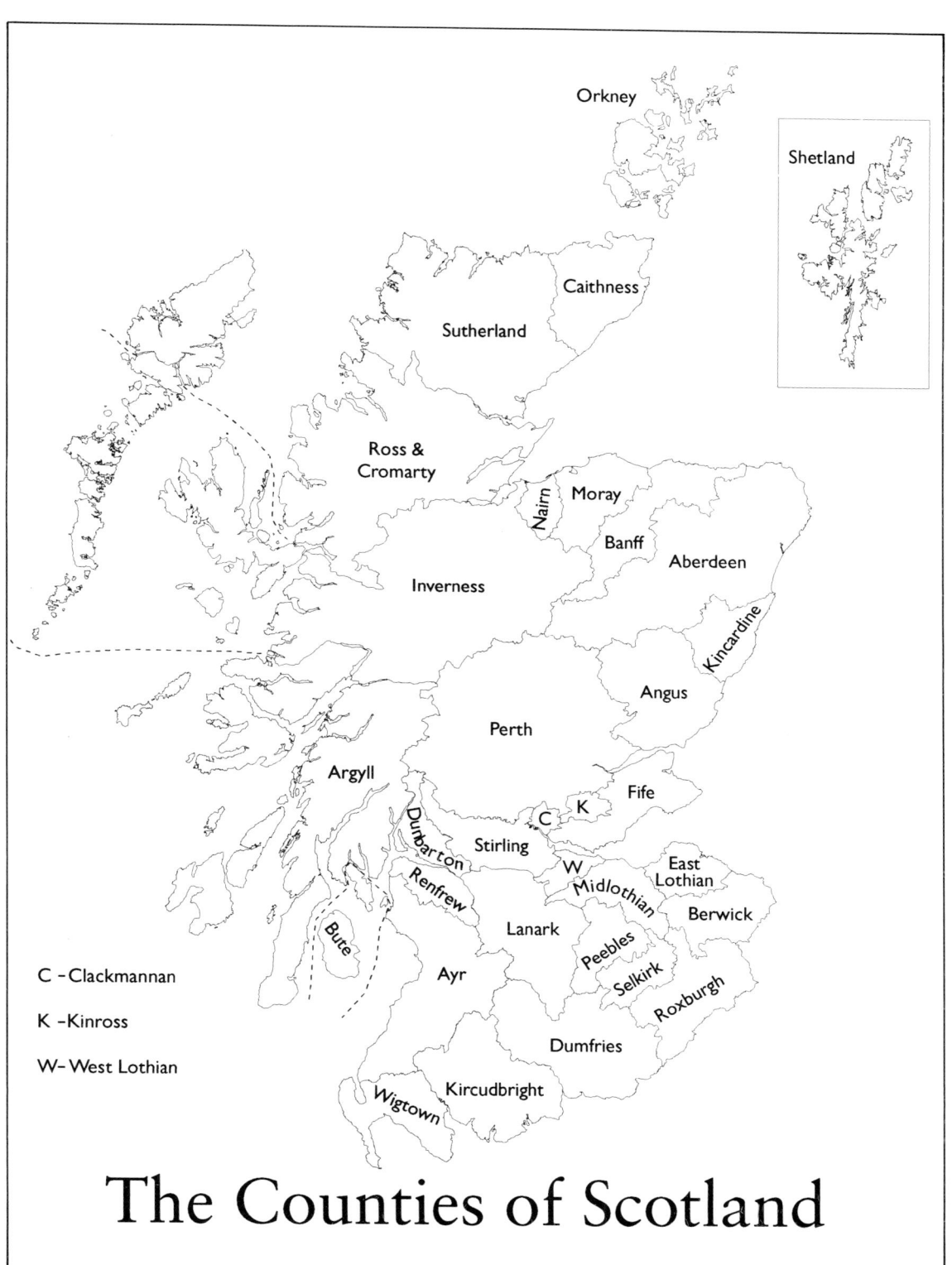

# Introduction

IN THE 1980s and early 90s, a series of major disasters such as the Piper Alpha explosion, the Exxon Valdez oil spill and a number of violent tropical storms caused much loss of life and environmental destruction. At the same time, various legal cases in the United States found against large corporations responsible for environmental contamination in earlier decades. These, together with growing concerns over global climate change, caused a major crisis of confidence in the global insurance market. Nowhere was this impact greater than in Lloyds of London. Although the hurricanes and oil spills had little direct impact on rural Scotland, a spate of land sales followed as Lloyds investors sought to raise the capital to pay debts. Some land agents spoke of a glut of land for sale which, if it had been released onto the open market, would have led to a collapse in land prices. The full effect on the rural economy will probably never be known but the fact that such distant events could have such dramatic consequences for land in Scotland is evidence enough of the unsatisfactory state of affairs that constitutes landownership in Scotland today.

The ownership and use of land is one of the most fundamental issues in any society and yet it is a subject which in Scotland remains poorly understood. Not only does ownership convey significant and far-reaching privileges to those in possession of land but the system and pattern of landownership has extensive economic, political, cultural, and environmental impacts on the economy and development of the country. In the final analysis, all economic activity relies on access to land and resources. How we as a society choose to define and distribute property rights and what obligations we place on their enjoyment has a profound bearing on not just economic activity but on the opportunities for the creation and distribution of wealth. Politically, land is important. Virtually every major political upheaval anywhere in the world has involved reforms of land law and in Scotland land reform has been of a substantial nature only when the forces driving it have threatened the perceived political stability of the country. There is a close, if various, association between land and political power in every country in the world.

Culturally, land and its ownership and use have shaped the outlook of the people of Scotland. Contemporary debates about landownership are a clear expression of a deep seated feeling, unaffected by two centuries of urbanisation, for the land. Whether expressed as national pride in landscape and wildlife or anger at abuses to land, the concerns are real and widely expressed in poems, books, music and plays.

Growing concerns over environmental damage to the planet have focused attention on the obligations we owe to future generations to protect and restore the planet. Problems arise however when our common inheritance is found not to be common at all but privately owned. Global environmental management requires a renegotiation of such rights if it is to be successful.

Landownership is a property system which in Scotland, under Scots law, ensures that every square inch of land and inland water together with the surrounding coastal waters and seabed, the ground down to the centre of the earth and up to the sky above is legally owned by somebody. This legal framework provides the basis of the relationship between the people of Scotland and their country. It is a framework which is still feudal and which owes its origins to a political and social system designed to exercise power in 11th-century Scotland. It was never designed as a system of property rights or as a way of managing land but rather evolved and adapted to accommodate the changing needs of those who have governed this country. In this adaptation lies one of the most important features of the system. Land tenure is not a static system; it is constantly evolving.

The most surprising thing about 20th-century feudal Scotland is not the character and behaviour of those who own it but the incredible survival and endurance of a system of property law that has been consigned to the history books in every other country in the world. Scotland's land laws represent not just the most distinctive aspect of Scots law, but also the least altered by any alien influence over their 900 years of evolution.

This book has been produced in response to the poorly informed debate that has often characterised discussions about landownership – a debate which has not been helped by the frequent media attention given to the more colourful and bizarre stories about rogue Dutchmen, offshore companies and eccentric lairds. The politics of envy and outrage whilst perfectly legitimate and providing some lively entertainment have not so far succeeded in overcoming any of the deep-rooted problems that exist. Nor is the debate helped by the persistent ignorance displayed by commentators and academics south of the border, who too often conveniently ignore the fact that the United Kingdom consists of more than just England.[1]

The book is in three sections. The first part summarises the historical development of feudal landownership in Scotland and concludes with a review of how it is understood today. The second section is an account of landownership in Scotland today. It analyses the patterns which emerge and explores the wider institution of Scottish landownership. Thirdly, the implications of what emerges are discussed. International comparisons are drawn, the landownership debate is characterised and crucial arguments are explored. This is developed into an agenda for land reform in Scotland.

It should be clarified at this early stage that this book does not seek to criticise landowners *per se*. Despite the undoubted entertainment this can provide and the long cultural traditions of doing so, it ultimately serves little purpose. Quite apart from the fact that Scotland is full of landowners who are eminently likeable, able and competent, landownership is too important a subject to be treated in this way.

Unfortunately, due to the nature of Scottish landownership, landowners as individuals necessarily loom large in any analysis of the subject. Precisely who owns Scotland should not matter. That it does is both a reflection of our desperate lack of information about landownership and a symptom of deeper problems of which the people involved are only the most obvious manifestation.

Finally, the pattern of landownership revealed in this book is described in its simplest measure, that of the acreage held by whom. Other measures such as land value are also valid and interesting but substantially more difficult to arrive at and are way beyond the resources of an independent author. As a result, the book concentrates exclusively on rural land and contains no account either of smaller landholdings or of urban land which, in any measure involving valuation, would come top of the list.

*Section 1*

# Chapter 1

# The Development of Feudalism

LANDOWNERSHIP IS A property system which embraces the whole of Scotland. Any landowner has a right of exclusive possession of land 'a caelo usque ad centrum' or 'from the sky to the centre of the earth'. The principal legal basis for landownership in Scotland is feudal tenure and the pattern of ownership outlined in this book has to be understood within this legal framework since it adds a 'vertical' dimension to property rights whereby more than one person may enjoy property rights over the same area of land.[1]

In Scots law an owner of land is entitled to use it as he or she pleases subject only to their feudal title and the various constraints enshrined in statutory and common law. This exclusive right of possession comprises both natural rights (such as legal protection against nuisance) and statutory rights to develop and use land within the laws governing development and land use.

Feudalism is a system of land tenure within which property rights are derived from an ultimate authority. In Scotland this authority is in legal theory God but in practice is the Crown which in the final analysis owns the whole country and is referred to as the Paramount Superior. All other landowners are vassals of the Crown but may themselves

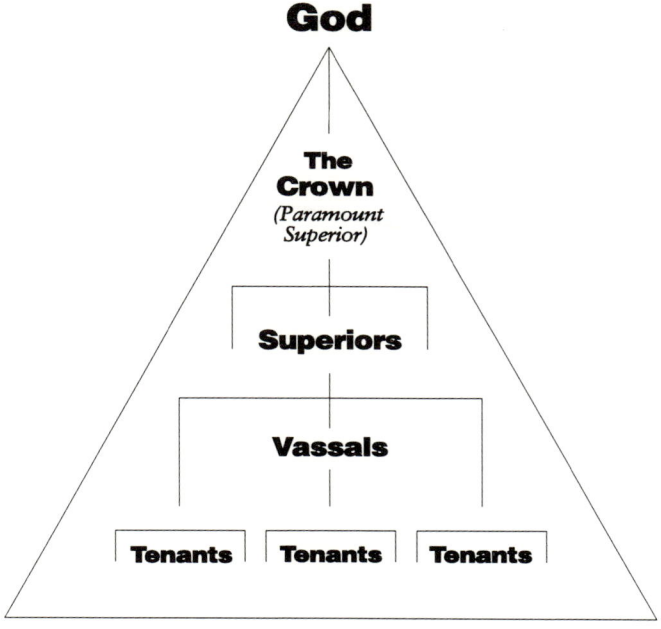

*A diagrammatic representation of the feudal system showing the hierarchical relationship between God and the Crown at the apex and vassals and tenants at the base.*

become feudal superiors by retaining certain rights and imposing certain obligations on those to whom they sell land. Such people in turn may become superiors through further retention and imposition of rights on other new owners who become their vassals. There is no limit to the number of times this process, known as feuing or subinfeudation, may occur and it adds a further dimension of ownership to that associated with the actual occupation of land (see diagram on p. 5).

Land which is sold need not of course be feud and can be sold outright. Whilst the process of subinfeudation creates a new feudal estate and a new superior-vassal relationship, with the former vassal now becoming a superior whilst still being a vassal of his or her superior, outright sale of land to another owner merely substitutes the interests of one vassal for another (or one superior for another).

Although any number of people can enjoy an interest in the same piece of land, in practice feudal rights are normally owned by three basic groups of people. At the top of the feudal pyramid is the Crown, from which all feudal authority derives. Certain Crown rights are reserved to the Crown and referred to as regalia. These include the sea within the limits of territorial waters, the foreshore between high and low water mark, the tidal stretches of rivers, precious metals and salmon fishings. To varying degrees the Crown is able to dispose of these interests to other people. The regalia majora (literally the greater royal rights) include the sea and tidal stretches of rivers and cannot be sold. Salmon fishings and precious metals on the other hand are regalia minora (lesser royal rights) and can be sold or otherwise disposed of. The Crown also owns land which, together with Crown rights, once formed the source of the monarch's income. Since 1760, however, the surplus income from the Crown Estate has been surrendered to parliament in exchange for the civil list which now funds the sovereign's activities. Crown property is not the property either of parliament or the reigning monarch but is part of the hereditary possessions of the sovereign 'in right of the Crown' and under the Crown Estate Act 1961 is managed by the Crown Estate Commissioners who have a duty to maintain and enhance the value of the Crown Estate. The Commissioners are appointed by and report to the Sovereign and to Parliament.

Below the Crown is the level of Superiority or, in legal terms, the 'dominium directum' (direct ownership). Superiors may typically retain mineral rights and can impose any number of burdens on land which they feu. These most commonly are rights of preemption (to have first right of buying back property should it be offered for sale in the future) or rights to control or share in the value of certain developments (for example house building). Since a new Superiority is created every time a piece of land is feud there may in theory be many superiors sharing an interest in a particular piece of land.

The third level of rights is that possessed by the vassal or 'dominium utile' (useful ownership) whose interests are most directly associated with the pattern of landownership described in this book. Vassals are constrained in their rights by the terms of their title deeds including any restrictions or burdens imposed by their feudal superior. Below the vassals are tenants whose occupancy and rights are derived from the vassal and today are usually governed by legislation.

Whilst feudal tenure is the dominant form of tenure in Scotland, there are exceptions of which the main one is alloidal tenure. Land held alloidally is held absolutely and under no superior and includes (or is commonly said to include) Crown land itself where no feuing has taken place, certain property belonging to the Church of Scotland, and land acquired by compulsory purchase. Udal tenure is a form of alloidal tenure which still exists in Orkney and Shetland. Its origins lie with the Vikings who didn't consider themselves to be vassals of anyone. An important distinguishing feature of udal tenure is partible inheritance, which allowed hereditary ownership by all children rather than by simply the eldest child (most commonly the son). This emphasises the need to view land tenure not as an isolated legal system but in the context of wider issues such as laws on succession.

Whilst many of the historic roles of superiors and vassals have long since disappeared, the continuation of a feudal system of land tenure means that in order to make any sense of the pattern of land ownership it is necessary to understand something of the history and development of feudal land tenure in Scotland.[2]

The origins of feudalism go deep into Scotland's history but are commonly associated with David I. Unlike the situation in England where feudalism was imposed by conquest, it developed gradually in Scotland. By assuming ultimate ownership of land, Scottish monarchs operated a system of patronage by granting land to lesser nobility in exchange for financial and military obligations. From the monarch down to the lowest of sub-tenants, the stakes were high if feudalism's obligations were not fulfilled since the Crown enjoyed the power of forfeiture and redistribution to others. The system itself was relatively easily fused with existing forms of tenure which, although little is known about them, were based loosely on kinship relationships. Chiefs of such groups, in so far as they had any association with particular pieces of territory, held rights under a reciprocal relationship with their kinship group who, in exchange for providing the chief with military support, could in turn count on the Chief's protection. The transformation of this mutual relationship between Chiefs and their people into a hierarchical relationship between the Chief and a higher external authority was the key change necessary to allow feudal authority to be exercised. Land became less of a territorial concept and more a form of property. Rights became attached to specific parcels of land rather than to specific individuals, authority for holding such rights derived from a higher authority rather than from a kinship group and, finally, these rights became directly heritable through primogeniture, passing upon death to the eldest son. Land in short was now property and traditional leaders were now landowners.

As feudalism gradually spread, so the indigenous forms of tenure disappeared and native chiefs as well as Anglo-Norman friends of the early Scottish kings were granted the earldoms and thanedoms, some of which still exist today. Wardholding was the term used to describe the principal obligation placed upon the beneficiaries of royal patronage in the centuries following the introduction of feudalism and involved the provision of military service to the monarch. This obligation could, in turn, be passed on to other vassals.

The Crown and other feudal superiors, through having the power to forfeit land and pass it to more loyal or able supporters, were able thus to exercise power without fear of contradiction provided they were careful. In addition, primogeniture ensured that lands whose owner died with no male heir reverted to the possession of the superior. Not surprisingly, strategic marriages became more important and, by the

15th century, wider kinship relationships of landowners through manrent (alliances to provide financial and military support) also added to the strictly feudal relationship with superiors thus extending the network of power from a purely hierarchical one to a more locally based pattern of political authority.

As an alternative to wardholding and other feudal obligations, superiors could demand financial payments in return for feudal charters. Feuing as it was known became commonplace by the 15th century and resulted in increased prosperity and power for the superior, who retained the power to resume land and charge for the renewal of feu charters. By the 1600s, therefore, land had become a commodity with monetary value. The social and economic power associated with landholding became more important than the earlier military power and landowning had become an important element in the development of modern Scotland. So much so that in 1617 the Register of Sasines was established as the legal register of heritable property, its purpose being to ensure the protection of private rights over land.

Considerable confusion surrounds the introduction of feudalism into the Highlands and Islands of Scotland. It is often popularly claimed that feudalism was introduced following the Jacobite defeat at Culloden and replaced older forms of communal and kinship tenure. This is wrong. Feudalism, whilst slower to penetrate this region, was nevertheless present from an early stage. The difference lay in the limited significance which was generally attached to feudal authority by Clan Chiefs who generally respected older Celtic traditions and relationships based on kinship. Crown authority was quite simply less well developed in parts of the Highlands than it was in the Lowlands. An important turning point in this came following the collapse of the Lordship of the Isles.

John, Lord of the Isles, had signed the Treaty of Westminster-Ardtornish in 1462 which gave him, in return for becoming Edward IV's liege, half of Scotland north of the Forth if and when Scotland was conquered by England. The forfeiture of the Lordship of the Isles in 1493 by an understandably furious James IV was the first of a series of attempts to assert control in the region where royal authority was weakest. In 1598, for example, James VI, who regarded the Highlanders as barbarous (and those on the Isles as utterly barbarous), passed an Act requiring all those who claimed to own land in the Highlands and Islands to produce their title deeds before the Scottish Privy Council. The MacLeods of Lewis, whose titles had been stolen by the MacKenzies, failed to oblige and the island was forfeited by the Crown who subsequently transferred it to a group of 12 merchants from Fife known as the Gentleman Adventurers of Fife. Despite the Adventurers being eventually forced to leave the island, this event underscored the political wisdom in Clan Chiefs ensuring they had proper Crown charters to their lands.

Kinship modified by feudalism is how the historian Professor Christopher Smout has described landownership in parts of the Highlands and Islands at this time. The more astute Clan Chiefs adopted a 'dual strategy' of retaining indigenous forms of kinship-based tenure and authority but backed up by keeping in with central authority in Edinburgh at the same time. Despite the limited impact of feudalism, its legal authority was to have devastating effects when the older clan system eventually collapsed and was to lead to the ultimate betrayal by Clan Chiefs of their clansmen who almost universally never accepted that a piece of paper from some distant monarch could ever usurp their rights. By the beginning of the 17th century and certainly by the end of it, landownership was a secure and significant institution in the politics and economics of Scotland. Landowners were ready to enjoy the fruits of political and economic power in the lead-up to the Union and in the major economic developments of the 18th and 19th centuries.

The 17th century saw the dramatic advance in the economic importance of landownership. Not only was there increased interest in securing and registering legally protected titles, but the economic importance of land was made manifest by the introduction of valuation rolls for taxation purposes. Most of the legislation of the Scots parliament in the 17th century concerned landownership and use. Land was a commodity which could be bought and sold and it was during the 17th century that the number of landowners stopped expanding and began to contract. A diluting pattern of ownership which had been developing for five centuries began to reconcentrate. In 1685 the entailment laws were introduced reflecting the need for increased security in possession of land in an active land market. These laws allowed land to be safeguarded against the claims of creditors in the event of bankruptcy. Family succession could be protected and the break up of estates could be prevented. Economic circumstances rather than political allegiance were therefore the chief determinant of successful landowning. The use of land for commercial purposes became well established and new practices began to emerge in forestry and agriculture.

It was in 1695 that the main Act for the division of commonties was passed. Commonties were areas of land held in common by neighbouring proprietors. Millions of acres of commonties survived the first five centuries of feudalism but by the end of the 19th century nearly all of it had been added to the private estates of Scotland's landowners. Because feudalism assumed that all land had to have a landowner, commonties were thus a form of private although undivided private property rather than genuine commons. The Acts which allowed for their division simply recognised what was already legal reality, that these lands were private but undivided. The closest contemporary example is provided by the rights over inland lochs where they form a boundary between properties. These rights are shared by neighbouring proprietors but remain undivided for obvious practical reasons.

By the beginning of the 18th century, landowners could begin to be identified into three distinct classes. The largest were the Great Landlords, the nobles and aristocracy who held their lands directly from the Crown and derived most of their wealth from their estates. Below them were the Lairds who might be relatives of the aristocracy but also included in their number people from the wider worlds of business and politics. Finally the 'Bonnet Lairds' held smaller estates and were the most numerous. Feudal tenure, however, continued to ensure that anyone holding land only did so under the authority of their Superior.

From the 18th century we begin to be much better informed about the pattern and nature of landownership. The overall number of landowners continued to decline so that where there were around 9500 landowners at the beginning of the century and around 8500 mid-century, by the start of the 19th century this figure had dropped to about 8000. The 18th century saw further developments in agricultural improvement and increased commercial exploitation of land. Feudal tenure was further reformed in the direction of a property system by the abolition of wardholding in 1747 and by allowing holders of feu charters to sell their land without having to obtain the permission of their feudal superior.

In parts of the Highlands the older understanding of land tenure based upon kinship rights, expressed in Gaelic as a 'duthchas' or 'kindness', whereby hereditary occupation of itself was sufficient to satisfy any counter claims of property rights was to receive a rude awakening when those Chiefs who had availed themselves with charters began to sell land to people with very different ideas about landownership or who subsequently embarked upon the evictions and clearance which was to lead eventually to the Crofters Holdings (Scotland) Act of 1886. Despite the beliefs of the indigenous people that the land of the Highlands belonged inalienably to the people, landlords had different ideas and believed that they were the outright possessors of the land.

The number of landowners in Scotland continued to decline, reaching 7637 in 1814. Throughout the 19th century 90% of Scotland continued to be held by less than 1500 landowners. Increased economic activity and the involvement of many landowners in commerce and empire led to land being regarded by its owners, if not by those consigned to make a living from it, as a status symbol. The romanticisation of the Highlands by Victorian writers and the purchase of Balmoral by Queen Victoria in 1852 underlined the transformation in external perceptions of the Highlands, for example, from a place of dark foreboding full of primitive people to a playground for the nouveau riche with whom the Scottish aristocracy was happy to associate. Landowners relied less on their land for a living and more on external business activities. Business failures, however, could threaten their estates and many landowners in the second half of the 19th century sought to protect their lands by transferring the title to trusts or by using the entailment laws. In Aberdeenshire, for example, the great majority of the 100 largest estates were entailed by this time.

The end of the 19th century witnessed unparalleled rural agitation in Scotland. Earlier resistance to agricultural improvement and enclosure, such as that of the Levellers in Galloway in 1724, had little impact on the consolidation of landowning power. The end of the 19th century, however, saw chronic agricultural depression particularly in the Highlands. Increased political agitation in Ireland was paralleled in Scotland where crofters and tenants in the Highlands demanded land reform to increase their security and protect against eviction and rapid rent rises. The 1886 Crofting Act introduced security of tenure, judicially reviewed rents, the right to bequeath tenancies to descendants and the right to compensation for improvements on outgoing. It was a watershed in Scottish land tenure law. Whilst it did nothing to address the fundamental grievance of crofters, which was their demand for the return of land now under sheep farms and deer forests, it was little short of revolutionary in a time accustomed to landowning power. It did not address the problems of the landless cottars and, just as significantly, it only applied to the counties of Argyll, Inverness, Ross & Cromarty, Sutherland, Caithness, Orkney and Shetland. Moves to include counties such as Aberdeenshire within its scope were defeated.

Scotland's feudal land laws, however, were still intact by the end of the 19th century. Crofters may have achieved limited but significant tenurial concessions but they were restricted both in place (the Crofting counties) and in scope (essentially restricted to agricultural tenancies). The pattern of large scale private landownership also survived the economic and political upheavals of the 19th century more or less intact.

Further reforms in the 20th century included the nationalisation of development rights under the post-war planning acts. In a rapidly industrialising society, it was no longer thought sufficient to rely on private interests to determine the development of the most important aspects of an industrial economy, namely, housing, industrial development and infrastructure. This century has seen increased public intervention in most aspects of the economy. Private landownership itself has decreased as a result of major state purchases of land by the Forestry Commission (FC), Agricultural Department, National Coal Board, and Ministry of Defence (MoD). In the period 1872 to 1970, the proportion of land held in estates of 1000 acres or more dropped from 92.8% to 62.8%.[3] The extent of the very largest estates also declined with the break up of the vast Sutherland Estate and Lord Leverhulme's estate on Lewis and Harris. The concentrated pattern of ownership within this 62.8%, however, remained as did the essential features of feudal tenure.

The ways in which property rights have changed over the centuries have involved both a consolidation of power over land and a contraction of earlier, wider, feudal rights. Feudalism itself has thus become of much less significance whilst common law, case law and statute have been of growing importance in defining the modern interpretation of the Scots law of property.

In the final years of this millennium, feudalism may finally be consigned to history, a thousand years after its introduction. Since 1969 in the White Paper on Land Tenure in Scotland,[4] successive governments have been committed to the abolition of the feudal system. In 1974, the Land Tenure Reform (Scotland) Act prohibited the creation of new feu duties (money payments to the feudal superior) and allowed for the redemption of existing ones. It did not, however, do anything to change feudal tenure.

In 1991 the Scottish Law Commission published its consultation paper, 'Property Law: Abolition of the Feudal System'. Despite the bold title, this paper essentially followed earlier proposals by focussing on the rather narrow perspective of conveyancing. Its proposals represent the Commission's early thinking and do not directly address many of the elements of feudalism. It proposes, for example, to finally abolish feu duties and to replace the superior–vassal relationship with one of absolute ownership. Importantly, however, the right of imposing real burdens or land conditions on land will still exist when land is sold and the proposals thus simply replace the powers of superiors with another form of private regulation. It outlines important reforms but, as will be argued later, a fresher and more comprehensive approach is required.

But the legal basis for landownership, though fundamental, is only one part of the picture. Legal systems are social and political constructs and wider political and historical events are therefore important. How land sales are regulated, what statutory requirements need to be met by owners, what the laws of inheritance are, how tenancies are governed and how the public interest is secured either by laws or through taxes and other financial relationships are all relevant.

How have these aspects of landownership affected the wider development of Scotland as a country? What does landownership in Scotland mean today? How has the ownership of land over the years affected the country? These are questions to which we now turn.

# Chapter 2

# Landownership in Scotland Today

## Historical Context

THE OWNERSHIP OF land in Scotland has a long history and, as its feudal origins make clear, is rooted in times when land had a very different significance in the politics and economy of Scotland. How it has developed over the centuries might therefore be thought to reflect the wider development of Scotland as a country.

Land had a very different political significance in early Scotland. The development of a stable sovereign state was conditional on not only securing control over land but on successfully exercising political power so as to ensure that things stayed that way. Feudalism introduced a simple and powerful system for regulating and influencing these struggles and strengthening the political power of the Crown. Its evolution to form the contemporary legal basis for landownership today despite having lost all of its rationale is one reason which makes its study so important and interesting.

Early industrialisation in Scotland led to the marginalisation of agrarian society and a steadily reduced role for land in the economy. A key turning point in this process was in 1688 when the so-called Glorious Revolution ended the absolute powers of the monarch and created a sovereign English parliament. Although such a constitutional reform never took place in Scotland, where constitutional theory continues to recognise that sovereignty lies with the people, the Union of 1707 resulted in a British parliament which in practice was a straightforward enlargement of the English parliament and which continued the assumptions which had underlain its creation as the 'Mother of Parliaments' 20 years earlier. As a result, Britain enjoyed a century and a half of relative political peace compared to most of the rest of Europe. Britain's rulers consisted of the landed gentry and capitalist merchants whilst most of Europe was still in the hands of absolute monarchs and feudal aristocrats. Scotland may still have been feudal but a good proportion of its landowners were distinctly and obviously ambitious commercially and exploited the opportunities presented both by Britain's colonial adventures and by subsequent industrialisation. Agrarian unrest, which did so much in the rest of Europe and throughout the world to shape political systems and cultures, was sporadic and seldom presented a real threat to central government. The one exception to this general trend was the unrest which preceded and followed the Crofters Act of 1886.

Political ideas about the role of land in the economy were the subject of heated debate towards the end of the 19th century. Social reformers such as the American Henry George were active in articulating ideas which argued that land was a key determinant in economic and social development. Unlike labour and capital, land was not merely another factor of production whose supply could fluctuate with the economy, but rather it represented a private monopoly interest which was in fixed supply. Land, he argued, was the common inheritance of humankind and should not be held as private property whose owners could capture the rising values created by rapidly developing economic activity.

This was a radical idea but one which drew its inspiration straight from classical thinkers such as the 18th-century Scottish economist, Adam Smith, as well as Rousseau, Locke and other less well-known philosophers such as Professor William Ogilvie of Aberdeen University whose 'Birthright in Land', published in the late 18th century, was a radical critique of the role of land in the economy.

Such thoughts are merely a reflection of how many of the world's political revolutions from the French to the Russian to the Irish and the Spanish have been directly stimulated or influenced by ideas about land and land reform.[1] It is no coincidence that one of the first things to be dealt with following political upheavals is the question of who should own the land.

Despite such movements, which undoubtedly had some influence on political thought, land in this country has been the centre of concern on only limited occasions and reforms that have been implemented have generally been no more than concessions. Scotland was not in a position to revolt over the land question.

Latterly, the State has sought to influence land use by grants and subsidies and, where it had an overwhelming strategic objective, by direct purchase. A comprehensive development planning framework was introduced in 1947 which ensured the rational development of the built environment. Private landownership, however, has never been fundamentally reformed.

The system of landownership therefore has survived for 900 years and today confers status and political power which, although diminished in important respects, has been developed seamlessly as a property system from the very beginnings of feudalism. For almost 300 of those years Scotland has not had the legislature which in most other European democracies has enabled programmes of land reform to be developed and implemented.

This remains a principal reason why landownership in Scotland remains both feudal and so much more concentrated than in other European countries. It is the reason why, despite the wider development of the Scottish economy, land tenure has been left in a position of uneasy association both with its feudal and aristocratic origins and with the ambitions and ideas of the present. Despite such a contradictory relationship, little has been done to try and and improve understanding of the subject.

## Towards a Modern Understanding

Studies of how landownership has shaped this country are notable by their scarcity. Aside from a few academic works, most general social and economic histories scarcely mention the subject outside periods such as the Clearances or the agricultural improvements era when its significance was more obvious.[2] Yet one only needs to look across the North Sea at countries like Norway to see how fundamental landownership has been in determining the economic and political development of a country through most if not all of its history. Even within Scotland one can look at Orkney and Shetland to see what a different system of land tenure has produced or at how successfully the 1886 Crofting Act has retained sizable populations in areas which without it would now almost certainly be empty.

Quite clearly, landownership has generally been neglected as a subject worthy of analysis partly because of lack of information about it but also because there has been a more or less universal unwillingness to reveal anything about the pattern of ownership. Successive governments of both left and right have seldom had any impact on this state of affairs. Government agencies moreover have often been closely associated with landowning interests and to this day remain hypersensitive about landownership information.

The only comprehensive and authoritative review of Scotland's landowning history to emerge in recent years was Callander's *A Pattern of Landownership in Scotland*.[3] The most remarkable thing to emerge from Callander's study is the incredible resilience of Scotland's land tenure system which has survived almost 900 years of Scottish history. Not only has the legal system survived but so too has the long association between many of Scotland's leading landowning families and their estates.

## Why Landownership Is Important Today

Landownership remains a politically contentious issue in Scotland. The ease with which interest is generated and passions aroused is well illustrated by the phenomenal support and media attention which was given to the campaign by the Assynt crofters to buy the North Lochinver estate on which they lived but which in 1992 was in the hands of receivers of a bankrupt Swedish property company, Scandinavian Property Services. The mobilisation of support for what proved to be perhaps the most important event in crofting history since the 1886 Crofting Act was not only skilfully handled but extended throughout Scotland. Few people were left untouched by the emotions that were aroused when they were finally successful. Their charismatic chairman, Alan Macrae, told a packed party the night they heard they were successful,

'It seems we have won the land and this is certainly a moment to savour. But my immediate thoughts are to wish that some of our forebears were here to share it. This is a historic blow which we have struck for people on the land right throughout the Highlands and Islands.'

Such appeals to history are very much justified in the context of the Highlands, where the events of last century continue to inform current attitudes and where the impacts of the Clearances are all too evident on the ground for those with an eye to see them. Elsewhere, in the Lowlands in particular, landownership seldom arouses such powerful feelings. The consolidation of landed power in the 19th century was neutralised as a focus for popular resistance by the ready availability of jobs in the growing industrial centres of central Scotland where radical politics was channelled into the developing labour movement.

Landownership, however, remains an important issue for Scotland.[4] Economically, it determines investment patterns, employment opportunities and local economic development. Culturally, land continues to inspire writers, poets, playwrights and singers.[5] Landowning patterns have an impact upon people's cultural and social outlook and aspirations as even a cursory examination of the effect of the Assynt Crofters' success on people there demonstrates. Environmentally, landowner motivation, land use decisions and the assumptions underlying property rights and obligations, can have marked effects on environmental stewardship standards.[6] In spiritual terms, land has long been and continues to be a powerful icon and influence in people's beliefs.[7]

But the system of property rights itself is not the only factor. The institutions that are created to underpin property rights, the fiscal policies to develop them and the powers to exploit them can individually and collectively result in radically different outcomes. One only needs to compare the former Soviet Union with Canada, for example, to see the difference. On the one hand the former Soviet Union nationalised all land following the 1917 revolution and managed it according to the principles of the command economy. Canada, with a similar proportion of 'nationalised land', although technically Crown land, pursued a capitalist economy where private interests manage and exploit public resources. The land in both cases is effectively public land but the outcomes are very different.

In contrast to urban areas, land tenure and landownership patterns in rural Scotland have a far greater impact on land use and development. This is due to the relatively more concentrated pattern of ownership in rural areas, its relatively greater importance in the economy, and the more limited significance of planning legislation. Three major factors emphasise this contrast.

The first of these is owner motivation.[8] This varies widely according to the type of landowner, their background and reasons for owning land, their financial circumstances and interests. Owner motivation ranges from strictly private enjoyment to outright profit maximisation. It includes the varying agendas of state bodies such as the Forestry Commission, conservation organisations such as the Royal Society for the Protection of Birds (RSPB) and the myriad of characters and bodies who are Scotland's landowners.

Second is the process by which landownership changes. The open market is frequently criticised for its crude emphasis on land as a marketable commodity where the ability to offer the highest price is the only qualification for holding land. Inheritance is equally open to criticism for its reliance on fortuitous parentage. Neither process is particularly discriminating in terms of assessing who is best placed or most deserving to occupy and use any particular parcel of land.

Finally there is the issue of land use incentives and development. Farmers, for example, are attracted to farming by an interest and commitment to it but also by virtue of the financial rewards it can offer. With the Common Agricultural Policy (CAP) and its emphasis on financial support to encourage high levels of production has developed the corporate investor landowner who is not interested in farming as such but in both the profit and capital gains that can be made. Financial support which may have been intended to support farmers is used as the basis for capitalist investors, many of whom may never see the farm or farms in question. Forestry is another very good example where, in order to encourage more tree planting, investors are induced to buy land and establish woodlands with grants from the government. Such people and institutions have a very different outlook on life than, for example, a resident farmer who plants a wood.

Professor Bryan McGregor, in the first John McEwen Memorial Lecture in 1993 argued that

'The impact of the land tenure system goes far beyond land use. It influences the size and distribution of an area's population; the labour skills and the entrepreneurial experiences of the population; access to employment and thus migration; access to housing; access to land to build new houses; the social structure; and the distribution of power and influence. In many areas of rural Scotland, large landowners play a crucial role in local development: they are the rural planners.'[9]

In Scotland today, under the dominant political consensus on private property rights, if you own land you are seen as the deliverer of important public policy objectives. Incentives, grants and subsidies can only go to those in possession of property rights. How these rights are defined dictates who can be involved. For example, a tenant farmer can plant a turnip, harvest it, sell it and benefit from the proceeds. The same farmer plants a tree and it belongs to the landowner. With no rights over trees, farmers are therefore disinclined to plant them. If the government of the day wants trees planted, it might consider whether the rights to do so are sufficiently well distributed to achieve its objectives. It is quite legitimate therefore to explore how such objectives might be achieved under different tenure and landownership regimes.

Just as the history of landownership is closely associated with the wider evolution of power in society, so the pattern of landownership continues to exert considerable influence on the attitudes of people, their aspirations and opportunities. A shift in this balance of power from the few to the many would in no way necessarily affect the ability of owners to manage their affairs but would introduce a broader sense of accountability to the wider public. In Scotland today the only criteria for obtaining access to land (and therefore the support available to develop it) are either wealth (or access to the necessary capital) or a fortuitous inheritance. Furthermore, whilst this may not in itself be a problem, in Scotland land prices are consistently above what ordinary people can afford and with so few people owning land the benefits of inheritance flow to a tiny number of lucky people.

Who these people are is not just a matter of some curiosity, it is the basis for debating how we should take matters forward, whether we are content with the status quo, whether we would like to see changes and if so why and how. That we remain substantially ignorant of who owns the territory many regard as 'their' country is not only frustrating and disturbing, it is also deeply shocking if we aspire to any control over our destiny.

Section I has attempted to outline something of the origins of landownership and tenure in Scotland as well as indicating why it remains important today. Before we can make any sense of the subject though, we need to know what the contemporary pattern associated with this system is. Who owns Scotland?

*Section II*

# Chapter 3

# Who Owns Scotland

WE ARE STILL very poorly informed about who owns Scotland, and the state of debate about landownership, frustrated as it has been by the lack of readily available information, is only the most obvious casualty. The reasons for having such information go beyond simple curiosity. Knowing who owns what is merely the beginning of a wider process of exploring more fundamental questions about landownership and use. More information would also assist greatly in the exercise of public duties by bodies as disparate as local authority roads departments, Scottish Natural Heritage (SNH) and the Scottish Environmental Protection Agency, to name but a few. It would be interesting to know just how much public money is spent trying to find out who owns land. In the course of research for this book it became abundantly clear that such information is widely needed by such agencies, is seldom easy to obtain, and that there is much wasted effort and repetition.

Despite obvious needs, information on the matter remains elusive. Aberdeen geographer, Sandy Mather, who has been one of a few academics to conduct serious research into the subject, commented in a recent paper:

'The ownership and occupancy of land in Scotland is an emotive subject on which it is difficult to carry out objective research. The fact that no comprehensive national inventory has been published during the twentieth century is significant. It is eloquent, if silent, testimony to the technical problems involved in such an exercise, and to the political sensitivity of the subject.'[1]

Such a state of affairs is nothing short of archaic and is usually regarded with disbelief by other European citizens who have grown accustomed to having such information readily provided as part of the normal workings of government.

This is not to suggest that a crude list of who owns the country is of any special value. It is however the first step in understanding and analysing the situation. Properly researched and presented, it can be of immense value to many people engaged in activities as diverse as regulating pollution, surveying, planning and studying wildlife. The fact that it arouses so much interest is a reflection both of the ignorance which has been generated by not having such information readily accessible and of the crude state of the debate about the subject. As one landowner put it to me in the course of this research, such a list can result in a situation whereby 'all manner of ideas, theories, conclusions, conspiracies and extrapolations may be extracted at the whim of the reader. This particularly as the reader seems to me likely to be the urban academic social engineer with head firmly stuck in what so frequently swirls around the tops of our Munros.'

Such a comment reveals a lot about the state of understanding of land ownership, of the state of landowner attitudes and of the gulf between urban and rural Scotland. Whilst I am in sympathy with some of what lies behind this view, the fact is that if we are to bridge any of the gulfs that currently exist in the understanding and interpretation of landownership in Scotland we need comprehensive, accurate and publicly available information. The fact that a partial picture may lead to all manner of theories, conspiracies and extrapolations is not an excuse for not making a start in providing more information but an argument for doing more.

The principal beneficiaries of more information on landownership may well be landowners themselves. Frequently characterised as hostile to such exercises, they may well find it helpful since nothing breeds misunderstandings and hostility more than a lack of real information. Indeed the very motives of this book have frequently been questioned in the course of my research, demonstrating the sensitivity bordering on hysteria which often surrounds what should be a straightforward issue of public interest. Equally, however, this exercise was welcomed by land owners and agents who in the past had found regular cause to consult John McEwen's *Who Owns Scotland*[2] to find out who owned particular areas of land. I trust that my enquiries may therefore be a cause of some material benefit to the very people who were so often critical of McEwen's work.

# Chapter 4

# Availability of Information

THE FIRST PROBLEM facing anyone interested in finding out who owns Scotland is where to obtain the information. Indeed there would be no need or interest in this book if there was wider access to accurate, comprehensive data presented in ways useful to the general public. It is one of the key purposes of this book therefore to stimulate and provoke better availability of information. This chapter outlines current available sources and reviews their origins and purpose as well as their usefulness as an aid to research.

Scotland remains better off than England and Wales with respect to the availability of information on landownership. The key problem is that much of it is not readily accessible in an easily usable form. Helpful work has been done by Sandy Mather in analysing the various sources of information.[1] His views accord on the whole with mine as to their usefulness.

## Existing Publications

Books which have been published to date on the subject are of course a useful starting point. There has only ever been one official survey of landownership in Scotland – that conducted by the government in 1872–73. The survey was carried out at a time of great land agitation in Ireland and the Highlands of Scotland and various politicians were concerned at the apparent concentration of land in a very few hands. As few as 30,000 people were alleged to dominate landownership in the UK. Lord Derby, the Prime Minister, himself an owner of 70,000 acres of England, was so incensed at what he claimed were the 'wildest and most reckless exaggerations' of land agitators, that he sponsored a parliamentary motion which was passed in 1872 to make a 'Return of Owners of Lands and Heritages'. Contrary to even the estimations of his critics, the survey revealed that only 7000 people owned 80% of the entire country, whilst in Scotland 659 people owned 80% with 50% owned by a mere 118. Over half of the Highlands was owned by just fifteen people.

John Bateman, himself a landowner, followed up the government survey by conducting further research which was published in 1883.[2] Bateman's *The Great Landowners of Britain and Ireland*, reprinted in 1971, remained the sole accessible source of information on landownership in Scotland until the remarkable work of an Aberdeen geographer, Roger Millman. The Proprietary Survey of Rural Scotland was begun as an offshoot of a study of how to effectively plan for the growth in outdoor recreational activities. It was sponsored by the Countryside Commission for Scotland (CCS) and the Highlands and Islands Development Board (HIDB) and also enjoyed the support of the Scottish Landowners' Federation. The survey involved determining the boundaries of all landholdings over 100 acres which were then plotted on a series of 6 inch and 1 inch maps and published in a series of papers in *Scottish Geographical Magazine* from 1969 to 1972.³ He also prepared over 10,000 index cards containing the names of proprietors but these were never published.

Other work in the 1970s involved various studies of public ownership of land⁴ as well as various local studies including the celebrated *Acreocracy of Perthshire* written by Alasdair Steven and published by Perth and Kinross Fabian Society.⁵ One of its researchers was a Perthshire forester named John McEwen.

Six years later, John McEwen published *Who Owns Scotland*, the first account of landownership in Scotland for over 100 years.⁶ McEwen derived his information from the maps and index cards prepared by Roger Millman and his book remains a milestone in Scottish social and political publishing which attracted interest not only from fellow radicals but, unsurprisingly, from Scotland's landowners. One John Christie of Lochdochart, a leading member of the Royal Scottish Forestry Society, of which John McEwen had been the only working forester ever to be President, wrote in the Society's magazine, '. . . it is sad when the family and friends of a very old man cannot dissuade him from exhibiting in print his envy of those more fortunate, hard-working and thrifty than himself and his ignorance of an industry in which he claims to have worked for a lifetime . . . My main regret is that the early thinnings of privately owned and managed woods may have been pulped to produce the paper upon which this silly little booklet was printed.'⁷

John McEwen had hit a sore point. One of the main criticisms levelled at his work was that it contained major inaccuracies. This was undoubtedly true but what was remarkable was that, despite them, the overall pattern of ownership which he presented was by and large accurate. Why he made mistakes (and he understated as well as overstated the extent of land holdings) is of some limited interest.

The maps he used were photocopies of Millman's maps which are lodged in the Scottish Record Office.⁸ There are three main sets. The first is a set of 1″ (1:63,360) maps giving rough coverage for the whole country. The second is a set of 2.5″ (1:25,000) maps which give greater detail and finally there is a neat set of 1″ maps transcribed from the first set by a student assistant. Roger Millman left extensive suggestions for tidying up his information with SRO staff. Unfortunately these were never followed up. As a result it seems that McEwen received copies of the first rough set which had two major deficiencies. They were roughly drawn and therefore not clear when photocopied and secondly they did not include some information contained on the 1:25,000 set.

Even taking his sources into account, it remains something of a mystery why McEwen made some of the errors he did. One clear reason is that the maps he obtained contained references to superiorities, farms having a feudal superior in common – the original, larger estate owner. These were marked as feud farms, but often interpreted by McEwen as being under one ownership. Of more importance are the alleged gaps in the Southern counties which resulted in some inaccuracies in McEwen's data. This is almost certainly the result of McEwen not having access to the most comprehensive of Millman's maps which are as comprehensive of the south as they are of the north.

Such errors, however, do not detract from the valuable work done by John McEwen whose book remains a remarkable achievement for a man of 90 years of age. What is more significant is the incredible fact that no-one else has attempted to abstract Millman's information to publish a more accurate account of landownership in

Scotland in 1970 and that even academic researchers continue to rely on the efforts of McEwen.[9] Millman's work therefore remains the only comprehensive survey of Scottish landownership undertaken in the 20th century and John McEwen has been the only person to analyse it and publish an account of who owns Scotland.

In the late 1970s and 1980s, several academic works appeared, most notably from Aberdeen University. One such study, *Land Ownership and Land Use in the Scottish Highlands* was based upon a sample survey of landholdings which revealed some useful information about the nature of Highland landownership. Other work by Professor Bryan MacGregor looked at owner motivation in north-west Sutherland, whilst Professor John Bryden, who as the HIDB agricultural economist had been centrally involved in its land politics, wrote up an important study of agrarian change in the Highlands which included useful information on the pattern of landownership.[10]

Unfortunately, information that is generated about who owns land in such studies almost always remains confidential in the interests of obtaining the necessary access to undertake the work. This has meant that, for example, an important study of landownership in Fife and north-west Sutherland which was produced for the Countryside Commission for Scotland as a pilot study looking at the feasibility of assembling a map-based register of landownership, had to keep its essential findings confidential.[11] It produced some beautiful maps and data but on the central questions of who owns Fife or Sutherland, nothing could be published.

A few localised studies of landownership have been published. Callander's account of Scottish landowning history contains a detailed analysis of Aberdeenshire; other studies, such as the Skye Data Atlas, which published ownership information for the Isle of Skye, have appeared. Crude maps of estates in mountain areas were published by the Scottish Landowners' Federation and the Mountaineering Council of Scotland in their publication *Heading for the Scottish Hills*. Estate boundaries are identified in relation to a base map which shows watercourses, roads and settlements. The maps, however, are only indicative, the data is incomplete and, of course, it covers only mountainous areas, principally areas containing Munros, mountains over 3000ft.[12]

## The Register of Sasines

The Register of Sasines is the authoritative legal source of information on heritable property (land and buildings) in Scotland and is one of the oldest legal registers of title to land anywhere in the world, having been established by an Act of the Scots Parliament in 1617. Designed as a public register, it contains details of virtually all heritable property in Scotland and registration is the primary device whereby property rights are secured. Its value as a source of information on landownership is restricted, however, in a number of ways. Firstly, the register is not map-based and so any search must begin with knowledge of either the place or the person concerned. This leads to the deeds for the property and searching the history of it is made straightforward by the creation of search sheets which contain a full history of the property concerned, including when it was sold to whom, what if any securities have been taken against it, and details of any long leases.[13]

The Search Sheets are only descriptive but are in many cases cross-referenced to plans. If the name of a person who owns land is known, the persons index can be used which leads relatively quickly to a specific property in any county where a history of the property can be quickly determined. Problems arise where a property is large and complex. Fathoming the exact nature of the interests of large landowners who may be involved in numerous property transactions is long and tedious. Much simpler, for example, is to find out who bought a specific farm or estate or how a specific farm was sold and split up.

In 1979, the Land Registration (Scotland) Act introduced the new Land Register which is slowly replacing the Register of Sasines. The main feature of the Land Register is that it provides a state-guaranteed title to property in the form of a Land Certificate. A once-and-for-all search is made of the title deeds, following which the certificate is issued. This Land Certificate henceforth provides the sole security over property and removes the need for repeated searches every time a property is sold. The Land Register is also map-based and associated with every Land Certificate is a plan. Starting in 1995 with Fife, the plans are being computerised. The new system is being introduced over a period with all counties being included by 2003. Since only a sale of property triggers actual registration, it will be many decades beyond that until all counties are covered by the new system. Provision does exist, however, by statutory instrument, for the Secretary of State to require all remaining interests in land to be registered. Sasines will thus eventually become a historical archive.

There is frequent misunderstanding as to the exact nature and purpose of the Register of Sasines, and it frequently has to defend itself against allegations of a lack of any proper register of landownership. Such criticism is often made but seldom justified since the Register was never designed as a cadastre* or map-based register for the purposes of identifying landholders from a glance at a map. The system is a legal register, designed to satisfy purchasers of the validity of title to a property. It contains over a million search sheets. Any attempt to find out who owns Scotland purely on the basis of the legal register is, unfortunately, not feasible.

Whilst the new Land Register improves the efficiency of conveyancing and reduces the possibilities of defective titles, it does not in itself do anything to address the most common criticism that it is virtually impossible to simply and cheaply find out who owns what particular parcel of land.

## Valuation Rolls

Agriculture and forestry have been de-rated for many years, but until April 1995, most landowners were paying shooting or sporting rates. The abolition of these rates is explored in greater detail in Chapter 9 but given that almost all land from large sporting estates down to medium size farms and blocks of private forestry was rated for shootings, valuation rolls as at April 1994 give an almost complete list of the names and addresses of all the principal proprietors.

---

* A cadastre is an official register of landownership showing details of ownership, boundaries, and valuation of land and property, often compiled for taxation purposes. It is distinct from a register of titles, which is compiled for legal purposes.

## Landowners

Private landowners are an obvious source of information but understandably vary in their willingness to divulge information. Their identity itself is of course often difficult to determine and this frustrates efforts at contact. The phone book and local contacts are often the only way to build up a picture of who is involved in any area. Land agents who are often responsible for day to day management can be a useful source of information but tend to be as variable in their willingness to cooperate as owners themselves. On a local level, for practical purposes, contact with owners may be adequate to serve local needs. At a county or national level, however, such an approach is best pursued to seek limited amounts of information from a selected number of owners. For example, the largest owners in an area, if cooperative, can supply information on boundaries which can then form the basis of completing the jigsaw by approaching smaller, neighbouring proprietors.

## Public Bodies

Public bodies owning land are generally cooperative in providing information for research purposes. Annual reports of the Forestry Commission, Crown Estate Commissioners and the Scottish Office Agriculture, Environment and Fisheries Department (SOAEFD) all contain information on the extent of their landholdings. Local authorities generally hold information on their own holdings for internal purposes and will usually provide details. Such information, however, is highly variable in scope and usefulness. For a proper understanding of these bodies' landholdings it is often necessary to visit the relevant organisation in person.

In addition to their own holdings, public bodies also hold information on private land. This ranges from the maps submitted to SOAEFD under the Integrated Administration and Control System (IACS) to maps prepared by the Forestry Commission and Scottish Natural Heritage (SNH) as part of their statutory duties. There remain great discrepancies in the attitude taken to some of this information by officials in these agencies. Some regard virtually all information as confidential whereas others are much more relaxed about it. A much more consistent and open approach to what is and what is not justifiably confidential needs to be developed before such sources can be of any real value.

## Sales Brochures

Land for sale in Scotland can either be advertised publicly on the open market or privately through the network of land and estate agents. It is difficult to know precisely how much land is sold on the open market and how much privately, but open market sales involve the production of a brochure which contains extensive information about the property, details of any restrictions in the title, rateable values, statutory designations, history and, importantly, a map. They are a very useful source of information about landownership and, when built up over a number of years, can provide an invaluable picture of landownership in any particular area.

# Chapter 5

# The Research Process

ANYONE TRYING TO find out who owns Scotland on a sudden whim would find the task well-nigh impossible and highly frustrating. A prerequisite for some form of success is a degree of general knowledge and awareness as to what the basic landownership pattern is. What is required beyond that is the time and the ability to pick up on the main sources quickly. Of additional advantage is contact with people who, if they don't know who owns what in different parts of the country, know others who do. A major part of the success in achieving the coverage presented here is down to the help I received from a large number of people across Scotland, some of whom had literally done the job already on a local scale.

In terms of coverage, my target was to account for the ownership of 75% of Scotland. In the event I achieved slightly less. Priority was given to accounting for the largest landholdings since these would go furthest in achieving the target coverage. All counties were therefore screened for their largest landholdings. Priority was given, however, to the ten largest counties in Scotland which together cover 70% of the country, namely, Inverness, Argyll, Ross & Cromarty, Perth, Sutherland, Aberdeen, Ayr, Dumfries, Lanark and Kirkcudbright. Even within these, however, availability of sources and pattern of holdings determined that some would end up well covered and others less so.

The information consists of four main elements, the owner, the name of the property, the acreage and the location with boundaries. Of these elements the most straightforward and readily accessible are the owner and property name. Greater difficulty was encountered in establishing the acreage and exact boundaries.

The process was not perfect given the time constraints. The priority was to identify the names of the principal landowners in each county. This was done largely by using the Valuation Rolls assembled by the Assessors Departments of Regional Councils for business rating purposes. A wide range of other published material from newspaper cuttings and books was assembled to complement this material. Boundaries were obtained from a wide range of public and private sources. The Red Deer Commission, for example, maintains maps of all the main estates within red deer range. The boundaries are broadly accurate and could be checked in many cases with various collections of sales brochures. Millman's maps were consulted for parts of the country where few other sources were available.

The extent of land in public ownership was determined from direct contact with the bodies concerned. A number of local studies have been done which cover specific areas and this information was incorporated. In several districts, local people helped to build up a picture from local knowledge.

At this stage, information which had been collated on maps was taken to various people around the country for verification. Even people whose instinct was not to cooperate with such an exercise found it difficult to resist pointing out errors and making corrections and in this way wider support was given than would have been the case had I presented people with a blank map.

The Register of Sasines was used to clear up confusing or contradictory information and to determine the identity of new owners of land which had been sold or split up.

Finally, I contacted a number of landowners directly where I had information which was either out of date, required additional confirmation not obtainable from any other known source, or where holdings were so large that this was the only practicable way of determining the current extent.

My enquiries to landowners and agents called for a degree of goodwill on their part since the information I supplied them with was often incomplete. A full explanation of the origin of such information would have been prohibitively time-consuming and expensive. Most who responded were helpful but some were distinctly unhelpful and a minority chose to misinterpret my enquiry as a gross intrusion on their privacy. Most respondents appeared quite comfortable with spending a little time to correct maps, acreages and details of ownership even to the extent of providing additional information on neighbouring proprietors. Of 258 owners contacted, 157 (61%) replied representing 72% of the acreage. Of this, only 9, representing less than 6% of owners but 13% of the acreage were unhelpful. They included some of the larger estates such as Roxburghe and Dunecht as well as several smaller ones.

Landowner involvement was interesting. To their credit, most were very helpful but landowners were clearly divided on whether and how to respond. This ambivalence was well illustrated by a notice that appeared in the *Bulletin of the Scottish Landowners' Federation* which is worth reproducing in full.

> PUBLICATIONS ON WHO OWNS SCOTLAND
> From time to time members may receive requests from authors for details of their landholdings. Before providing or confirming any information, members should consider very carefully the use to which it may be likely to be put. Where owners do not wish to cooperate and are asked to confirm or alter inaccurate information provided by an author, they may wish to respond simply by stating that the information is inaccurate.
> *SLF Bulletin* September 1995.

This is a pretty silly piece of advice since the best way of preventing inaccurate information being published is to take the opportunity to correct it. Declining to do so merely reinforces arguments to have this information more readily available. Any criticisms of inaccuracy against this book's findings should be considered against such a background of secrecy and paranoia.

A handful of owners had no problem with information about their landholdings being published but only on condition that nothing 'political' was done with it. I leave it to their judgment whether this is the case but would suggest that whatever one's views on the subject of landownership in Scotland, there can be nothing lost by the straightforward publication of factual material. How people choose to interpret such material is an entirely separate matter and it is unhelpful to attempt to influence this by placing conditions on the publication of the hard facts.

Given that McEwen was widely criticised and his work discredited by landowners for its inaccuracies, it is interesting to note how landowners themselves have been prone to exaggeration.

In numerous articles in landowning journals, inaccurate figures are given. Brahan estate in Ross-shire for example was stated as being 4000 acres in the SLF journal by their own forestry advisor but in reply to my enquiry this was claimed to be incorrect. Paul van Vlissingen, the owner of Letterewe estate in Wester Ross, was credited with owning 100,000 acres in an interview in the *Field* magazine. The various properties making up his landholding amount to 81,000 acres. Factors of estates were particularly prone to exaggerate acreages, often working with the same figures that might have been accurate in the 1950s but had substantially diminished since then. Several landowners, on the other hand, denied owning as much land as I suggested but when boundaries were clarified found that they were indeed proprietors of some very large areas of land.

It should be emphasised from the outset that the information on landownership contained in this book is not and does not claim to be a 100% accurate factual statement of the pattern of landownership in Scotland today. Such an analysis would take the kind of time and resources which although, as will be argued later, need not be too onerous, are beyond the means of this author. Instead, what is presented is an account of landownership in Scotland which is as accurate a picture as it is possible to generate using available public and private sources. There are inevitably inaccuracies and mistakes and I look forward to these being identified.

# Chapter 6

# *The Tables and Maps*

THE INFORMATION PRESENTED on the following tables follows the pattern of McEwen with the addition of maps, identification where known of beneficial owners, and a grid reference. The following points should be noted regarding the information presented.

The analysis is presented based on the 33 counties of Scotland which were abolished following the 1975 reorganisation of local government. They continue, however, to be the basis for organising the Register of Sasines and the Land Register. In addition, most historical information on landownership is organised on the basis of counties and therefore it continues to be the logical unit to work with.

The data is presented in terms of who owns Scotland. In other words, it is broken down on the basis of landowners. Any one landowner may own more than one landholding in a county and indeed may own landholdings across Scotland. Data for each county is edited to identify the total land held by each owner within the county and data for the whole of Scotland is edited to eliminate multiple ownerships across Scotland. Landowners who own land in more than one county are identified in Appendix 2. The threshold for inclusion in the tables is a minimum landholding of 1000 acres in total across Scotland. All owners of such holdings are identified in the county tables where the holding in that county exceeds 500 acres.

For the purposes of this research a single ownership is defined as any single discrete natural or legal person (an individual, company etc.) except where these are, to all intents and purposes, representative of the same owner. For example, many large estates owned by a single family are split into several ownerships. Cawdor Estate in Nairnshire, for example, is held in five separate ownerships. Typically in such cases, the castle or stately home will be held separate from the land, woodlands may be held separately from the farmland and the bulk of the estate may be in several family trusts. Invercauld Estate, for example, is now owned by several trusts with Alwyn Farquharson himself owning Invercauld House and a bit of land surrounding it. In such cases, I have had to make a decision as to whether to treat such trusts as new landowners or as part of the former single ownership. In the vast majority of cases I have treated them as a single ownership particularly if the beneficiaries of such trusts are the same people and if management regimes continue to treat the estate as one entity. Most cases of such splits are to do with the tax planning of the owners in question and do not represent a meaningful fragmentation of landholdings. Indeed in the case of trusts, they are almost always established precisely to prevent the break-up of holdings.

Landowners are identified wherever possible by their legal status. Many landowners do not hold land individually but through companies and private trusts. These are created for financial and taxation reasons. Private trusts are legal entities which are created by someone (the truster) passing over ownership to trustees who become the legal owners and who are under an obligation to administer the property on behalf of the beneficiaries. Any person can simultaneously be any two of these three parties. The truster can also be a trustee or a beneficiary, even the sole trustee or beneficiary. A sole trustee cannot however be the sole beneficiary. Companies are also often the legal owners of land. Buccleuch Estates Ltd. for example was set up as early as 1923. Such companies are controlled by the shareholders which in the case of Buccleuch Estates Ltd include the Duke of Buccleuch and his son, the Earl of Dalkeith. Where such trusts or companies are the legal owners, I have attempted to identify the 'principal interest', that is to say the principal truster or beneficiary (of trusts) or Directors (of companies).

This is not of course so simple. Private trusts are, as the term implies, private and unless they have successfully negotiated charitable status with the Inland Revenue, remain private. There is no public record of the identities of the people involved. Companies on the other hand are generally registered in Companies House in Edinburgh which includes all companies registered either in Scotland or England as well as foreign companies with branches or a place of business in Scotland. A search of company records was undertaken for a selection of companies. This identified at the very least whether they were actually registered or not. Any which were not by deduction must be offshore companies.

Some offshore companies are registered under Section 691 of the Companies Act. This section requires registration where the company intends to establish a place of business in Scotland. It also requires the identification of the person resident in the UK who is competent to conduct business on the company's behalf. Land which is used as the basis for trading operations such as the leasing of land is usually therefore registered. In contrast, offshore companies which hold land for the private enjoyment of the beneficiaries are not registered. Burnden Park Investments Ltd., for example, which owns the Scardroy Estate in Ross & Cromarty, whilst registered in the British Virgin Islands with 3 Bermudan directors, is registered under Section 691 and includes Angus MacKenzie of the accounting firm in Inverness as a Director. Greentop Lands and Estates Ltd., which is the Scottish branch of Greentop Lands and Estates AG registered in Liechtenstein, is also registered and includes, in addition to three Danish directors, Ian Edward of Ledingham and Chalmers, Solicitors in Aberdeen. On the other hand, companies such as Smech Ltd. (Ross and Cromarty) and Andras Ltd. (Inverness and Banff) are not registered anywhere in the UK. Appendix 3 contains a full list of directors of a selection of the companies owning land in Scotland.

A grid reference is given which, on an Ordnance Survey map, will allow the property in question to be identified. The grid square identified will usually locate a central point of the property or the principal residence associated with it. In association with the maps this should make it relatively straightforward to locate the landholdings fairly accurately.

Finally, it is worth pointing out the main contrast between this survey and that carried out by Roger Millman. His survey was virtually comprehensive down to 100 acres. The abstraction of data of the number of holdings above, for example, 1000 acres could reasonably be expected to be even more comprehensive therefore and was the basis of John McEwen's work. The survey conducted for this current book however was not as comprehensive and whilst it is unlikely that any properties above 5000 acres are excluded, there will be some below that extent which certainly are.

# Key to Maps and Tables

## The Maps

The maps show the landholdings referred to in the tables and are annotated with numbers. Where possible holdings are shown with their complete boundaries. Where information has been unavailable or unreliable they are indicated by a dot.

The grey shading ▓ indicates Forestry Commission land.

Letters in holdings on the maps refer to public sector landowners as follows:

a  SOAEFD
b  Local authorities
c  SNH
d  MoD
e  Highlands and Islands Enterprise
f  British Coal

Because of the small scale of the maps, holdings may contain within them other holdings of up to 100 acres in extent which are not shown.

Maps were generated by digitising boundaries which had been drawn on the 1:50,000 Series OS maps. The finished artwork was prepared using Corel Draw. Digitising and artwork were produced by Mega Ram, Portree, Isle of Skye.

## The Tables

See text for details of how the tables have been generated. The following annotations have been used.

(part)  indicates land held contiguously with land in a neighbouring county.
\*  indicates a landowner (other than national organisations such as the Scottish Wildlife Trust and National Trust for Scotland) with land in at least another county. See Appendix 2 for details.

Public landholdings are listed to indicate the land owned by public bodies. See Appendices 4, 5 and 6 for full details.

A comparison of the distribution of landholdings between 1970 and 1995 is presented. This shows the distribution of holdings over 1000 acres in the county.

For reasons of space, in many cases the full name of the landowner has had to be abbreviated.

# Aberdeenshire
# 1,261,333 acres

Aberdeenshire is still a county of contrasts between large inland estates on Deeside and Donside and smaller estates and farms in coastal Buchan. Although nothing much has changed in the overall pattern of landownership since 1970, the larger estates comprising good mixed and arable farms have continued to fragment. A number have been sold to the farming tenants such as Bonnykelly Estate and others, such as Castle Fraser Estate have been split up and sold.

Aberdeenshire was the subject of a detailed study by Deeside author Robin Callander whose book, *A Pattern of Landownership in Scotland*, provides a detailed analysis of the historical development of landownership in this county.

The main estates are still virtually as they were in 1970 with very little change in ownership. Most significant perhaps was the purchase of the Mar Lodge Estate in 1995 (see Box 3 page 184). Other estates such as Invercauld are now in the hands of Trustees. Some estates such as Glentanar have seen some internal changes in ownership within the family.

Private investment forestry has made very little impact in Aberdeenshire. Most of the big estates tend to have a long tradition of forest management and although new forestry has appeared it has involved little in the way of ownership changes.

A feature of the farmland market has been the dramatic number of sales to people from the south of England in the late 1980s fuelled by the huge price rises being experienced in the English property market. It was possible to sell a modest holding in England and buy a substantial farm in Buchan. This has died down and many aspirant good-lifers are reported to have returned home, perhaps not finding the rigour of the Buchan climate to their liking!

I encountered rumours of speculation in Aberdeenshire farms by Dutch drug dealers laundering their ill-gotten gains. These remain to be substantiated.

Information on landownership in Aberdeenshire in terms of the exact extent and boundaries of properties is amongst the most accurate available due to the fact that Callander made enquiries of proprietors in the mid-80s and my own research involved direct contact with 50 owners in the county, to which I received an 80% response rate. The vast majority were helpful. Allathan Associates, however, the agents for the Marquess of Huntly, kindly informed me that my information was 'substantially incorrect in all respects. Beyond what is a matter of public record, we do not feel it serves any purpose to divulge precise details of property titles.'

One of the biggest owners in the county, the Dunecht Estates, declined to confirm my findings due to the estate being held by Trustees following the death of Viscount Cowdray in January 1995. The factor could confirm that 'the plans you sent are inaccurate in several major respects, but I am not authorised to assist you with specific information'.

Aberdeenshire shares much in common with the other north-east counties of Moray, Nairn, Banff, Kincardine and Angus in having large areas of good quality land held in relatively large estates and with high proportions of families who have held the land for many generations. There have been dramatic changes when looked at over a period of centuries but Aberdeenshire remains a county where one shouldn't expect any overnight revolutions.

# Aberdeen

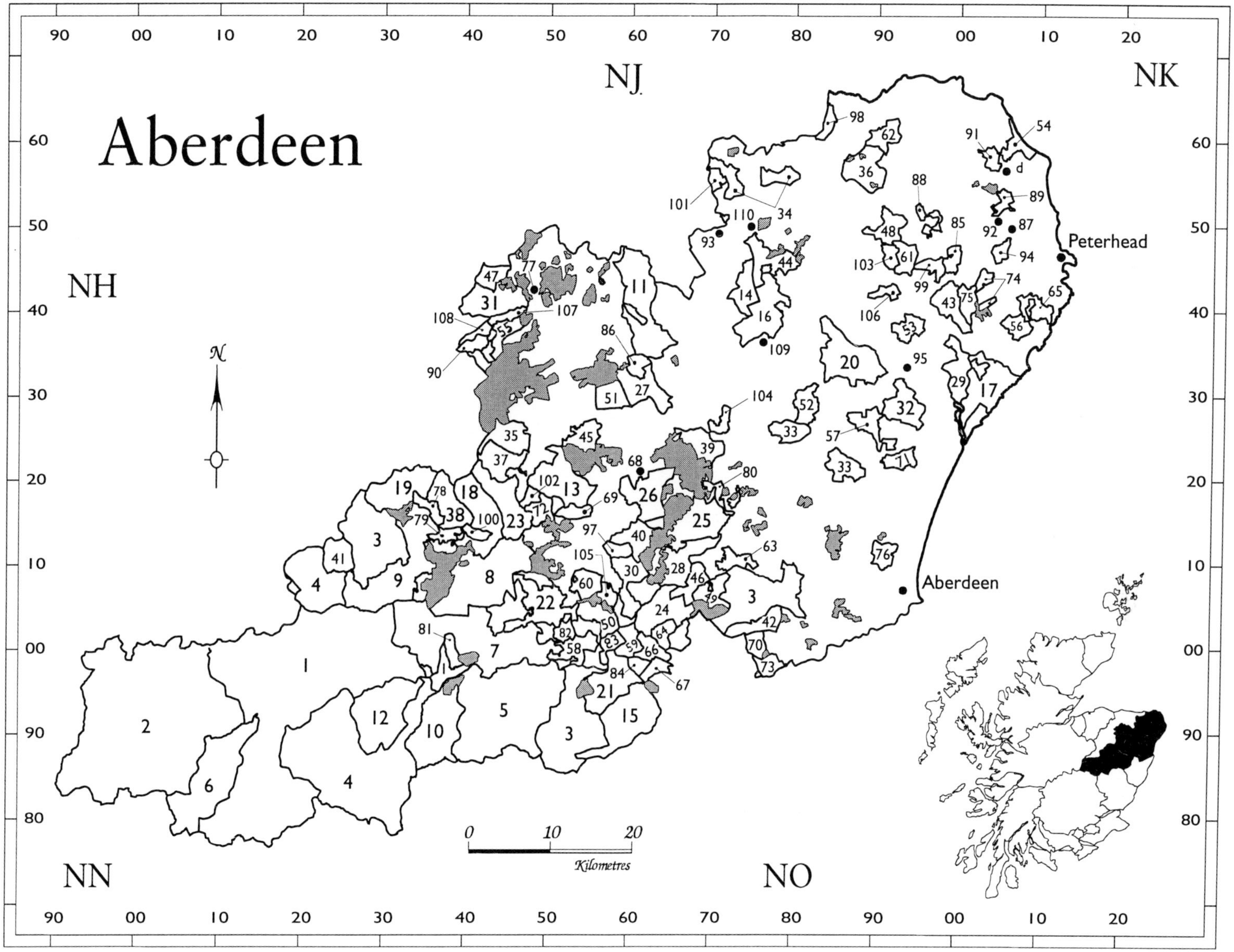

# Aberdeenshire

| NO. | PROPRIETOR | PROPERTY | PRINCIPAL INTEREST | ACREAGE | GRID REF. |
|---|---|---|---|---|---|
| 1 | Captain A.A.C. Farquharson's Invercauld Trusts * | Invercauld (part) | Capt A.A.C. Farquharson | 87500 | NO 1792 |
| 2 | National Trust for Scotland | Mar Lodge and others | | 73582 | NO 0989 |
| 3 | Viscount Cowdray & Trusts * | Dunecht & others | | 65600 | NJ 7507 |
| 4 | The Queen and Trustees of Balmoral * | Balmoral & Delnadamph | | 50370 | NO 2594 |
| 5 | Glen Tanar Trusts | Glen Tanar | Michael A. Bruce | 29150 | NO 4795 |
| 6 | Captain A.A.A.D.M. Ramsay | Mar | | 25143 | NO 0984 |
| 7 | Edward Humphrey & the Wester Coull Trust | Dinnet & Wester Coull | | 23800 | NJ 4400 |
| 8 | Trustees of Tillypronie Trust | Tillypronie & Towie | Hon. Philip Astor | 15000 | NJ 4307 |
| 9 | Candacraig Trust | Candacraig | Falconer A. Wallace | 14000 | NJ 3411 |
| 10 | Sir Ian Okeover-Walker Bt. | Glenmuick | | 13000 | NO 3690 |
| 11 | BMF Group * | Bognie | Alex Gordon Morison | 11700 | NJ 6141 |
| 12 | John Howard Seton Gordon of Abergeldie | Abergeldie | | 10200 | NO 2992 |
| 13 | Alan McLean | Littlewood | | 8460 | NJ 5118 |
| 14 | Trustees of Aberdeen Endowments Trust | Towie Barclay & others | | 8008 | NJ 7443 |
| 15 | Donald H.M. & Andrew M.L. Farquharson | Finzean | | 7900 | NO 5993 |
| 16 | Sir Andrew G. Forbes-Leith Bt. and family | Fyvie | | 7720 | NJ 7639 |
| 17 | Sir Richard Suttons Settled Estates | Slains | | 7574 | NK 0430 |
| 18 | Frogmore Investments Ltd. | Glenkindie | See Appendix 3 | 7300 | NJ 4214 |
| 19 | Georgina Tulloch | Glenbuchat North | | 7200 | NJ 3318 |
| 20 | Trustees of Haddo and Earl of Haddo | Haddo | | 7047 | NJ 8633 |
| 21 | Nicol Brothers | Ballogie | | 6500 | NO 5795 |
| 22 | The MacRobert Trust Estate | MacRobert Trust Estate | | 6500 | NJ 4905 |
| 23 | Kildrummy (Jersey) Ltd. | Kildrummy & Towie | Peter & Hylda Smith | 6200 | NJ 4516 |
| 24 | Thomas Innes of Learney | Learney | | 5900 | NJ 6304 |
| 25 | Monymusk Land Co. & Monymusk Estate | Monymusk | Sir Archibald Grant | 5486 | NJ 6815 |
| 26 | Master of Forbes & Trusts | Forbes | | 5200 | NJ 6219 |
| 27 | | Drumossie House | | 5200 | NJ 6328 |
| 28 | Trustees of the Cluny Estates | Cluny Estates | | 5000 | NJ 6912 |
| 29 | Captain David W.S. Buchan & Children's Trust | Auchmacoy & Auchleuchries | | 4935 | NJ 9930 |
| 30 | Andrew Salvesen | Findrack & Tillyfour | | 4600 | NJ 6005 |
| 31 | James R. Ingleby | Invermarkie | | 4500 | NJ 4239 |
| 32 | Mrs Robert & C.I.R. Wolrige Gordon | Esslemont | | 4500 | NJ 9230 |
| 33 | Barra Trust & Straloch Trust | Barra & Straloch | Major Francis C.Q. Irvine | 4250 | NJ 7925 |
| 34 | Bruce Urquhart | Craigston Estate | | 4200 | NJ 7655 |
| 35 | Alisdair J. Barlas | Craig | | 4200 | NJ 4624 |
| 36 | | Sligo Estate | | 4200 | NJ 8857 |
| 37 | Hans Depre | Clova | | 3950 | NJ 4522 |
| 38 | Mrs Isabel J.B. Sole | Glenbuchat South | | 3800 | NJ 3815 |
| 39 | Pittodrie Estate Ltd. | Pittodrie & Bennachie | | 3500 | NJ 6923 |
| 40 | | Tonley | | 3200 | NJ 6013 |
| 41 | | Allargue | | 3000 | NJ 2609 |
| 42 | Cullerlie Trust | Cullerlie | | 3000 | NJ 7602 |
| 43 | | Skelmuir | | 3000 | NJ 9841 |
| 44 | D.R.M. James-Duff & Trusts | Hatton | | 2700 | NJ 7546 |
| 45 | Knockespock Estate Co. | Knockespock | | 2680 | NJ 5424 |
| 46 | R.L.O. Fyffe | Corsindae | | 2500 | NJ 6808 |

**Aberdeenshire**

| # | Owner | Estate | Notes | Area | Grid Ref |
|---|---|---|---|---|---|
| 47 | L.A. & P.M. Gordon-Duff | Drummuir (part) | | 2500 | NJ 4344 |
| 48 | Andrew Dingwall-Fordyce | Brucklay | | 2340 | NJ 9150 |
| 49 | | Midmar | | 2250 | NJ 7005 |
| 50 | William A.J. Davie, | Lumphanan | | 2200 | NJ 5703 |
| 51 | | Wardhouse | | 2200 | NJ 5630 |
| 52 | Meldrum Estate | Old Meldrum | | 2200 | NJ 8129 |
| 53 | | Arnage | | 2200 | NJ 9337 |
| 54 | Royal Society for the Protection of Birds | Loch of Strathbeg | | 2029 | NK 0758 |
| 55 | ON MARKET | Grumack | | 2028 | NJ 4437 |
| 56 | Trustees of John Anderson | Teuchan | | 2000 | NK 0738 |
| 57 | Udny & Dudwick Estates | Udny & Dudwick | | 2000 | NJ 8826 |
| 58 | Aboyne Castle Estate Trustees | Aboyne | Marquis of Huntly | 2000 | NJ 5299 |
| 59 | Andrew E.H. Bradford | Kincardine | | 2000 | NJ 6000 |
| 60 | Trustees of Lt. Col. Forbes | Corse | | 2000 | NJ 5407 |
| 61 | | Clackriach | | 2000 | NJ 9346 |
| 62 | | Boyndlie | | 2000 | NJ 9162 |
| 63 | C.R. Ratcliffe & family | Courtcairn & Kinnernie | | 1800 | NJ 7211 |
| 64 | Craigmyle Estates Ltd. | Craigmyle | | 1800 | NJ 6301 |
| 65 | Usborne & Son (London) Ltd. | Longhaven | | 1700 | NK 1039 |
| 66 | Trustees of James Allan | Midbeltie | | 1700 | NJ 6200 |
| 67 | Sluie Estate Trust | Sluie | R. Strang-Steel | 1700 | NO 6296 |
| 68 | C.E.I. Harding | Brindy | | 1500 | NJ 6120 |
| 69 | Hamish C. McLean | Breda | | 1500 | NJ 5416 |
| 70 | James C.A. & Alexander J.A. Burnett | Crathes & Leys (part) | | 1500 | NJ 7500 |
| 71 | William K.A.J. Chambers Hunter | Tillery | | 1500 | NJ 9122 |
| 72 | I.M. Smith | Brux | | 1500 | NJ 4916 |
| 73 | Craigie Farm Estates | Park | | 1500 | NO 7898 |
| 74 | Trustees of Alfred E. Jones | Ludquharn | | 1500 | NK 0242 |
| 75 | | Kinmundy | | 1500 | NK 0041 |
| 76 | | Grandhome | | 1500 | NJ 9011 |
| 77 | Crown Trust Fund | Drumdelgie | | 1401 | NJ 4842 |
| 78 | ON MARKET | Glenbuchat Forest | | 1391 | NJ 3516 |
| 79 | ON MARKET | Ben Newe Forest | | 1317 | NJ 3713 |
| 80 | Corsindae & Fetternear Farms | Fetternear & Whitehaugh | R. Fyffe | 1300 | NJ 7217 |
| 81 | Crannach Woodland Partnership | Crannach | Robin Callander and others | 1261 | NJ 3899 |
| 82 | Alistair J. Lilburn | Coull | | 1250 | NJ 5102 |
| 83 | M. Calvert | Dessmuir & Dess | | 1250 | NJ 5700 |
| 84 | | Tillydrine | | 1250 | NO 6098 |
| 85 | A. Howie | West Knock | | 1200 | NJ 9845 |
| 86 | | Foundland | | 1200 | NJ 6034 |
| 87 | Stephen and Susan Mackie | Rora & Balquhindachy | | 1160 | NK 0649 |
| 88 | ON MARKET | Forest of Deer | | 1103 | NJ 9650 |
| 89 | Herbst Peat & Energy (Scotland) | Rora and St Fergus Moss | | 1047 | NK 0451 |
| 90 | Jolyon V. Robinson & S.W. Robinson | Beldorney | | 1030 | NJ 4136 |
| 91 | ON MARKET | Crimongate | | 1012 | NK 0458 |
| 92 | Alessandro Muratori | Rora Moss | | 1000 | NK 0450 |
| 93 | Andrew D. Tennant | Muiresk | | 1000 | NJ 7049 |
| 94 | Excrs of D. M. Godsman & N. M. Godsman | Cairngall | | 1000 | NK 0447 |
| 95 | Trustees of David W. Stewart | Turnerhall | | 1000 | NJ 9333 |
| 96 | Electricity Supply Nominees * | Logie & Craigievar | | 1000 | |
| 97 | Mrs Flora M.M. Williams | Lynturk | | 1000 | NJ 5912 |
| 98 | ON MARKET | Troup (part) | | 1000 | NJ 8362 |
| 99 | Geordie Burnett-Stuart | Dens & Crichie | | 1000 | NJ 9745 |

## Aberdeenshire

| # | Owner | Property | Acres | Grid Ref |
|---|---|---|---|---|
| 100 | Irene Bell Tawse | Culquoich | 1000 | NJ 4113 |
| 101 | Mrs D.A. Stancioff | Dunlugas | 1000 | NJ 6955 |
| 102 | Trustees of Ardhuncart Estate | Ardhuncart | 1000 | NJ 4817 |
| 103 | | Old Maud | 1000 | NJ 9146 |
| 104 | | Logie | 1000 | NJ 7025 |
| 105 | | Camphill | 1000 | NJ 5706 |
| 106 | | Barrack | 1000 | NJ 9142 |
| 107 | Thomas Ingleby | Aswanley | 1000 | NJ 4439 |
| 108 | Malcolm Hay | Edinglassie (part) | 800 | NJ 4137 |
| 109 | Co-op Wholesale Society Ltd. * | Petty | 550 | NJ 7636 |
| 110 | Captain John Hay of Delgatie * | Delgatie | 500 | NJ 7550 |
| | TOTAL | | 685124 | |
| | Aberdeenshire land area | | 1261333 | |
| | % of county accounted for | | 54.3% | |

### PUBLIC LANDHOLDINGS

| | | | |
|---|---|---|---|
| Forestry Commission | Various properties | 59135 | |
| b. Grampian Regional Council | Various properties | 1914 | |
| c. SNH | See Appendix 5 | 450 | |
| d. MoD | See Appendix 6 | 484 | |
| TOTAL | | 61983 | |
| % of county | | 4.9% | |

### CHANGES IN THE DISTRIBUTION OF LANDHOLDINGS BY SIZE 1970 - 1995

| | 1970 | | | 1995 | | |
|---|---|---|---|---|---|---|
| Acreage threshold | Acres | % of county | No. of owners | Acres | % of county | No. of owners |
| > 100 000 | 0 | 0% | 0 | 0 | 0% | 0 |
| > 75 000 | 75000 | 5.9% | 1 | 87500 | 6.9% | 1 |
| > 50 000 | 191800 | 15.2% | 3 | 277052 | 22.0% | 4 |
| > 40 000 | 191800 | 15.2% | 3 | 277052 | 22.0% | 4 |
| > 30 000 | 191800 | 15.2% | 3 | 277052 | 22.0% | 4 |
| > 20 000 | 342200 | 27.1% | 9 | 355145 | 28.2% | 7 |
| > 10 000 | 491600 | 39.0% | 21 | 419045 | 33.2% | 12 |
| > 5 000 | 639300 | 50.7% | 44 | 526240 | 41.7% | 28 |
| > 1 000 | 926600 | 73.5% | 154 | 683274 | 54.2% | 107 |

# Angus

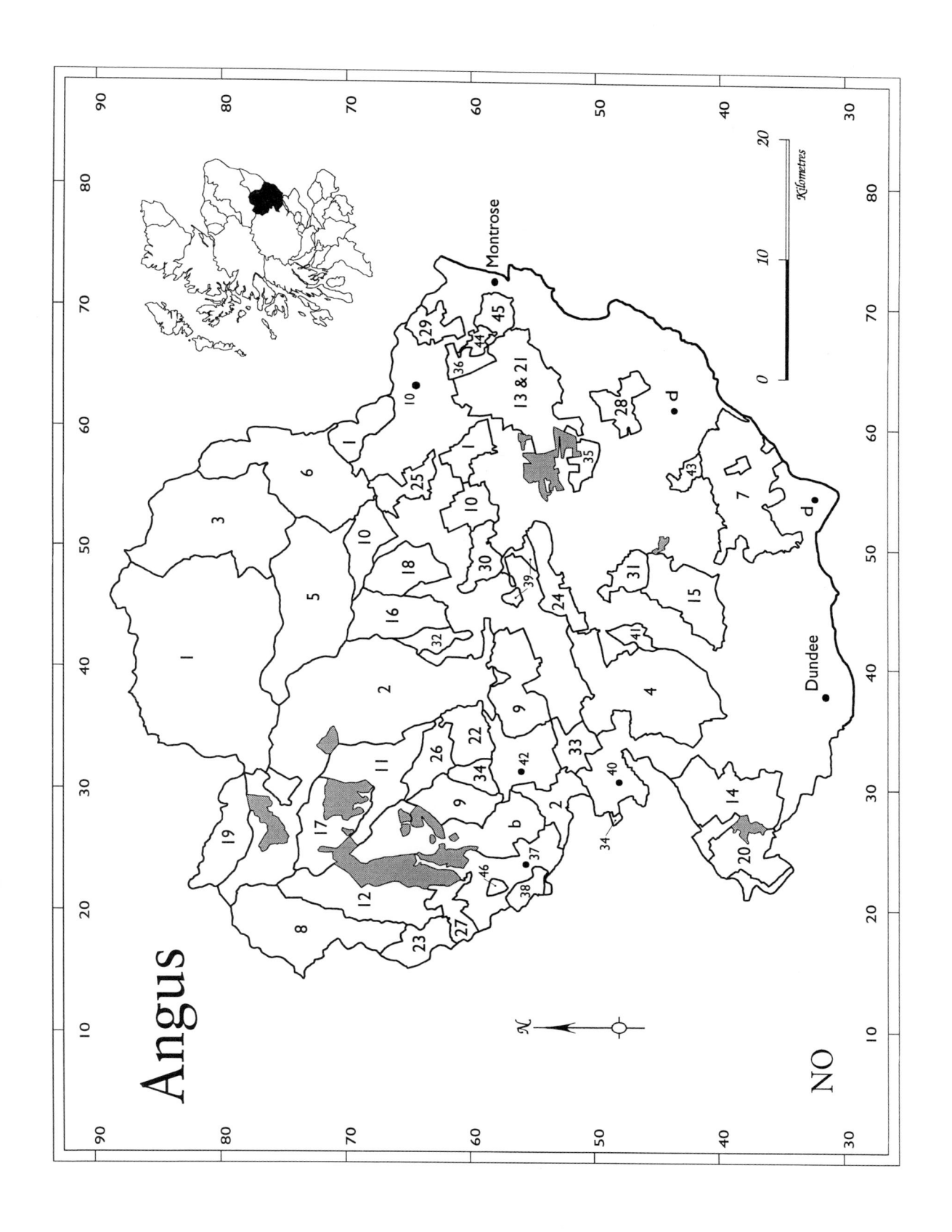

# Angus
## 559,090 acres

Angus was described by John McEwen as 'an aristocratic, even royal county'. This is still accurate. The Queen and the Earls of Airlie, Strathmore, Southesk, Dalhousie, Woolton and other members of the aristocracy own 141,456 acres or 25% of the county.

Banking and finance is responsible for large areas also with the Keswicks, Commercial Union Assurance, and Prudential Assurance owning 38,400 acres.

Like Aberdeen, Angus conducts its affairs with an air of discreetness. Everyone knows each other. It is not the place for flamboyancy. Things get done by the subtle but effective network that is the Angus Establishment. One has the feeling that the county has seen a low rate of turnover in land with few real newcomers. It was rather a surprise, therefore, to find out that the Tulchan Estate in Glenisla, for so long in the ownership of the Earl of Inchcape, had been sold to a German couple, Gunther Maxmillian Johannes Kuhnle and Frau Renate Hedwig Mina Kuhnle.

Most owners in Angus were helpful in clarifying ownership information. Cluttons, for example, the Chartered Surveyors, were particularly helpful and appreciative of my efforts to ensure accurate information as were others such as the Earl of Southesk. Strathmore Estate on the other hand pointed out that my information was not correct, that the acreage was 'a good deal lower than that suggested by you', the boundaries were 'correspondingly inaccurate' but that 'unfortunately it is not our policy to make public a great deal of information about the Estate and regret that I am unable to help you further'. It is hardly surprising therefore that we remain so ignorant about landownership in Scotland. It is quite revealing also that of the owners or agents who chose not to help clarify information, many were members of the Royal Institute of Chartered Surveyors, the very people who are campaigning for greater openness with respect to information about property through their Domesday 2000 initiative (see page 204).

| NO. | PROPRIETOR | PROPERTY | PRINCIPAL INTEREST | ACREAGE | GRID REF. |
|---|---|---|---|---|---|
| 1 | Dalhousie 1964/1971 Trust | Dalhousie Estates | Earl of Dalhousie & Lord Ramsay | 47200 | NO 5959 |
| 2 | Earl of Airlie & Lord Ogilvie | Airlie Estates | | 37300 | NO 2952 |
| 3 | Millden Estate Ltd. | Millden | See Appendix 3 | 18700 | NO 5478 |
| 4 | Strathmore Estates (Holding) Ltd. | Strathmore | Earl of Strathmore | 17300 | NO 3846 |
| 5 | Henry Keswick * | Hunthill | | 16800 | NO 4771 |
| 6 | Derald H. & Mrs Ruttenberg | Gannochy | | 14600 | NO 5970 |
| 7 | Commercial Union Assurance Co. plc | Panmure | | 13600 | NO 5437 |
| 8 | Tulchan of Glenisla Forest Ltd. | Tulchan | See Appendix 3 | 12500 | NO 1872 |
| 9 | Rt. Hon. Lord Lyell | Kinnordy & Balintore | | 10500 | NO 3655 |
| 10 | Careston Ltd. | Careston Estates | Jamie Campbell Adamson | 9000 | NO 5068 |
| 11 | C.H. & Miss E.A. Maitlands 1988 Trust | Balnabooth or Glentairie | | 8700 | NO 3267 |
| 12 | J.P.O. Gibb & A.J.R. Gibb | Glenisla | | 8100 | NO 1964 |
| 13 | Prudential Assurance Co. Ltd. | Southesk & Rossie School | | 8000 | NO 6653 |
| 14 | Sir James A. Cayzer | Kinpurnie & Lundie | | 8000 | NO 2836 |
| 15 | Fothringham Estate Co. Ltd. * | Fothringham | Robert Steuart Fothringham | 6500 | NO 4644 |
| 16 | Earl of Woolton | Glenogil | | 6400 | NO 4463 |
| 17 | Miss A.J. Strutts Protective Trust | Glenprosen | | 5400 | NO 2968 |

**Angus**

| | | | | | |
|---|---|---|---|---|---|
| 18 | Rothesay Trust Ltd. | Fern | | 5000 | NO 4766 |
| 19 | The Queen and Trustees of Balmoral * | Bachnagairn | | 4900 | NO 2579 |
| 20 | Trustees of W.N. Graham-Menzies | Hallyburton | | 4600 | NO 2438 |
| 21 | Southesk Settlement | Southesk | Lord Southesk | 4500 | NO 6357 |
| 22 | Pearsie Estate Company Ltd. | Pearsie | | 4000 | NO 3458 |
| 23 | James Gammell & Son Ltd. | Alrick | | 3700 | NO 1962 |
| 24 | Captain H.L. Gray-Cheape's 1986 Settlement | Carsegray | | 3700 | NO 4653 |
| 25 | Balnamoon Farms Company | Balnamoon | Carnegy Arbuthnott family | 3500 | NO 5563 |
| 26 | Lednathie Estate Ltd. | Lednathie | | 3400 | NO 3363 |
| 27 | Brewlands Land & Forestry | Brewlands | Brian G. Ivory | 2800 | NO 1960 |
| 28 | Robert D. Ramsay | Boysack & Kinblethmont | | 2700 | NO 6249 |
| 29 | Excrs of Sir Ewan G. MacPherson-Grant | Craigo | | 2200 | NO 6964 |
| 30 | Angus Neish | Tannadyce | | 2000 | NO 4857 |
| 31 | Bartholomew E.E. Smith | Lour | | 2000 | NO 4746 |
| 32 | Ian M.C.E. Clow | Baikies | | 2000 | NO 4263 |
| 33 | Lindertis Co. Ltd. | Lindertis | | 1800 | NO 3351 |
| 34 | Silvie Estates Company | Auldallan & Silvie | | 1700 | NO 3158 |
| 35 | P.S.H. Management Corporation | Guthrie | | 1500 | NO 5650 |
| 36 | William L. Mackie & Son | Balwyllo | | 1500 | NO 6559 |
| 37 | | Kilry | | 1500 | NO 2355 |
| 38 | James & Andrew Younger | Knowehead | | 1300 | NO 2354 |
| 39 | Lord and Lady Glendyne | Finavon & Craigeassie | | 1156 | NO 4557 |
| 40 | Ian Ivory | Ruthven & Cardean | | 1150 | NO 3047 |
| 41 | Roderick H.W. Munro | Kinnetties | | 1100 | NO 4247 |
| 42 | Kenneth G. Farquharson | Kinclune | | 1000 | NO 3155 |
| 43 | Trustees of late Cdr. Thomas C.A.H. Ouchterlony | Guynd | | 1000 | NO 5641 |
| 44 | National Trust for Scotland | House of Dun | | 936 | NO 6759 |
| 45 | Scottish Wildlife Trust | Montrose Basin & others | | 506 | NO 6957 |
| 46 | Electricity Supply Nominees Ltd. * | Kilry Estate Woodlands | | 500 | NO 2157 |
| | Total | | | 316248 | |
| | Angus land area | | | 559090 | |
| | % of county accounted for | | | 56.6% | |

**PUBLIC LANDHOLDINGS**

| | | |
|---|---|---|
| Forestry Commission | Various properties | 10122 |
| b. Tayside Regional Council | Lintrathen & others | 9970 |
| c. SNH | See Appendix 5 | 395 |
| d. MoD | See Appendix 6 | 3418 |
| TOTAL | | 23905 |
| % of county | | 4.3% |

**CHANGES IN THE DISTRIBUTION OF LANDHOLDINGS BY SIZE 1970 - 1995**

| | 1970 | | | 1995 | | |
|---|---|---|---|---|---|---|
| Acreage threshold | Acres | % of county | No. of owners | Acres | % of county | No. of owners |
| > 100 000 | 0 | 0% | 0 | 0 | 0% | 0 |
| > 75 000 | 0 | 0% | 0 | 0 | 0% | 0 |
| > 50 000 | 0 | 0% | 0 | 0 | 0% | 0 |
| > 40 000 | 43800 | 7.8% | 1 | 47200 | 8.4% | 1 |
| > 30 000 | 75200 | 13.5% | 2 | 84500 | 15.1% | 2 |
| > 20 000 | 75200 | 13.5% | 2 | 84500 | 15.1% | 2 |
| > 10 000 | 224400 | 40.1% | 12 | 188500 | 33.7% | 9 |
| > 5 000 | 265400 | 47.5% | 18 | 253600 | 45.4% | 18 |
| > 1000 | 408400 | 73.0% | 80 | 314306 | 56.2% | 43 |

# Argyll
## (1)

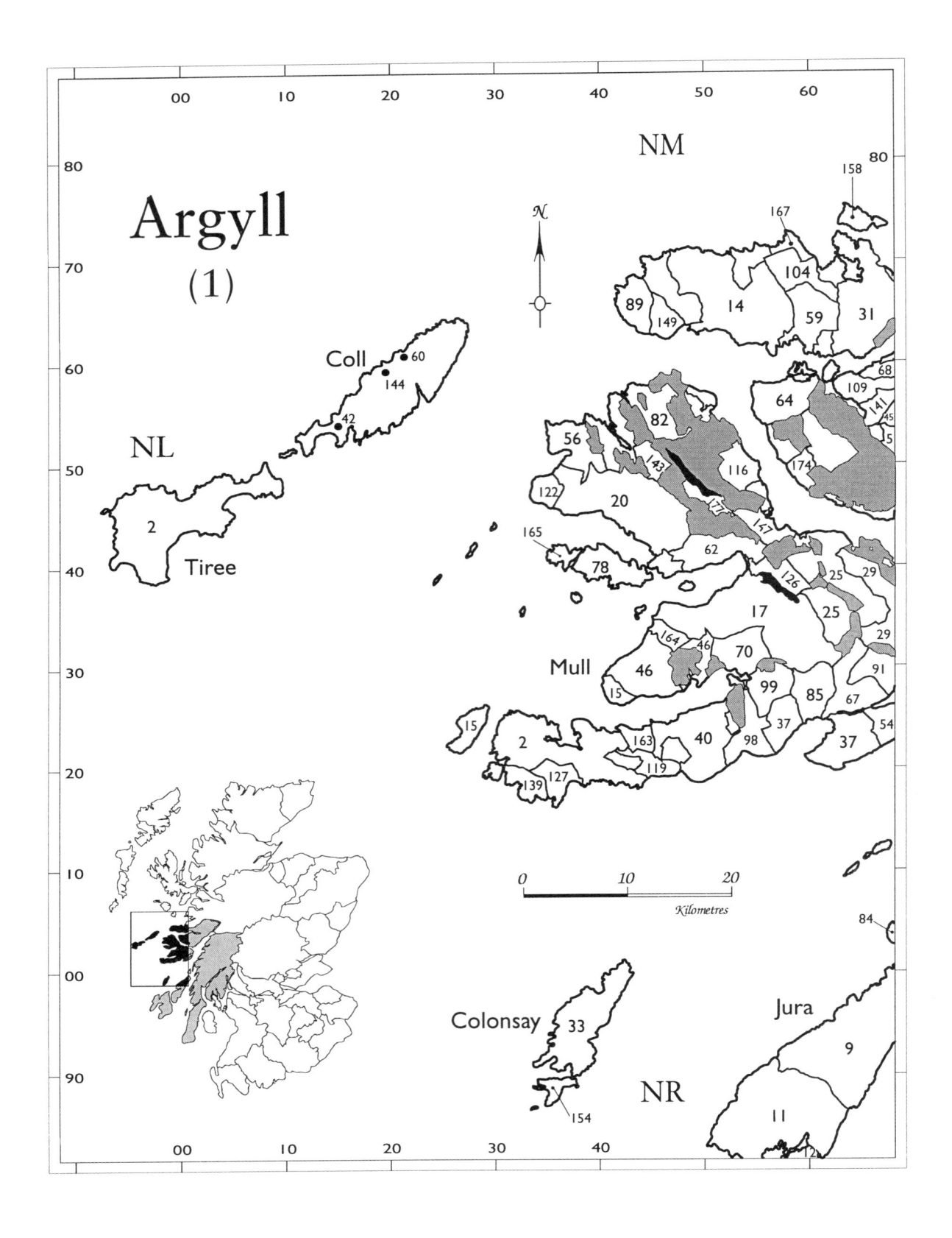

# Argyll
## (2)

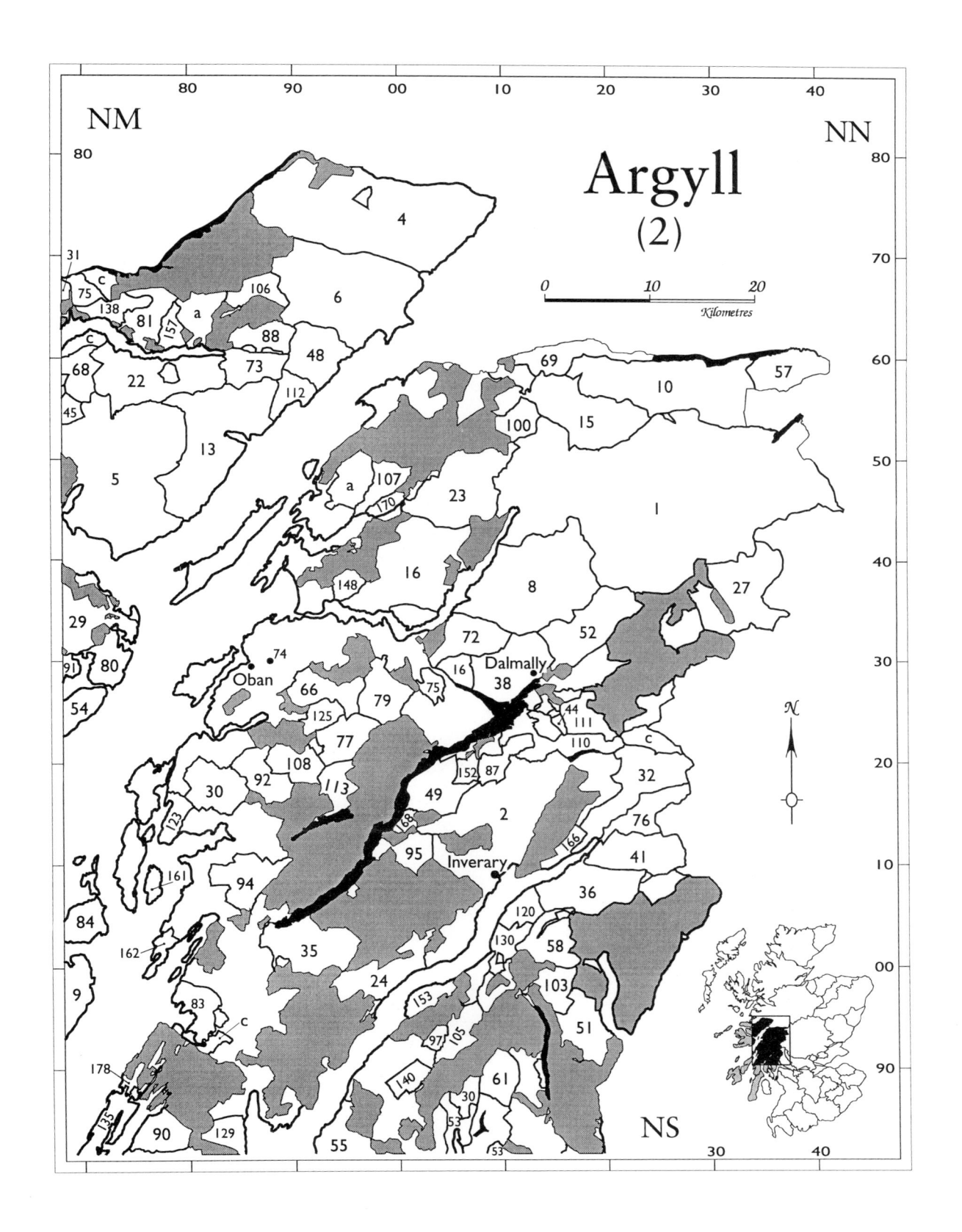

# Argyll (3)

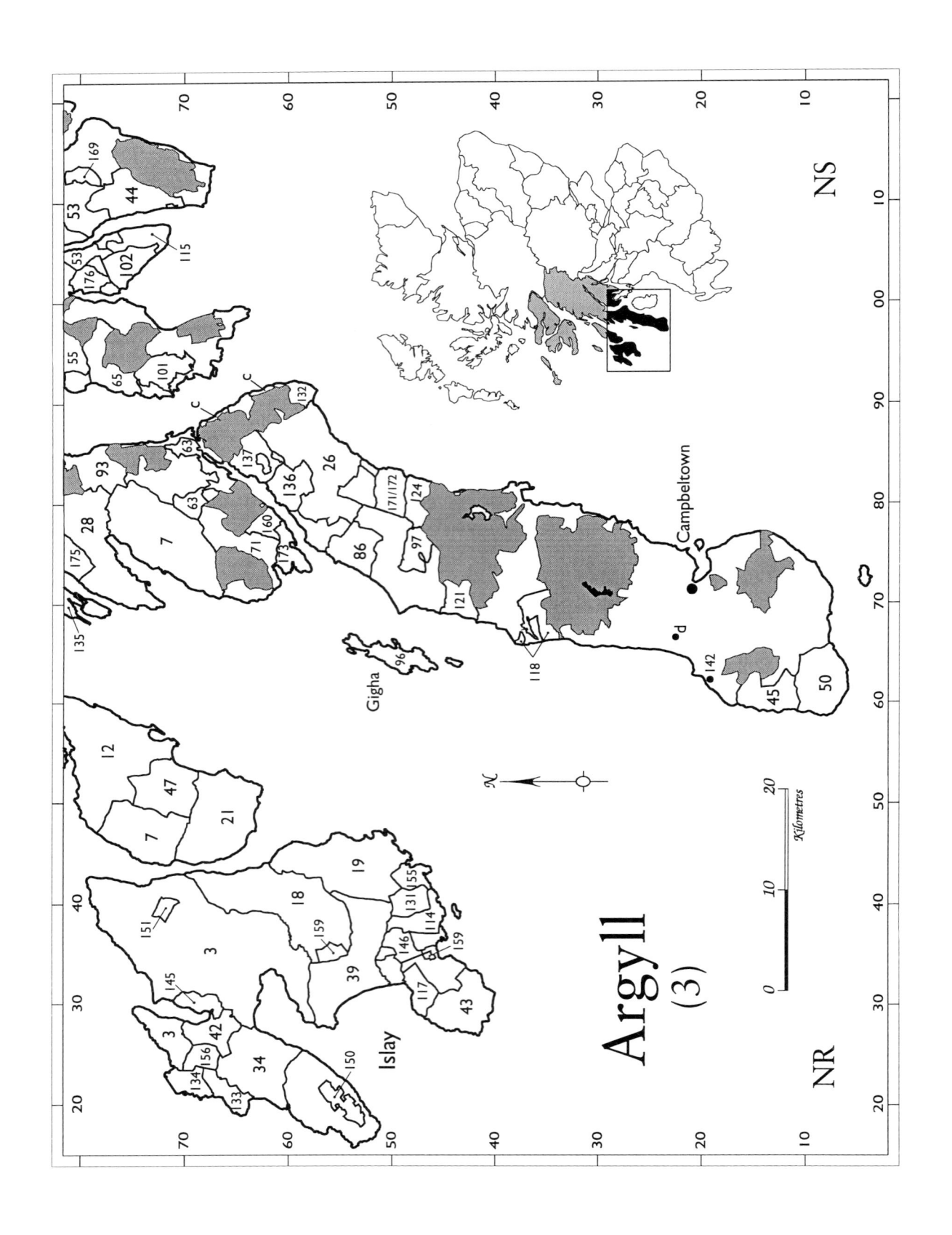

## Argyllshire
## 1,990,522 acres

The second largest county in Scotland has witnessed marked changes in landownership over the last 25 years. Private forestry has transformed western Argyll from mid-Kintyre north to Oban and Dalmally and a substantial number of new landowners have appeared, particularly overseas interests.

The overall pattern, however, has remained remarkably unchanged over this period with a similar distribution of holdings over 5000 acres. One of the few estates to have been broken up is the Ardkinglass Estate, formerly owned by Michael Noble, the former Secretary of State for Scotland, and his brother John. Upon Michael's death, his part passed to his four daughters who have split it up. John Noble has sold his share to D.P. Sumison. On the other hand, the financier Robert Fleming has expanded his estate and now owns 73,200 acres. Together with his cousins, who own Glenkinglass and Duilleter, the combined holding covers 118,700 acres of northern Argyll. Most of the bigger holdings have survived with relatively few estates changing hands other than the expected number of changes as one generation gives way to another.

The main structural changes have been at the smaller end of the scale where, with the massive increase in private forestry, many hill farms and small estates have sold off land. At the lower end of the holding range therefore a very different picture emerges. Not only has private forestry brought in new owners but Argyll has experienced an influx of new owners in small estates. Among the newcomers is Keith Schellenberg who will presumably be looking for a quieter life after his stewardship of the Isle of Eigg ended in tears.

Of greatest significance perhaps has been the dramatic increase in ownership by overseas interests who now own over 100,000. Danish and Swedish involvement has been most pronounced, accounting for almost half of this. The Danish Jensen Foundation which operates under the company Greentop Lands and Estates Ltd. owns 11,914 acres including the 9650 acre Claonaig Estate (see Box 2, page 148).

The Swedish government owns 6726 acres at Knockdow and Dalmally, having bailed out Nordbanken, a Swedish bank, which in turn had a bad debt from the original owner of the Knockdow Estate, Keith Olsson, who owned the estate under a Dutch-registered company Proprium Knockdow Ltd. Controversy over this particular estate was heightened when it was revealed that the Forestry Commission had awarded it a grant of £400,000 for tree planting.

Other newcomers are the Saxe Coburg Gotha Family Trust, the Saxon ducal family of which Queen Victoria's husband Prince Albert was a member. It is unclear who is behind this trust today, but the name of Count Rudi von Pezold was mentioned to me frequently in my enquiries. He is reputed to own more land but it is difficult to find out since he is thought to operate under a number of names, one of which is Illaria Ltd. which owns land in Lanarkshire.

There are perhaps more royal connections, with reports from a local farmer that the Queen Mother owns some forestry land.

Other interesting characters include Nicholas KS Wills, chairman of the Eclectic American Catalogue Ltd. and owner of the Otter Estate who lists among his recreations in *Who's Who* 'trying to farm in the Highlands'.

The Pension Funds are major investors in forestry in Argyll with Eagle Star Insurance Company owning over 10,000 acres and others, such as the tobacco giant Gallaher Pension Fund owning 4254 acres across the county.

Argyll strikes me as a rather sad place, where many of the local farmers have sold up and a new breed of wealthy overseas buyer has moved in. This is a feeling that is shared by many people in Argyll whom I spoke to, who have seen the forestry plantations spread over the hills and the farmers disappear. Argyll, as much as anywhere, convinces me that we could do things better.

| NO. | PROPRIETOR | PROPERTY | PRINCIPAL INTEREST | ACREAGE | GRID REF. |
|---|---|---|---|---|---|
| 1 | Robert Fleming & Trusts | Blackmount & Glen Etive | | 88900 | NN 2842 |
| 2 | Trustees of the 10th Duke of Argyll | Argyll Estates | | 60800 | NM 3323 |
| 3 | Islay Estates Company | Islay Estate | Lord Margadale | 49500 | NR 3362 |
| 4 | John M. Guthrie * | Conaglen | | 37000 | NM 9372 |
| 5 | Ardtornish Estate Co. Ltd. | Ardtornish | Raven family | 34100 | NM 7047 |
| 6 | R.M.M. Maclean of Ardgour | Ardgour | | 27900 | NM 9467 |
| 7 | Sir William J. Lithgow | Inver & Ormsary | | 24700 | NR 4471 |
| 8 | Hon Mrs D.C. Fleming & Hon Mrs L.F. Schuster | Glenkinglass | | 23200 | NN 1638 |
| 9 | Ardlussa Estate | Ardlussa | C.H. Fletcher | 21700 | NR 6487 |
| 10 | Vicomte Adolphe de Speolbergh | Altnafeadh (part) | | 20000 | NN 2955 |
| 11 | Lindsay C.N. Bury | Ruantallen | | 19700 | NR 5083 |
| 12 | Viscount Astor | Tarbert | | 19500 | NR 5577 |
| 13 | Yeoman (Morvern) Ltd. | Kingairloch & Glensanda | Angela Yeoman | 19000 | NM 8353 |
| 14 | John C. Grisewood | Ardnamurchan | | 18199 | NM 5165 |
| 15 | National Trust for Scotland | Glencoe, Iona & Burg | | 17625 | NN 1754 |
| 16 | Sarah Hope Troughton | Ardchattan Priory | | 16780 | NM 9735 |
| 17 | Viscount Massereene & Ferrard | Benmore | | 16600 | NM 5438 |
| 18 | Dunlossit Trustees Ltd. | Dunlossit | Bruno L. Schroder | 16500 | NR 4065 |
| 19 | Western Heritable Investments Ltd. | Ardtalla/Kintour | Sir John & Sandy Mactaggart | 14300 | NR 4654 |
| 20 | Torloisk Trustees * | Torloisk | Capt A.A.C. Farquharson | 14000 | NM 4145 |
| 21 | A.W.A. Riley-Smith of Jura | Ardfin | | 13100 | NR 4763 |
| 22 | Wefri A/S & Lurga Ltd. | Laudale | See Appendix 3 | 12500 | NM 7459 |
| 23 | Establissement Entraide et Solidarite | Glenure & Glencreran | P. Zvegintz & Dominic Collinet | 12300 | NN 0146 |
| 24 | Sir Ilay Mark Campbell of Succoth | Cumlodden | | 12200 | NS 0098 |
| 25 | Trustees of John A. & Dorothy A. Stancer | Glenforsa | | 12086 | NM 6138 |
| 26 | Greentop Lands & Estates Ltd. * | Claonaig & others | | 11914 | NR 7956 |
| 27 | Lord Trevor | Auch | | 11900 | NN 3235 |
| 28 | Duncan H. Rogers | Ellary & Castle Sween | | 11800 | NR 7376 |
| 29 | Christopher James | Torosay | | 10600 | NM 7235 |
| 30 | Eagle Star Insurance Co. Ltd. * | Cairnbaan & others | | 10017 | NS 0687 |
| 31 | C.B. Holman's Settlement Trustees | Shielbridge & Laga | | 10000 | NM 6565 |
| 32 | D.P. Sumison | Ardkinglas | | 10000 | NN 2318 |
| 33 | The Hon D.A. Howard | Colonsay | | 9880 | NR 3793 |
| 34 | D. Doyle | Foreland | | 9600 | NR 2664 |
| 35 | Major William Warde-Aldam | Ederline | | 9150 | NM 8702 |
| 36 | Catherine How | Ardno | | 8900 | NN 1508 |
| 37 | John James Corbett | Laggan & Glenbyre | | 8700 | NM 6224 |

**Argyllshire**

| | | | | | |
|---|---|---|---|---|---|
| 38 | E. Smith & Sons | Castles | | 8470 | NN 1329 |
| 39 | Laggan Estate Ltd. | Laggan | | 8100 | NR 2855 |
| 40 | Pennyghael Estates Ltd. | Pennyghael | Phil Collins & Genesis | 7900 | NM 5023 |
| 41 | Johnny M. Turnbull | Strone | | 7500 | NN 2211 |
| 42 | Royal Society for the Protection of Birds | Loch Gruinart, Coll & others | | 7388 | NR 2767 |
| 43 | Robert Montgomery | Kinnabus | | 6800 | NR 2942 |
| 44 | Securum | Knockdow & Creagan | | 6726 | NS 1070 |
| 45 | Scottish Wildlife Trust | Largiebaan and Rahoy Hills | | 6642 | NR 6014 |
| 46 | Messrs M. & A. Holman | Kilfinichen | | 6435 | NM 4429 |
| 47 | Lord Vestey & Hon. Mark Vestey | Forest | | 6400 | NR 5370 |
| 48 | Orion Holdings | Inversanda | C.S. Bailey | 6200 | NM 9359 |
| 49 | John & Catherine T. MacPherson | Balliemeanoch | | 6200 | NN 0116 |
| 50 | Terra Firma Trustees Ltd. | Carskiey | | 6193 | NR 6107 |
| 51 | Peter Ferguson | Carrick | | 5900 | NS 1994 |
| 52 | Richard D. Schuster | Duiletter | | 5900 | NN 1530 |
| 53 | Ardtaraig Farming Co. | Ardtaraig | | 5779 | NS 0682 |
| 54 | Robert Lionel Corbett | Craggan | | 5500 | NM 7027 |
| 55 | Baron van Lynden | Ballimore & Otter Ferry | | 5400 | NS 9283 |
| 56 | Navimar SA | Calgary | | 5200 | NM 3751 |
| 57 | Lord Pearson of Rannoch | Cruach (part) | | 5200 | NN 3657 |
| 58 | John Campbell & Sons | Succoth | | 5200 | NN 1302 |
| 59 | Captain J.E.C. Elliot | Glenborrodale | | 5000 | NM 6065 |
| 60 | Ferndale Ltd. | Gallanach & Cliad Farms | Neil Smith | 4920 | NM 2257 |
| 61 | Glenmassan Ltd. | Glen Massan | Stefan von Geijer | 4900 | NS 1087 |
| 62 | Killiechronan Estates Ltd. | Killiechronan | J.L. Leroy | 4805 | NM 5441 |
| 63 | Ileene & Neil Duncan | Stonefield Farms | | 4731 | NR 8069 |
| 64 | J.M.V. Horsman | Drimnin | | 4700 | NM 5554 |
| 65 | Nicholas Kenneth Spencer Wills | Otter | | 4562 | NR 9278 |
| 66 | Mrs E.V. McCorquodale's Trust | Dunach | | 4500 | NM 9227 |
| 67 | Peter R. Corbett | Kinlochspelvie | | 4500 | NM 6526 |
| 68 | Neils Tandrup & Viggo & Helle Sorensen | Glencripesdale | | 4500 | NM 6758 |
| 69 | Alcan Highland Estates Ltd. | Caolasnacon | | 4400 | NN 1460 |
| 70 | Trustees of Robert D.G. Laing | Ardvergnish | | 4400 | NM 5329 |
| 71 | Hilda May Coates | Carse House | | 4400 | NR 7461 |
| 72 | 1990 Trust for Lewis Heriot-Maitlands Issue | Glenoe | | 4400 | NN 0534 |
| 73 | B. Dowson | Carnoch Farm | | 4355 | NM 8460 |
| 74 | M.A. Mackay-James | Glencruitten | | 4272 | NM 8729 |
| 75 | Gallacher Pensions Trust Ltd. * | Resipole, Fanans & others | | 4254 | NM 7066 |
| 76 | Anastasia de Lapp | Achadunan | | 4200 | NN 2013 |
| 77 | William Dickie | Musdale | | 4200 | NM 9322 |
| 78 | Hon. Mrs Jean Howard | Ulva | | 4200 | NM 4439 |
| 79 | Gorstain Enterprises Ltd. | Barguillean | S. & E. Macdonald & J. Marshall | 4100 | NM 9828 |
| 80 | Col M.P. de Klee | Auchnacraig | | 4000 | NM 7330 |
| 81 | | Ardery | | 4000 | NM 7562 |
| 82 | Janet Nelson | Glengorm | | 4000 | NM 4357 |
| 83 | Robin N.L. Malcolm | Poltalloch | | 4000 | NR 7995 |
| 84 | The Rt. Hon. Lord Sandys | Scarba | | 3700 | NM 7004 |
| 85 | George T. Sassoon | Ben Buie | | 3700 | NM 6027 |
| 86 | John D. Pollock | Ronachan | | 3700 | NR 7454 |
| 87 | Midland Bank Pension Trust Ltd. * | Bovuy, Inistrynich & Cladich | | 3561 | NN 1121 |
| 88 | Messrs C. Walton Ltd. | Carnoch North | | 3535 | NM 8662 |
| 89 | | Achasnig Farm | | 3500 | NM 4366 |
| 90 | | Inverlussa | | 3500 | NR 7783 |

*The Tables and Maps*

## Argyllshire

| # | Owner | Estate | Notes | Acres | Grid Ref |
|---|---|---|---|---|---|
| 91 | Ardura Estate | Ardura | | 3500 | NM 6830 |
| 92 | | Lagganmore | | 3500 | NM 8520 |
| 93 | Kenneths of Stronachullin | Stronachullin | | 3500 | NR 8479 |
| 94 | John MacNicol & Sons | Turnalt, Barbreck | | 3500 | NM 8407 |
| 95 | James Angus Roderick Neil McGrigor | Ardchonnell | | 3468 | NM 9812 |
| 96 | Holt Leisure Parks Trust Ltd. | Gigha | | 3400 | NR 6449 |
| 97 | Vecata A/S | Narachan & Kilbridemore | | 3384 | NR 7547 |
| 98 | M. Horton | Carsaig & Kinloch | | 3200 | NM 5321 |
| 99 | Timothy Laing Family Fund | Rossal | Timothy J. Laing | 3200 | NM 5527 |
| 100 | Domenico Felice Berardelli * | Gleanleacnamuidhe | | 3200 | NN 1155 |
| 101 | ON MARKET | Ardmarnock Forest | | 3173 | NR 9372 |
| 102 | Bute Estate Ltd. * | Ardentraive etc. | | 3090 | NS 0374 |
| 103 | William Montgomery | Invernoaden | | 3000 | NS 1297 |
| 104 | Assina, Charles and Johannes H.J. MacQueen | Gortoneorn Estate | | 3000 | NM 5968 |
| 105 | Angus Anthony Fletcher of Dunans | Dunans | | 3000 | NS 0491 |
| 106 | William & Donald William MacPherson | Ariundle | | 2945 | NM 8666 |
| 107 | | Invernahyle | | 2900 | NM 9644 |
| 108 | Rev. L.H. Robertson | Bragleenmore | | 2900 | NM 9020 |
| 109 | Rahoy Estate Co. | Rahoy | | 2840 | NM 6356 |
| 110 | Trustees of Brigadeer R.W.L. Fellowes | Cladich | | 2839 | NN 0921 |
| 111 | Sybil J.A. Crerar & J&A Crerar | Brackley | | 2700 | NN 1826 |
| 112 | Geoffrey D.C. Burns | Kilmalieu | | 2700 | NM 8955 |
| 113 | | Drissaig | | 2700 | NM 9415 |
| 114 | Hendrick E. Ten Cate | Kilbride | | 2500 | NR 3846 |
| 115 | Calum M. Sinclair & others | South Hall | | 2500 | NS 0672 |
| 116 | John S.W. Chilvers | Ardnacross | | 2500 | NM 5449 |
| 117 | | Kintra | | 2500 | NR 3248 |
| 118 | Glenbarr Farms | Glenbarr | Angus C. Macalister of Genbarr | 2500 | NR 6636 |
| 119 | | Scoor & Beach | | 2447 | NM 4420 |
| 120 | Mount Castle 1985 Trust * | Ardchyline | Duchess of Abercorn | 2350 | NN 1106 |
| 121 | Keith Schellenberg | Killean | | 2234 | NR 7044 |
| 122 | Somerset Charrington | Treshnish | | 2220 | NM 2741 |
| 123 | Charles Huntington Struthers | Ardmaddy | | 2200 | NM 7816 |
| 124 | G.H.F.S.Nickerson | Cour | | 2200 | NR 8248 |
| 125 | Robert Craig | Kilbride | | 2200 | NM 9124 |
| 126 | Nichola Anne Harmer | Gruline | | 2200 | NM 5440 |
| 127 | Aenas A. Mackay & Araminta Hall | Ardalanish | | 2200 | NM 3719 |
| 128 | Electricity Supply Nominees * | Cowal Farm & Glen Fearna | | 2120 | |
| 129 | Saxe Coburg Gotha Family Trust | Ardrishaig | Count Rudi von Pezold | 2104 | NR 8383 |
| 130 | Sir Fitzroy Maclean | Strachur Estate | | 2000 | NN 1106 |
| 131 | John G. MacGowan | Callumkill | | 2000 | NR 4046 |
| 132 | M.E. James | Skipness | | 2000 | NR 9057 |
| 133 | I. Warren | Coull Farm | | 2000 | NR 2064 |
| 134 | Dr Anderson | Smaull | | 2000 | NR 2168 |
| 135 | A.C. Pollock | Tayvallich | | 2000 | NR 7387 |
| 136 | J.J.G. McCallum | Gartnagrenoch | | 2000 | NR 7959 |
| 137 | Jimmy Mceachern | Achnacarnan Farm | | 2000 | NR 8363 |
| 138 | Peter Sinclair | Resipole Farm | | 2000 | NM 7264 |
| 139 | | Knockvologen | | 2000 | NM 3119 |
| 140 | Robert E.A. & Margaret McVicar | Achanelid | | 1875 | NS 0087 |
| 141 | | Rahoy Deer Farm | | 1850 | NM 6655 |
| 142 | Joan & Laura-Lynn Dixon | Ballygroggan | | 1843 | NR 6219 |

**Argyllshire**

| | | | | | |
|---|---|---|---|---|---|
| 143 | Hugh & Lorna Boa | Aintuim | | 1808 | NM 4351 |
| 144 | Major N.V. MacLean Bristol | Grishipoll | | 1800 | NM 1959 |
| 145 | Tony Archibald | Craigens | | 1800 | NR 2967 |
| 146 | Execs. of Matthieu Speltham | Leorin | Nicholas Joseph Speltham | 1788 | NR 3548 |
| 147 | | Glenaros | | 1700 | NM 5544 |
| 148 | | Achnaba | | 1700 | NM 9436 |
| 149 | | Ormsaig | | 1700 | NM 4663 |
| 150 | L. & L. de Meuss D'Argenteuil & A. Bortonowski | Ballimony Woodlands | | 1676 | NR 1954 |
| 151 | Terry Ramsden | Bunnahabhain | | 1546 | NR 3972 |
| 152 | | Upper Sonachan Woodland | | 1500 | NN 0619 |
| 153 | Euan Maclachlan | Castle Lachlan | | 1500 | NS 0195 |
| 154 | Adam Bergius | Oronsay | | 1500 | NR 3588 |
| 155 | | Kildalton | | 1500 | NR 4347 |
| 156 | Dr D. Berry | Coille | | 1500 | NR 2468 |
| 157 | | Ranachan Farm | | 1500 | NM 7861 |
| 158 | Robert Devereux | Eilean Shona | | 1340 | NM 6473 |
| 159 | Mr & Mrs Stevenson | Avenvogie & An Curran | | 1300 | NR 3556 |
| 160 | | Dunmore | | 1300 | NR 7861 |
| 161 | Dowager & Viscount Selbey | Shuna | | 1200 | NM 7608 |
| 162 | Youngers family | Craignish | | 1200 | NM 7601 |
| 163 | Haighall Holdings Ltd. | Ardchrishnish & Ormsaig | Annetta Heusdens & Bois Labesse | 1200 | NM 4664 |
| 164 | | Balnahard | | 1200 | NM 4534 |
| 165 | Roc Sandford | Gometra | | 1170 | NM 3641 |
| 166 | Arthur Goddard | Ardkinglas Forest | | 1160 | NN 1510 |
| 167 | John Charles Humphrey Hart | Acairsaid | | 1000 | NM 5872 |
| 168 | Ernest Crawford & others | Blarghour | | 1000 | NM 9913 |
| 169 | B.I.C.C. Group Pension Trust Ltd. * | Glenkin Woodlands | | 1000 | NS 1279 |
| 170 | | Creagan | | 1000 | NM 9744 |
| 171 | Messrs Neil & Robert McBurney | Crossaig | | 1000 | NR 8151 |
| 172 | Frank Shannon Settlement Trustees | Crossaig | | 1000 | NR 8152 |
| 173 | Alastair, Eden & Damien Kinneil | Ardpatrick | | 1000 | NR 7559 |
| 174 | Mrs M. Lauder & Mr W. Lauder | Killundine | | 1000 | NM 5849 |
| 175 | Richard F. Tuthill | Creag a Mhadaidh | | 1000 | NR 7280 |
| 176 | | Ardachuple | | 1000 | NS 0179 |
| 177 | | Tenga | | 1000 | NM 5145 |
| 178 | Gong Hill Ltd. * | Carsaig | | 800 | NR 7387 |
| | Total | | | 1196749 | |
| | Argyllshire land area | | | 1990522 | |
| | % of county accounted for | | | 60.1% | |

**PUBLIC LANDHOLDINGS**

| | | |
|---|---|---|
| Forestry Commission | Various properties | 415045 |
| a. SOAEFD | See Appendix 4 | 8144 |
| c. SNH | See Appendix 5 | 7872 |
| d. MoD | See Appendix 6 | 987 |
| TOTAL | | 432048 |
| % of county | | 21.7% |

## Argyllshire

**CHANGES IN THE DISTRIBUTION OF LANDHOLDINGS BY SIZE 1970 - 1995**

|  | 1970 | | | 1995 | | |
|---|---|---|---|---|---|---|
| Acreage threshold | Acres | % of county | No. of owners | Acres | % of county | No. of owners |
| > 100 000 | 0 | 0% | 0 | 0 | 0% | 0 |
| > 75 000 | 0 | 0% | 0 | 88900 | 4.5% | 1 |
| > 50 000 | 198800 | 10.0% | 3 | 149700 | 7.5% | 2 |
| > 40 000 | 281100 | 14.1% | 5 | 199200 | 10.0% | 3 |
| > 30 000 | 377000 | 18.9% | 8 | 270300 | 13.6% | 5 |
| > 20 000 | 440300 | 22.1% | 11 | 387800 | 19.5% | 10 |
| > 10 000 | 777767 | 39.1% | 36 | 698421 | 35.1% | 32 |
| > 5 000 | 983767 | 49.4% | 68 | 884684 | 44.4% | 59 |
| > 1000 | 1262167 | 63.4% | 185 | 1195949 | 60.1% | 177 |

# Ayr

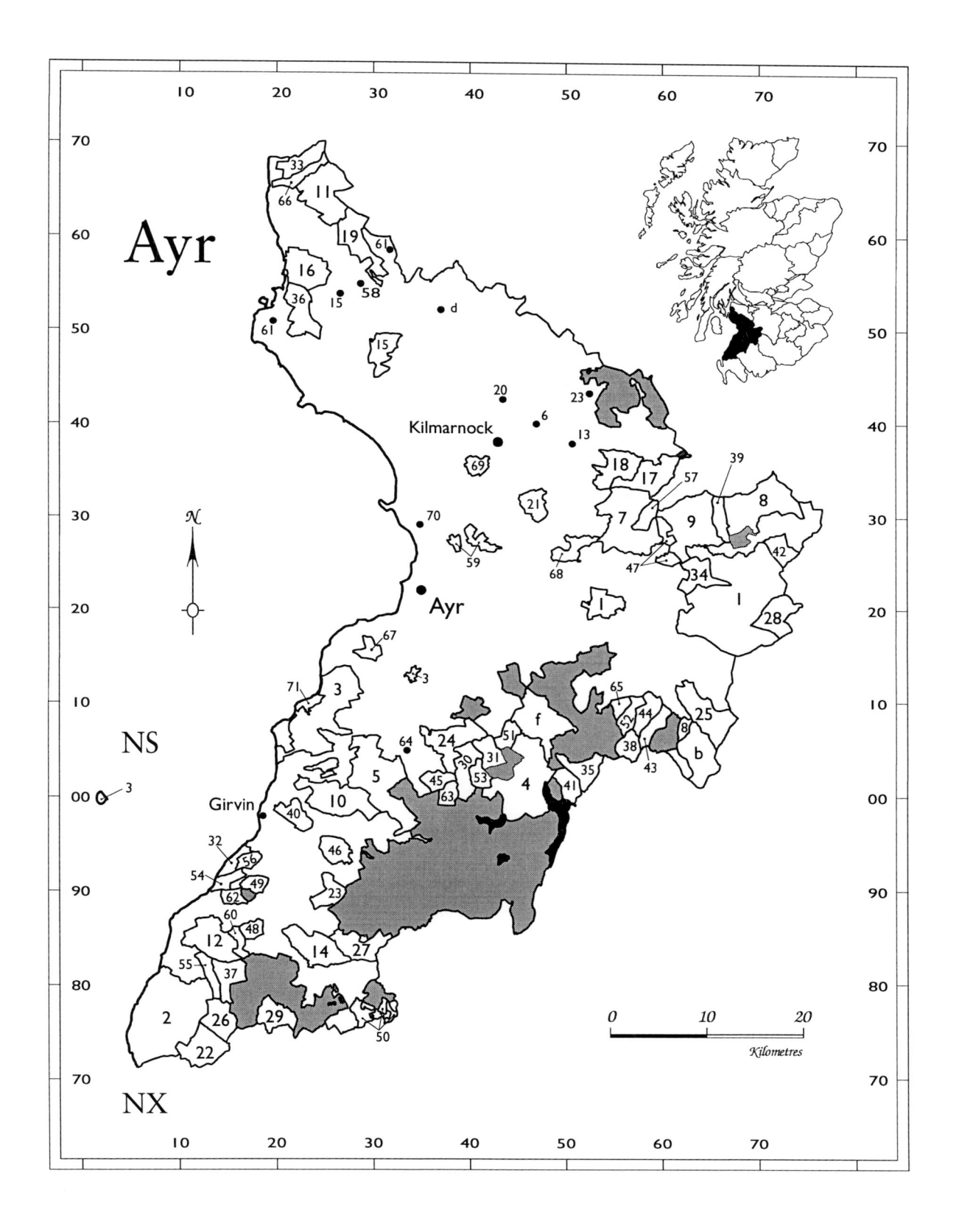

NS

NX

## Ayrshire
## 724,234 acres

Ayrshire is the largest county in the lowlands and includes some of the most productive land in the country for dairy and vegetable products. The number of large estates has continued to decline but the quality of information here is particularly poor. I sought the help of the estate agents Cluttons in Ayr, who manage many of the estates in Ayrshire. Unlike others who, if they could not help, at least passed my enquiries onto the relevant owner, Cluttons simply replied that they could be of no assistance.

Changes include the sale of the Muirkirk estate to Dunlin Ltd. from Northamptonshire whose Director, J.H. Richmond-Watson, also owns Arnisdale Estate in Inverness-shire. They have cleared the estate of its sheep stock and are now restoring the ground for grouse shooting with the close involvement of the Game Conservancy. This is something which is happening increasingly over the country.

Adam Wilson and Sons, the Ayr timber merchants, have bought parts of the old Avondale Estate, the bulk of which is in Lanarkshire. H.H. Roesner Land and Forestry Management is an offshore registered company believed to be controlled by Germans which has bought a significant part of the Lanfine Estate formerly owned by Baron Rotherwick of the Cayzer family. They also own land at Sallachy in Sutherland.

Private forestry incentives have also produced a number of new owners with land in other parts of Scotland, such as Gong Hill Ltd., another offshore registered company with interests in Argyll.

Fred Olsen, the Norwegian industrialist, owns 1200 acres at Dalreoch which, like his estate in Kirkcudbrightshire, he seems to have speculated with to raise business finance. Having paid £565,000 for it in August 1980, he promptly sold it six days later for £5,200,000 to two companies, A/S Quatro and A/S Cinco Ltd. They in turn sold it in 1991 to Cinco Ltd. and Forrest Estate Ltd. for £6,389,000. A Standard Security was taken out in 1995 with Christiania Bank og Kreditkasse. Quite how regularly such inflated deals are carried out on land in Scotland is, of course, unclear. It would be of some concern if we were to discover that significant parts of the country are mortgaged to the hilt for dubious overseas business deals.

| NO. | PROPRIETOR | PROPERTY | PRINCIPAL INTEREST | ACREAGE | GRID REF. |
|---|---|---|---|---|---|
| 1 | Bute Estate Ltd. * | Dalblair & Dumfries House | | 19600 | NS 5420 |
| 2 | Glenapp Estate Co Ltd. * | Glenapp | Earl of Inchcape | 13000 | NX 0980 |
| 3 | Cassillis Estate | Cassilis | Earl of Ailsa | 10000 | NX 0299 |
| 4 | Craigengillan Estates Co. Ltd. | Craigengillan | A.D.B. Gavin | 8600 | NS 4602 |
| 5 | Sir Charles Fergusson | Kilkerran | | 8000 | NS 3003 |
| 6 | Pension Fund Property Unit Trust | Kilmarnock Estates | | 8000 | NS 4740 |
| 7 | R.G. McIntyre's Trust | Sorn | | 7900 | NS 5426 |
| 8 | Dunlin Ltd. * | Muirkirk & Lochingirroch | J.H. Richmond-Watson | 7817 | NS 6931 |
| 9 | R.L. & M.H. Tufnell | Nether Whitehaugh | | 6200 | NS 6129 |
| 10 | N.J.F. Dalrymple-Hamilton | Bargany | | 6000 | NS 2400 |
| 11 | Brisbane Glen Estate Co. Ltd. | Outerwards | | 5362 | NS 2366 |
| 12 | Lord Richard Wellesley & Duchess of Wellington | Knockdolian | | 4700 | NX 1285 |
| 13 | Lady Jean Campbell of Loudoun | Loudoun | | 4400 | NS 5037 |

**Ayrshire**

| | | | | | |
|---|---|---|---|---|---|
| 14 | Mohan Singh Atwal | Kildonan | | 4000 | NX 2283 |
| 15 | Blair Trust Company | Blair & Plann | V.J. Borwick | 3500 | NS 3048 |
| 16 | Earl of Glasgow | Kelburn | | 3200 | NS 2156 |
| 17 | Adam Wilson & Sons Ltd. | Avondale (part) | | 3200 | NS 5834 |
| 18 | H.H. Roesner Land & Forestry (Scotland) Ltd. * | Lanfine | | 3200 | NS 5536 |
| 19 | Thomas Logan | Plan | | 3200 | NS 3057 |
| 20 | Alexander George & Co. | Rowallan | | 3000 | NS 4342 |
| 21 | John Findlay | Carnell & Damhead | | 3000 | NS 4632 |
| 22 | | Dalnigap (part) | | 3000 | NX 1371 |
| 23 | Eagle Star Insurance Co. Ltd. * | Lamdoughty & Craigends | | 2848 | NX 2491 |
| 24 | James Hunter Blair | Blairquhan | | 2700 | NS 3605 |
| 25 | Dalhanna Farming Co. | Lochbrowan (part) | Angus Campbell | 2700 | NS 6209 |
| 26 | | Lagafater | | 2500 | NX 1476 |
| 27 | Black Clauchrie Estate Co. | Black Clauchrie | | 2500 | NX 2984 |
| 28 | Illaria Ltd. | Carmacoup & Penbreck (part) | Count Rudi von Pezold | 2500 | NS 7119 |
| 29 | Trustees of Robert Carswell | Chirmorrie | | 2200 | NX 2176 |
| 30 | Andrew Paton & Co. | Craig & Genoch & Largs | | 2000 | NS 3902 |
| 31 | James Kay | Gass | | 2000 | NS 4105 |
| 32 | John Melville & Sons | Ardwell | | 2000 | NX 1694 |
| 33 | Lord Montgomerie | Fardens | | 2000 | NS 2166 |
| 34 | | Boghead Farm | | 2000 | NS 6324 |
| 35 | Scottish Amicable Life Assurance Society * | Glenmuck & Brownhill (part) | | 1800 | NS 5102 |
| 36 | R.A. Montgomerie | Crosbie & Southannan Moor | | 1700 | NS 2351 |
| 37 | John Scott | Balkissock | | 1600 | NX 1381 |
| 38 | Refuge Farms Ltd. * | Various properties | | 1566 | NS 5605 |
| 39 | A. Woodburn & Sons | Netherwood | | 1500 | NS 6528 |
| 40 | Anthony Howat | Enoch & Brae | | 1500 | NX 2198 |
| 41 | Eriff Estates | Eriff | | 1500 | NS 5100 |
| 42 | John Murray | Crossflat | | 1500 | NS 7127 |
| 43 | Martin Sloot | Monquhill | | 1500 | NS 5806 |
| 44 | Peter Hyslop | Brockloch | | 1500 | NS 5910 |
| 45 | Thomas Murray & Sons Ltd. | Dalmorton | | 1500 | NS 3701 |
| 46 | Alexander Fergusson | Alton Albany | | 1470 | NX 2693 |
| 47 | Gong Hill Ltd. * | Auchenlongford | | 1435 | NS 5928 |
| 48 | Fred Olsen Ltd. * | Dalreoch | | 1200 | NX 1686 |
| 49 | Hugh Paton | Millenderdale | | 1200 | NX 1690 |
| 50 | J. Sanders & Mrs Beale | Drumlamford | | 1200 | NX 2876 |
| 51 | James McWhirter | Grimmet | | 1200 | NS 4406 |
| 52 | Mrs Alvean Kerr | Dalleagles | | 1200 | NS 5710 |
| 53 | Robert & Mrs Margaret McTaggart | Glenauchie | | 1200 | NS 4201 |
| 54 | Straid Farms Ltd. | Straid | | 1200 | NX 1390 |
| 55 | William Stevenson & Son | Balrazzie | | 1200 | NX 1281 |
| 56 | Scottish Wildlife Trust | Grey Hills & others | | 1178 | NX 1793 |
| 57 | | Blacksidend | | 1100 | NS 5728 |
| 58 | R. Fuchs | Moorpark & others | | 1053 | NS 3055 |
| 59 | Robert Angus | Ladykirk | | 1050 | NS 3826 |
| 60 | Alexander D. McEwen | Bardrochat | | 1000 | NX 1585 |
| 61 | Hunterston Estates Ltd | Campbelton & Cockston | | 1000 | NS 1950 |
| 62 | John Lambie | Knockdaw | | 1000 | NX 1589 |
| 63 | John McWhirter & Co. Ltd. | Linfairn | | 1000 | NS 3801 |
| 64 | Katrina Geddes | Kirkbride | | 1000 | NS 3304 |
| 65 | Robert Laurie | Knockburnie | | 1000 | NS 5610 |
| 66 | Scott Farms Ltd. | Barr & Thirdpart | | 1000 | NS 2065 |

## Ayrshire

| | | | | |
|---|---|---|---|---|
| 67 | W. & R. Kerr & Sons | Sauchrie Mains & Craigskean | 1000 | NS 3014 |
| 68 | | Mauchline | 1000 | NS 4926 |
| 69 | | Caprington | 1000 | NS 4036 |
| 70 | Co-op Wholesale Society Ltd. * | Monktonhill | 590 | NS 3429 |
| 71 | National Trust for Scotland | Culzean | 579 | NS 2309 |

| | |
|---|---|
| Total | 212048 |
| Ayrshire land area | 724234 |
| % of county accounted for | 29.3% |

### PUBLIC LANDHOLDINGS

| | | |
|---|---|---|
| Forestry Commission | Various properties | 95362 |
| b. Strathclyde Regional Council | Craigdarroch | 4200 |
| d. MoD | See Appendix 6 | 1186 |
| f. British Coal | Burnton | 4000 |
| TOTAL | | 104748 |
| % of county | | 14.5% |

### CHANGES IN THE DISTRIBUTION OF LANDHOLDINGS BY SIZE 1970 - 1995

| | 1970 | | | 1995 | | |
|---|---|---|---|---|---|---|
| Acreage threshold | Acres | % of county | No. of owners | Acres | % of county | No. of owners |
| > 100 000 | 0 | 0% | 0 | 0 | 0% | 0 |
| > 75 000 | 0 | 0% | 0 | 0 | 0% | 0 |
| > 50 000 | 0 | 0% | 0 | 0 | 0% | 0 |
| > 40 000 | 0 | 0% | 0 | 0 | 0% | 0 |
| > 30 000 | 0 | 0% | 0 | 0 | 0% | 0 |
| > 20 000 | 21100 | 2.9% | 1 | 0 | 0% | 0 |
| > 10 000 | 64200 | 8.9% | 4 | 42600 | 5.9% | 3 |
| > 5 000 | 127300 | 17.6% | 12 | 100479 | 13.9% | 11 |
| > 1000 | 189100 | 26.1% | 43 | 210879 | 29.1% | 69 |

## Banffshire
## 403,054 acres

Banffshire is a long and skinny county working its way from the Cairngorm plateau down the east bank of the Spey to the fishing towns of Buckie and Banff. It remains dominated by large estates, the biggest five alone accounting for just under half of the county.

The Crown Estate Commissioners remain the biggest owners with their holdings at Glenlivet and at Auchindoun. Glenlivet was the focus of the Glenlivet Development Project undertaken by the Crown Estates in the late 80s. The Commissioners agreed to take a 'more positive' role than that of the traditional landlord and 'actively encourage a wide range of economic activity, including diversification on their let farms'. This has included allowing tenants to benefit from the management of woodlands for example, which by law they are not normally entitled to. The project has demonstrated the possibilities that a flexible approach to ideas and support for a wide range of development measures can bring to the kind of area which is often regarded as having limited scope for economic development.

One estate which could apparently do with such an approach is Glenfiddich and Cabrach, once owned separately but now owned by a company called Golden Lane Securities whose directors are Michael Cutting, Christopher Moran and Anthony Ehrenzweig. Local sources tell me of access problems, depopulated farms and a decaying Glenfiddich Lodge. Such are the results of a laissez-faire, free market approach to landownership and the rural economy.

Another newcomer to Banffshire is the mysterious Andras Ltd., an offshore company controlled by an unknown but exceedingly wealthy Malaysian businessman, who owns Glenavon Estate. Sir Seton Wills, who bought the estate for £100,000 in 1963, ended up in 1995 reputedly putting the same amount annually into running the place and deciding that enough was enough. One of the last of the Wills family to own land in Scotland, he sold out for £6.1 million in 1995. The sale, which I learnt of from a local person and which *The Herald* then ran as a front-page exclusive, prompted a flurry of media interest in overseas ownership of land in Scotland.

Seafield Estates did not reply to my enquiries and, in the absence of any better information, their holdings in Banffshire are recorded as they were by Millman in 1970.

# Banff

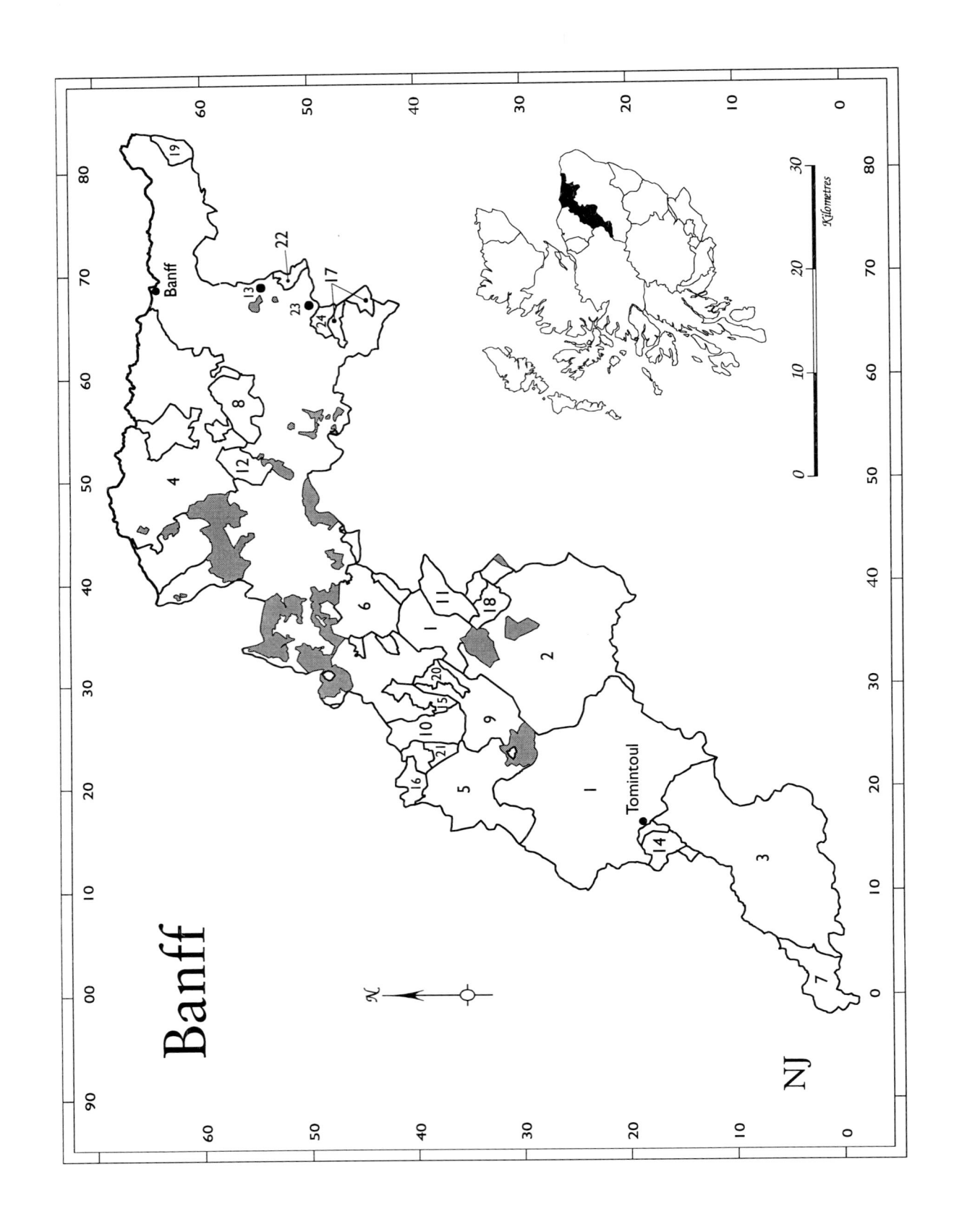

## Banffshire

| NO. | PROPRIETOR | PROPERTY | PRINCIPAL INTEREST | ACREAGE | GRID REF. |
|---|---|---|---|---|---|
| 1 | Crown Estate Commissioners | Glenlivet & Auchindoun | | 57700 | NJ 1922 |
| 2 | Golden Lane Securities Ltd. | Glenfiddich & Cabrach | See Appendix 3 | 41500 | NJ 3132 |
| 3 | Andras Ltd. * | Glenavon | | 41200 | NJ 1205 |
| 4 | Earl of Seafield * | Seafield Estates | | 35000 | NJ 5066 |
| 5 | C. Macpherson-Grant Russell & Ballindalloch Trust | Ballindalloch (part) | | 14200 | NJ 1736 |
| 6 | L.A. & P.M. Gordon-Duff | Drummuir (part) | | 7400 | NJ 3844 |
| 7 | Royal Society for the Protection of Birds | Upper Glen Avon | | 4500 | NJ 0102 |
| 8 | Charles Marshall | Park | | 4200 | NJ 5857 |
| 9 | Reckitt | Ben Rinnes | | 4200 | NJ 2634 |
| 10 | Kinermony Ltd. | Kinermony & Shenval | | 4200 | NJ 2541 |
| 11 | Malcolm Hay | Edinglassie (part) | | 3500 | NJ 4138 |
| 12 | John B. Innes | Edingight | | 2700 | NJ 5155 |
| 13 | BMF Group * | Bognie | Alec Gordon Morison | 2300 | NJ 6854 |
| 14 | Delnabo Estate Ltd. | Delnabo | See Appendix 3 | 2200 | NJ 1417 |
| 15 | Horsens Folkeblad Foundation * | Conval | | 2170 | NJ 2839 |
| 16 | Dr Catherine Wills | Phones | | 2000 | NJ 1940 |
| 17 | | Ardfour | | 2000 | NJ 6547 |
| 18 | D. Anthony Sharp | Lesmurdie | | 2000 | NJ 3932 |
| 19 | ON MARKET | Troup (part) | | 1748 | NJ 8362 |
| 20 | W.G. & G.I. Macpherson | Glenrinnes | | 1400 | NJ 3138 |
| 21 | Michael Woodcock | Carron | | 1300 | NJ 2337 |
| 22 | Forglen Estate (Hong Kong) Ltd. | Forglen | | 1263 | NJ 6951 |
| 23 | John Mutch | Carnousie | | 1000 | NJ 6749 |
| 24 | Colin P.L. Oliphant | Netherdale | | 1000 | NJ 6548 |
| | Total | | | 240681 | |
| | Banffshire land area | | | 403054 | |
| | % of county accounted for | | | 59.7% | |

### PUBLIC LANDHOLDINGS

| | | |
|---|---|---|
| Forestry Commission | Various properties | 19977 |
| TOTAL | | 19977 |
| % of county | | 5.0% |

### CHANGES IN THE DISTRIBUTION OF LANDHOLDINGS BY SIZE 1970 - 1995

| | 1970 | | | 1995 | | |
|---|---|---|---|---|---|---|
| Acreage threshold | Acres | % of county | No. of owners | Acres | % of county | No. of owners |
| > 100 000 | 0 | 0% | 0 | 0 | 0% | 0 |
| > 75 000 | 0 | 0% | 0 | 0 | 0% | 0 |
| > 50 000 | 57700 | 14.3% | 1 | 57700 | 14.3% | 1 |
| > 40 000 | 98800 | 24.5% | 2 | 140400 | 34.8% | 3 |
| > 30 000 | 132700 | 32.9% | 3 | 175400 | 43.5% | 4 |
| > 20 000 | 132700 | 32.9% | 3 | 175400 | 43.5% | 4 |
| > 10 000 | 179900 | 44.6% | 7 | 189600 | 47.0% | 5 |
| > 5 000 | 211800 | 52.5% | 11 | 197000 | 48.9% | 6 |
| > 1000 | 284700 | 70.6% | 40 | 240681 | 59.7% | 24 |

*The Tables and Maps*

# Berwick

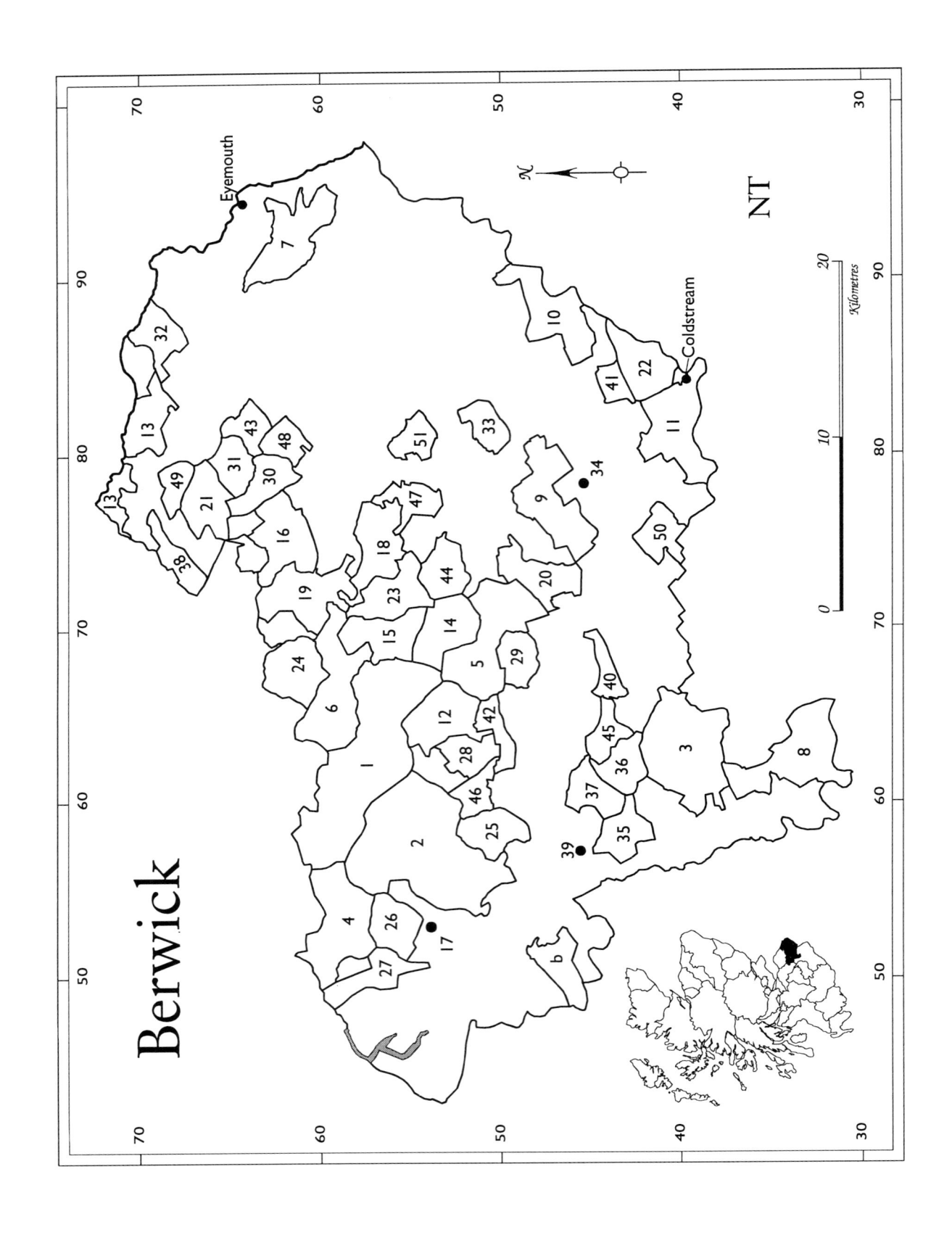

## Berwickshire
## 292,535 acres

Berwickshire is still a very aristocratic county, with three Dukes (Roxburghe, Northumberland and Sutherland) and two Earls (Haddington and Home).

It is the Scottish county which apparently receives most EU agricultural subsidy of any Scottish county. That such a wealthy county enjoys such a privilege says all that needs to be said about why the Common Agricultural Policy needs to be reformed.

The Duke of Roxburghe is the largest landowner in the county, although I have to rely on Millman's maps cross-referenced to the Valuation Rolls to determine this with any confidence. Roxburghe Estates have a policy of not disclosing information on landownership and could not confirm any of the details I sent them.

The Burncastle grouse moor was sold by Baron Biddulph to the Duke of Northumberland for £5 million in 1990. The grouse economy appears to be healthy in one part of the country at least.

Most of the estates above 5000 acres that John McEwen reported have fragmented markedly. How reliable this is, however, is uncertain. McEwen was not working with the best of the Millman maps for southern Scotland and hence his claims of poor coverage could be responsible for more errors being made in the region. Millman covered southern Scotland just as comprehensively as northern Scotland, as his map published in *Scottish Geographical Magazine* in 1972 shows.

| NO. | PROPRIETOR | PROPERTY | PRINCIPAL INTEREST | ACREAGE | GRID REF. |
|---|---|---|---|---|---|
| 1 | 2nd Roxburghe Discretionary Trustees * | Byrecleugh & Rawburn | Duke of Roxburghe | 10100 | NT 6358 |
| 2 | The Northumberland Estates | Burncastle | Duke of Northumberland | 9000 | NT 5351 |
| 3 | The Earl of Haddington | Mellerstain | | 7000 | NT 6539 |
| 4 | Faccombe Estates Ltd. * | Tollishill | See Appendix 3 | 4558 | NT 5158 |
| 5 | Thomas Elliot | Bedshiel & Greenlaw Moor | | 4200 | NT 6851 |
| 6 | Andrew W. Pate & Andrew A.W. Pate | Horseupcleugh & Redpath | | 4200 | NT 6658 |
| 7 | David I. Liddell-Grainger | Ayton | | 3700 | NT 9361 |
| 8 | Trustees of Ellesmere 1939 Settlement * | Mertoun | Duke of Sutherland | 3500 | NT 6131 |
| 9 | Major Alexander R. Trotter | Charterhall | | 3200 | NT 7647 |
| 10 | Ladykirk Estates Ltd. | Ladykirk | | 3000 | NT 8845 |
| 11 | Douglas & Angus Estates Ltd. * | The Hirsel | | 3000 | NT 8240 |
| 12 | Mrs Janet R.L. Campbell | Wedderlie | | 2700 | NT 6351 |
| 13 | Frank J. Usher of Dunglass | Dunglass (part) | | 2600 | NT 7671 |
| 14 | Kettelshiel Partners | Kettleshiel Farm & Polwarth | | 2500 | NT 7051 |
| 15 | Fraser M.S. & Michael J.S. Charles | Longformacus | | 2500 | NT 6957 |
| 16 | William S.J. Dobie | Abbey St Bathans | | 2500 | NT 7562 |
| 17 | James M. Sharp & Trustees | Longcroft etc. | | 2369 | NT 5252 |
| 18 | Lynn A. Wilson | Whitchester | | 2272 | NT 7258 |
| 19 | Iveagh Trustees | Ellemford | | 2270 | NT 7360 |
| 20 | Marchmont Farms Ltd. | Marchmont | | 2250 | NT 7448 |
| 21 | R.W. Walker, J.A. Hardie & P. Rothwell | Blackburn | | 2200 | NT 7766 |
| 22 | The Sir Ilay Campbell Settlement | Lennel | | 2200 | NT 8540 |

## Berwickshire

| | | | | | |
|---|---|---|---|---|---|
| 23 | Christine M.G. Rodger | Stobswood | | 2200 | NT 7156 |
| 24 | W.S. Landale | Cranshaws | | 2000 | NT 6861 |
| 25 | | Blythe | | 1750 | NT 5849 |
| 26 | Captain Gerald Maitland-Carew | Glenburnie Moor | | 1731 | NT 5456 |
| 27 | | Hillhouse | | 1700 | NT 5055 |
| 28 | Thomas F. Macfarlane | Flass Farm | | 1700 | NT 6251 |
| 29 | Marjory Little | Halliburton | | 1500 | NT 6748 |
| 30 | N.S. Salvesen | Quixwood | | 1500 | NT 7963 |
| 31 | W. & I. Arnott & Nigel S. Salvesen | Butterdean | | 1500 | NT 8064 |
| 32 | | Lumsdaine | | 1500 | NT 8769 |
| 33 | Kimmerghame A. & M. Trust | Kimmerghame | | 1400 | NT 8151 |
| 34 | Trustees of J. M. Menzies & Kames Dairies Ltd. | Kames etc. | John Menzies | 1390 | NT 7845 |
| 35 | I.R. & W.B. Scott Aiton | Legerwood | | 1250 | NT 5943 |
| 36 | Hon Mrs M.A. Christian | Upper Huntlywood | | 1250 | NT 6143 |
| 37 | J.W. Fullerton & Sons | Corsbie & Kirkhill | | 1200 | NT 6044 |
| 38 | David A. Hinton | Fulfordlees | | 1200 | NT 7669 |
| 39 | Colin J. Anderson | Boon | | 1099 | NT 5745 |
| 40 | Peter & Michael Aitchison | East Gordon | | 1000 | NT 6743 |
| 41 | J.R. Calder & Son | Skaithmuir | | 1000 | NT 8443 |
| 42 | Thomas E. Walker | Cammerlaws | | 1000 | NT 6550 |
| 43 | John R. Prentice | Brockholes | | 1000 | NT 8263 |
| 44 | L.L. Macvie & Co. | Langtonlees | | 1000 | NT 7353 |
| 45 | Thoresway Farming Co. Ltd. | Greenknowe | | 1000 | NT 6443 |
| 46 | A.G. & R. Haliburton | Raecleugh | | 1000 | NT 6151 |
| 47 | Alexander D. Hay | Duns Castle | | 1000 | NT 7754 |
| 48 | William T. Kemp | Drakemyre | | 1000 | NT 8162 |
| 49 | E.M. Houston | Bowshiel | | 1000 | NT 7768 |
| 50 | James D. Greig | Eccles | | 1000 | NT 7641 |
| 51 | The Rt. Hon. the Lord Palmer | Manderston | | 1000 | NT 8154 |
| | Total | | | 119689 | |
| | Berwickshire land area | | | 292535 | |
| | % of county accounted for | | | 40.9% | |

### PUBLIC LANDHOLDINGS

| | | |
|---|---|---|
| Forestry Commission | Various properties | 431 |
| b. Ettrick & Lauderdale District Council | Lauder Common | 1990 |
| TOTAL | | 2421 |
| % of county | | 0.8% |

### CHANGES IN THE DISTRIBUTION OF LANDHOLDINGS BY SIZE 1970 - 1995

| | 1970 | | | 1995 | | |
|---|---|---|---|---|---|---|
| Acreage threshold | Acres | % of county | No. of owners | Acres | % of county | No. of owners |
| > 100 000 | 0 | 0% | 0 | 0 | 0% | 0 |
| > 75 000 | 0 | 0% | 0 | 0 | 0% | 0 |
| > 50 000 | 0 | 0% | 0 | 0 | 0% | 0 |
| > 40 000 | 0 | 0% | 0 | 0 | 0% | 0 |
| > 30 000 | 0 | 0% | 0 | 0 | 0% | 0 |
| > 20 000 | 0 | 0% | 0 | 0 | 0% | 0 |
| > 10 000 | 12900 | 4.4% | 1 | 10100 | 3.5% | 1 |
| > 5 000 | 89700 | 30.7% | 12 | 26100 | 8.9% | 3 |
| > 1000 | 160300 | 54.8% | 46 | 119689 | 40.9% | 51 |

# Bute

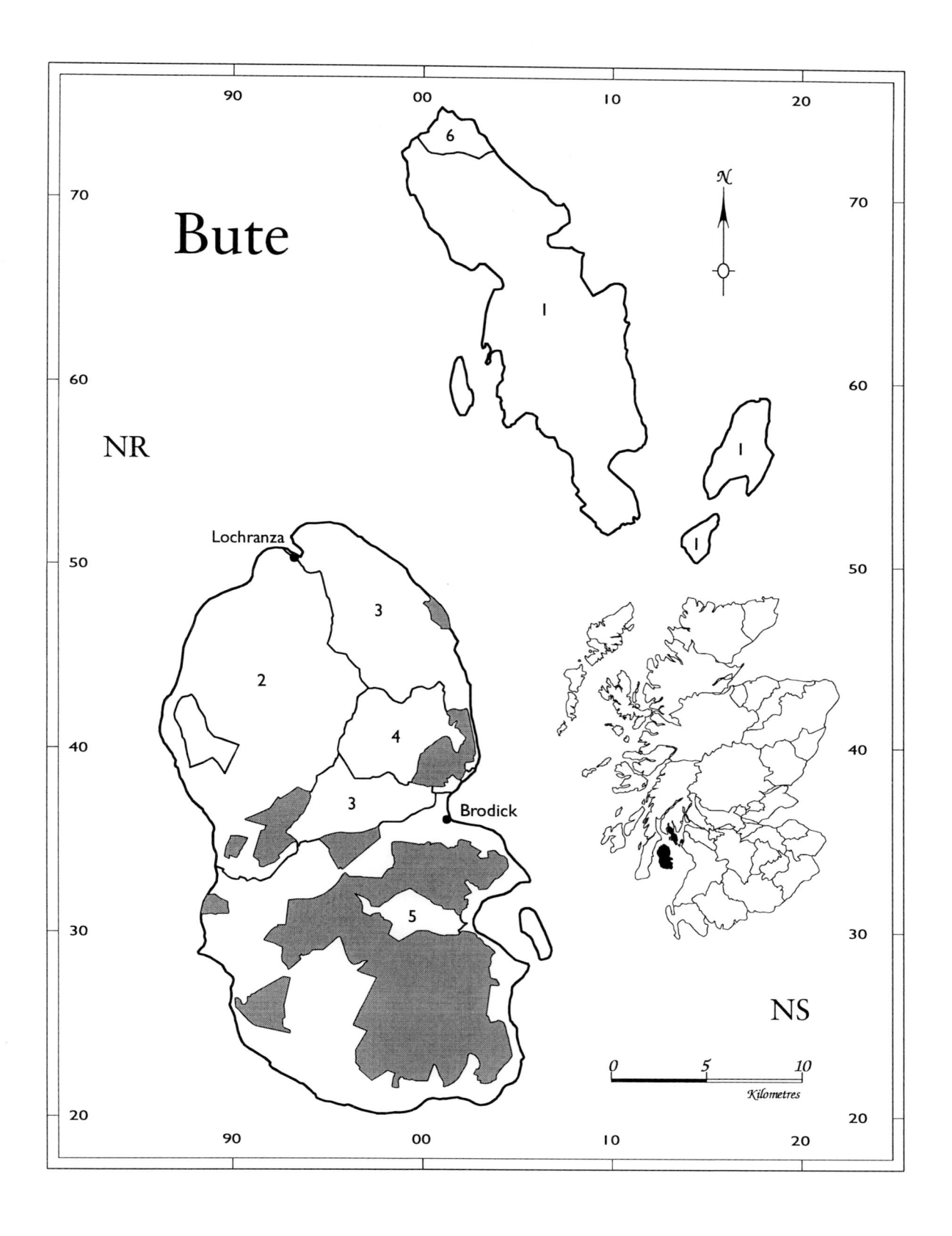

NR

NS

Lochranza

Brodick

0  5  10
Kilometres

# Bute
## 139,711 acres

Bute is dominated by Bute Estates who own almost all of the island of Bute. The county's other major landowners are the Forestry Commission, which owns large areas of Arran together with Dougarie and Arran Estates. Charles Fforde, the owner of Arran Estates, was involved in controversy a number of years ago over proposals to charge geology students who come to Arran regularly to study the wonderful granite. He is also reported to insist on sizable sums of money for minutes of waiver, the agreements needed from a feudal superior if burdens are to be removed from one's title.

| NO. | PROPRIETOR | PROPERTY | PRINCIPAL INTEREST | ACREAGE | GRID REF. |
|---|---|---|---|---|---|
| 1 | Bute Estate Ltd. * | Bute Estate | Marquess of Bute | 31300 | NS 0664 |
| 2 | Stephen Gibbs | Dougarie | | 24908 | NR 8837 |
| 3 | Charles J.G. Fforde | Arran Estate | | 16300 | NR 9845 |
| 4 | National Trust for Scotland | Brodick | | 5434 | NR 9840 |
| 5 | J.K. & C. Bone | Glenkiln | | 1700 | NS 0130 |
| 6 | Sir Richard Attenborough | Rhubodach | | 1500 | NS 0273 |
| | Total | | | 81142 | |
| | Bute land area | | | 139711 | |
| | % of county accounted for | | | 58.1% | |

**PUBLIC LANDHOLDINGS**

| | | | |
|---|---|---|---|
| Forestry Commission | Various properties | | 27170 |
| TOTAL | | | 27170 |
| % of county | | | 19.4% |

**CHANGES IN THE DISTRIBUTION OF LANDHOLDINGS BY SIZE 1970 - 1995**

| | 1970 | | | 1995 | | |
|---|---|---|---|---|---|---|
| Acreage threshold | Acres | % of county | No. of owners | Acres | % of county | No. of owners |
| > 100 000 | 0 | 0% | 0 | 0 | 0% | 0 |
| > 75 000 | 0 | 0% | 0 | 0 | 0% | 0 |
| > 50 000 | 0 | 0% | 0 | 0 | 0% | 0 |
| > 40 000 | 0 | 0% | 0 | 0 | 0% | 0 |
| > 30 000 | 0 | 0% | 0 | 31300 | 22.4% | 1 |
| > 20 000 | 81500 | 58.3% | 3 | 56208 | 40.2% | 2 |
| > 10 000 | 81500 | 58.3% | 3 | 72508 | 51.9% | 3 |
| > 5 000 | 87600 | 62.7% | 4 | 77942 | 55.8% | 4 |
| > 1000 | 99800 | 71.4% | 12 | 81142 | 58.1% | 6 |

## Caithness
## 438,943 acres

Caithness contains some of the most infertile yet environmentally special land in Scotland. It also has the most fertile land in northern Scotland and the highest population density of any of the crofting counties (Shetland, Orkney, Caithness, Sutherland, Ross & Cromarty, Inverness and Argyll). Together with Orkney, Caithness has the highest proportion of owner-occupied crofts, those which have been bought by their tenants under the 1976 Crofting Reform Act.

Caithness has seen big changes in both the pattern of landownership and the people involved since 1970. The structural changes are associated with the frantic expansion of private forestry on the peatlands which caused a raging controversy in the mid-80s. Fuelled by low land prices, a forestry company called Fountain Forestry went round London financial advisers persuading wealthy clients who had high exposure to income tax to invest in tree plantations against which tax could be written off. New landowners such as Terry Wogan, Shirley Porter and Alex 'Hurricane' Higgins arrived to join the traditional Sinclairs, Gunns, Swansons and Pottingers. The environmental controversy, together with the publicity surrounding the tax breaks, ensured that in the 1988 Budget, forestry was removed completely from the tax system and the mechanism which was fuelling afforestation in some of the most sensitive parts of the country was abolished.

The Nature Conservancy Council (NCC), which had been highly critical of the afforestation activities, published a report called *Birds, Bogs and Forestry* in 1987. Robert Cowan, Chairman of the HIDB described it as 'the most swingeing act of excessive zeal yet seen from the NCC in the Highlands and Islands'. Publication of the report in London served to alienate some people in the Highlands who were offended by what was considered an insensitive and arrogant approach by the agency. Afforestation in Caithness and Sutherland was to prove the death knell for the NCC. It was replaced by the Nature Conservancy Council for Scotland in 1991 and merged with the Countryside Commission for Scotland to form Scottish Natural Heritage a year later.

Land use changes of this magnitude could not take place without the unregulated market in land and uncoordinated land use policy which Scotland is still suffering from. Bad land use, as the Caithness and Sutherland controversy shows, can claim more victims than just the land.

The vast Dunbeath and Glutt estates are on the market at the time of writing and have been so for most of 1995.

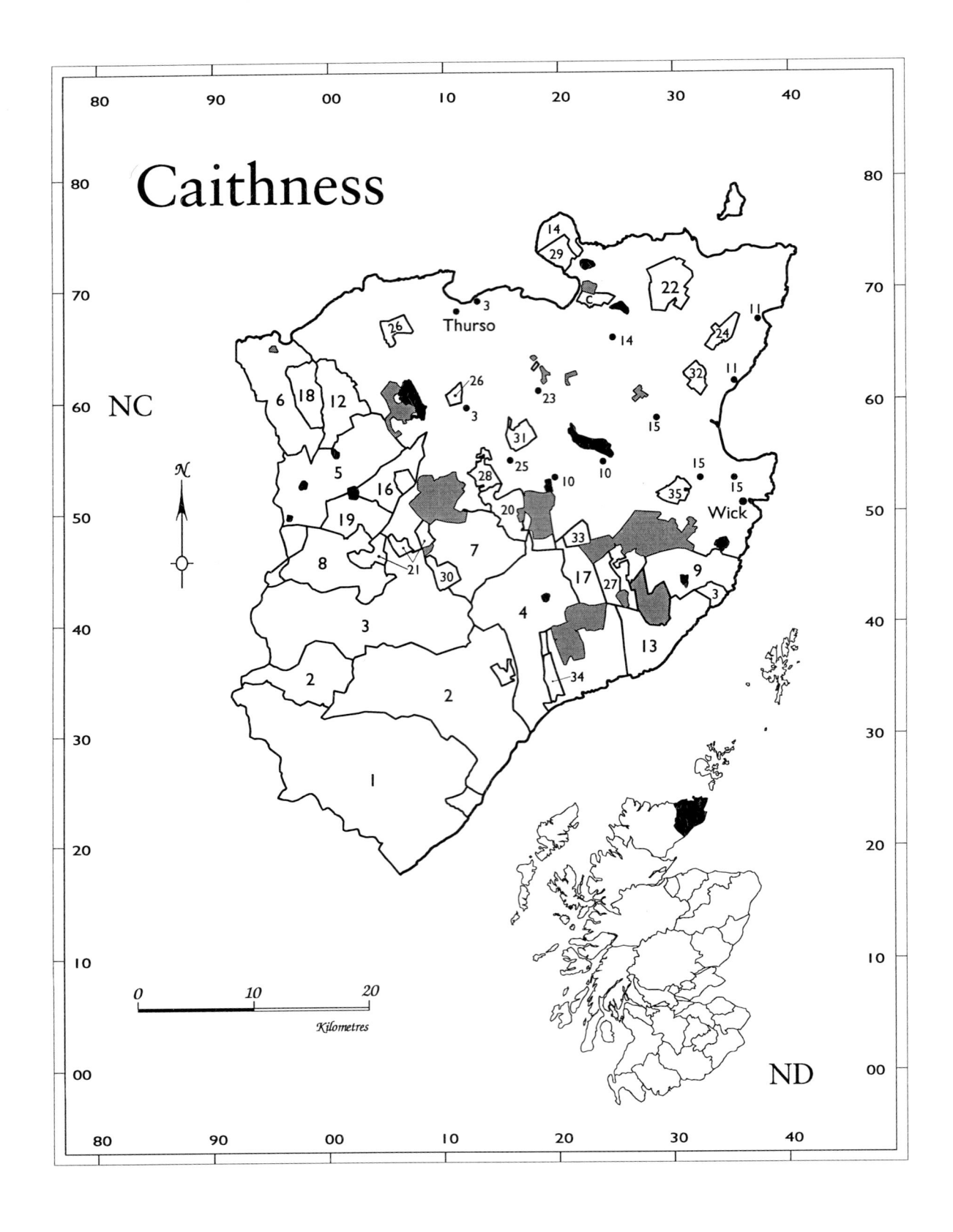

# Caithness

## Caithness

| NO. | PROPRIETOR | PROPERTY | PRINCIPAL INTEREST | ACREAGE | GRID REF. |
|---|---|---|---|---|---|
| 1 | Wellbeck Estates Company Ltd. | Langwell & Braemore | Lady Anne Cavendish-Bentinck | 45000 | ND 0325 |
| 2 | ON MARKET | Dunbeath & Glutt | | 37400 | ND 1034 |
| 3 | Viscount Thurso of Ulbster | Dalnawillan & Thurso | | 36800 | NC 0240 |
| 4 | Messrs W. & R. Palmer | Latheronwheel | | 20000 | ND 1832 |
| 5 | Sir R. & Lady I.H. Black | Shurrery | | 13600 | ND 0356 |
| 6 | Sandside Estates Ltd. | Sandside | Geoffrey Minter | 9600 | NC 9565 |
| 7 | Strathmore Sportings Ltd. | Strathmore | Stuart WM Threipland | 9500 | ND 1047 |
| 8 | Various clients | Altnabreac & Lochdu | See Appendix 2 | 8937 | ND 0045 |
| 9 | Thrumster Estate Ltd. | Thrumster | Harmsworth family | 7000 | ND 3445 |
| 10 | Sir Ralph H. Anstruther Trustees | Watten & Backlass Moss | | 6833 | ND 1953 |
| 11 | I.J. Spencer-Thomas | Freswick & Keiss Estates | | 5300 | ND 3767 |
| 12 | John F Swanson | Clyth | | 4700 | ND 2938 |
| 13 | Various clients | Broubster & Claise Brice | See Appendix 2 | 4377 | ND 0059 |
| 14 | Helen B. Hamilton | Dunnet & Moss of Greenland | | 4200 | ND 2075 |
| 15 | Trustees of the late Sir George Duff-Dunbar | Ackergill & Myrelandhorn | | 4000 | ND 3553 |
| 16 | Clarence G.S. Munro | Dorrery Farm | | 3787 | ND 0754 |
| 17 | Alistair F. Sinclair | Munsary | | 3200 | ND 2145 |
| 18 | Siemens Benefits Scheme Ltd. | Limekiln & Whitewell | | 3063 | NC 9860 |
| 19 | Donald & Mrs M Carmichael | Dorrery Forest | | 3000 | ND 0754 |
| 20 | ON MARKET | Dale Farm South | | 2909 | ND 1550 |
| 21 | Securities Management Trust Ltd. | Cnoc a Bhothain & others | | 2900 | ND 0646 |
| 22 | Andrew G. Simpson * | Philips Mains | | 2340 | ND 2972 |
| 23 | P.D. McCanlis | Stemster & Brabsterdorran | | 2000 | ND 1761 |
| 24 | Messrs Matheson | Stroupster | | 1971 | ND 3465 |
| 25 | J.I. Falconer | Spittal Mains | | 1697 | ND 1554 |
| 26 | Crown Estates Commissioners | Lythmore & Scotscalder | | 1640 | ND 0566 |
| 27 | Property & Financial Syndications Ltd. | Camster | | 1600 | ND 2541 |
| 28 | B. Plumley & Son | Dale Farm Estate North | | 1217 | ND 1353 |
| 29 | Keith H. Draper | House of the Northern Gate | | 1200 | ND 2071 |
| 30 | Royal Society for the Protection of Birds | Carn nam Muc | | 1166 | ND 1044 |
| 31 | Messrs Steve C. & Tom B. Pottinger | Banniskirk | | 1052 | ND 1657 |
| 32 | Shirley Porter | Moss of Quintfall | | 1000 | ND 3162 |
| 33 | Annie M.E. Cumming & Williamina J. Thomson | Kensary | | 1000 | ND 2248 |
| 34 | H.I.T. Gunn | Latheron Estate | | 1000 | ND 1933 |
| 35 | J. & Mrs M.H. Brims | Thuster | | 1000 | ND 2851 |
| | Total | | | 255989 | |
| | Caithness land area | | | 438943 | |
| | % of county accounted for | | | 58.3% | |

### PUBLIC LANDHOLDINGS

| | | | |
|---|---|---|---|
| Forestry Commission | Various properties | | 18912 |
| a. SOAEFD | See Appendix 4 | | 3926 |
| c. SNH | See Appendix 5 | | 894 |
| TOTAL | | | 23732 |
| % of county | | | 5.4% |

### CHANGES IN THE DISTRIBUTION OF LANDHOLDINGS BY SIZE 1970 - 1995

| | 1970 | | | 1995 | | |
|---|---|---|---|---|---|---|
| Acreage threshold | Acres | % of county | No. of owners | Acres | % of county | No. of owners |
| > 100 000 | 0 | 0% | 0 | 0 | 0% | 0 |
| > 75 000 | 0 | 0% | 0 | 0 | 0% | 0 |
| > 50 000 | 52600 | 12.0% | 1 | 0 | 0% | 0 |
| > 40 000 | 100600 | 22.9% | 2 | 45000 | 10.3% | 1 |
| > 30 000 | 134400 | 30.6% | 3 | 119200 | 27.2% | 3 |
| > 20 000 | 161900 | 36.9% | 4 | 139200 | 31.7% | 4 |
| > 10 000 | 262700 | 59.8% | 11 | 152800 | 34.8% | 5 |
| > 5 000 | 304100 | 69.3% | 17 | 199970 | 45.6% | 11 |
| > 1000 | 351200 | 80.0% | 35 | 255989 | 58.3% | 35 |

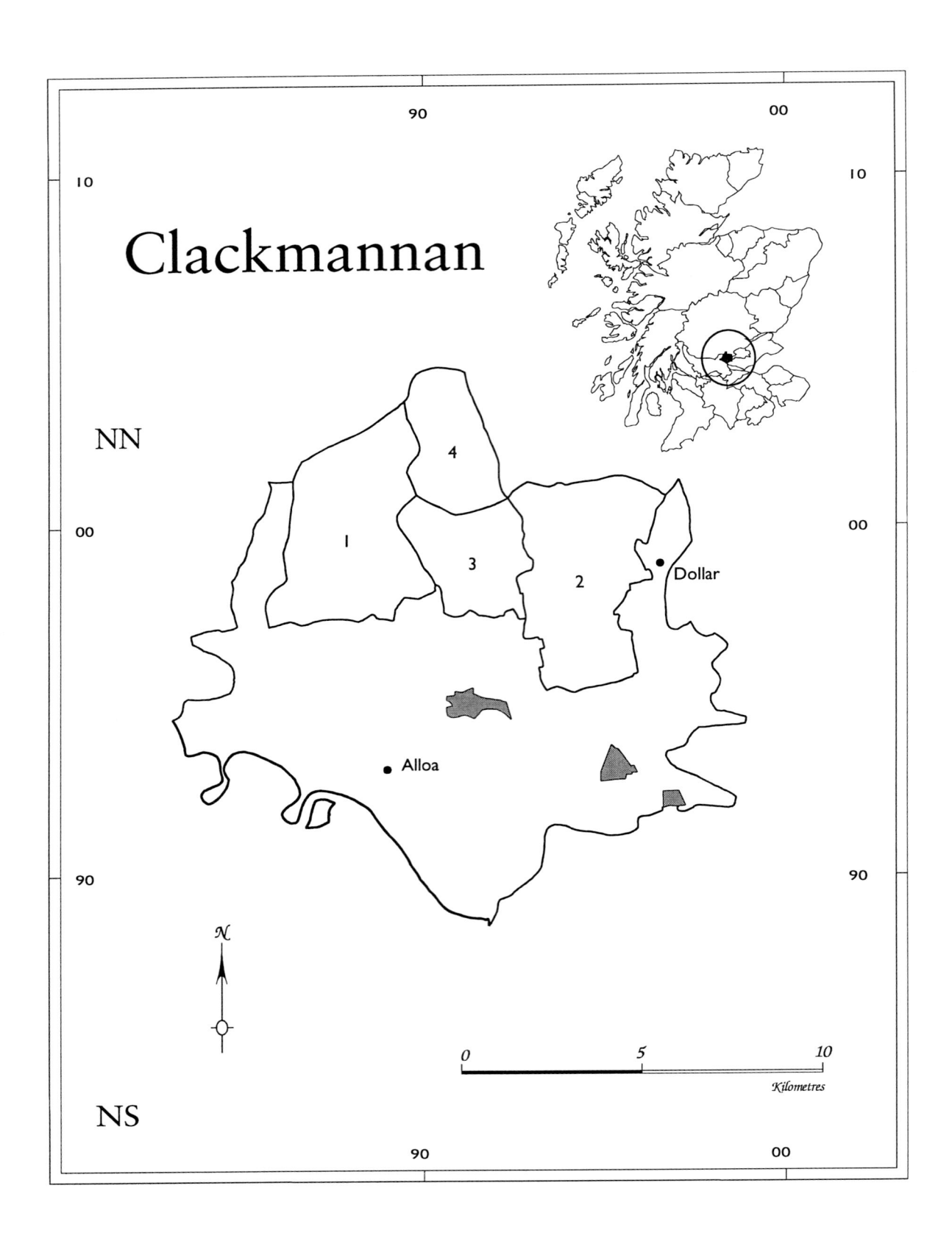

# Clackmannan

# Clackmannanshire
## 34,860 acres

The smallest county in Scotland is so small that there are more than fifty estates in the country that are bigger than this entire county.

The few large landholdings are concentrated in the Ochil Hills. I have not spent as much time as I could have investigating landownership in Clackmannanshire. With limited time and resources, it proved more productive to concentrate on the larger counties.

Private forestry again has been responsible for the main changes in the pattern of landownership together with the sale of some tenant farms to their occupiers. British Coal own a fair amount of land here, much of it under agricultural tenancies. The wholesale disposal of its estate on the instructions of government has caused a fierce debate concerning the prices being demanded of farmers and those in Clackmannan have been at the forefront of a campaign to allow them to buy their farms at a fair price, something which has proven hard to agree upon.

| NO. | PROPRIETOR | PROPERTY | PRINCIPAL INTEREST | ACREAGE | GRID REF. |
|---|---|---|---|---|---|
| 1 | J. Miller | Rhodders | | 5000 | NS 8899 |
| 2 | | Glencarse and Harvieston | | 4200 | NS 9397 |
| 3 | | Tillycoultry | | 2000 | NS 9198 |
| 4 | Colin Campbell | Backhills Farm | | 1350 | NN 9002 |
| | Total | | | 12550 | |
| | Clackmannanshire land area | | | 34860 | |
| | % of county accounted for | | | 36.0% | |

**PUBLIC LANDHOLDINGS**

| | | |
|---|---|---|
| Forestry Commission | Various properties | 539 |
| TOTAL | | 539 |
| % of county | | 1.5% |

**CHANGES IN THE DISTRIBUTION OF LANDHOLDINGS BY SIZE 1970 - 1995**

| | 1970 | | | 1995 | | |
|---|---|---|---|---|---|---|
| Acreage threshold | Acres | % of county | No. of owners | Acres | % of county | No. of owners |
| > 100 000 | 0 | 0% | 0 | 0 | 0% | 0 |
| > 75 000 | 0 | 0% | 0 | 0 | 0% | 0 |
| > 50 000 | 0 | 0% | 0 | 0 | 0% | 0 |
| > 40 000 | 0 | 0% | 0 | 0 | 0% | 0 |
| > 30 000 | 0 | 0% | 0 | 0 | 0% | 0 |
| > 20 000 | 0 | 0% | 0 | 0 | 0% | 0 |
| > 10 000 | 0 | 0% | 0 | 0 | 0% | 0 |
| > 5 000 | 5000 | 14.3% | 1 | 5000 | 14.3% | 1 |
| > 1 000 | 26800 | 76.9% | 13 | 12550 | 36.0% | 4 |

# Dumfries

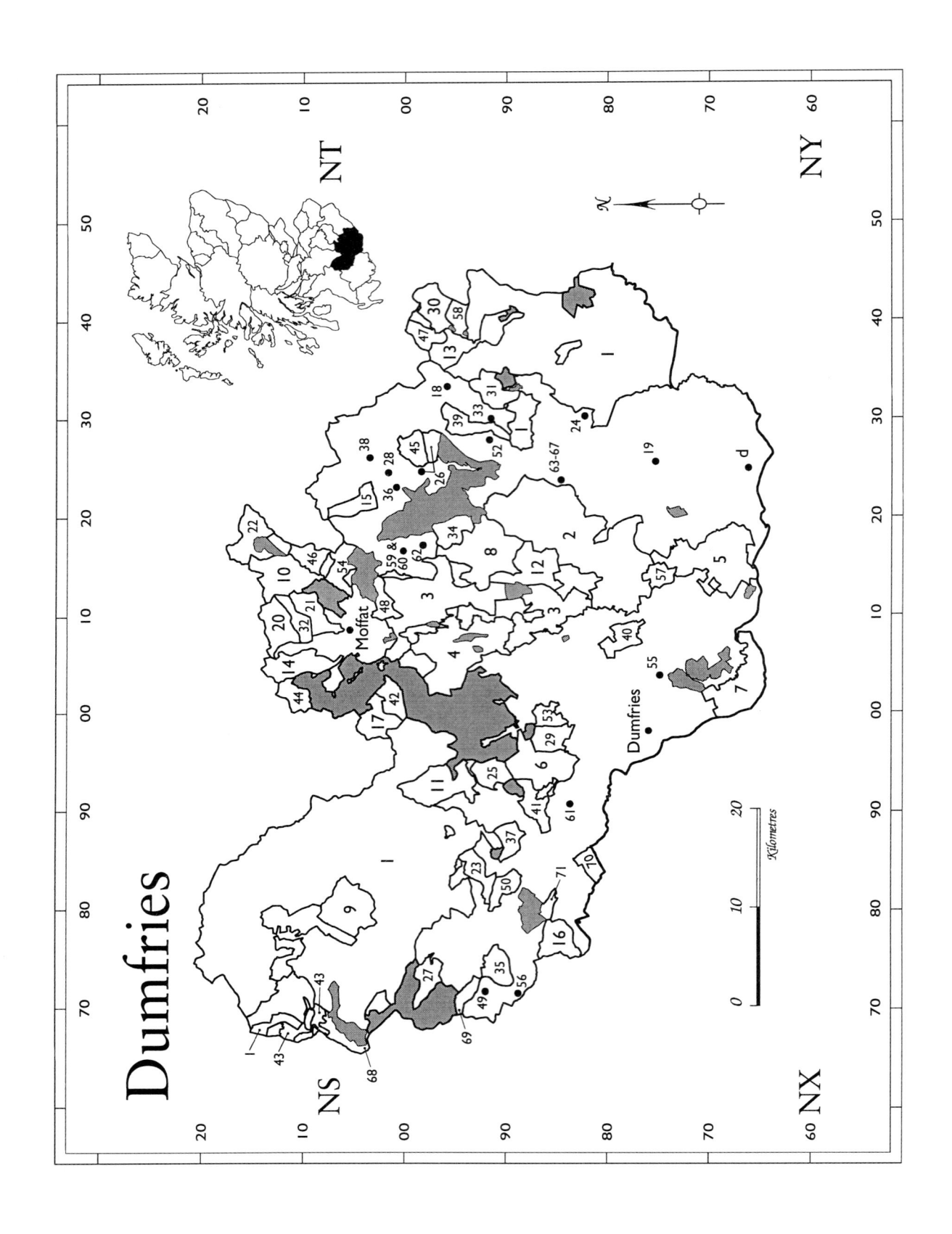

# Dumfriesshire
## 688,112 acres

Dumfriesshire is dominated by the Queensberry and Langholm estates of the Duke of Buccleuch. The other major landowners are the Forestry Commission and the vast private holdings in the Eskdalemuir forest which have been developed over the past 20 years.

Private forestry has transformed the face of Dumfriesshire since Millman did his survey in 1970. Typically, at the time private investors would buy land and plant it. They would be assessed under Schedule D taxation which allowed for all expenditure to be written off against tax. After ten years, the plantations would be sold, free of capital gains tax, to another investor, often a pension fund, who would be assessed under Schedule B taxation which only requires tax to be paid on the bare land value of the plantation. By the early 80s, therefore, most of the private forestry in Dumfriesshire was owned by pension funds. The Michelin Pension Fund alone owned over 6000 acres. New investors appeared in Dumfriesshire in the early 90s, among them Owl Forestry, an offshore company believed to be German-owned. Timber processors such as Shotton plc and Kronospan from Wales are also now major forest owners in the region.

In the hills above Moniaive, another new type of owner has emerged. Appin forest, which was planted in the early 70s, was bought in 1993 by Foster & Cranfield, a London-based auction company recently specialising in auctioning life assurance policies. It has in turn been auctioning syndicate shares in the property. The market for forestry land is thus constantly being adapted to new 'investment products'.

Other than forestry, landownership in Dumfries has remained fairly stable over the past 25 years.

| NO. | PROPRIETOR | PROPERTY | PRINCIPAL INTEREST | ACREAGE | GRID REF. |
|---|---|---|---|---|---|
| 1 | Buccleuch Estates Ltd. * | Queensberry & Liddesdale | | 167200 | NX 8599 |
| 2 | Trustees of Sir J.W. Buchanan-Jardine's Trust | Castlemilk | Sir A.R.J. Buchanan-Jardine Bt. | 24500 | NY 1577 |
| 3 | Crown Estate Commissioners | Applegirth | | 17493 | NY 1084 |
| 4 | Earl of Annandale & Hartfell | Annandale | | 12500 | NY 0694 |
| 5 | S.A. Birbecks 1972 Child's Settlement | Hoddom & Kinmount | | 10000 | NY 1572 |
| 6 | Sir David Landale | Dalswinton | | 5489 | NX 9484 |
| 7 | Lady Herries & Lady Mary Mumford | Caerlaverock | | 5050 | NY 0265 |
| 8 | Trustees of Alex R. Tulloch | Gillesbie | | 5000 | NY 1691 |
| 9 | R.A. & J.B. Greenshield | Eliock | | 4996 | NS 8007 |
| 10 | John & Wendy Barker | Capplegill | | 4875 | NT 1409 |
| 11 | Matthew & Robert Weir | Townhead and Townfoot | | 4320 | NX 9198 |
| 12 | Michael Jardine-Paterson | Balgray | | 3824 | NY 1486 |
| 13 | John Higgs | Arkleton | | 3700 | NY 3791 |
| 14 | Shotton plc | Raecleugh | | 3500 | NT 0411 |
| 15 | | Nether Cassock | | 3201 | NT 2303 |
| 16 | Peter Kennedy-Moffat | Lochurr | | 3000 | NX 7685 |
| 17 | George R. & James T. Blacklidge | Blairmack | | 2736 | NS 9902 |
| 18 | Tilhill Economic Forestry clients | Stennieswater | | 2632 | NY 3395 |
| 19 | Michael H., C. & Sir Ian Johnson-Ferguson | Springkell | | 2600 | NY 2575 |
| 20 | | Newton | | 2564 | NT 0710 |

## Dumfriesshire

| | | | | | |
|---|---|---|---|---|---|
| 21 | J.A. Thomson | Archbank | | 2500 | NT 0906 |
| 22 | National Trust for Scotland | Gray Mare's Tail | | 2279 | NT 1814 |
| 23 | R.H. Gladstone | Cappenoch | | 2200 | NX 8493 |
| 24 | Alastair E.H. Salvesen | Westwater Farm | | 2195 | NY 3082 |
| 25 | Scottish Amicable Life Assurance Society * | Auchencairn Wood | | 2102 | NX 9390 |
| 26 | Kronospan * | Davington & Craighaugh | | 2081 | NY 2697 |
| 27 | Foster & Cranfield syndicate | Appin Forest | | 2076 | NX 7397 |
| 28 | | Drumfedling | | 2042 | NT 2401 |
| 29 | Andrew Duncan | Newlands | | 2000 | NX 9785 |
| 30 | | Burnfoot | | 2000 | NY 3996 |
| 31 | Cayzer Trust Co. Ltd. | Westerhall | Peter Buckley | 2000 | NY 3189 |
| 32 | | Granton | | 2000 | NT 0910 |
| 33 | Cmdr. Colin J. Balfour | Georgefield | | 2000 | NY 2991 |
| 34 | | Waterhead | | 2000 | NY 1994 |
| 35 | J.H.A. Sykes | Craigdarroch | | 2000 | NX 7490 |
| 36 | Turner & Newall (Staff) Pension Trustees | Garwald & Finniegill | | 1986 | NY 1998 |
| 37 | A.J.J. Hunter-Arundell | Barjarg | | 1905 | NX 8790 |
| 38 | Owl Forest Ltd. * | Aberlosk Forest | | 1905 | NT 2603 |
| 39 | Lt. Col. Raymond Johnson-Ferguson | Westerkirk Mains | | 1800 | NY 2991 |
| 40 | Malcolm Bell-MacDonald | Rammerscales | | 1800 | NY 0877 |
| 41 | Mr & Mrs E Matthews | Blackwood | | 1760 | NX 9087 |
| 42 | ON MARKET | Kinnelhead | | 1712 | NT 0301 |
| 43 | ON MARKET | High Cairn & Carcarse | | 1707 | NS 6808 |
| 44 | | Harthope | | 1700 | NT 0212 |
| 45 | John I. Cartner | Clerkhill | | 1700 | NY 2698 |
| 46 | | Bodesbeck Farm | | 1700 | NT 1509 |
| 47 | | Eweslees Farm | | 1590 | NY 3897 |
| 48 | | Breconside | | 1500 | NT 1002 |
| 49 | Alex B. Hall | Craiglearan | | 1500 | NX 7192 |
| 50 | Stenhouse Estates Ltd. | Maxwelton | Paul H.A. Stenhouse | 1382 | NX 8289 |
| 51 | Alderleaf Ltd. | Eskdalemuir | | 1358 | |
| 52 | Lord Tanlaw | Lyneholm & Tanlawhill | | 1358 | NY 2791 |
| 53 | ON MARKET | Glenae | | 1288 | NX 9985 |
| 54 | Euan F. & Elizabeth Gordon | Crofthead | | 1230 | NT 1205 |
| 55 | David Sloan | Rigghead & Belridding | | 1202 | NY 0374 |
| 56 | | Minnygryle | | 1200 | NX 7188 |
| 57 | Captain John Bell-Irving | Whitehill | | 1200 | NY 1474 |
| 58 | | Unthank | | 1200 | NY 3894 |
| 59 | Parsons Forestry Partnership & John Wyld | Dryfhead & Finniegill | | 1118 | NY 1699 |
| 60 | Earl of Inchcape * | Dryfehead | | 1085 | NY 1699 |
| 61 | Thomas and Shiela Bell | McMurdoston & McCubbington | | 1076 | NX 9083 |
| 62 | Halifax Building Society Pension Nominees Ltd. * | Finniegill | | 1075 | NY 1798 |
| 63 | Halliday | Peasby Hall 5 | | 1060 | NY 2384 |
| 64 | Halliday | Peasby Hall 4 | | 1060 | NY 2384 |
| 65 | Halliday | Peasby Hall 3 | | 1060 | NY 2384 |
| 66 | Halliday | Peasby Hall 2 | | 1060 | NY 2384 |
| 67 | Halliday | Peasby Hall 1 | | 1060 | NY 2384 |
| 68 | Dalhanna Farming Co. | Lochbrowan (part) | Angus Campbell | 1000 | NS 6706 |
| 69 | | Glenjaan | | 1000 | NX 7194 |
| 70 | J.W. Clark-Maxwell | Speddoch | | 1000 | NX 8482 |
| 71 | Refuge Farms Ltd. * | Bogrie | | 759 | NX 8085 |
| | Total | | | 369751 | |
| | Dumfriesshire land area | | | 688112 | |
| | % of county accounted for | | | 53.7% | |

**Dumfriesshire**

**PUBLIC LANDHOLDINGS**

| | | |
|---|---|---|
| Forestry Commission | Various properties | 55938 |
| a. SOAEFD | See Appendix 4 | 576 |
| d. MoD | See Appendix 6 | 2431 |
| TOTAL | | 58945 |
| % of county | | 8.6% |

**CHANGES IN THE DISTRIBUTION OF LANDHOLDINGS BY SIZE 1970 - 1995**

| | 1970 | | | 1995 | | |
|---|---|---|---|---|---|---|
| Acreage threshold | Acres | % of county | No. of owners | Acres | % of county | No. of owners |
| > 100 000 | 177700 | 25.8% | 1 | 167200 | 24.3% | 1 |
| > 75 000 | 177700 | 25.8% | 1 | 167200 | 24.3% | 1 |
| > 50 000 | 177700 | 25.8% | 1 | 167200 | 24.3% | 1 |
| > 40 000 | 177700 | 25.8% | 1 | 167200 | 24.3% | 1 |
| > 30 000 | 213400 | 31.0% | 2 | 167200 | 24.3% | 1 |
| > 20 000 | 213400 | 31.0% | 2 | 191700 | 27.9% | 2 |
| > 10 000 | 257593 | 37.4% | 5 | 231693 | 33.7% | 5 |
| > 5 000 | 372893 | 54.2% | 24 | 247232 | 35.9% | 8 |
| > 1000 | 451993 | 65.7% | 59 | 368992 | 53.6% | 70 |

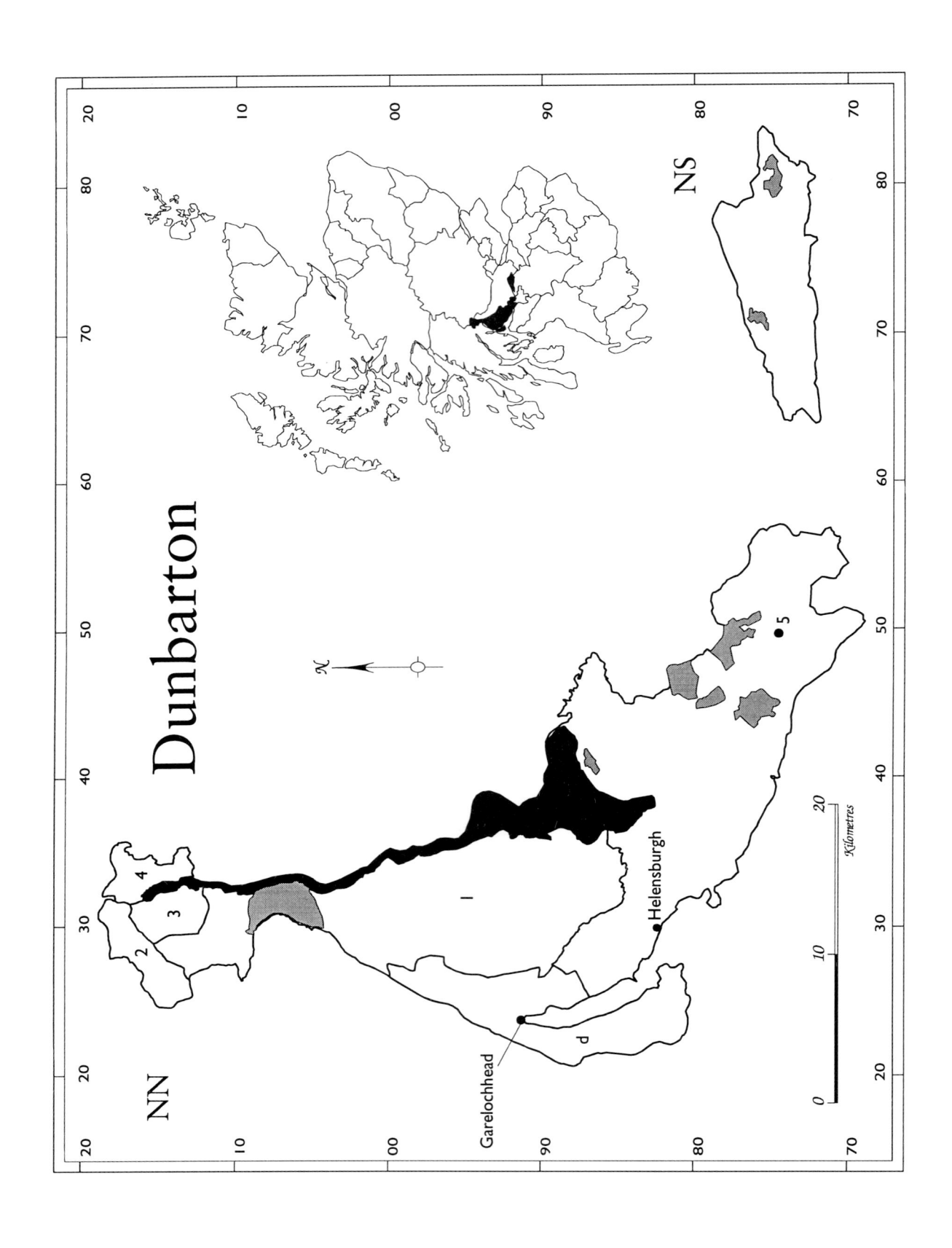

# Dunbarton

## Dunbartonshire
## 154,462 acres

Dunbartonshire remains dominated by Luss Estate, now owned by Luss Estates Company whose directors include Sir Ivar Colquhoun of Luss Bt. DL JP and Michael Wigan, owner of the Borrobol Estate in Sutherland.

The Ministry of Defence owns over 10,000 acres in the county, centred around the Gare Loch. These holdings represent 20% of their total Scottish estate, more than in any other county in Scotland.

Apart from the four large estates at the head of Loch Lomond, the rest of Dunbartonshire is owned by farmers. The Forestry Commission owns the Kilpatrick Hills Woodlands which were placed on the market to be sold in 1994 and withdrawn following concerns over loss of public access.

| NO. | PROPRIETOR | PROPERTY | PRINCIPAL INTEREST | ACREAGE | GRID REF. |
|---|---|---|---|---|---|
| 1 | Luss Estates Company | Luss | See Appendix 3 | 50000 | NS 3095 |
| 2 | Dr Frischmann | Garabal | | 4118 | NN 3117 |
| 3 | D. Fisher | Stuckindroin | | 3500 | NN 3114 |
| 4 | Lowe brothers | Ardleish Lodge | | 2700 | NN 3215 |
| 5 | | Cochno Farm | | 1800 | NS 4974 |
| | Total | | | 62118 | |
| | Dunbartonshire land area | | | 154462 | |
| | % of county accounted for | | | 40.2% | |

**PUBLIC LANDHOLDINGS**

| | | | |
|---|---|---|---|
| Forestry Commission | Various properties | | 5327 |
| d. MoD | See Appendix 6 | | 10870 |
| TOTAL | | | 16197 |
| % of county | | | 10.5% |

**CHANGES IN THE DISTRIBUTION OF LANDHOLDINGS BY SIZE 1970 - 1995**

| | 1970 | | | 1995 | | |
|---|---|---|---|---|---|---|
| Acreage threshold | Acres | % of county | No. of owners | Acres | % of county | No. of owners |
| > 100 000 | 0 | 0% | 0 | 0 | 0% | 0 |
| > 75 000 | 0 | 0% | 0 | 0 | 0% | 0 |
| > 50 000 | 0 | 0% | 0 | 50000 | 32.4% | 1 |
| > 40 000 | 42700 | 27.6% | 1 | 50000 | 32.4% | 1 |
| > 30 000 | 42700 | 27.6% | 1 | 50000 | 32.4% | 1 |
| > 20 000 | 42700 | 27.6% | 1 | 50000 | 32.4% | 1 |
| > 10 000 | 42700 | 27.6% | 1 | 50000 | 32.4% | 1 |
| > 5 000 | 42700 | 27.6% | 1 | 50000 | 32.4% | 1 |
| > 1000 | 103300 | 66.9% | 28 | 62118 | 40.2% | 5 |

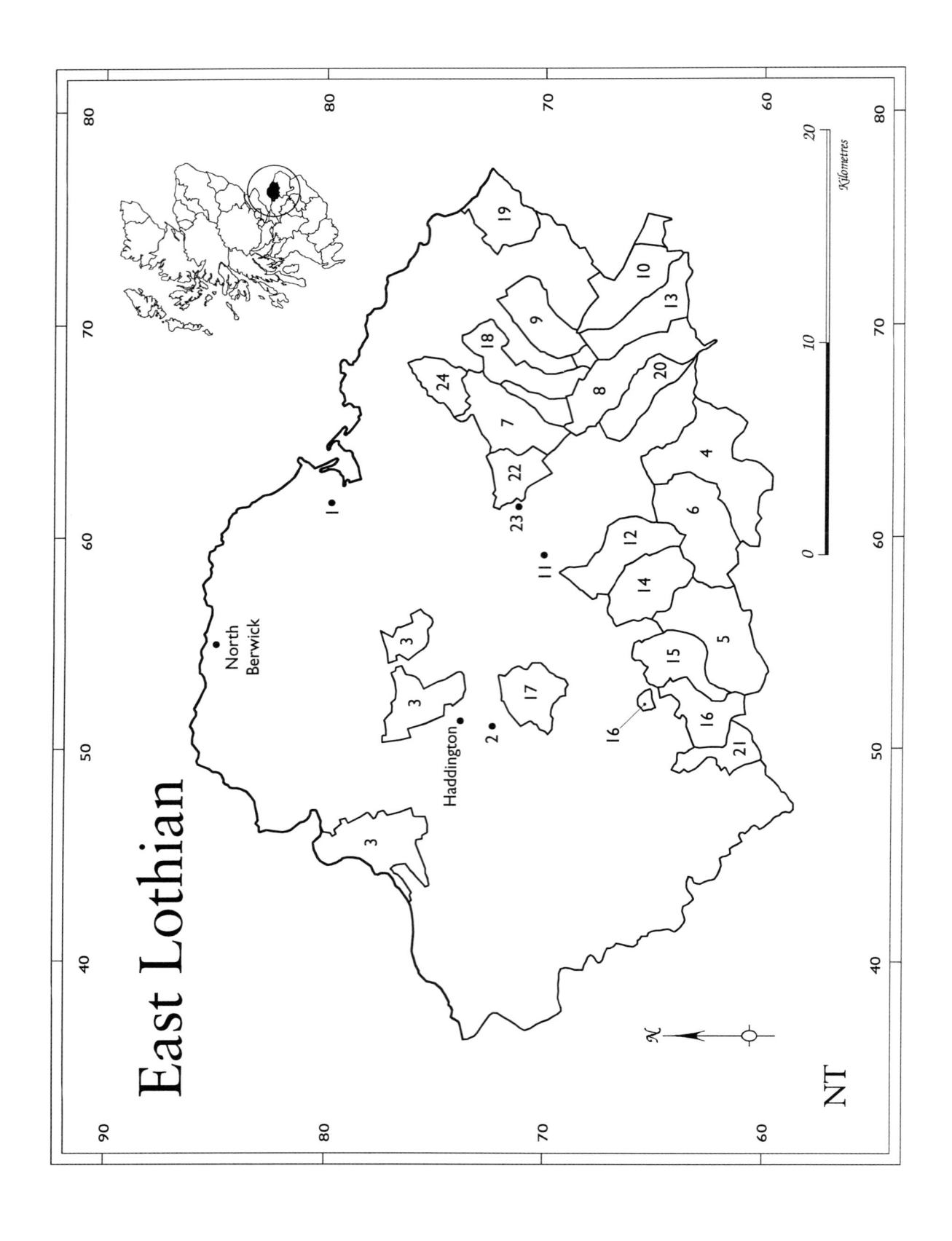

# East Lothian

## East Lothian
## 171,044 acres

Despite it being on my doorstep, I had difficulty finding information on East Lothian. More time for fieldwork would have produced a more comprehensive survey but, given its small size, I chose to prioritise other areas where enquiries proved more profitable. Access to SOAEFD information would be of great assistance for this county, one of the richest farming areas in the country.

The aristocracy still own land in East Lothian with the Haddington (Lord Binning is the son of the Earl of Haddington), Hamilton and Wemyss earldoms heading the list. Land prices in East Lothian continue to benefit from better access to Edinburgh, and hobby farming is beginning to compete with productive agriculture.

East Lothian remains a county of landed wealth, much of it recently generated in the finance houses of Edinburgh. Exclusive golf courses for gentlemen add to the attraction (for men) as does a favourable climate.

| NO. | PROPRIETOR | PROPERTY | PRINCIPAL INTEREST | ACREAGE | GRID REF. |
|---|---|---|---|---|---|
| 1 | Trustees of Lord Binning | Tyninghame | | 6000 | NT 6179 |
| 2 | Duke of Hamilton & Brandon | Hamilton Estates | | 5200 | NT 5172 |
| 3 | Earl of Wemyss Trust * | Wemyss Estates | | 4700 | NT 4578 |
| 4 | Peter Straker-Smith | Priestlaw | | 4200 | NT 6463 |
| 5 | Faccombe Estates Ltd. * | The Hope | See Appendix 3 | 3675 | NT 5663 |
| 6 | | Mayshiel Farm | | 3000 | NT 6264 |
| 7 | | Halls Farm | | 2700 | NT 6572 |
| 8 | Penny & Giles Inter plc | Harehead & Crichness | Professor William A. Penny | 2408 | NT 6963 |
| 9 | | Aikengall | | 2000 | NT 7170 |
| 10 | | Middle Monynut | | 2000 | NT 7264 |
| 11 | | Nunraw Abbey | | 2000 | NT 5970 |
| 12 | | Snawdon | | 2000 | NT 5867 |
| 13 | Refuge Farms Ltd. * | Upper Monynut | | 2000 | NT 6966 |
| 14 | | Newlands | | 2000 | NT 5766 |
| 15 | | Longyester | | 1800 | NT 5465 |
| 16 | | Newton Hall | | 1700 | NT 5265 |
| 17 | | Coulstoun | | 1500 | NT 5270 |
| 18 | | Woodhall | | 1400 | NT 6872 |
| 19 | Frank J. Usher of Dunglass | Dunglass (part) | | 1400 | NT 7671 |
| 20 | | Bothwell Farm | | 1200 | NT 6764 |
| 21 | John Elliot | Stobshiel Estate | | 1156 | NT 4963 |
| 22 | | Deuchrie | | 1100 | NT 6271 |
| 23 | | Stoneypath | | 1000 | NT 6171 |
| 24 | | Spott | | 1000 | NT 6775 |
| | Total | | | 57139 | |
| | East Lothian land area | | | 171044 | |
| | % of county accounted for | | | 33.4% | |

**PUBLIC LANDHOLDINGS**

No significant public landholdings

**CHANGES IN THE DISTRIBUTION OF LANDHOLDINGS BY SIZE 1970 - 1995**

| | 1970 | | | 1995 | | |
|---|---|---|---|---|---|---|
| Acreage threshold | Acres | % of county | No. of owners | Acres | % of county | No. of owners |
| > 100 000 | 0 | 0% | 0 | 0 | 0% | 0 |
| > 75 000 | 0 | 0% | 0 | 0 | 0% | 0 |
| > 50 000 | 0 | 0% | 0 | 0 | 0% | 0 |
| > 40 000 | 0 | 0% | 0 | 0 | 0% | 0 |
| > 30 000 | 0 | 0% | 0 | 0 | 0% | 0 |
| > 20 000 | 0 | 0% | 0 | 0 | 0% | 0 |
| > 10 000 | 13000 | 7.6% | 1 | 0 | 0% | 0 |
| > 5 000 | 33600 | 19.6% | 4 | 11200 | 6.5% | 2 |
| > 1 000 | 75800 | 44.3% | 30 | 57139 | 33.4% | 24 |

# Fife

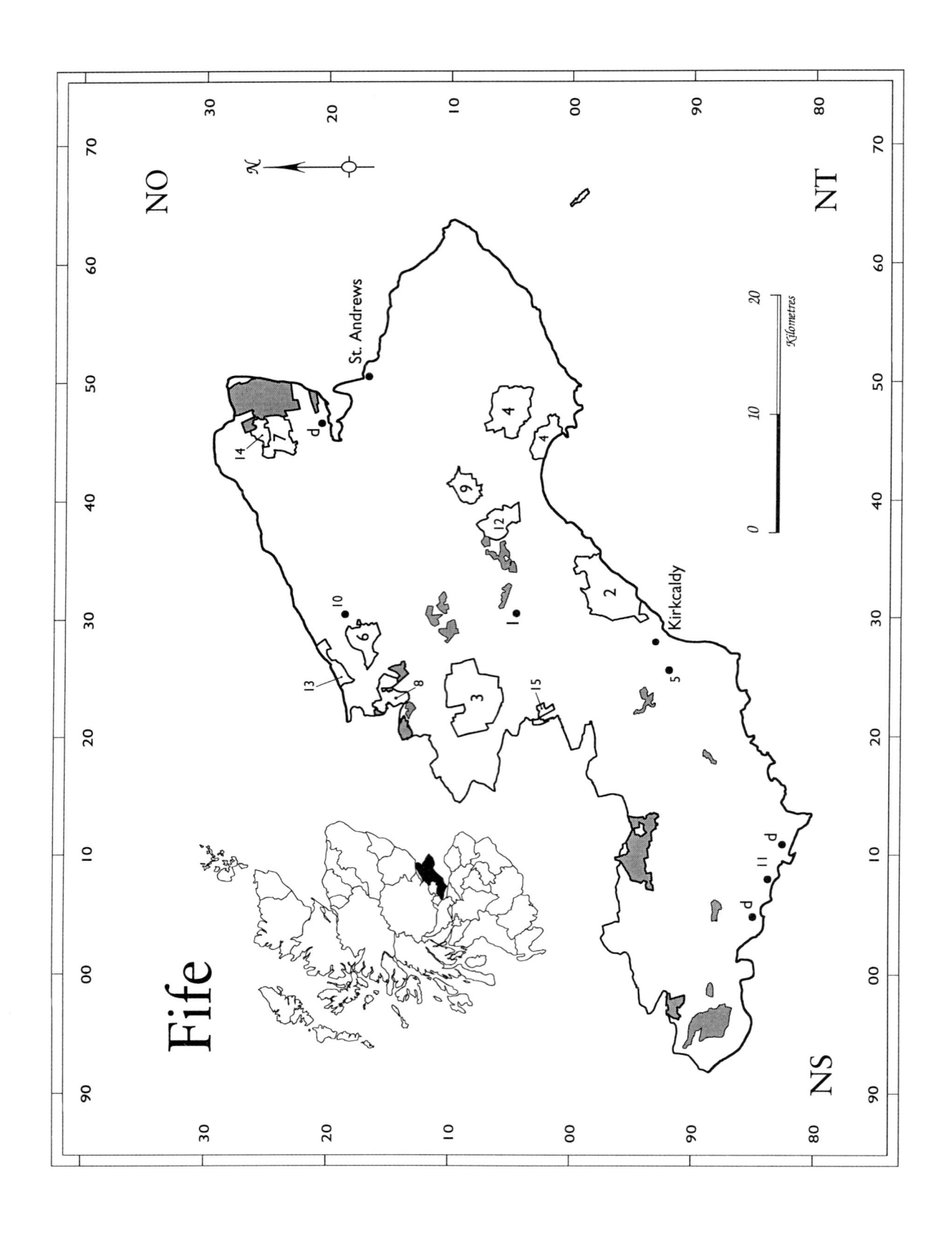

## Fife
## 322,856 acres

John McEwen managed to account for over a third of Fife from Millman's maps. I tried to update his work but managed only to reliably account for a mere 9.5%. Substantial information was assembled for much of the rest of the county but remains to be verified. The former Countryside Commission for Scotland sponsored research on landownership in Fife and produced some beautiful maps. Unfortunately the data on who owns the land remains confidential.

Fife became an 'operational county' of the new Land Register and the first to be supported by computerised mapping.

| NO. | PROPRIETOR | PROPERTY | PRINCIPAL INTEREST | ACREAGE | GRID REF. |
|---|---|---|---|---|---|
| 1 | Jean Balfour * | Balbirnie | | 5000 | NO 3004 |
| 2 | Wemyss Estate Trustees | Wemyss | | 5000 | NT 3295 |
| 3 | Falkland Estates Ltd. | Falkland | | 4500 | NO 2207 |
| 4 | Lord Balneil | Balcarres | | 4000 | NO 4707 |
| 5 | Richard R.L. Munro Ferguson * | Raith | | 2000 | NT 2591 |
| 6 | H.H. Turcan & partners | Lindores & Dunbog | | 1600 | NO 2616 |
| 7 | Faskally Investments Ltd. | Craigie | | 1500 | NO 4524 |
| 8 | Keneth Fraser | Pitcairlie | | 1140 | NO 2314 |
| 9 | Fraser & Trish Morrison | Teasses | | 1132 | NO 4008 |
| 10 | Frank Bethune | Ayton & Denmuir | | 1000 | NO 3018 |
| 11 | Earl of Elgin | Broomhall | | 1000 | NT 0783 |
| 12 | V.J. & Andrew Gilmour | Montrave | | 1000 | NO 3706 |
| 13 | Legal & General Assurance (Pensions Ltd.) | Parkhill & Ballinbreich | | 1000 | NO 2518 |
| 14 | Andrew G. Simpson * | Vicarsford Farm | | 500 | NO 4524 |
| 15 | ON MARKET | Arnot Estate (part) | | 440 | NO 2002 |
| | Total | | | 30812 | |
| | Fife land area | | | 322856 | |
| | % of county accounted for | | | 9.5% | |

**PUBLIC LANDHOLDINGS**

| Forestry Commission | Various properties | 9323 |
|---|---|---|
| c. SNH | See Appendix 5 | 299 |
| d. MoD | See Appendix 6 | 2983 |
| TOTAL | | 12605 |
| % of county | | 3.9% |

**CHANGES IN THE DISTRIBUTION OF LANDHOLDINGS BY SIZE 1970 - 1995**

| | 1970 | | | 1995 | | |
|---|---|---|---|---|---|---|
| Acreage threshold | Acres | % of county | No. of owners | Acres | % of county | No. of owners |
| > 100 000 | 0 | 0% | 0 | 0 | 0% | 0 |
| > 75 000 | 0 | 0% | 0 | 0 | 0% | 0 |
| > 50 000 | 0 | 0% | 0 | 0 | 0% | 0 |
| > 40 000 | 0 | 0% | 0 | 0 | 0% | 0 |
| > 30 000 | 0 | 0% | 0 | 0 | 0% | 0 |
| > 20 000 | 0 | 0% | 0 | 0 | 0% | 0 |
| > 10 000 | 0 | 0% | 0 | 0 | 0% | 0 |
| > 5 000 | 48400 | 15.0% | 8 | 10000 | 3.1% | 2 |
| > 1000 | 111300 | 34.5% | 41 | 29872 | 9.3% | 13 |

## Inverness-shire
## 2,695,094 acres

The biggest county in Scotland takes in Inverness, Strathspey, Ben Nevis, Morar and Knoydart, the Isles of Skye and Rum and Harris, the Uists, Benbecula and Barra. It is a county of high mountains and long glens and some of Scotland's best known islands.

Inverness-shire remains a county of big estates and increasingly so. In 1970 59.2% of the county was covered by estates larger than 5000 acres; the proportion is now 66.1%. This is probably due to parts of some estates which were split up being added to the estates of neighbours and the amalgamation of several properties under one ownership. It could simply be due to McEwen having missed some properties now covered. Certainly there has been some concentration. For example, Eira Drysdale now has what were once four estates, the John Muir Trust now has 23,648 acres covering three estates and Lord Dulverton now owns Eileanreach, Fassifern and Glen Fionnlighe.

On the other hand, there have been several major fragmentations in ownership. The most spectacular of these has been the virtual disappearance of the ancient lands of the Lovat family. Simon Fraser, who inherited the Lovat Estates from his father in 1964, died in 1994, leaving massive debts. He had sold the entire estate to one of his companies, Highlands and Islands Oil and Gas Co. Ltd for £6,005,966 and mortgaged the lot. The 29,600 acre Braulen Estate was sold in 1990 and the 12,000 North Morar Estate in 1994. The remaining 19,500 acres were sold in lots in 1995, with 6500 acres being kept for the new schoolboy Lord Lovat. The purchasers had not been registered in Sasines at the time of writing. A reduction from 76,000 acres to 6500 acres represents one of the last and most dramatic collapses and business failures of the old aristocratic order in the Highlands.

Another estate to have been broken up, although this time with a profitable outcome, is the Knoydart Estate. Once owned by the infamous Nazi sympathiser Lord Brocket, the estate passed through various hands including those of Lord Hesketh, a government spokesman in the House of Lords during the 1980s. He bought it for £250,000 in 1972 and sold it in April 1973 for £1.5 million. Philip Rhodes, who bought it in 1984, proceeded to split it up further, making a profit of over £1 million. The estate is on the market again at the time of writing, although a company, Kinloch Investments Co. Ltd., is reported to be negotiating a deal.

Other ownership changes include the sale of the North Harris Estate, Corrour, Glen Feshie, and Ben Alder, the latter having proven a bad buy for Dutchman Marcus Johannes Antonius Maria Diks whose wife, having spent two wet August weeks in Ben Alder Lodge, reportedly gave her husband an ultimatum: Ben Alder Estate or our marriage! Having paid £1.5 million in July 1992, he chose to sell it the following January for £1,335,500. It is now 75% owned by Agro Invest Overseas Ltd., a company controlled by Urs Schwarzenbach, and 25% by Christopher, Bridget, Zahra, Emma, Arabella, Jessica, Charles and George Hanbury. They are spending a fortune demolishing and rebuilding two stalker's cottages, a dog kennel, stables and the lodge for a reported cost of £5 million, no doubt to accommodate all those children.

The island of Scarp provides a good example of how land speculation operates in Scotland. Once part of the Amhuinnsuidhe Estate, it was sold by the Swiss company Enessey Co. SA in 1978 to a Panama company Tewera SA for £100. The Swiss owners associated with this company, Mr & Mrs Daniel Fiaux, spent a fair amount of money doing up the schoolhouse. On 2 February 1983, Tewera SA sold it to Libco (No. 3) Ltd. for £50,000. A Mr Nazmudin Virani appeared on the scene, visited Scarp once and discovered he could do very little with it since it is all under crofting tenure. On his way home he popped into a firm of solicitors in Portree, asking if there were any more Scottish islands on the market. There were not. Soon afterwards, an agent from London arrived on Scarp and began surveying the island for development as a tourist resort. When confronted with the fact that this would be impossible, due to the entire island being under crofting tenure, he said that these plans were not to be implemented but to be used as the basis of obtaining a bank loan. On 7 March 1983, Libco (No. 3) Ltd. sold the island to Orbitglen Ltd. for £500,000. On 23 January 1985, a Standard Security was raised against the island in favour of the Bank of Credit and Commerce International Societe Anonyme Licensed Deposit Taker (BCCI). BCCI was later to become infamous in the Western Isles when it went bust taking a good deal of the Council's money with it. Mr Virani, it turned out, was a director of BCCI and Scarp was put on the market in 1995 and eventually sold to an Anderson Duke Bakewell from Wallingford in Oxfordshire for £155,055 with the consent of the liquidators of BCCI. An interesting aside is that the titles to Scarp contain a feudal burden prohibiting the development of tourism. Quite who imposed these is unclear but it may have been Sir Hereward Wake, a former owner who liked his privacy. He is remembered as having persuaded Lord Burton, then an Inverness County Councillor and Chairman of the Roads Committee, of the need for a bypass around Amhuinnsuidhe Castle. The main road runs past the front door which, whilst common in most high streets in the land, was not good enough for Sir Hereward. The bypass was never built.

The controversy over the Isle of Eigg further underlines the precarious future which many communities face in the hands of the bizarre characters who frequent this part of the world and whom we have allowed to run so many places as idle hobbies. At the time of writing the owner, Marlin Eckhard (otherwise known as Maruma), had mortgaged the island and was under investigation by the Stuttgart police for alleged tax irregularities.

Inverness-shire remains a county wasted by a century and more of neglect and abuse. Land reform, together with a programme of ecological restoration, resettlement and sensible investment could transform it into the productive, prosperous and lively place that it should be.

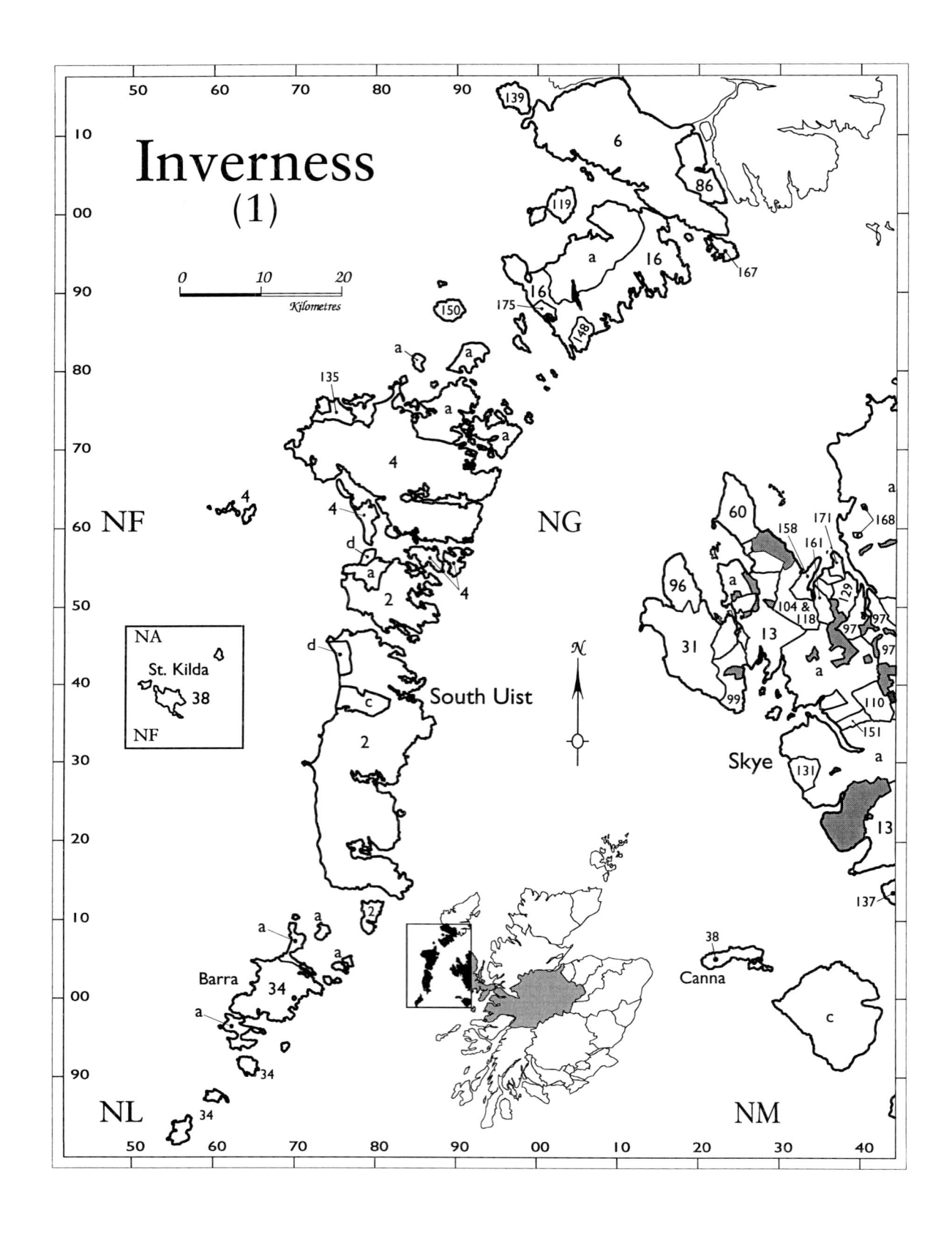

# Inverness
## (1)

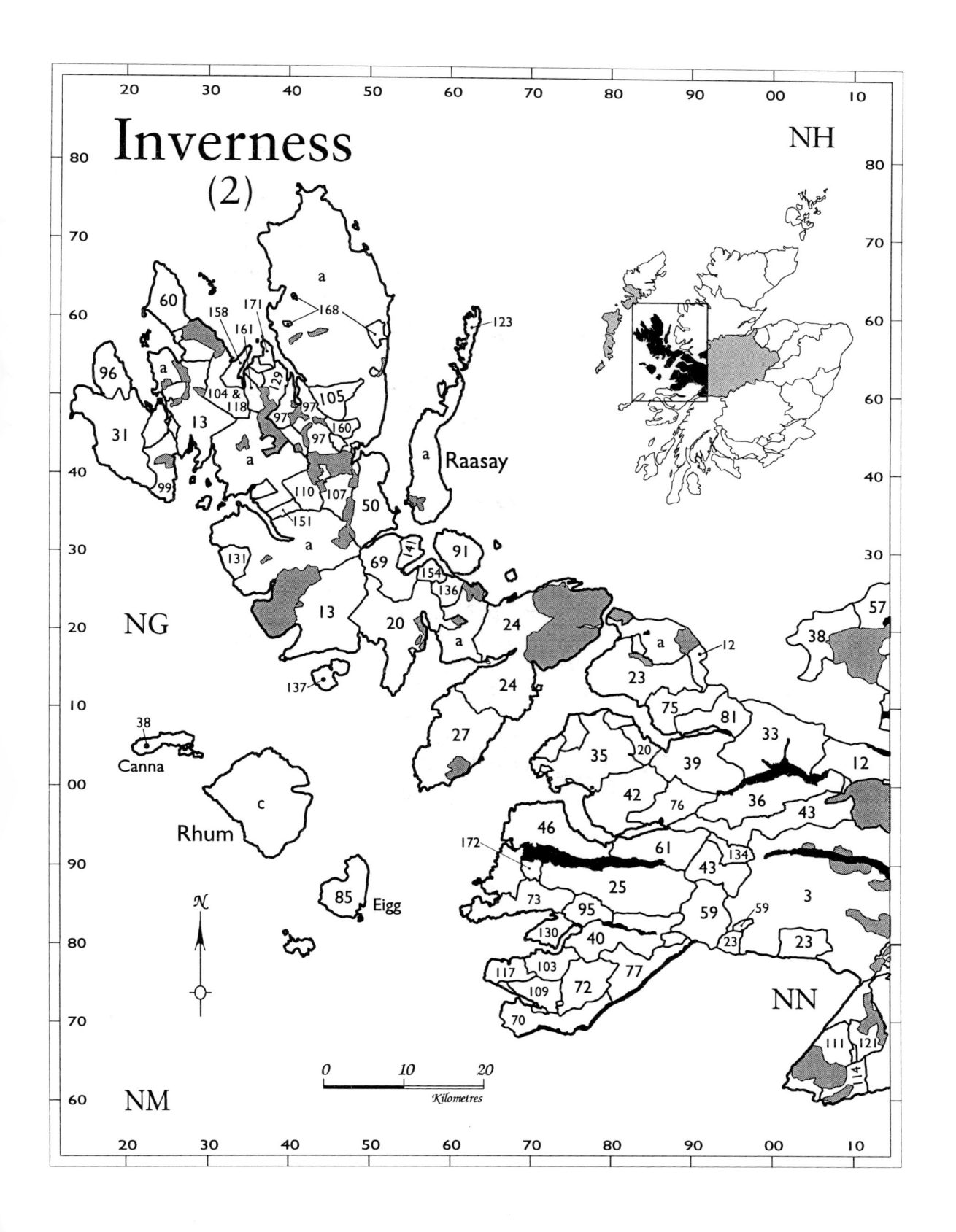

# Inverness (2)

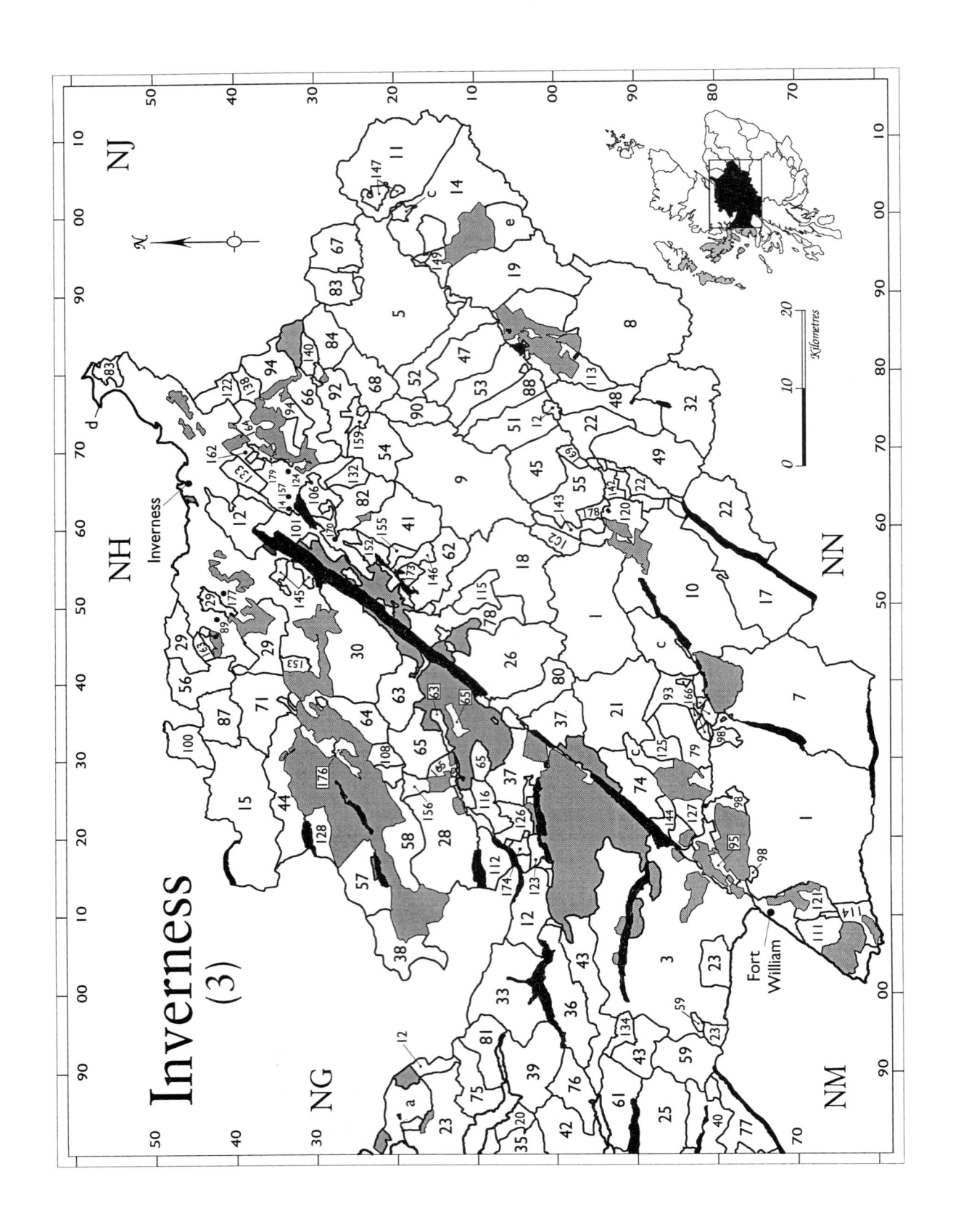

# Inverness (3)

## Inverness-shire

| NO. | PROPRIETOR | PROPERTY | PRINCIPAL INTEREST | ACREAGE | GRID REF. |
|---|---|---|---|---|---|
| 1 | Alcan Highland Estates Ltd. | Mamore & Glenshero | | 112400 | NN 2270 |
| 2 | South Uist Estates Ltd. | South Uist & Islands | See Appendix 3 | 92000 | NF 8030 |
| 3 | Lochiel Estates | Achnacarry | Sir Donald A. Cameron | 76000 | NN 1787 |
| 4 | North Uist Estate Trust 1990 | North Uist & Islands | Earl of Granville & family | 62200 | NF 8070 |
| 5 | Earl of Seafield & Viscount Reidhaven * | Seafield Estates | | 50000 | NH 9018 |
| 6 | North Harris Estate Ltd. | Amhuinnsuidhe (part) | Jonathan & Lady Marcia Bulmer | 49900 | NB 0308 |
| 7 | Joseph & Lisbet Koerner | Corrour | | 48210 | NN 4069 |
| 8 | Will Woodlands | Glen Feshie | | 42000 | NN 8493 |
| 9 | Coignafearn Estate Company Ltd. | Coignafearn | See Appendix 3 | 38000 | NH 6815 |
| 10 | Ardverikie Estate Ltd. | Ardverikie | Patrick Gordon Duff-Pennington | 37800 | NN 5087 |
| 11 | Lady Pauline Ogilvie Grant Nicholson | Revack & Dorbrack (part) | | 34000 | NJ 0817 |
| 12 | Burton Property Trust * | Dochfour & Glenquoich | Lord Burton | 31000 | NH 6039 |
| 13 | John Macleod of Macleod | Dunvegan & Glen Brittle | | 30600 | NG 2449 |
| 14 | Royal Society for the Protection of Birds | Abernethy & others | | 29627 | NJ 0116 |
| 15 | Andras Ltd. * | Braulen | | 29600 | NH 2338 |
| 16 | Rodney M. Hitchcock | Bays of Harris | | 26400 | NG 1193 |
| 17 | Agro Invest Overseas Ltd. & Hanbury family | Ben Alder | Urs Schwarzenbach & C. Hanbury | 26000 | NN 5778 |
| 18 | Charles R. Connell & Co. Ltd. * | Garragie & Stronelairig | | 25200 | NH 5211 |
| 19 | Rothiemurchus Estate Trust | Rothiemurchus | John Grant | 24000 | NH 9208 |
| 20 | The John Muir Trust | Strathaird, Torrin & Knoydart | | 23648 | NG 5318 |
| 21 | D.K.D. & G.M.L Buckle | Braeroy | | 23500 | NN 3391 |
| 22 | Eira Drysdale | Drumochter & Ralia | | 23400 | NN 6379 |
| 23 | Gilbert M. H. Wills (Lord Dulverton) | Eileanreach & others | | 22400 | NG 8017 |
| 24 | Iain Noble | Fearann Eilean Iarmain | | 22000 | NG 6912 |
| 25 | Ferranti Meters Ltd. | Meoble & Lettermorar | Mr M.Z. de Ferranti | 21000 | NM 7987 |
| 26 | Hillhouse Ests. Ltd. | Glendoe & Ardachy | Greville E.M. & H.R.M. Vernon | 20700 | NH 4009 |
| 27 | Clan Donald Lands Trust | Clan Donald Estate | | 20500 | NG 6006 |
| 28 | Thomas D. Girvan & David M. Girvan | Ceannacroc | | 19500 | NH 2211 |
| 29 | ON MARKET | Beaufort Castle Estate | | 19500 | NH 5042 |
| 30 | Balmac Forest Ltd. | Balmacaan | | 19300 | NH 3925 |
| 31 | Glendale Crofters Ltd. | Glendale | | 19000 | NG 1749 |
| 32 | Gaick Estate Ltd. | Gaick | See Appendix 3 | 18500 | NN 7584 |
| 33 | Andrew D. Gordon * | Wester Glenquoich | | 18000 | NG 9906 |
| 34 | The MacNeill of Barra | Barra & Islands | | 17500 | NF 6800 |
| 35 | ON MARKET | Knoydart Estate | | 17200 | NG 7505 |
| 36 | I. & H. Brown * | Glen Kingie | | 15250 | NN 0297 |
| 37 | Glengarry Estate Trust | Invergarry & Aberchalder | Miss Jean Ellice | 15000 | NH 3403 |
| 38 | National Trust for Scotland | Affric, Canna & St Kilda | | 14440 | |
| 39 | W. Gordon Gordon of Lude | Barrisdale | | 14100 | NG 9002 |
| 40 | Inverailort Estate | Inverailort & Ranachan | | 13100 | NM 7681 |
| 41 | Dunmaglass Estate Partnership | Dunmaglass | Sir Jack Hayward | 13000 | NH 5922 |
| 42 | Kilchoan Estate Ltd. | Kilchoan | Eric Delwart | 12800 | NM 7798 |
| 43 | Ronald Schmitt | Glen Dessary | | 12600 | NM 9290 |
| 44 | Sir John & Mr Anthony Fuller | Glencannich (part) | | 12600 | NH 2032 |
| 45 | Avion Holdings SPA | Glen Banchor & Strone | | 12200 | NH 6702 |
| 46 | Nevis Estates Ltd. | Nevis Estates | See Appendix 3 | 12000 | NM 6993 |
| 47 | Alvie Trust | Alvie & Dalraddy | Jamie Williamson | 11600 | NH 8407 |
| 48 | Michael Hone | Glentromie | | 11400 | NN 7796 |
| 49 | Hon. Michael J. & Nichola Samuel | Etteridge, Phones & Cluaich | | 11300 | NN 6892 |
| 50 | Iona O'Connor, Cleodie MacKinnon & C. Leslie | Braes | | 11100 | NG 4935 |
| 51 | Lucas Aardenburg | Pitmain | | 10800 | NH 7402 |

*The Tables and Maps*

## Inverness-shire

| # | Owner | Estate | Notes | Acres | Grid Ref |
|---|---|---|---|---|---|
| 52 | Major F.S. MacLaren Webster | Kinrara | | 10600 | NH 8708 |
| 53 | John C. Forbes-Leith | Dunachton & Kincraig | | 10400 | NH 8104 |
| 54 | W. & E. Benyon & D. Campbell | Glen Mazeran | | 10300 | NH 7422 |
| 55 | Roy Tylden-Wright & partners | Cluny | | 10250 | NN 6494 |
| 56 | Hon. E. Maurice W. Robson * | Erchless | | 10000 | NH 4140 |
| 57 | Tasmin Ltd. | North Affric | John Watson | 9900 | NH 1823 |
| 58 | Reynout Kwint | Wester Guisachan | | 9875 | NH 1920 |
| 59 | Michael R. Warren | Glenfinnan | | 9700 | NM 9183 |
| 60 | Mr van der Veen | Waternish | | 9600 | NG 2657 |
| 61 | Mrs Ian R.S. Bond | North Morar | | 9600 | NM 8592 |
| 62 | Hon. Alex A.M. Fraser | Corriegarth | | 9500 | NH 5016 |
| 63 | Poul Johansen | Glenmoriston Lodge | | 9250 | NH 3719 |
| 64 | D. Lindsay & M.H. Girvan | Corrimony | | 9100 | NH 3730 |
| 65 | Dundreggan Estate Ltd. | Dundreggan | Julio Amos & Katkut Anstalt | 9000 | NH 3214 |
| 66 | Lord MacPherson of Drumochter. | Tomals & Kyllachy | | 8700 | NH 7630 |
| 67 | The Calthorpe Trust | Muckrach | | 8600 | NH 9825 |
| 68 | Hon. E.R.H. Wills | Clune | | 8500 | NH 7823 |
| 69 | Central Skye Hotels Ltd. | Sconser | | 8400 | NG 5129 |
| 70 | Westminster (Liverpool) Trust Co. | Lochshiel | Corlett family | 8400 | NM 7270 |
| 71 | Over Rankeilour Farms Ltd. | Struy | Angus Spencer-Nairn | 8400 | NH 3841 |
| 72 | Trustees of Glenmoidart Est. | Glenmoidart | Mrs J. Lees-Millais | 8400 | NM 7472 |
| 73 | Amphill Investments | Arisaig | Xavier Namy | 8320 | NM 6984 |
| 74 | David A. Macleod | Glen Gloy & Glenfintaig | | 8200 | NN 2689 |
| 75 | J.H. Richmond-Watson * | Arnisdale | | 8150 | NG 8410 |
| 76 | Carnoch Ltd. | Camusrory | J. Crosthwaite-Eyre | 8129 | NM 8595 |
| 77 | Lt. Col. & D.H. Gray-Cheape | Glenaladale | | 8100 | NM 8275 |
| 78 | Lady Serena Bridgeman | Dell | | 8000 | NH 4816 |
| 79 | Edmund Luxmore | Glenspean | | 7665 | NN 3485 |
| 80 | Graham Biggs | Cullachy | | 7600 | NH 3706 |
| 81 | Henry Charles Birkbeck | Kinlochourn | | 7600 | NG 9309 |
| 82 | Wylie Valley Farming Ltd. | Aberarder & Ruthven | Robin Clark | 7500 | NH 6225 |
| 83 | Earl of Cawdor's Marriage Settlement Trustees | Cawdor (part) | | 7400 | NH 9027 |
| 84 | Tinsley Branston Farms Ltd. | Corrybrough | See Appendix 3 | 7400 | NH 8129 |
| 85 | Eigg Islands Ltd. | Isle of Eigg | Marlin Eckhard | 7400 | NM 4686 |
| 86 | Svenno SA/Loch Seaforth Crofters Ltd. | North Harris | Helene Panchaud | 7000 | NB 2004 |
| 87 | C. Frank Spencer-Nairn | Culligran | | 6900 | NH 3841 |
| 88 | Alan W.M. MacPherson-Fletcher | Balavil | | 6700 | NH 7902 |
| 89 | Simon Fraser | Lovat Estate | | 6500 | NH 4842 |
| 90 | Sir Edward B. Greenwell | Dalmigavie | | 6400 | NH 7419 |
| 91 | Trustees of J.G. Walford's Settlement | Scalpay | | 6400 | NG 6030 |
| 92 | Major Colin MacKenzie | Glen Kyllachy & Farr | | 6400 | NH 7523 |
| 93 | Eastaff Estates Ltd. | Tulloch | | 6100 | NN 3380 |
| 94 | John McIntosh of McIntosh | Moy | | 6000 | NH 7735 |
| 95 | Domenico Felice Berardelli * | Glen Mama & Achindaul | | 5922 | NM 7484 |
| 96 | Olaus Martin | Husabost | | 5200 | NG 1752 |
| 97 | Major John L. MacDonald | Tote, Bernisdale & Skeabost Bridge | | 5100 | NG 4149 |
| 98 | ON MARKET | Killiechonate Forest | | 5045 | NN 2479 |
| 99 | MacDonald Brothers | Orbost | | 5000 | NG 2543 |
| 100 | Kirkbi Estates Ltd. | Strathconon (part) | Kjeld Kirk Christiansen | 5000 | NH 3246 |
| 101 | Lt. Col. Angus I. Cameron | Aldourie & Old Clune | | 4900 | NH 6037 |
| 102 | Jane B. Ramsden & Hugh Morrison | Dalchully & Coull | | 4900 | NN 5800 |
| 103 | Captain J.A.P. Forbes | Roshven | | 4700 | NM 7278 |
| 104 | | Greshornish Woodlands II | | 4689 | NG 3249 |
| 105 | Borve & Annishader Township Ltd. | Borve & Annishader | | 4500 | NG 4448 |
| 106 | Lord Gray of Contin & others | Brin Farr | | 4400 | NH 6629 |
| 107 | Murdo Nicolson | Glenvarragill | | 4200 | NG 4740 |

## Inverness-shire

| # | Owner | Property | Other | Acres | Grid Ref |
|---|---|---|---|---|---|
| 108 | John Grigg & Anthony Grigg | Hilton | | 4200 | NH 3021 |
| 109 | Mrs Nino Stewart | Kinlochmoidart | | 4200 | NM 7073 |
| 110 | Keith Duckworth | Tungadal Forest | | 4090 | NG 4238 |
| 111 | Dr Sybrand F.C. & Feya S.J. Heerma van Voss | Blar a' Chaoruinn | | 4050 | NN 0966 |
| 112 | Abbey Commercial Investments Ltd. | Bunloinn | | 4006 | NH 1707 |
| 113 | G.P. Christie | Killiehuntly | | 4000 | NN 7998 |
| 114 | Callart Estate | Callart | | 4000 | NN 0960 |
| 115 | S.R. Waldron | Killin | | 4000 | NH 5209 |
| 116 | Achlain Estates Ltd. | Achlain | | 4000 | NH 2409 |
| 117 | Mrs Llewellyn & J.C. & A. Steuart (Trustees) Ltd. | Glenuig | | 3700 | NM 6776 |
| 118 | J. Ford & C. McColgan | Greshornish Woodlands I | | 3582 | NG 3249 |
| 119 | John Mackay | Taransay Island | | 3500 | NB 0002 |
| 120 | Richard, Adrian & John Miller | Cat Lodge | | 3500 | NN 6392 |
| 121 | D. Cameron | Glen Nevis | | 3500 | NN 1267 |
| 122 | Marigold E. Macrae | Clava (part) | | 3500 | NH 7741 |
| 123 | Mrs Dorte Aamann-Christensen * | Rona & Ardochy | | 3496 | NG 6257 |
| 124 | John Shaw of Tordarroch | Tordarroch | | 3200 | NH 6733 |
| 125 | | Cranachan | | 3200 | NN 3187 |
| 126 | Michael George Dawson | Ardochy | | 3147 | NH 2104 |
| 127 | Blairour Farming Co. | Blairour & Tirindrish | | 3000 | NN 2282 |
| 128 | Mr Hay | Mullardoch (part) | | 3000 | NH 2029 |
| 129 | Hugh MacDonald | Tayinloan | | 3000 | NG 3752 |
| 130 | Mr Sandeman | Ardnish | | 3000 | NM 7281 |
| 131 | Neil Campbell | Talisker Farm | | 3000 | NG 3230 |
| 132 | Sir Patrick Grant & Lady Carolyn Grant | Achvraid | | 2700 | NH 6626 |
| 133 | Michael A. Williamson | Leys | | 2700 | NH 6840 |
| 134 | Post Office Staff Superannuation Scheme * | Glendessary & Glenpean | | 2541 | NM 9591 |
| 135 | R.C. Macaulay (Kirkibost) Ltd. | Vallay & Griminish | Macaulay family | 2500 | NF 7776 |
| 136 | Nicolson | Stollamus Farm | | 2500 | NG 5925 |
| 137 | Tex Geddes and Nicholas Martin | Soay | | 2500 | NG 4413 |
| 138 | | Dalriach | | 2500 | NH 7637 |
| 139 | Anderson Duke Bakewell | Scarp | | 2488 | NA 9615 |
| 140 | Patrick H. Grant | Inverbrough & Balnespic | | 2400 | NH 8130 |
| 141 | Chas Hodges | Sconser | | 2349 | NG 5530 |
| 142 | Campbell Slimon | Breakachy & Crubenbeg | | 2200 | NN 6492 |
| 143 | Donald J. Wilson | Blaragie & Glenmarkie | | 2200 | NN 6095 |
| 144 | ON MARKET | Glenfintaig | | 2133 | NN 2086 |
| 145 | ON MARKET | Abriachan Forest | | 2132 | NH 5434 |
| 146 | Hon. A.A.M. Fraser | Wester Aberchalder | | 2078 | NH 5519 |
| 147 | Horsens Folkeblad Foundation * | Revack Forest | | 2066 | NO 0222 |
| 148 | Rodel Crofting Lands Ltd. | Rodel | Donnie MacDonald & others | 2000 | NG 0584 |
| 149 | Captain A.D.M. MacGregor | Pityoulish | | 2000 | NH 9214 |
| 150 | Oliver Plunkett | Pabbay | | 2000 | NF 8988 |
| 151 | Murdo MacDonald | Meadale | | 2000 | NG 3835 |
| 152 | Mrs Sewell | Farraline & Errogie | | 2000 | NH 5621 |
| 153 | Carn Mor Woodland Conservancy Ltd. | Kilmartin | | 1940 | NH 4230 |
| 154 | William Batey & Co (Exports) Ltd. | Strollamus | | 1800 | NG 5727 |
| 155 | Sporting Agency Ltd. | Easter Aberchalder | Alex Catto | 1800 | NH 5619 |
| 156 | Professor & Mrs M.E.D. Poore | Balnacarn | | 1800 | NH 2713 |
| 157 | A.W. Freed, MP Executive Pension Fund & others | Duntelchaig | | 1779 | NH 6231 |
| 158 | Angus Beaton | Greshornish | | 1729 | NG 3353 |
| 159 | ON MARKET | Garbole Forest | | 1726 | NH 7424 |
| 160 | Ronald MacSween | Drumuie | | 1700 | NG 4546 |
| 161 | Ruaraidh E.M.R. Hilleary | Edinbane | | 1700 | NG 3551 |

## Inverness-shire

| | | | | | |
|---|---|---|---|---|---|
| 162 | ON MARKET | Drummossie Forests | | 1688 | NH 6938 |
| 163 | ON MARKET | Cluanie | | 1583 | NH 4544 |
| 164 | G. Maxwell Smith | Lairgandour | | 1500 | NH 7237 |
| 165 | C.G. & N.D. Harris & Brian W. Bonnyman | Dalchreichart | | 1500 | NH 2912 |
| 166 | Various owners | Tulloch Let Woodlands | See Appendix 2 | 1500 | NN 3381 |
| 167 | John S. Taylor | Scalpay | | 1500 | NG 2395 |
| 168 | ON MARKET | North Skye Woodlands | | 1282 | NG 5058 |
| 169 | Trustees of M.J. Haywood's 1974 Trust | Biallaid | | 1250 | NN 7098 |
| 170 | Alex & John MacPherson | Dunchea & Abersky | | 1200 | NH 5827 |
| 171 | Donald MacLeod | Lyndale | | 1200 | NG 3755 |
| 172 | Malcolm Hugh Spence | Scamadale | | 1200 | NM 7090 |
| 173 | | Migovie | | 1200 | NH 5418 |
| 174 | Alexander A.C. & Susan M. Cruickshank | Ardochy (Ghrianach) | | 1055 | NH 1804 |
| 175 | John L.V. Lomas | Kyles | | 1000 | NA 9987 |
| 176 | J. & Donald Fraser | Guisachan Farm | | 1000 | NH 3026 |
| 177 | Belladrum Forestry Partnership | Belladrum | Aidan J.M. Gibbs | 1000 | NH 5241 |
| 178 | J. Graham Grant | Gaskbeg | | 1000 | NN 6294 |
| 179 | Lord Mackay of Clashfern & others | Inverarnie | | 1000 | NH 6933 |

| | | |
|---|---|---|
| Total | | 1986260 |
| Inverness-shire land area | | 2695094 |
| % of county accounted for | | 73.7% |

### PUBLIC LANDHOLDINGS

| | | |
|---|---|---|
| Forestry Commission | Various properties | 316887 |
| a. SOAEFD | See Appendix 4 | 190709 |
| c. SNH | See Appendix 5 | 49894 |
| d. MoD | See Appendix 6 | 3116 |
| e. HIE | Cairngorm Estate | 5802 |
| TOTAL | | 566408 |
| % of county | | 21.0% |

### CHANGES IN THE DISTRIBUTION OF LANDHOLDINGS BY SIZE 1970 - 1995

| | 1970 | | | 1995 | | |
|---|---|---|---|---|---|---|
| Acreage threshold | Acres | % of county | No. of owners | Acres | % of county | No. of owners |
| > 100 000 | 103200 | 3.8% | 1 | 112400 | 4.2% | 1 |
| > 75 000 | 455600 | 16.9% | 5 | 280400 | 10.4% | 3 |
| > 50 000 | 620800 | 23.0% | 8 | 392600 | 14.6% | 5 |
| > 40 000 | 848400 | 31.5% | 11 | 532710 | 19.8% | 8 |
| > 30 000 | 782900 | 29.0% | 12 | 704110 | 26.1% | 13 |
| > 20 000 | 944900 | 35.1% | 19 | 1042085 | 38.7% | 27 |
| > 10 000 | 1348500 | 50.0% | 46 | 1445425 | 53.6% | 56 |
| > 5 000 | 1594161 | 59.2% | 81 | 1781481 | 66.1% | 100 |
| > 1000 | 1755661 | 65.1% | 142 | 1986260 | 73.7% | 179 |

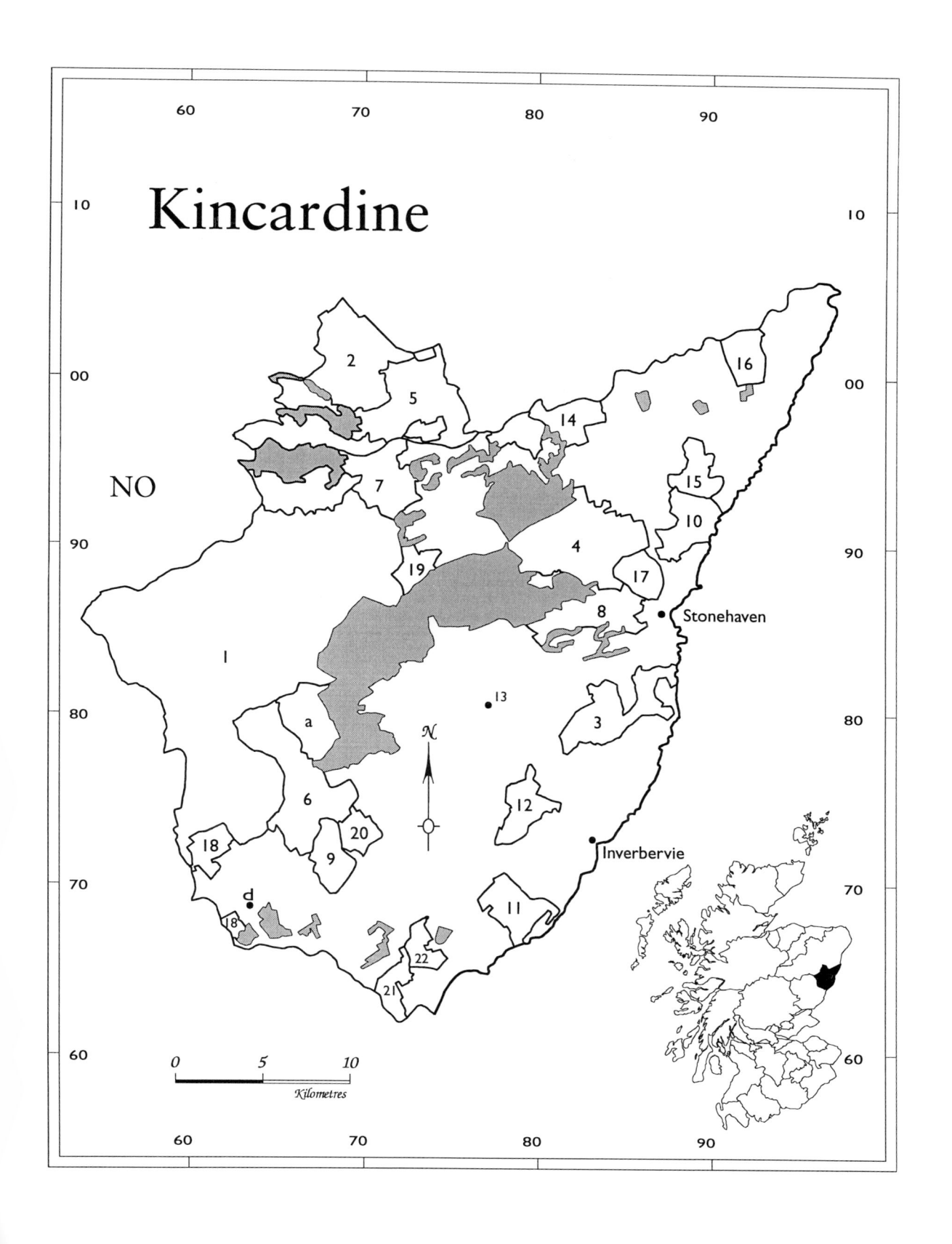

# Kincardine

NO

# Kincardineshire
## 244,248 acres

More work needs done to determine the current pattern of ownership in Kincardineshire and here, the greater availability of public information from SOAEFD would help. Nevertheless, I enjoyed a fair amount of help from the owners I contacted which, together with a few other reliable sources, has allowed me to account for just under half of the county.

The unwillingness of the Dunecht Estates to help means that I cannot explain the apparent loss of 10,000 acres from the 21,600 acres accounted for by McEwen. Whether they ever existed or whether they have indeed been sold can only be determined by further detailed investigation in the Registers of Sasines into the large number of transactions that an estate like this is engaged in.

Sir William Gladstone is still by far and away the largest proprietor in the county, owning virtually all the hill ground not held by the Forestry Commission. His enthusiasm for trees and the large grants that are available to plant them got him into controversy over a large planting scheme in Glen Dye.

| NO. | PROPRIETOR | PROPERTY | PRINCIPAL INTEREST | ACREAGE | GRID REF. |
|---|---|---|---|---|---|
| 1 | C.A. Gladstone & Gladstone 1987 Settlement | Fasque Estates | Sir William Gladstone | 47700 | NO 6475 |
| 2 | Viscount Cowdray & Trusts * | Dunecht & others (part) | | 11000 | NJ 6802 |
| 3 | Mrs M.C. Miller | Barras | | 6200 | NO 8381 |
| 4 | Richard I. Holman-Baird | Rickarton | | 6000 | NO 8388 |
| 5 | James C.A. & Alexander J.A. Burnett | Crathes & Leys (part) | | 5200 | NO 7398 |
| 6 | Mrs K. Lagneau | Fettercairn & Luthermuir | | 5000 | NO 6573 |
| 7 | Mary C. Rodwell | Tilquhillie | | 2700 | NO 7193 |
| 8 | | Fetteresso | | 2700 | NO 8485 |
| 9 | Thornton Estate | Thornton | Ian S. Thornton-Kemsley | 2000 | NO 6871 |
| 10 | Trustees of Aberdeen Endowments Trust | Muchalls | | 2000 | NO 8992 |
| 11 | Brotherton Estates Ltd. | Brotherton | | 2000 | NO 7967 |
| 12 | Hon. J.K.O. Arbuthnott | Arbuthnott | | 2000 | NO 7975 |
| 13 | A.C.S. & E.M.S. Macphie | Glenbervie | | 1850 | NO 7780 |
| 14 | | Ashentilly | | 1700 | NO 8297 |
| 15 | Duke of Fife | Elsick | | 1600 | NO 8994 |
| 16 | Capt Kenneth I.H. Lumsden | Banchory & Leggart | | 1565 | NJ 9102 |
| 17 | Ury Estate Ltd. | Ury | William Wisley | 1500 | NO 8588 |
| 18 | Heather Gray | Arnhall & Dalladies | | 1200 | NO 6169 |
| 19 | ON MARKET | Shillofad Forest | | 1055 | NO 7389 |
| 20 | ON MARKET | Bents & Kilnhill | | 1044 | NO 6972 |
| 21 | Mr Lewis & Partners | Morphie | | 1000 | NO 7164 |
| 22 | Morphie Farms Ltd. | Ecclesgreig | Lt. Cmdr. Michael Forsyth-Grant | 1000 | NO 7365 |
| | Total | | | 108014 | |
| | Kincardineshire land area | | | 244248 | |
| | % of county accounted for | | | 44.2% | |

## PUBLIC LANDHOLDINGS

| | | |
|---|---|---|
| Forestry Commission | Various properties | 24506 |
| a. SOAEFD | See Appendix 4 | 3952 |
| d. MoD | See Appendix 6 | 486 |
| TOTAL | | 28944 |
| % of county | | 11.9% |

## CHANGES IN THE DISTRIBUTION OF LANDHOLDINGS BY SIZE 1970 - 1995

| | 1970 | | | 1995 | | |
|---|---|---|---|---|---|---|
| Acreage threshold | Acres | % of county | No. of owners | Acres | % of county | No. of owners |
| > 100 000 | 0 | 0% | 0 | 0 | 0% | 0 |
| > 75 000 | 0 | 0% | 0 | 0 | 0% | 0 |
| > 50 000 | 0 | 0% | 0 | 0 | 0% | 0 |
| > 40 000 | 47700 | 19.5% | 1 | 47700 | 19.5% | 1 |
| > 30 000 | 47700 | 19.5% | 1 | 47700 | 19.5% | 1 |
| > 20 000 | 69300 | 28.4% | 2 | 47700 | 19.5% | 1 |
| > 10 000 | 69300 | 28.4% | 2 | 58700 | 24.0% | 2 |
| > 5 000 | 102100 | 41.8% | 7 | 81100 | 33.2% | 6 |
| > 1000 | 178100 | 72.9% | 47 | 108014 | 44.2% | 22 |

# Kinross

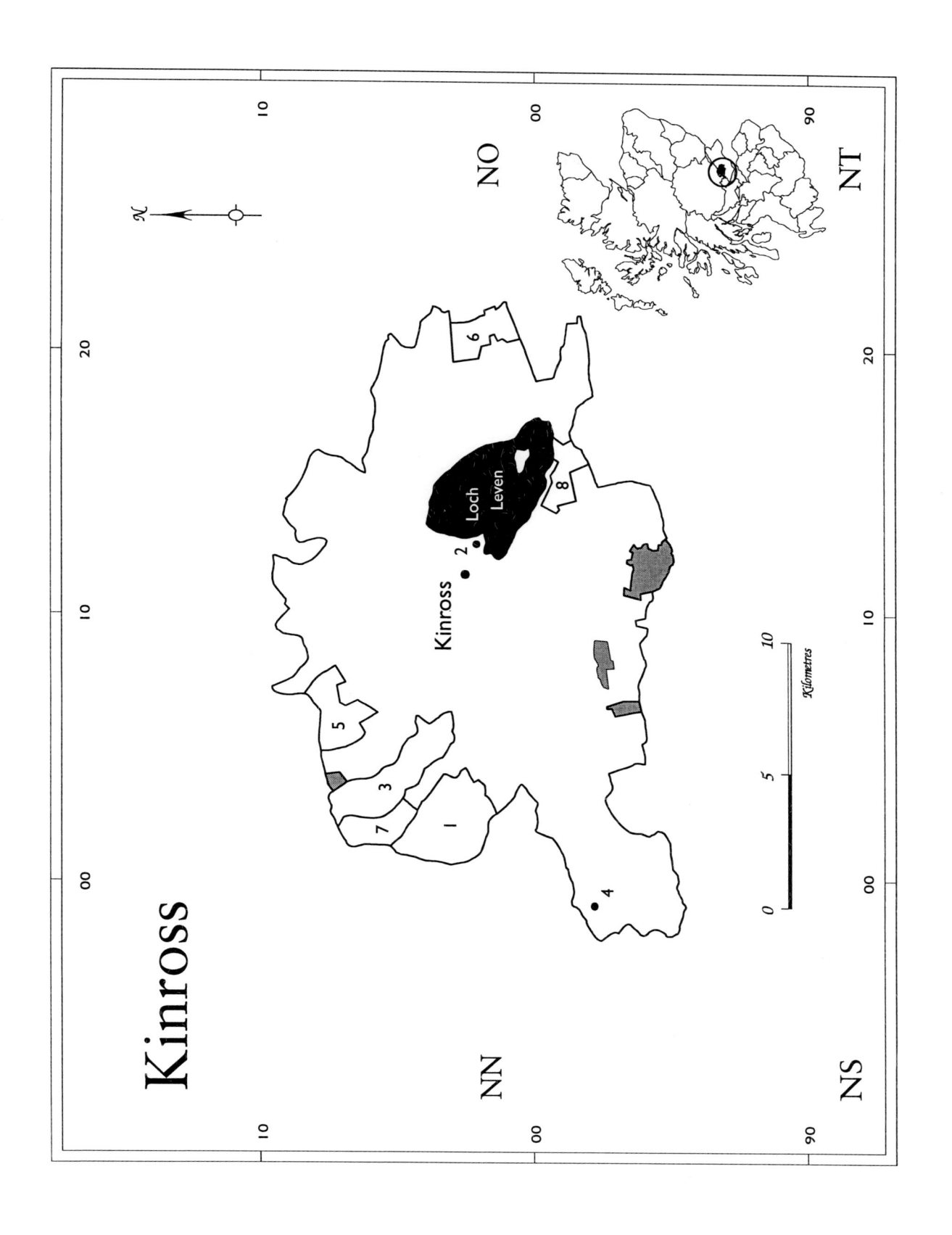

## Kinross-shire
## 52,392 acres

Kinross-shire is the second smallest county in Scotland and has no large estates. It is dominated by farms, many of which are on good quality soils around Loch Leven. The one significant landowner is Sir David Montgomery whose family have owned land around Kinross for centuries.

| NO. | PROPRIETOR | PROPERTY | PRINCIPAL INTEREST | ACREAGE | GRID REF. |
|---|---|---|---|---|---|
| 1 | 1990 Trust for P.R. Heriot-Maitland's Issue | Fossoway | | 1500 | NO 0202 |
| 2 | Kinross Estate Co. | Kinross Estate | Sir David Montgomery Bt. | 1100 | NO 1202 |
| 3 | William & Jean S. Paterson | Craighead Farm | | 1100 | NO 0404 |
| 4 | Robert C. Stewart | Blairingone & Arndean | | 1000 | NT 9897 |
| 5 | Eagle Star Insurance Company * | Blackhill & Touchie Wood | | 1000 | NO 0607 |
| 6 | ON MARKET | Arnot Estate (part) | | 600 | NO 2002 |
| 7 | John Paterson * | Earnieside Farm | | 600 | NO 0105 |
| 8 | Royal Society for the Protection of Birds | Vane Farm | | 568 | NT 1598 |
| | Total | | | 7468 | |
| | Kinross-shire land area | | | 52392 | |
| | % of county accounted for | | | 14.3% | |

**PUBLIC LANDHOLDINGS**

| | | | |
|---|---|---|---|
| Forestry Commission | Various properties | | 808 |
| TOTAL | | | 808 |
| % of county | | | 1.5% |

**CHANGES IN THE DISTRIBUTION OF LANDHOLDINGS BY SIZE 1970 - 1995**

| | 1970 | | | 1995 | | |
|---|---|---|---|---|---|---|
| Acreage threshold % | Acres | % of county | No. of owners | Acres | % of county | No. of owners |
| > 100 000 | 0 | 0% | 0 | 0 | 0% | 0 |
| > 75 000 | 0 | 0% | 0 | 0 | 0% | 0 |
| > 50 000 | 0 | 0% | 0 | 0 | 0% | 0 |
| > 40 000 | 0 | 0% | 0 | 0 | 0% | 0 |
| > 30 000 | 0 | 0% | 0 | 0 | 0% | 0 |
| > 20 000 | 0 | 0% | 0 | 0 | 0% | 0 |
| > 10 000 | 0 | 0% | 0 | 0 | 0% | 0 |
| > 5 000 | 0 | 0% | 0 | 0 | 0% | 0 |
| > 1000 | 18400 | 35.1% | 9 | 5700 | 10.9% | 5 |

## Kirkcudbrightshire
## 574,024 acres

Kirkcudbright is dominated by the Forestry Commission's holdings in the Galloway Forest Park and at Dalbeattie and Mabie which cover 146,506 acres or 25% of the entire county. In common with the rest of Galloway, many of the large estates of the nobility have disappeared. The transformation of the region is well described by R.H. Campbell in his book *Owners and Occupiers*.[1]

In recent years much of the uplands of Kirkcudbrightshire has changed hands as hill farmers have sold out to the new breed of overseas investor who are continuing the process of afforestation which has transformed the hills of Galloway. Danish interests are well represented with Mr Søren Engaard at Moorbrook and Strahana, and Greentops Lands and Estates Ltd. at Margree. Over the hill at Manquhill, Count Stanislaus Czermin-Kinsky has secured a place for the Austrian aristocracy.

The sale of hill farms to forestry investors represents much of what is wrong with the current system of landownership and use. Most other countries in Europe have a strong tradition of farm-forestry where cooperatives manage the forests and farmers manage the individual farm holdings. This is perfectly possible here if we had the political will. It would also call for some vision from hill farmers who, whilst sympathetic to ideas of integration, still by and large want to be sheep farmers. More critically, they stubbornly insist on the right to sell their farms to the highest bidder if it is in their interests. We cannot build up a stable and prosperous rural economy with an unregulated market in land.

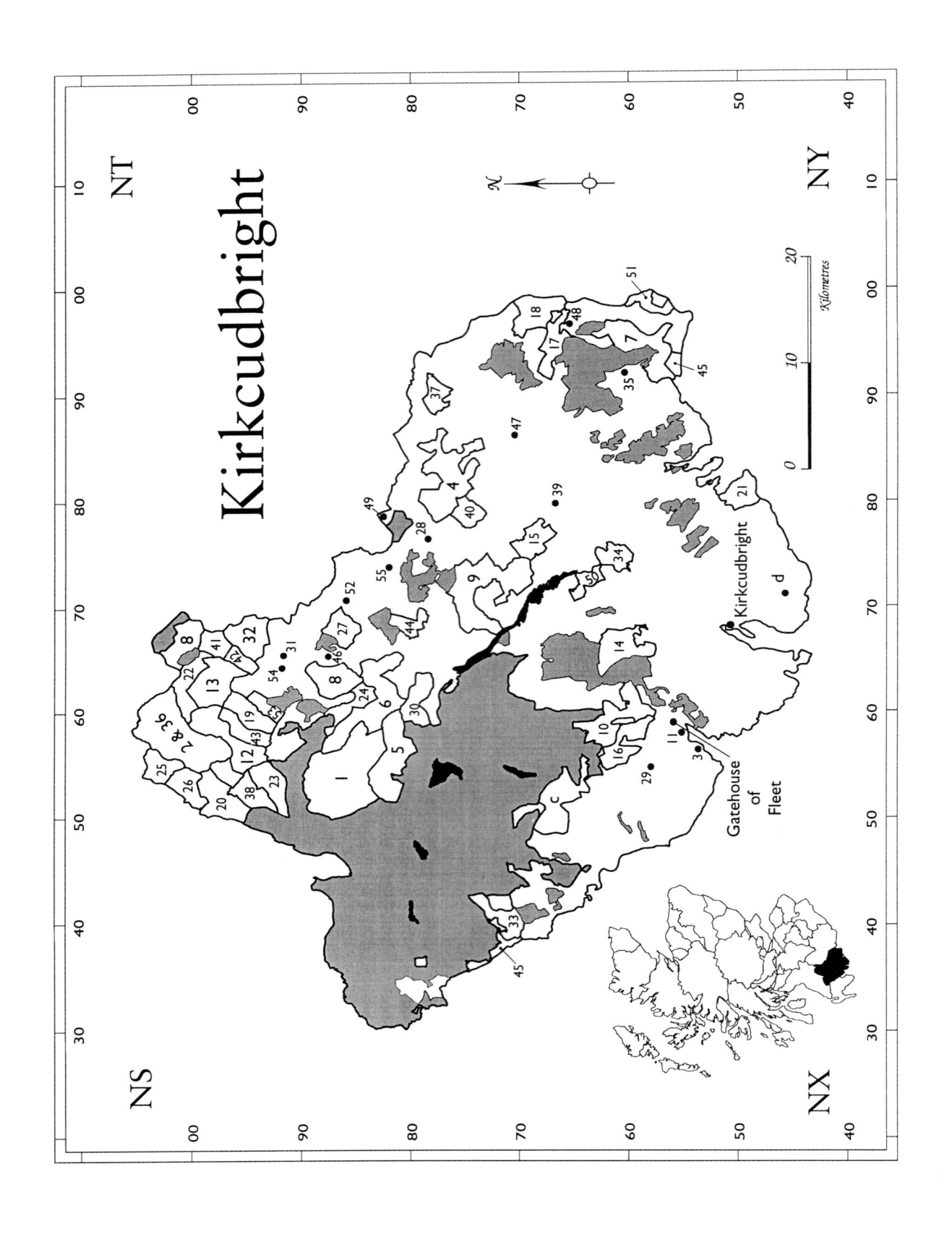

# Kirkcudbright

## Kirkcudbrightshire

| NO. | PROPRIETOR | PROPERTY | PRINCIPAL INTEREST | ACREAGE | GRID REF. |
|---|---|---|---|---|---|
| 1 | Cinco Ltd. and Forrest Estate Ltd. * | Forrest Estate | Fred Olsen | 11586 | NX 5586 |
| 2 | Electricity Supply Nominees Ltd. * | Carsphairn Forest & others | | 10497 | NS 5701 |
| 3 | Kirkdale Trust | Cardoness | R.W. Rainsford-Hanney | 7500 | NX 5355 |
| 4 | Henry Keswick * | Glenkiln | | 5681 | NX 8477 |
| 5 | Nick Roper-Caldbeck | Garroch Farm | | 5000 | NX 5981 |
| 6 | Lord Sinclair | Knocknalling Estate | | 5000 | NX 5984 |
| 7 | Robert Thomas | Southwick | | 4700 | NX 9560 |
| 8 | R. Fergusson | Barlaes, Mackilston & Lorg | | 4500 | NX 6385 |
| 9 | John M.A. Yerburgh & Trustees | Barwhillanty | | 4000 | NX 7270 |
| 10 | P. & J. Murray Usher & Murray Usher Foundation | Cally | Peter & James Murray Usher | 4000 | NX 6060 |
| 11 | Cordia Co. Ltd. | Ardwall, Margrie & Lochside | A.P. McCulloch | 4000 | NX 5854 |
| 12 | Colin W. Campbell | Holm of Daltallochan | | 3700 | NX 5594 |
| 13 | Søren Engaard | Moorbrock & Strahanna | | 3500 | NX 6296 |
| 14 | Lairdmannoch Enterprises | Lairdmannoch | | 3338 | NX 6559 |
| 15 | Auchendolly Trust | Auchendolly & Muil Farm | Sir J.C.L. Keswick | 3250 | NX 7668 |
| 16 | Anthony Gilbey | Rusko | | 2500 | NX 5958 |
| 17 | Davenport-Greenshields | Shambellie | | 2468 | NX 9566 |
| 18 | F.P. Maxwell | Kirkconnell | | 2200 | NX 9868 |
| 19 | Frank Hunter-Blair | Marbrack | | 2200 | NX 5993 |
| 20 | Eagle Star Life Assurance Co. Ltd. * | Drumjohn & Blackcraig | | 2153 | NX 5297 |
| 21 | Group Captain G.K. Gilroy | Auchencairn | | 2000 | NX 8150 |
| 22 | MacMillan & Partners | Dalquhairn | Peter Seed | 2000 | NX 6599 |
| 23 | Carol Cathcart | Garryhorn | | 2000 | NX 5493 |
| 24 | Earlston & Sanquhar Trusts | Earlston Estate | Callander Estates | 2000 | NX 6184 |
| 25 | Scottish Amicable Life Assurance Society * | Glenmuck & Brownhill (part) | | 1885 | NS 5502 |
| 26 | | Meadowhead Farm | | 1800 | NX 5299 |
| 27 | Greentops Lands and Estates Ltd. * | Margree | | 1800 | NX 6786 |
| 28 | Norman McQueen | Upper Barr | | 1780 | NX 7678 |
| 29 | I.R.S. Bond | Glen | | 1727 | NX 5457 |
| 30 | Captain Richard Agnew | Glenlee | | 1700 | NX 6180 |
| 31 | Wagfal Ltd. & others | Blackmark & Carroch | | 1602 | NX 6591 |
| 32 | Count Stanislaus Czermin-Kinsky | Manquhill | | 1600 | NX 6794 |
| 33 | Dr J. Radcliffe | Drannandow Farm | | 1548 | NX 3970 |
| 34 | National Trust for Scotland | Threave | | 1492 | NX 7560 |
| 35 | D.F. Culham Farms Ltd. | Boreland | | 1484 | NX 9260 |
| 36 | Refuge Farms Ltd. * | Deughwater | | 1464 | NS 5500 |
| 37 | Benjamin Weatherall | Crochmore | | 1425 | NX 8977 |
| 38 | Alastair & Susan Gordon | Woodhead | | 1404 | NX 5395 |
| 39 | James Biggar | Chapelton | | 1375 | NX 7966 |
| 40 | Andrew Dalton | Crofts | | 1325 | NX 7973 |
| 41 | W.H. Smith Pension Fund * | Corlae | | 1321 | NX 6597 |
| 42 | Jean Balfour * | Auchrae Hill | | 1321 | NX 6596 |
| 43 | Lt. Col. A. John Clark-Kennedy | Knockgray | | 1300 | NX 5793 |
| 44 | Various owners | Troquhain | | 1263 | NX 6879 |
| 45 | Royal Society for the Protection of Birds | Wood of Cree & Mersehead | | 1257 | NX 3871 |
| 46 | Malcolm S. Norgate | Glenshimmeroch | | 1225 | NX 6587 |
| 47 | D. & R. Kerr | Crochmore | | 1150 | NX 8670 |
| 48 | James Kingan & Sons Ltd. | Lochhill | | 1117 | NX 9665 |
| 49 | J.W. McConnel | Tower of Lettrick | | 1100 | NX 7882 |
| 50 | James Neil | Boreland of Balmaghie | | 1080 | NX 7263 |
| 51 | General Accident Fire & Life Assurance Co. Ltd. * | Arbigland | | 1064 | NX 9957 |
| 52 | | Holmhead | | 1028 | NX 7085 |

## Kirkcudbrightshire

| | | | | |
|---|---|---|---|---|
| 53 | | Furmiston | 1001 | NX 6092 |
| 54 | Pringle | Stroanpatrick & Cornharrow | 1000 | NX 6491 |
| 55 | J.F.S. Gourlay Farmers | Monybuie | 1000 | NX 7382 |
| | Total | | 142411 | |
| | Kirkcudbrightshire land area | | 574024 | |
| | % of county accounted for | | 24.8% | |

### PUBLIC LANDHOLDINGS

| | | |
|---|---|---|
| Forestry Commission | Various properties | 146506 |
| c. SNH | See Appendix 5 | 3247 |
| d. MoD | See Appendix 6 | 4716 |
| TOTAL | | 154469 |
| % of county | | 26.9% |

### CHANGES IN THE DISTRIBUTION OF LANDHOLDINGS BY SIZE 1970 - 1995

| | 1970 | | | 1995 | | |
|---|---|---|---|---|---|---|
| Acreage threshold | Acres | % of county | No. of owners | Acres | % of county | No. of owners |
| > 100 000 | 0 | 0% | 0 | 0 | 0% | 0 |
| > 75 000 | 0 | 0% | 0 | 0 | 0% | 0 |
| > 50 000 | 0 | 0% | 0 | 0 | 0% | 0 |
| > 40 000 | 0 | 0% | 0 | 0 | 0% | 0 |
| > 30 000 | 0 | 0% | 0 | 0 | 0% | 0 |
| > 20 000 | 0 | 0% | 0 | 0 | 0% | 0 |
| > 10 000 | 10700 | 1.9% | 1 | 22083 | 3.8% | 2 |
| > 5 000 | 58700 | 10.2% | 8 | 45264 | 7.9% | 6 |
| > 1000 | 91800 | 16.0% | 24 | 142411 | 24.8% | 55 |

# Lanark

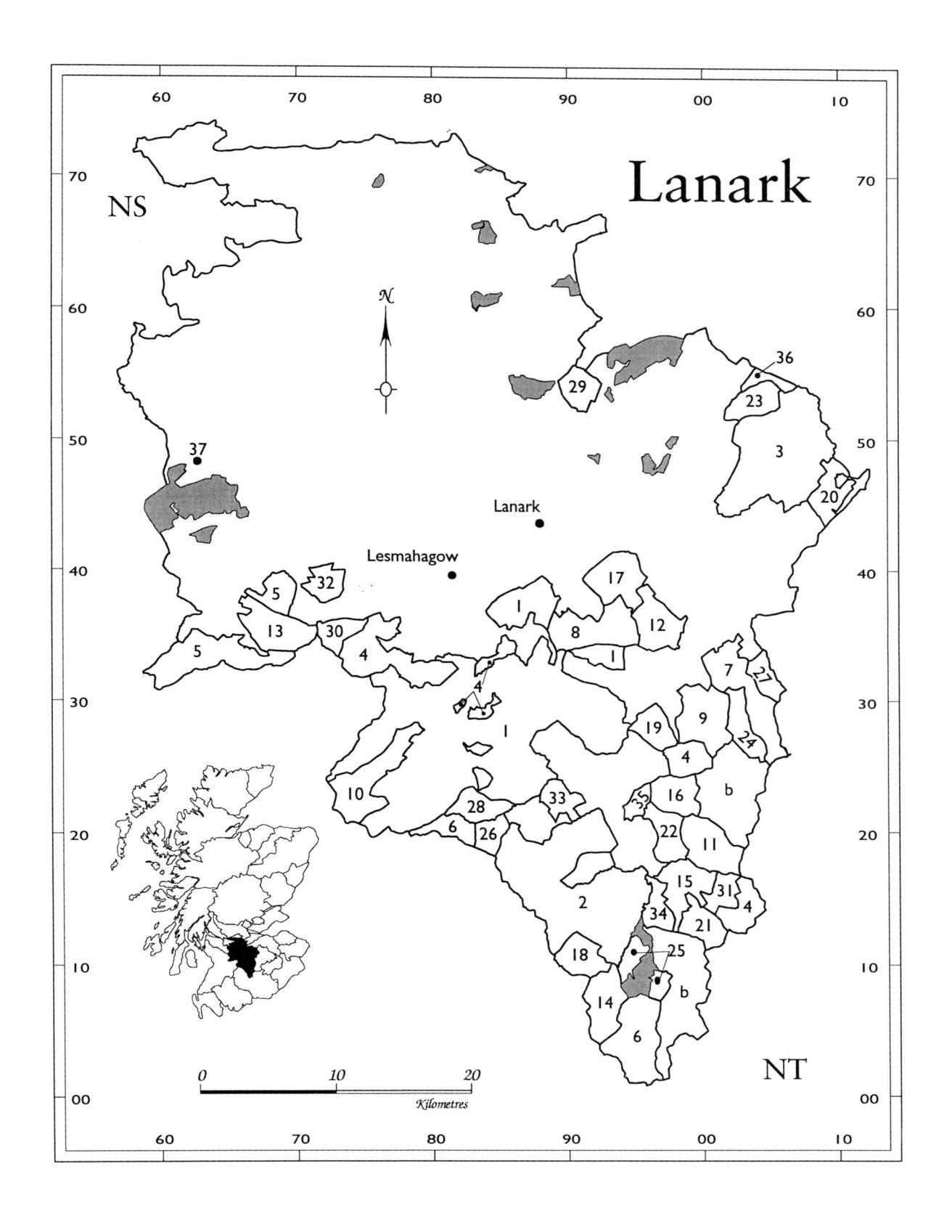

# Lanarkshire
## 574,473 acres

All the big estates have reduced in size since Millman's survey. The largest, Douglas and Angus, is down to 30,000 acres from 48,000 in 1970 and Lee & Carnwath Estates are only 12,500 acres compared to 20,000 acres in 1970. Other large estates such as Lord Rotherwick's Lanfine Estate have now been split up and Adam Wilson and Sons, the timber merchants from Ayr, now have much of what is left of the former Avondale Estates.

Again, with access to more information held by the government, it would be possible to account for more of this large county.

One of the most useful purposes to which a cadastral survey could be put, according to Roger Millman, is the design and layout of new roads. Knowledge of who the proprietors are and their business would enable road engineers to design roads that caused as little disturbance as possible to owners and minimised, for example, the need for underpasses for livestock. The construction of the new M74 has kept the South-west branch of the Scottish Landowners' Federation busy for the past few years. A straightforward cadastral register would have given everyone an easier time.

| NO. | PROPRIETOR | PROPERTY | PRINCIPAL INTEREST | ACREAGE | GRID REF. |
|---|---|---|---|---|---|
| 1 | Douglas & Angus Estates * | Douglas Estates | Earl Home | 30000 | NS 8431 |
| 2 | Hopetoun Estate Development Co. * | Leadhills & Glencaple | Marquess of Linlithgow | 18300 | NS 9214 |
| 3 | A.M. MacDonald Lockhart | Lee & Carnwath Estates | | 12500 | NT 0648 |
| 4 | Electricity Supply Nominees * | Cumberhead & others | | 8869 | NS 7734 |
| 5 | Adam Wilson & Sons Ltd. | Avondale (part) | | 7200 | NS 6735 |
| 6 | Buccleuch Estates Ltd. * | Daerhead & Whitecleugh | | 5700 | NS 9603 |
| 7 | McCosh Brothers | Culter Allers | | 4700 | NT 0331 |
| 8 | J. & A. Galloway Ltd. | Lochyloch | | 4400 | NS 9336 |
| 9 | Mr & Mrs Maxwell Stuart | Baitlaws Farm | | 4000 | NS 9830 |
| 10 | Illaria Ltd. | Carmacoup & Penbreck (part) | Count Rudi von Pezold | 3700 | NS 7423 |
| 11 | Charles Coubrough & Co. | Whelphill | | 3500 | NS 9920 |
| 12 | ON MARKET | St Johns Kirk Estate | | 3390 | NS 9736 |
| 13 | | Dungavel | | 3200 | NS 6735 |
| 14 | The Firm of Troloss Farm | Troloss | | 3000 | NS 9108 |
| 15 | ON MARKET | Little Clyde & Crookedstane | | 2540 | NS 9816 |
| 16 | Mr J.A. Craig | Normangill | | 2500 | NS 9722 |
| 17 | Richard Carmichael | Carmichael & Eastend | | 2300 | NS 9238 |
| 18 | Execs. of D. Batthurst & Mr Noble | Over Fingland Farm | | 2068 | NS 9209 |
| 19 | | Hartside | | 2000 | NS 9628 |
| 20 | Dolphinton Estate | Dolphinton | | 1975 | NT 1046 |
| 21 | N. Ireland Local Govt. Superannuation Committee * | Bidhouse | | 1742 | NT 0012 |
| 22 | John & Alan Wight | Midlock Farm | | 1700 | NS 9521 |
| 23 | John G. Hamilton | Dykefoot | | 1700 | NT 0252 |
| 24 | James & Hazel Brown | Birthwood | | 1700 | NT 0230 |
| 25 | Halifax Building Society Pension Nominees Ltd. * | Watermeetings & Hitteril Hill | | 1500 | NS 9511 |
| 26 | Robert A. Dalglish | Nether Whitecleugh | | 1500 | NS 8319 |
| 27 | Anthony Bertram | Nisbet | | 1500 | NT 0332 |
| 28 | | Stonehill Farm | | 1485 | NS 8421 |
| 29 | C. Henderson Hamilton | Birniehall Farm | | 1400 | NS 9052 |
| 30 | Trustees of W.M. Todd | Logan | | 1300 | NS 7435 |
| 31 | Lord Craigmyle "E" Settlement | Upper Howecleugh | | 1242 | NT 0014 |
| 32 | Enga Ltd. | Hareshawhead | See Appendix 3 | 1200 | NS 7239 |
| 33 | Trustees of Joseph Arthur, Baron Rank | Gilkerscleugh | | 1045 | NS 8922 |

| | | | | | |
|---|---|---|---|---|---|
| 34 | Mr & Mrs Peter Knowles-Brown | Crookedstane | 1000 | NS 9615 |
| 35 | R.H. Paton | Castle Farm | 1000 | NS 9521 |
| 36 | R. & D.H. Doig | Dykehead | 1000 | NT 0353 |
| 37 | Greentop Lands & Estates Ltd. * | Cleughearn | 500 | NS 6248 |
| | Total | | 148356 | |
| | Lanarkshire land area | | 574473 | |
| | % of county accounted for | | 25.8% | |

## PUBLIC LANDHOLDINGS

| | | |
|---|---|---|
| Forestry Commission | Various properties | 6660 |
| a. SOAEFD | See Appendix 4 | 883 |
| b. Strathclyde Regional Council | Campshead & Daer | 12000 |
| TOTAL | | 19543 |
| % of county | | 3.4% |

## CHANGES IN THE DISTRIBUTION OF LANDHOLDINGS BY SIZE 1970 - 1995

| | 1970 | | | 1995 | | |
|---|---|---|---|---|---|---|
| Acreage threshold | Acres | % of county | No. of owners | Acres | % of county | No. of owners |
| > 100 000 | 0 | 0% | 0 | 0 | 0% | 0 |
| > 75 000 | 0 | 0% | 0 | 0 | 0% | 0 |
| > 50 000 | 0 | 0% | 0 | 0 | 0% | 0 |
| > 40 000 | 48000 | 8.4% | 1 | 0 | 0% | 0 |
| > 30 000 | 48000 | 8.4% | 1 | 30000 | 5.2% | 1 |
| > 20 000 | 91000 | 15.8% | 3 | 30000 | 5.2% | 1 |
| > 10 000 | 102000 | 17.8% | 4 | 60800 | 10.6% | 3 |
| > 5 000 | 114700 | 20.0% | 6 | 82569 | 14.4% | 6 |
| > 1000 | 172700 | 30.1% | 34 | 147856 | 25.7% | 36 |

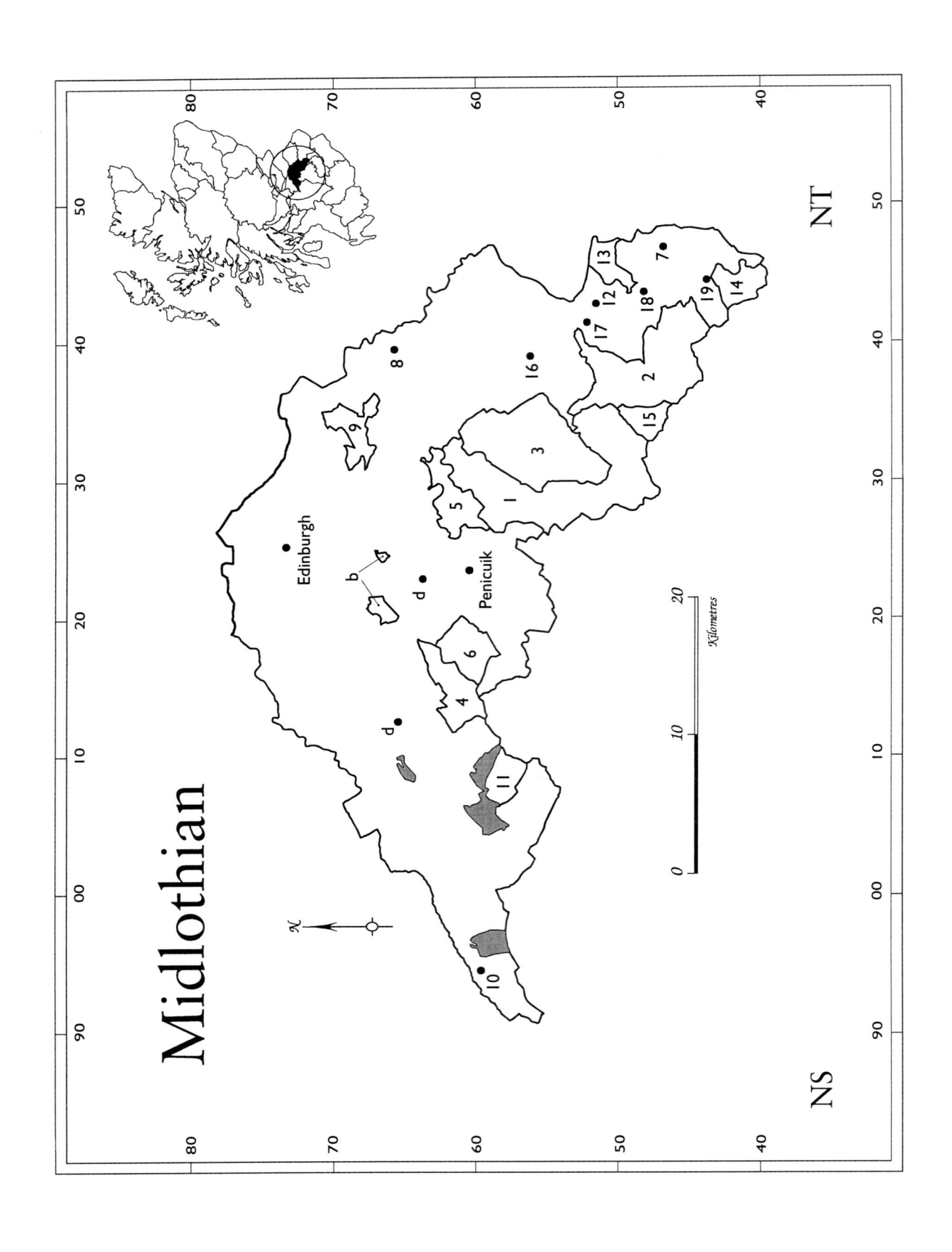

# Midlothian

# Midlothian
## 234,389 acres

Midlothian remains dominated by a few large properties, namely Dalmeny, Arniston and the Borthwick Estates.

Midlothian is the busiest section of the Register of Sasines in Edinburgh due to the sheer volume of property transactions in Edinburgh and I was reluctant to spend much time dodging the numerous professional searchers ushered in on the back of Thatcher's civil service reforms. There are other sources of information for Midlothian – surveys which have been done for various planning purposes – but time did not permit me to chase these up.

| NO. | PROPRIETOR | PROPERTY | PRINCIPAL INTEREST | ACREAGE | GRID REF. |
|---|---|---|---|---|---|
| 1 | Earl of Rosebery * | Dalmeny Estates | | 11000 | NT 3057 |
| 2 | Malcolm Borthwick | Nether Shiels, Corsehope & Raeshaw | | 10400 | NT 4146 |
| 3 | Mrs Bekker-Dundas | Arniston | | 10100 | NT 3259 |
| 4 | Colin Peters | Bavelaw | | 3500 | NT 1662 |
| 5 | Crown Estate Commissioners | Whitehill | | 3461 | NT 2861 |
| 6 | | Eastside | | 2500 | NT 1860 |
| 7 | Robert Hall | Cathpair & Little Cathpair | | 2500 | NT 4746 |
| 8 | Richard Callander | Prestonhall | | 2300 | NT 3965 |
| 9 | Buccleuch Estates Ltd. | Dalkeith House | | 2000 | NT 3368 |
| 10 | Hew Hamilton | Handaxwood | | 2000 | NS 9459 |
| 11 | ON MARKET | Colzium | | 1835 | NT 0858 |
| 12 | Hon. John H. Borthwick | Crookston & others | | 1700 | NT 4251 |
| 13 | Afton Settlement Trustees | Burnhouse Mains | | 1500 | NT 4449 |
| 14 | LB Plastic Ltd. * | Bowland & Fernihirst | Leon G. Litchfield | 1500 | NT 4439 |
| 15 | M.J.F. & F.M.S. Charles | Dewar Farm | | 1450 | NT 3448 |
| 16 | Douglas Kibble | Falahill Farm | | 1200 | NT 3956 |
| 17 | James C. & James S. Helm | Haltree | | 1100 | NT 4152 |
| 18 | James B. & Christine Hendry | Symington | | 1100 | NT 4348 |
| 19 | Margaret Barr * | Lugate | | 1000 | NT 4443 |
| | Total | | | 62146 | |
| | Midlothian land area | | | 234389 | |
| | % of county accounted for | | | 26.5% | |

**PUBLIC LANDHOLDINGS**

| | | | | |
|---|---|---|---|---|
| Forestry Commission | Various properties | | 2663 | |
| a. SOAEFD | See Appendix 4 | | 496 | |
| b. Lothian Regional Council | Bonaly, Hillend & others | | 1153 | |
| d. MoD | See Appendix 6 | | 2176 | |
| TOTAL | | | 6488 | |
| % of county | | | 2.8% | |

**CHANGES IN THE DISTRIBUTION OF LANDHOLDINGS BY SIZE 1970 - 1995**

| | 1970 | | | 1995 | | |
|---|---|---|---|---|---|---|
| Acreage threshold | Acres | % of county | No. of owners | Acres | % of county | No. of owners |
| > 100 000 | 0 | 0% | 0 | 0 | 0% | 0 |
| > 75 000 | 0 | 0% | 0 | 0 | 0% | 0 |
| > 50 000 | 0 | 0% | 0 | 0 | 0% | 0 |
| > 40 000 | 0 | 0% | 0 | 0 | 0% | 0 |
| > 30 000 | 0 | 0% | 0 | 0 | 0% | 0 |
| > 20 000 | 0 | 0% | 0 | 0 | 0% | 0 |
| > 10 000 | 32900 | 14.0% | 3 | 31500 | 13.4% | 3 |
| > 5 000 | 59400 | 25.3% | 7 | 31500 | 13.4% | 3 |
| > 1 000 | 119200 | 50.9% | 35 | 62146 | 26.5% | 19 |

*The Tables and Maps*

# Moray

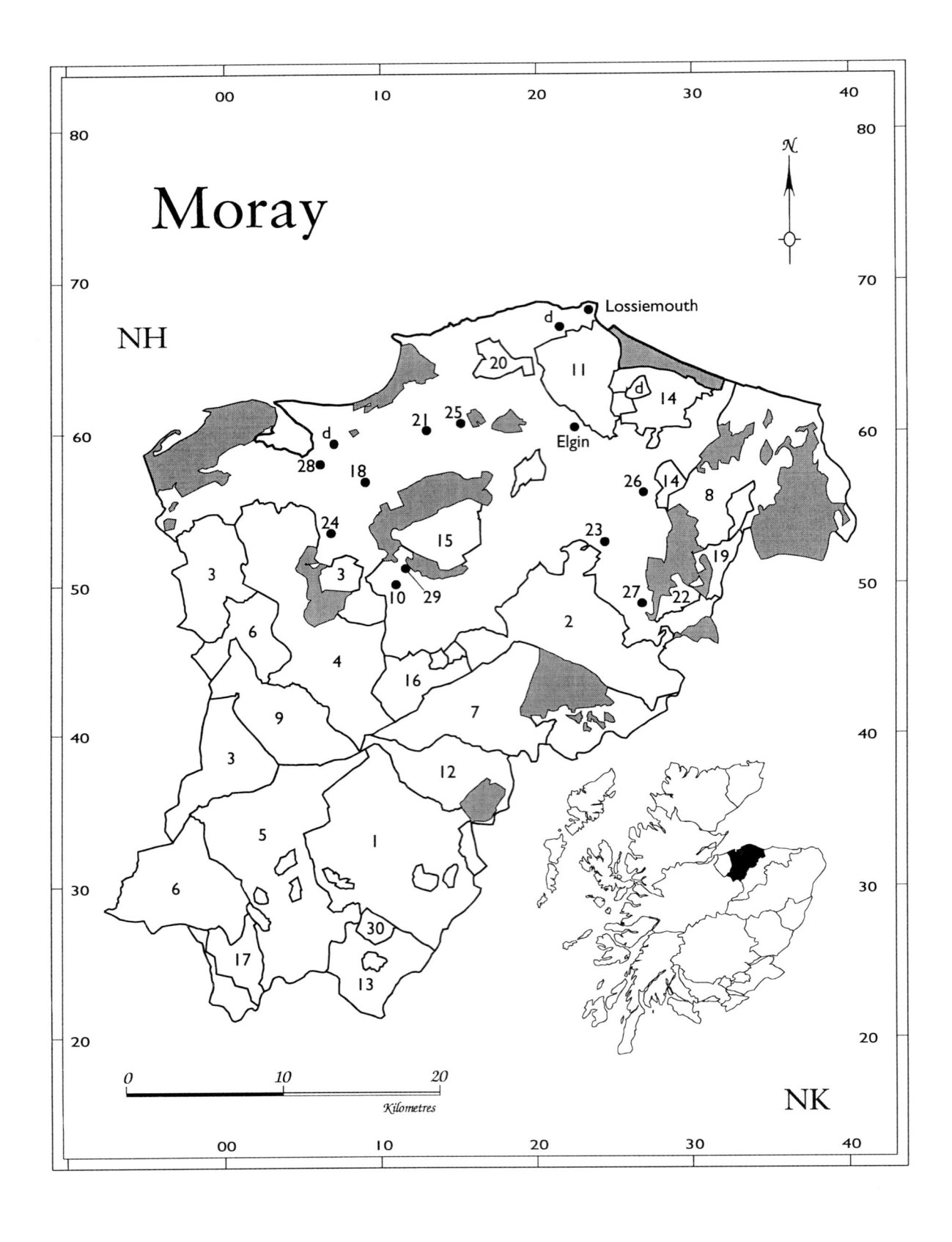

NH

Lossiemouth
Elgin

NK

## Moray
## 304,931 acres

Despite major reductions in the holdings of, for example, the Seafield Estates, Moray still remains a county of large landowners with 12 estates accounting for over half of it. Tulchan Estate appears as a new estate, sold by the Seafield Estate first to Ennessy Co., the past owners of Mar Lodge in Aberdeenshire and Amhuinnsuidhe Estate in Harris. It now belongs to Leon Litchfield, the boss of LB (Plastics) which makes plastic fittings for double-glazed windows. Seafield has also sold land to the Laing family who now own substantial parts of both Moray and Nairnshire. I have to rely on Millman's maps to derive the remains of the Seafield Estate. They never replied to my enquiries which is perhaps not surprising as I understand that they generally take a pretty dim view of anyone expressing an interest in their affairs.

John McEwen wrote with feeling about Moray, having worked there for several years and described how on a blazing July day he was out shovelling gravel, making estate roads for the opening of the grouse season on Altyre Estate. He would no doubt be pleased to read the thoughts of the laird of Altyre, Sir William Gordon Cumming Bt., in *Scottish Forestry* who, in response to the decline in grouse numbers concludes,

> The degradation caused by the burning and heavy grazing cannot be naturally corrected unless the land is returned to its natural state which provided a degree of fertility in the first place, i.e. a mixed woodland scenario. The creation of an extensive mixed forest is the only way to correct the abuse of the land in question. As landowners we are custodians and most privileged; we must not abuse that privilege by continuing to support the unsupportable.[2]

I can empathise both with John McEwen's thoughts and Sir William's having spent time as a forestry student fighting against Sitka Spruce farming and trying to find support for a more sympathetic way to both restore the land and develop a sustainable economy.

Eagle Star disposed of their Rothes Estate in 1994 to Broadland Properties and Edinmore Properties. Broadland own land on the Black Isle and its Director, John Guthrie, owns Conaglen in Argyll. Edinmore is a subsidiary of Caledonia Investments, owned by the Cayzer family who have extensive landholding interests around Scotland. They bought the estate for £4,797,000 and, having disposed of 2093 acres of the original 18,591, raised £1,690,289 in proceeds.

Again, landowners in Morayshire were generally quite helpful apart from one who was obviously quite offended by my approach. The fact that in this particular case I had increased the area attributed to him by McEwen (McEwen made as many understatements of acreages as he did overstatements) gave particular offence. Perhaps I should have made it clear that this was based on a reassessment of Millman's maps together with the acreage quoted in a press release issued by the Game Conservancy who held one of their annual jamborees on his estate.

## Moray

| NO. | PROPRIETOR | PROPERTY | PRINCIPAL INTEREST | ACREAGE | GRID REF. |
|---|---|---|---|---|---|
| 1 | Tulchan Estate Co. * | Tulchan | Leon G. Litchfield | 20000 | NJ 1335 |
| 2 | Broadland Estates Ltd & Edinmore Properties Ltd. * | Rothes | J.M. Guthrie & Cayzer family | 16861 | NJ 2349 |
| 3 | Moray Estates Development Company * | Moray Estates | Earl of Moray | 16500 | NH 9955 |
| 4 | Sir William Gordon Cumming Bart. | Altyre | | 16300 | NJ 0254 |
| 5 | Earl of Seafield * | Seafield Estates | | 16000 | NJ 0237 |
| 6 | Execs of Alexander G. Laing MC | Logie & Lochindorb | Alasdair Laing | 15500 | NJ 0150 |
| 7 | Dr Catherine Wills | Knockando | | 13800 | NJ 2042 |
| 8 | Crown Estate Commissioners | Fochabers | | 13290 | NJ 3459 |
| 9 | Mark & Robert J. Laing | Dunphail & Glenernie | | 8400 | NJ 0147 |
| 10 | David H. Houldsworth | Dallas Estate | | 7500 | NJ 1052 |
| 11 | Alexander A. Dunbar | Pitgaveny | | 6500 | NJ 2465 |
| 12 | Ballindalloch Trust | Ballindalloch | Clare Macpherson-Grant Russell | 5700 | NJ 1440 |
| 13 | Lady Pauline Ogilvie Grant Nicholson | Revack & Dorbrack (part) | | 4700 | NJ 0825 |
| 14 | Sir Iain, Mark, Christopher & Margaret Tennant | Innes | | 4565 | NJ 2765 |
| 15 | J.R.H. Wills | Pluscarden | | 3546 | NJ 1456 |
| 16 | Post Office Staff Superannuation Scheme * | Dallas (Glenlossie) | | 3310 | NJ 1247 |
| 17 | F. Laing | Glenbeg | | 2700 | NJ 0027 |
| 18 | Hamish J. Lochore | Burgie | | 2500 | NJ 0859 |
| 19 | R.P.W. Millar | Orton | | 1700 | NJ 3153 |
| 20 | Sir Archibald R. Dunbar | Duffus | | 1440 | NJ 1768 |
| 21 | General Accident Fire & Life Assurance Co. Ltd. * | W. Alves & Kirkton of Alves | | 1143 | NJ 1262 |
| 22 | Barbara C. Cheyne or Turcan | Sourden Wood | | 1034 | NJ 2951 |
| 23 | John A. Cruickshank | Coleburn | | 1000 | NJ 2455 |
| 24 | Allan G. Shiach & Mrs K. Shiach | Blervie House | | 1000 | NJ 0655 |
| 25 | ALIH (Farms) Ltd. | Ardgye | | 1000 | NJ 1562 |
| 26 | Trustees of Sylvester F. Christie | Blackhills | | 1000 | NJ 2658 |
| 27 | Duncan M. Dunbar-Naismith | Glen of Rothes | | 1000 | NJ 2652 |
| 28 | Trust for J.M. & Lt. Col. A.P. Grant Peterkin | Grangehall | | 1000 | NJ 0660 |
| 29 | Michael Gibson | Edinvale | | 1000 | NJ 1153 |
| 30 | | Tom an Uird | | 1000 | NJ 0930 |
| | Total | | | 190989 | |
| | Moray land area | | | 304931 | |
| | % of county accounted for | | | 62.6% | |

**PUBLIC LANDHOLDINGS**

| | | |
|---|---|---|
| Forestry Commission | Various properties | 29567 |
| d. MoD | See Appendix 6 | 3570 |
| TOTAL | | 33137 |
| % of county | | 10.9% |

**CHANGES IN THE DISTRIBUTION OF LANDHOLDINGS BY SIZE 1970 - 1995**

| | 1970 | | | 1995 | | |
|---|---|---|---|---|---|---|
| Acreage threshold | Acres | % of county | No. of owners | Acres | % of county | No. of owners |
| > 100 000 | 0 | 0% | 0 | 0 | 0% | 0 |
| > 75 000 | 0 | 0% | 0 | 0 | 0% | 0 |
| > 50 000 | 57500 | 18.9% | 1 | 0 | 0% | 0 |
| > 40 000 | 57500 | 18.9% | 1 | 0 | 0% | 0 |
| > 30 000 | 57500 | 18.9% | 1 | 0 | 0% | 0 |
| > 20 000 | 81400 | 26.7% | 2 | 20000 | 6.6% | 1 |
| > 10 000 | 146190 | 47.9% | 7 | 128251 | 42.1% | 8 |
| > 5 000 | 173690 | 57.0% | 11 | 156351 | 51.3% | 12 |
| > 1000 | 217190 | 71.2% | 31 | 190989 | 62.6% | 30 |

# Nairn

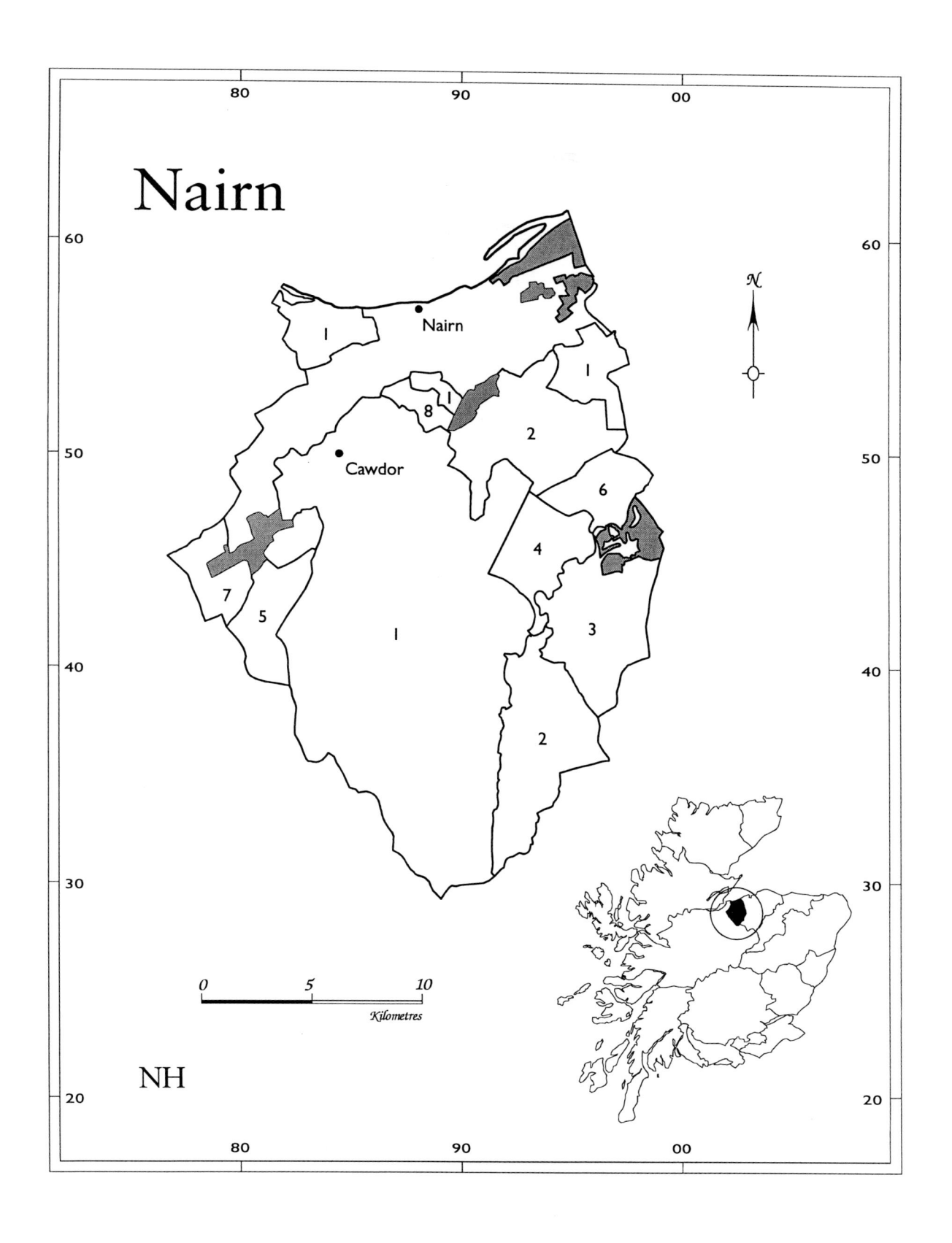

NH

# Nairnshire
## 104,252 acres

Nairnshire is a tiny county half of which is accounted for by just one estate, Cawdor. Curiously, McEwen only attributed 38,300 acres to this estate despite it having been clearly larger on Millman's maps. As with many of the large estates in Scotland today, it is now in the hands of Trustees. A number of trusts are the legal owners of the estate but it is in effect one holding since the current Earl of Cawdor is the sole beneficiary of most of it.

Trusts are increasingly used to defray problems with inheritance tax and capital gains taxes. They have a perpetual life, are secretive, and can seriously undermine the wider public interest. Trustees are legally obliged to follow the terms of the truster, the person who gave the property into the care of the trust. Years afterwards, trustees can make decisions which reflect outdated priorities. Where before, at least people could know who the landowner was, trustees are usually anonymous, and beneficiaries may take little interest if someone else is running their affairs. If we are serious about the redistribution of land and opportunity, private trusts should be prohibited from owning land.

There is not much more to say about Nairnshire, other than everyone I spoke to here was helpful, courteous and pleasant.

| NO. | PROPRIETOR | PROPERTY | PRINCIPAL INTEREST | ACREAGE | GRID REF. |
|---|---|---|---|---|---|
| 1 | Cawdor Trusts | Cawdor (part) | Earl of Cawdor | 49400 | NH 8449 |
| 2 | Lethen Estate Trustees | Lethen & Dunearn | E.J. Brodie | 12800 | NH 9351 |
| 3 | Lord Balgonie | Glenferness | | 6500 | NH 9342 |
| 4 | Hon. V.P.H. Wills | Dulsie Wood | | 3000 | NH 9244 |
| 5 | Rathy, Hassan & Armstrong | Holme Rose Grouse Moor | | 3000 | NH 8142 |
| 6 | Lord Laing's 1961 Settlement Trust | Coulmony | A.R. Laing | 2000 | NH 9747 |
| 7 | Marigold E. Macrae | Clava (part) | | 1500 | NH 7342 |
| 8 | C.J. MacKintosh-Walker | Geddes | | 1000 | NH 8852 |
| | Total | | | 79200 | |
| | Nairnshire land area | | | 104252 | |
| | % of county accounted for | | | 76.0% | |

**PUBLIC LANDHOLDINGS**

| | | |
|---|---|---|
| Forestry Commission | Various properties | 3463 |
| TOTAL | | 3463 |
| % of county | | 3.3% |

**CHANGES IN THE DISTRIBUTION OF LANDHOLDINGS BY SIZE 1970 - 1995**

| | 1970 | | | 1995 | | |
|---|---|---|---|---|---|---|
| Acreage threshold | Acres | % of county | No. of owners | Acres | % of county | No. of owners |
| > 100 000 | 0 | 0% | 0 | 0 | 0% | 0 |
| > 75 000 | 0 | 0% | 0 | 0 | 0% | 0 |
| > 50 000 | 0 | 0% | 0 | 0 | 0% | 0 |
| > 40 000 | 0 | 0% | 0 | 49400 | 47.4% | 1 |
| > 30 000 | 38300 | 36.7% | 1 | 49400 | 47.4% | 1 |
| > 20 000 | 38300 | 36.7% | 1 | 49400 | 47.4% | 1 |
| > 10 000 | 54200 | 52.0% | 2 | 62200 | 59.7% | 2 |
| > 5 000 | 59700 | 57.3% | 3 | 68700 | 65.9% | 3 |
| > 1000 | 76800 | 73.7% | 11 | 79200 | 76.0% | 8 |

# Orkney

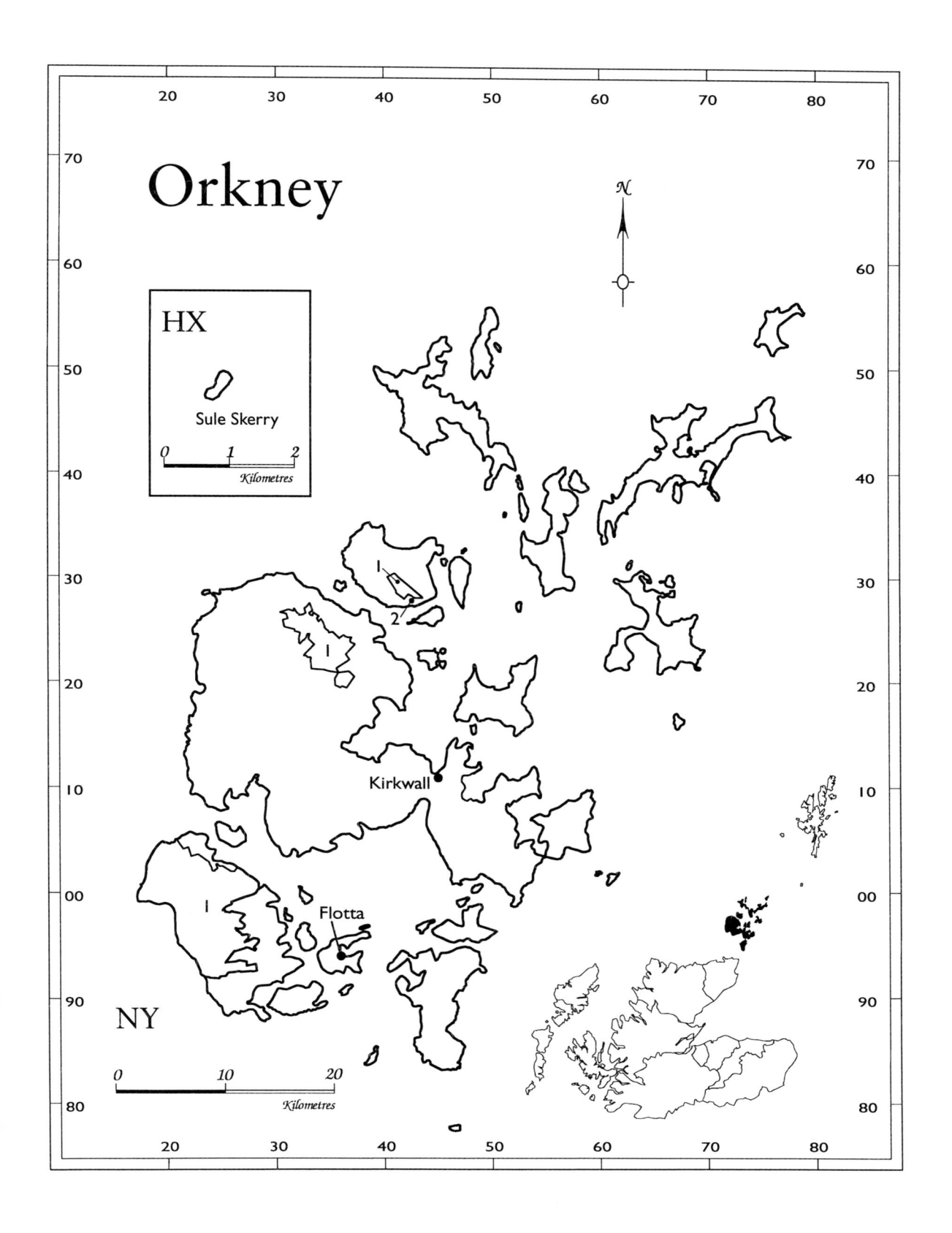

HX

Sule Skerry

NY

## Orkney
**240,848 acres**

Orkney is a fertile place and mainly made up of owner-occupied farms. Many of the big estates were split up in the early part of this century. Failure to obtain access to the relevant information means that little can be reported about Orkney. Indeed, it has been impossible to readily determine anything about landownership in this county. More time to make relevant local contacts and enquiries in the Register of Sasines would yield a better picture.

Udal law has, however, been an important influence in the pattern of owner occupied holdings, since property was inherited and subdivided among the children rather than all accruing to the eldest child. This provides a stark contrast with feudalism and primogeniture which perpetuates the concentration of private property.

I would like to learn more about Orkney and its landowning history.

| NO. | PROPRIETOR | PROPERTY | PRINCIPAL INTEREST | ACREAGE | GRID REF. |
|---|---|---|---|---|---|
| 1 | Royal Society for the Protection of Birds | North Hoy & others | | 15056 | ND 2298 |
| 2 | | Trumland | | 1900 | HY 4227 |

| | | |
|---|---|---|
| Total | | 16956 |
| Orkney land area | | 240848 |
| % of county accounted for | | 7.0% |

**PUBLIC LANDHOLDINGS**

No significant public landholdings

**CHANGES IN THE DISTRIBUTION OF LANDHOLDINGS BY SIZE 1970 - 1995**

| | 1970 | | | 1995 | | |
|---|---|---|---|---|---|---|
| Acreage threshold | Acres | % of county | No. of owners | Acres | % of county | No. of owners |
| > 100 000 | 0 | 0% | 0 | 0 | 0% | 0 |
| > 75 000 | 0 | 0% | 0 | 0 | 0% | 0 |
| > 50 000 | 0 | 0% | 0 | 0 | 0% | 0 |
| > 40 000 | 0 | 0% | 0 | 0 | 0% | 0 |
| > 30 000 | 0 | 0% | 0 | 0 | 0% | 0 |
| > 20 000 | 0 | 0% | 0 | 0 | 0% | 0 |
| > 10 000 | 0 | 0% | 0 | 15056 | 6.3% | 1 |
| > 5 000 | 0 | 0% | 0 | 15056 | 6.3% | 1 |
| > 1000 | 0 | 0% | 0 | 16956 | 7.0% | 2 |

# Peebles

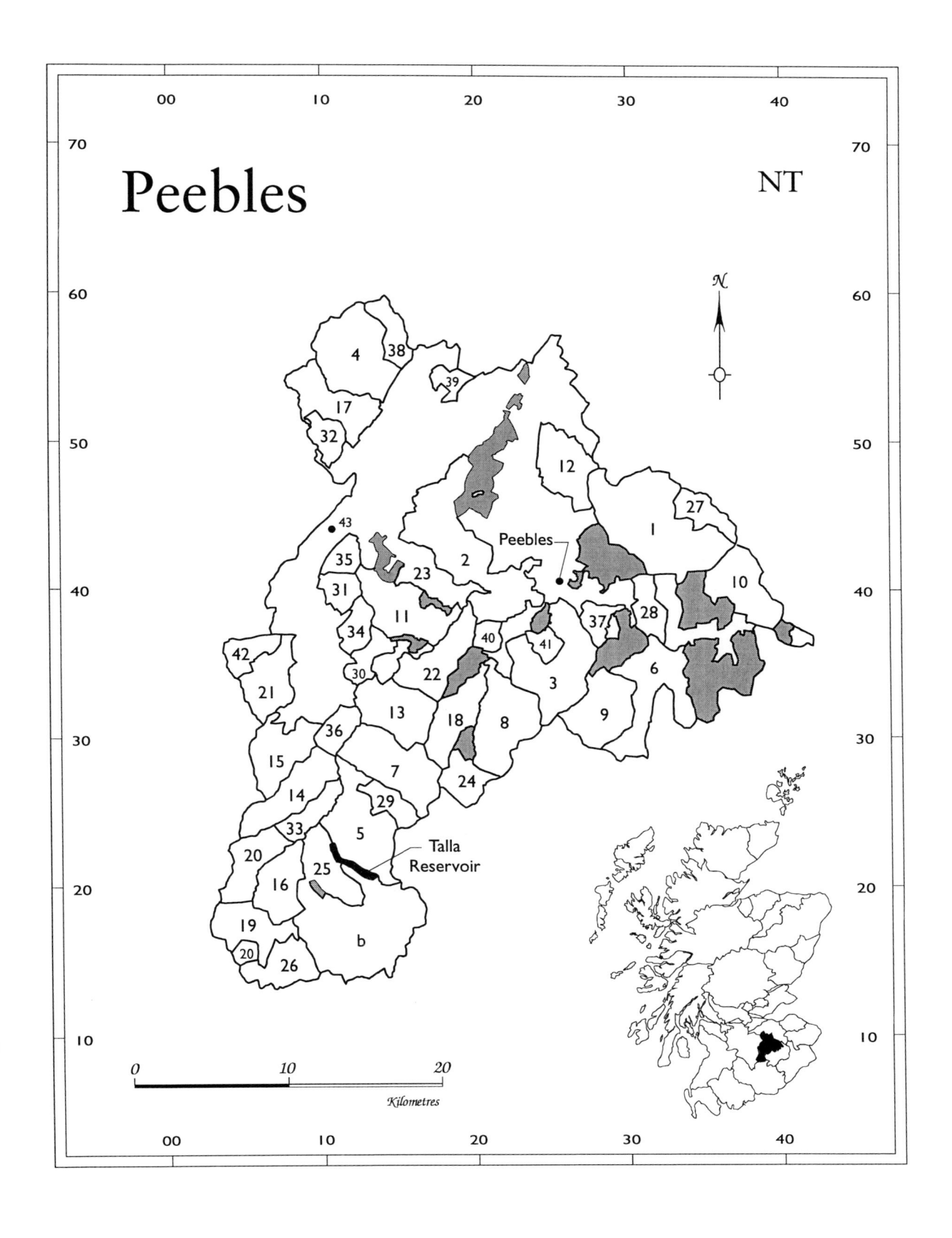

NT

# Peeblesshire
## 222,240 acres

McEwen described Peeblesshire as a small, quiet county. The Earls of Rosebery and Wemyss are still the largest owners although the Wemyss estates are held in trusts, one of which is Lady Benson's, whose Barns Estate was featured in a recent edition of *Shooting Times*, described as the Scottish home of Elizabeth and David Benson. Lady Elizabeth is the daughter of the Earl of Wemyss and March and married to David Benson, Chairman of Kleinwort and Charter Investment Trust.

Much of the information gathered for this book came from publications such as *Shooting Times*, *The Field*, *Harpers & Queen*, the *Financial Times*, and *Who's Who*. Taken together, these sources alone would probably reveal more than half the landowners in Scotland with a bit of detective work.

Peeblesshire of course contains the River Tweed which, as it is a major salmon river, means land on its banks is precious, provided of course there are riparian fishing rights. This appears to be the case in Peeblesshire although elsewhere in Scotland many salmon fishings have been sold off to wealthy syndicates.

The only major newcomers to Peeblesshire are the private forestry investors, among them the pension fund for the European Centre for Nuclear Research (CERN) which gave me cause for some anxiety when I first encountered it!

| NO. | PROPRIETOR | PROPERTY | PRINCIPAL INTEREST | ACREAGE | GRID REF. |
|---|---|---|---|---|---|
| 1 | Earl of Rosebery * | Rosebery Estates | | 9900 | NT 3045 |
| 2 | Lady E. Bensons Trust & Lord Wemyss Trust * | Wemyss Estates | Earl of Wemyss | 9400 | NT 2139 |
| 3 | Mary Coltman | Haystoun | | 6700 | NT 2635 |
| 4 | Gavin Marshall | Baddinsgill | | 5500 | NT 1355 |
| 5 | Multioptique International Ltd. & EGW (UK) Ltd. | Hearthstanes & Glenrusco | E.W. Glatt | 5400 | NT1323 |
| 6 | Flora Maxwell-Stuart | Traquair | | 5200 | NT 3235 |
| 7 | David H. Baxendale | Stanhope | | 4650 | NT 1527 |
| 8 | Glenrath Farms | Glenrath & Langhaugh Moor | John P. Campbell | 4500 | NT 2133 |
| 9 | Tessa M. Tennant | Glen House | | 4200 | NT 2933 |
| 10 | Sir David Thomson Bt. | Holylee | | 4200 | NT 3937 |
| 11 | Hugh L. & Charles R. Seymour | Stobo | | 3950 | NT 1736 |
| 12 | Christine M. Reid | Portmore & West Loch | | 3516 | NT 2548 |
| 13 | Trustees of Mrs S. Lukas Trust for Grandchildren | Drumelzier Place | | 3500 | NT 1431 |
| 14 | Bemeco Vastgoed BV | Kingledores | | 3500 | NT 1028 |
| 15 | Miss Brohda & Trustees of late Stephen Brown | Glencotho | | 3400 | NT 0829 |
| 16 | David Moffat & Sons | Hawkshaw | | 3000 | NT 0722 |
| 17 | The North Slipperfield Sporting Company | North Slipperfield | | 3000 | NT 1251 |
| 18 | Archibald Smellie | Posso | | 3000 | NT 2033 |
| 19 | CERN (European Org. for Nuclear Research) * | Badlieu | | 2964 | NT 0518 |
| 20 | Electricity Supply Nominees Ltd. * | Tweedsmuir Forest | | 2964 | NT0922 |
| 21 | Yelstan Property Co. | Mitchell Hill | David Marshall | 2700 | NT 0733 |
| 22 | Dawyck Estates Ltd. | Dawyck | | 2700 | NT 1635 |
| 23 | ON MARKET | Easter & Wester Happrew | | 2650 | NT1839 |
| 24 | Mr C.M. Couborough | Manorhead Farm | | 2000 | NT 1927 |
| 25 | Gerald Walsh Discretionary Settlement Trust | Menzion | | 2000 | NT 0923 |
| 26 | | Earlshaugh | | 1700 | NT 0714 |

**Peeblesshire**

| 27 | Mrs L. & Mr L. McVie | Blackhopebyre | 1700 | NT 3444 |
|---|---|---|---|---|
| 28 | John G. Hogg | Glenormiston | 1500 | NT 3138 |
| 29 | Messrs. M.H.J.S. Statham | Patervan Farm | 1500 | NT 1425 |
| 30 | Andrew & James Warnock | Rachan & Dreva | 1500 | NT 1335 |
| 31 | Trustees of Peter Smith & Son | Stirkfield | 1500 | NT 1040 |
| 32 | ON MARKET | Ferniehaugh | 1450 | NT 1049 |
| 33 | Kenneth R. Reive | Oliver Farm | 1300 | NT 0924 |
| 34 | A.K.M.C.C. Elliot & others | Broughton Place | 1250 | NT 1137 |
| 35 | W.A.B. Noble | Lochurd Farm | 1250 | NT 1143 |
| 36 | Alexander C. Welsh | Mossfennan Farm | 1250 | NT 1131 |
| 37 | Dr W McKelvey & Lady A. Buchan Hepburn | Kailzie House Mains | 1200 | NT 2738 |
| 38 | Peter & Douglas Miller | Fairliehope | 1000 | NT 1556 |
| 39 | Douglass Scarff | Deepsyke | 1000 | NT 1853 |
| 40 | Matthew R. Barr | Woodhouse Farm | 1000 | NT 2037 |
| 41 | Lt. Col. Aidan Sprot | Crookston Farm | 1000 | NT 2436 |
| 42 | Ian M. & Jennifer M. Roper-Caldbeck | Thripland & Pyatknowe | 1000 | NT 0435 |
| 43 | Greentop Lands & Estates Ltd. * | Netherurd Mains | 500 | NT 1044 |

| Total | 127094 |
|---|---|
| Peeblesshire land area | 222240 |
| % of county accounted for | 57.2% |

**PUBLIC LANDHOLDINGS**

| Forestry Commission | Various properties | 15716 |
|---|---|---|
| b. Lothian Regional Council | Fruid & Talla | 5800 |
| TOTAL | | 21516 |
| % of county | | 9.7% |

**CHANGES IN THE DISTRIBUTION OF LANDHOLDINGS BY SIZE 1970 - 1995**

| | 1970 | | | 1995 | | |
|---|---|---|---|---|---|---|
| Acreage threshold | Acres | % of county | No. of owners | Acres | % of county | No. of owners |
| > 100 000 | 0 | 0% | 0 | 0 | 0% | 0 |
| > 75 000 | 0 | 0% | 0 | 0 | 0% | 0 |
| > 50 000 | 0 | 0% | 0 | 0 | 0% | 0 |
| > 40 000 | 0 | 0% | 0 | 0 | 0% | 0 |
| > 30 000 | 0 | 0% | 0 | 0 | 0% | 0 |
| > 20 000 | 0 | 0% | 0 | 0 | 0% | 0 |
| > 10 000 | 28200 | 12.7% | 2 | 0 | 0% | 0 |
| > 5 000 | 71300 | 32.1% | 9 | 42100 | 18.9% | 6 |
| > 1000 | 112800 | 50.8% | 27 | 126594 | 57.0% | 42 |

# Perth
## (1)

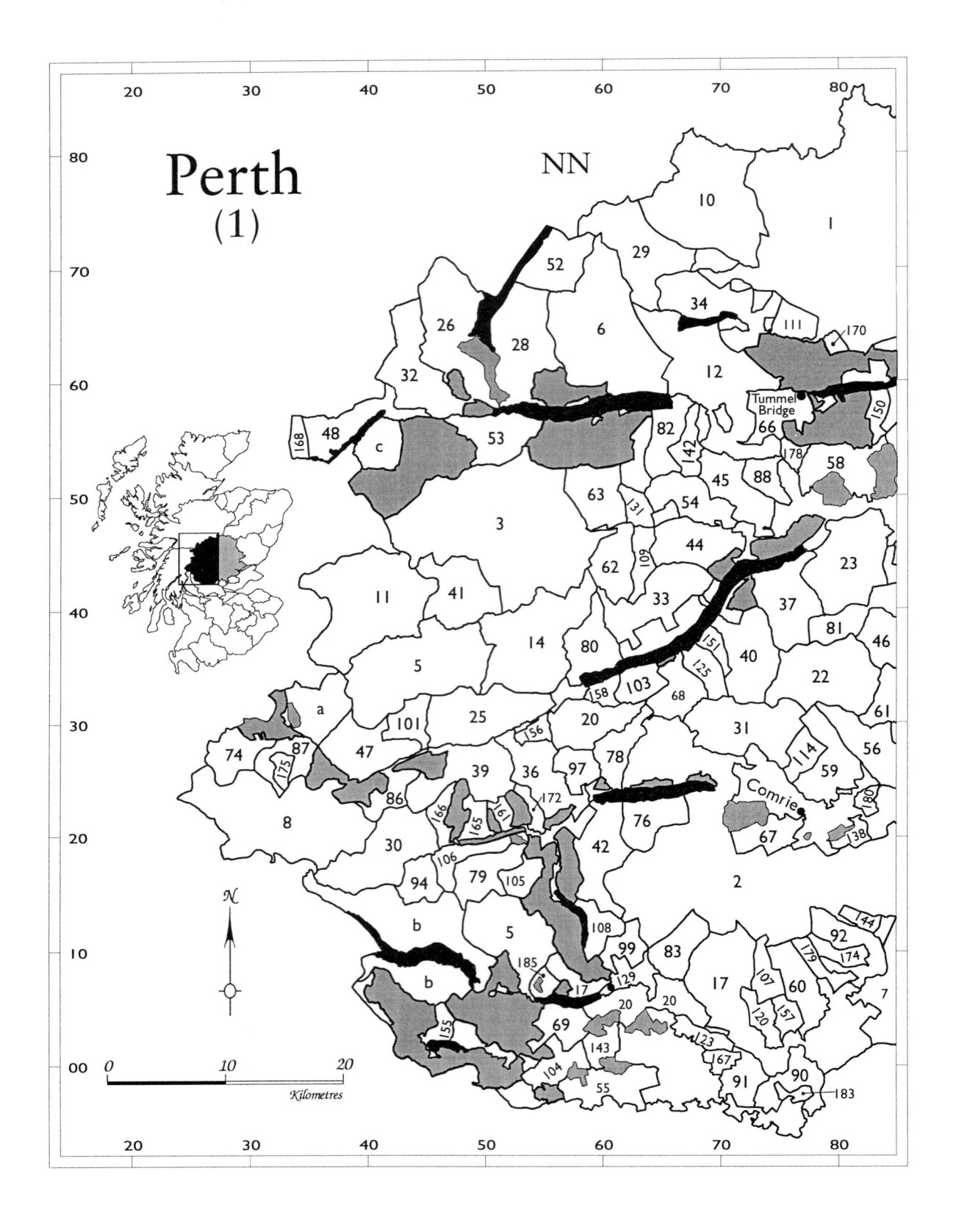

NN

Tummel Bridge

Comrie

# Perth (2)

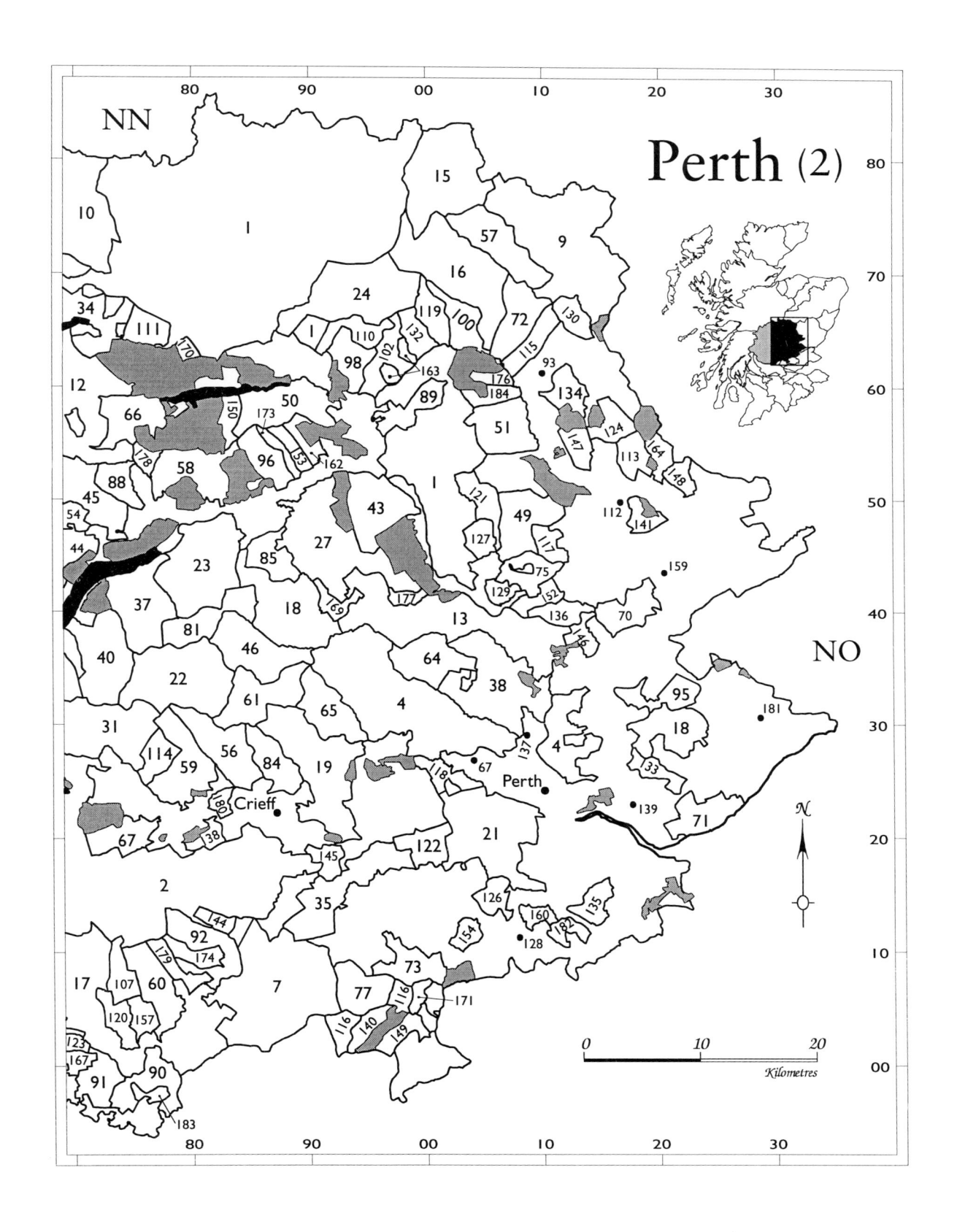

## Perthshire
## 1,595,804 acres

Perthshire is a substantial and important county which, whilst it has seen some dilution in the concentrated pattern of ownership reported by McEwen, is still dominated by a few dozen major owners. Neither has there has been much change in the people involved. The names listed in McEwen remain for the most part very familiar and most estates are still with the same families that held them when Millman was undertaking his survey. Sir Edward Wills, who owned Meggernie Estate, is one of the few to have disappeared. Newcomers include Sir Ian Lowson who, under a variety of companies including Tay and Torridon Estates Ltd. and Culfargie Estates Ltd., owns the Lochan Estate and land to the east of Perth.

Established landowners have prepared for change, however, and Atholl Estates is now owned by various trusts including the Bruar Trust and Sarah Troughton, the half-sister of the late Duke of Atholl. I have recorded Atholl Estates as still one holding however since, like many other large estates, changes are being made in ownership which have everything to with internal estate polices towards tax exposure and nothing to do with breaking up these landholdings.

Private forestry has been responsible for the few changes that have taken place, with the Midland Bank now owning over 10,000 acres above Aberfeldy and a Spanish gentleman, Senor Raphael Cruz Conde owning over 5000 acres in Glenample.

The activities of the Al Tajir family from Dubai, owners of the Blackford Estate, continue to attract media interest and deservedly so given reports of farms being abandoned and £200,000 in set-aside payments to one of the wealthiest families in the world. Local people are speaking publicly now for the first time since the early 70s when the estate was bought by Al Tajir, although even in the latest BBC Scotland investigation in the autumn of 1995, one person withdrew at the last minute. Twenty-five years of silence is damning testimony to a landownership system which most other civilised countries have consigned to their museums of rural life.

Perthshire's acres deserve better than the insidious neglect of the Al Tajirs or the blasted hills of Breadalbane.

## Perthshire

| NO. | PROPRIETOR | PROPERTY | PRINCIPAL INTEREST | ACREAGE | GRID REF. |
|---|---|---|---|---|---|
| 1 | Bruar Trust, Sarah Troughton & The Blair Trust | Atholl Estates | Sarah Troughton | 148000 | NN 8666 |
| 2 | Baroness Willoughby de Eresby | Drummond Estates | | 63200 | NN 6815 |
| 3 | Beverley Jane Malim | Meggernie & Lochs | | 36500 | NN 5546 |
| 4 | Trustees for Visc. Stormont & Earl of Mansfield | Scone Estates | | 33800 | NN 9631 |
| 5 | John B. Cameron | Glen Lochay & Glen Finglas | | 26400 | NN 5210 |
| 6 | Astel Ltd. | Craiganour | Viscount Wimborne | 20200 | NN 6159 |
| 7 | Blackford Farms Ltd. | Blackford Farms | See Appendix 3 | 20000 | NN 8505 |
| 8 | Felicity A. Richardson | Glenfalloch | | 20000 | NN 3219 |
| 9 | Invercauld Estates Trust * | Invercauld (part) | Capt A.A.C. Farquharson | 19000 | NO 1274 |
| 10 | Executors of Hilda C. Pilkington | Dalnacardoch | | 18000 | NN 6775 |
| 11 | Invermearan Estates Ltd. | Invermearan | See Appendix 3 | 16500 | NN 4142 |
| 12 | Captain Ian C. de Sales la Terriere | Dunalastair & Crossmount | | 15500 | NN 7158 |
| 13 | Robert Steuart Fothringham * | Murthly & Drumour | | 14000 | NO 0739 |
| 14 | The Upper Boreland Trust | Boreland | Judge R.A.R. Stroyan QC | 13800 | NN 5535 |
| 15 | Spearman Trustees | Fealar | James Teacher | 13000 | NO 0079 |
| 16 | David Heathcoat Amory | Glen Fernate & Glen Loch | | 13000 | NO 0465 |
| 17 | Moray Estates Development Company * | Doune & Milton of Callander | Lord Doune | 12900 | NN 7103 |
| 18 | Tay & Torridon, Bandirran & Culfargie Ests. Ltd. | Lochan, Bandirran & others | Sir Ian Lowson Bt. | 12800 | NN 8937 |
| 19 | Abercairny Estates Ltd. | Abercairny Estates | William Drummond Moray | 12500 | NN 9122 |
| 20 | Cambusmore Estate Trustees | Cambusmore & Acharn | Captain J.N.B. Baillie-Hamilton | 11681 | NN 6605 |
| 21 | Dupplin Trust & The 4th Lord Forteviot | Dupplin Estate | Dewar family | 11600 | NO 0519 |
| 22 | Lady Mary E.L. Whitaker & David G. Bosanquet | Auchnafree | | 11400 | NN 8133 |
| 23 | Robert A. Price | Bolfracks | | 11200 | NN 8248 |
| 24 | Andrew D. Gordon * | Lude | | 11100 | NN 8865 |
| 25 | Emma F.H. Paterson | Auchlyne Estate | | 10611 | NN 5129 |
| 26 | Abacus Trust Co. | Camusericht | David Irvine & L.H. Kerfoot | 10400 | NN 5158 |
| 27 | Midland Bank Ltd. * | Griffin Forest | | 10240 | NN 9046 |
| 28 | Adrian J.M. van Well | Talladh-a-Bheithe | | 9900 | NN 5362 |
| 29 | Brian R. Adams | Dalnaspidal | | 9900 | NN 5974 |
| 30 | Braes Farming Co. | Inverlochlarig | Mr MacNaughton | 9600 | NN 4318 |
| 31 | James F. Priestly | Invergeldie | | 9600 | NN 7427 |
| 32 | Hamish McCorquodale | Dunan | | 9100 | NN 4757 |
| 33 | National Trust for Scotland | Ben Lawers | | 8266 | NN 6540 |
| 34 | I.J. Mackinlay's Trust | Auchleeks | Donald Mackinlay | 8100 | NN 7264 |
| 35 | Sir William Denby Roberts | Strathallan | | 8100 | NN 9115 |
| 36 | Trustees of Derek Russell Hunniset | Edinchip & Glen Dubh | | 7900 | NN 5523 |
| 37 | A. & J. Duncan Millar | Remony & Acharn | | 7900 | NN 7643 |
| 38 | Eagle Star Insurance Co. Ltd. * | Pitlandie & Strathord | | 7500 | NO 0730 |
| 39 | Judith Bowser | Suie Estate | | 7500 | NN 5129 |
| 40 | Moncrieffe Farm Partnership | Ardtalnaig | | 7200 | NN 7039 |
| 41 | William H. Porter | Cashlie | | 7200 | NN 4841 |
| 42 | Senor Raphael Cruz Conde | Glenample | | 6950 | NN 5916 |
| 43 | Constance C. Ward | Kinnaird | | 6700 | NN 9849 |
| 44 | C.A. Ramsay Partnership | South Chesthill | Major General C.A. Ramsay | 6500 | NN 6947 |
| 45 | ON MARKET | Glen Lyon | | 6235 | NN 7347 |
| 46 | Cadogan Estates (Agricultural Holdings) Ltd. | Glenquaich | See Appendix 3 | 6200 | NN 8537 |
| 47 | William J. Christie | Loch Dochart | | 6180 | NN 4327 |
| 48 | Lord Pearson of Rannoch | Cruach (part) & Corrie Carie | | 6000 | NN 3657 |
| 49 | W. & W.I. Bruges | Laighwood | | 6000 | NO 0649 |
| 50 | Pitlochry Estate Trust | Cluniemore & Duntanlich | Major Sir David Butter | 5900 | NN 8858 |

*The Tables and Maps*

## Perthshire

| # | Owner | Estate | Notes | Acres | Grid |
|---|---|---|---|---|---|
| 51 | Sir George Nairn's 1970 Trust | Pitcarmick | | 5700 | NO 0856 |
| 52 | Compania Financiera Waterville SA | Corrievarkie | | 5700 | NN 5572 |
| 53 | Herbert A. & Theresa M. Heinzel | Finnart | | 5644 | NN 5157 |
| 54 | Islay K. Molteno | North Chesthill | | 5400 | NN 6650 |
| 55 | Archibald D. & Sir Ronald Orr Ewing | Cardross | | 5400 | NS 6097 |
| 56 | Glen Turret Estates Ltd. | East Glen Turret | | 5400 | NN 8327 |
| 57 | Dalmunzie Ltd. | Dalmunzie | | 5400 | NO 0971 |
| 58 | Nicholas F. Fane Waterers' (Landscape) Ltd. | Farleyer | Nicholas Fane | 5325 | NN 8052 |
| 59 | Sidebell Ltd. | Fordie & West Glen Turret | See Appendix 3 | 5307 | NN 7922 |
| 60 | Cromlix Estate Co. | Cromlix | | 5200 | NN 7806 |
| 61 | Robert A. Montgomerie | West Glenalmond | | 5000 | NN 8532 |
| 62 | James & Emily M. Anderson | Roro Estate | | 5000 | NN 6044 |
| 63 | Mrs R. Whewell | Innerwick | | 5000 | NN 5947 |
| 64 | The Earl of Shelbourne | Glenshee | | 5000 | NO 0135 |
| 65 | Glenalmond Estate Ltd. | Glenalmond | | 4900 | NN 9328 |
| 66 | Mary C. Horsfall | Kynachan & Braes of Foss | | 4900 | NN 7556 |
| 67 | Patrick C.G. Wilson * | Aberuchill & East Methven | | 4550 | NN 7421 |
| 68 | John Taylor | Ardeonaig | | 4400 | NN 6632 |
| 69 | Greentop Lands and Estates Ltd. * | Invertrossachs & others | | 4332 | NN 5604 |
| 70 | Meikleour Estate Trust | Meikleour | Marquess of Lansdowne | 4200 | NO 1639 |
| 71 | Jason Trust & West Errol Trust | Errol Park | L.D. Heriot Maitland | 4200 | NO 2422 |
| 72 | J. & R. Manning | Dirnanean | | 4200 | NO 0663 |
| 73 | Cloan Estate Trust | Cloan Estate | Richard Haldane | 4200 | NN 9809 |
| 74 | John & Margaret Burton | Cononish | | 4200 | NN 3028 |
| 75 | Viscount Chelsea's Settlement Trust E.F.F. | Snaigow Estate | Earl & Countess Cadogan | 4000 | NO 0844 |
| 76 | Ardvorlich Estate Ltd. | Ardvorlich | Alexander Stewart | 4000 | NN 6322 |
| 77 | Gleneagles Estate Trust | Gleneagles | Martin Haldane | 4000 | NN 9308 |
| 78 | Timothy & Charmian Holcroft | Glenbeich | | 4000 | NN 6124 |
| 79 | John Thom | Ballimore | | 4000 | NN 5117 |
| 80 | Archibald C. MacNab | Tirarthur & Morenish | | 3829 | NN 5936 |
| 81 | Garrows Farm Ltd. | Garrows | | 3700 | NN 8240 |
| 82 | Leo G.D. Barclay | Innerhadden | | 3700 | NN 6657 |
| 83 | McLaren & Wood of Bracklinn | West Bracklinn | | 3700 | NN 6508 |
| 84 | Charles M.M. Crichton | Monzie | | 3500 | NN 8724 |
| 85 | ON MARKET | Moness | | 3272 | NN 8748 |
| 86 | Fulton C. Ronald | Benmore Farm | | 3200 | NN 4125 |
| 87 | Martin & Rona Cruickshank | Auchreoch | | 3200 | NN 3327 |
| 88 | C.M. Buchan | Garth | | 3200 | NN 7451 |
| 89 | Seabright Ltd. | Ballyoukan | Sir D.W. Hardy | 3150 | NN 9656 |
| 90 | Keir & Cawdor Estates Ltd. | Keir Estate & Leny | See Appendix 3 | 3000 | NS 7798 |
| 91 | Blair Drummond Estate | Blair Drummond | Richard Muir | 3000 | NS 7398 |
| 92 | Braco Castle Farms | Braco Castle | N.J. Muir | 3000 | NN 8211 |
| 93 | C. Steel & Trust of Maud A. Clarks Grandchildren | Ashintully | | 3000 | NO 1061 |
| 94 | Blaircreich Forestry Trust | Blaircreich | | 3000 | NN 4317 |
| 95 | James M. Sinclair | Dunsinnan | | 2800 | NO 1632 |
| 96 | Edradynate Ltd. | Edradynate & The Ward | Michael Campbell | 2800 | NN 8852 |
| 97 | ON MARKET | Glenogle | | 2750 | NN 5824 |
| 98 | Alastair F. Ferguson | Baledmund | | 2700 | NN 9459 |
| 99 | G., G., & W. Cameron & B. Fetherston | Farmston | | 2550 | NN 6008 |
| 100 | Ronald P. Thorburn | Straloch | | 2500 | NO 0364 |
| 101 | Alan W. & Nikki Cory-Wright | Auchessan | | 2500 | NN 4427 |
| 102 | Colonel R.S. Stewart-Wilson MC | Balnakeilly | | 2500 | NN 9559 |
| 103 | C. Andrew & J. Anderson | Camusurich | | 2500 | NN 6335 |
| 104 | John Mungo Ingleby | Malling | | 2500 | NN 5600 |
| 105 | William Hendry | Immeroin | | 2500 | NN 5317 |
| 106 | Muirlaggan Forest Partnership | Muirlaggan | Prof. W. & P. MacKenzie | 2480 | NN 5119 |

**Perthshire**

| | | | | | |
|---|---|---|---|---|---|
| 107 | J. Cameron (Graziers) Ltd. | The Bows | | 2450 | NN 7306 |
| 108 | B.I.C.C. Group Pension Trust Ltd. * | Ardchullarie More | | 2435 | NN 5813 |
| 109 | R. Cliffe-Jones | Roromore | | 2367 | NN 6346 |
| 110 | Andrew Mackinnon | Urrard | | 2250 | NN 9063 |
| 111 | David Martin | Blairfettie | | 2200 | NN 7564 |
| 112 | McCosh Brothers | Mains, Easter Mause etc. | | 2200 | NO 1649 |
| 113 | George A.D. & Henry D. Church | Rannagulzion | | 2200 | NO 1751 |
| 114 | Lt. Col. Martin G.T. Robb | Carroglen | | 2200 | NN 7626 |
| 115 | Robin Stormonth Darling | Balvarran | | 2200 | NO 0762 |
| 116 | Glen Devon Estates Ltd. | Glen Devon | Daniel C. McNee | 2200 | NN 9704 |
| 117 | Jenners Ltd. | Forneth | | 2000 | NO 0945 |
| 118 | Smythe family | Methven | | 2000 | NO 0425 |
| 119 | John P. Colman | Tarvie | | 2000 | NO 0164 |
| 120 | Captain David S. Bowser | Argaty Estate | | 2000 | NN 7303 |
| 121 | Lt. Col. Archibald M. Lyle | Riemore | | 2000 | NO 0549 |
| 122 | A.J.B. Jardine Paterson | Gask | | 2000 | NN 9918 |
| 123 | D. & J. Dickson | Lanrick Estate | | 2000 | NN 6802 |
| 124 | S. & C. Ferguson | Corb & Shieldrum | | 2000 | NO 1656 |
| 125 | Kenneth Taylor & Sons | Dall | | 2000 | NN 6735 |
| 126 | Wemyss Estate Management | Invermay | | 2000 | NO 0616 |
| 127 | Alpin F. MacGregor of Cardney | Cardney | | 1800 | NO 0445 |
| 128 | Marshall | Mains of Struie | | 1800 | NO 0711 |
| 129 | Highland Properties BV | Dungarthill & Gartchonzie | | 1700 | NO 0641 |
| 130 | Finegand Estate Ltd. | Finegand & Corrydon | D.M. Kirke-Smith | 1700 | NO 1466 |
| 131 | John Walker | Slatich Farm | | 1700 | NN 6347 |
| 132 | Charles Bremeridge | Clunskea | | 1700 | NO 0063 |
| 133 | Mrs M.A. Steele & Co. | Evelick & Nether Durdie | | 1700 | NO 1825 |
| 134 | Alan Wass & Anthony Pay | W. & E. Bleaton & Soilzarie | | 1700 | NO 1159 |
| 135 | Streetfield Property Co. | Balmanno & Blairstruie | | 1700 | NO 1415 |
| 136 | Executors of Mrs Mary G.S. Dunphie | Delvine | | 1700 | NO 1240 |
| 137 | I. & H. Brown and Fordoun Estates Ltd. * | Battleby and others | | 1600 | NO 0829 |
| 138 | | Strowan House | | 1500 | NN 8121 |
| 139 | Major David Walter | Balthayock | | 1500 | NO 1723 |
| 140 | Helen C. Cramb & Ian Alsop | Glensherup Farm | | 1500 | NN 9504 |
| 141 | A.L. Rattray | Craighall | | 1500 | NO 1748 |
| 142 | Col. J.H. Horsfall DSO MC | Dalchosnie | | 1500 | NN 6757 |
| 143 | Mrs J.M.S. Graham | Rednock Estate | | 1500 | NN 5900 |
| 144 | J. & S. Davidson | Beannie Farm | | 1500 | NN 8211 |
| 145 | Charles R. Connell & Co. (Colquhalzie Farms) Ltd. * | Colquhaalzie Farms | | 1500 | NN 9117 |
| 146 | | Ballathie | | 1471 | NO 1436 |
| 147 | | Persie | | 1300 | NO 1354 |
| 148 | Paul R. Ramsay | Bamff | | 1300 | NO 2251 |
| 149 | George Allan | Glenquey | | 1300 | NN 9803 |
| 150 | Penelope M. McKerrow | Lick | | 1250 | NN 8258 |
| 151 | Tullich Farmers | Wester Tullich | Duncan Millar | 1250 | NN 6837 |
| 152 | Glendelvine Estate Trust | Glendelvine | Sir Gavin Lyle Bt. | 1200 | NO 0941 |
| 153 | Viscountess Ridley | Findynate | | 1200 | NN 8953 |
| 154 | Wilfred & Mrs Beryl Meadows | Balquhandy | | 1200 | NO 0311 |
| 155 | Renaya-Stahl Anstalt | Drumlean | | 1200 | NN 4802 |
| 156 | Dalgety Pension Trust * | Wester Lix | | 1200 | NN 5429 |
| 157 | Sir Colin Campbell Bart. | Kilbryde Castle | | 1200 | NN 7503 |
| 158 | | Cuildochart | | 1100 | NN 5932 |
| 159 | Co-op Wholesale Society Ltd. * | Rosemount & others | | 1100 | NO 2043 |
| 160 | Rossie Ochil Enterprises Ltd. | Rossie Ochil Farm | Stephen Smith | 1089 | NO 0813 |
| 161 | ON MARKET | Tulloch Farm | | 1077 | NN 5120 |
| 162 | Tate & Lyle plc | Pitcastle | | 1070 | NN 9053 |
| 163 | ON MARKET | Brerachan & Kinnaird | | 1017 | NO 9760 |

## Perthshire

| | | | Acres | Grid Ref |
|---|---|---|---|---|
| 164 | J.M. Mitchell & Sons | Tullymurdoch | 1000 | NO 1952 |
| 165 | Gilmour & Joy Cumming | Monachyle Beag | 1000 | NN 4820 |
| 166 | Robert Louis | Monachyle Mhor | 1000 | NN 4620 |
| 167 | Gartincaber Estate Ltd. | Gartincaber | 1000 | NN 7000 |
| 168 | Vicomte Adolphe & Diane M. de Spoelbergh | Altnafeadh (part) | 1000 | NN 3454 |
| 169 | Emily, Ivor & R.S. Salvesen | Scotston | 1000 | NN 9042 |
| 170 | Sofaelde Scov-OG Ejen Domsselskab A/S | Achanruie & Balnacraig | 1000 | NN 7963 |
| 171 | John Paterson * | Boreland | 1000 | NN 9804 |
| 172 | Rennie Iain K. Little | Auchleskine | 1000 | NN 5421 |
| 173 | Messrs Norman Jackson (Farmers) Ltd. | Derculich | 1000 | NN 8952 |
| 174 | M.J. Hunt's Trustees | Feddal | 1000 | NN 7909 |
| 175 | Michael Pilkington | Strathfillan | 1000 | NN 3226 |
| 176 | Anthony G. Reid | Balnakilly Farm | 1000 | NO 0760 |
| 177 | Francis, Ferelith, Alice & Thomas Salvesen | Ballinloan | 1000 | NN 9742? |
| 178 | H.S. McAdam | Glengoulandie | 1000 | NN 7652 |
| 179 | Sheila Macgregor | Knoxfauld & Cambushinnie | 1000 | NN 7907 |
| 180 | Archibald D. McDiarmid | Locherlour Estate | 1000 | NN 8223 |
| 181 | Hon. Mrs Caroline Best | Rossie Priory | 1000 | NO 2830 |
| 182 | Pryde Foundation | Fordel     Y.R.F. Walton | 1000 | NO 1312 |
| 183 | General Accident Fire & Life Assurance Co. Ltd. * | Lecropt & Ochtertyre | 1000 | NS 7697 |
| 184 | | Balchrochan | 1000 | NO 0759 |
| 185 | | Lendrick Farm | 1000 | NN 5507 |
| | Total | | 1127878 | |
| | Perthshire land area | | 1595804 | |
| | % of county accounted for | | 70.7% | |

### PUBLIC LANDHOLDINGS

| | | | Acres |
|---|---|---|---|
| | Forestry Commission | Various properties | 150726 |
| a. | SOAEFD | See Appendix 4 | 5782 |
| b. | Strathclyde Regional Council | Loch Katrine | 21000 |
| c. | SNH | See Appendix 5 | 3704 |
| | TOTAL | | 181212 |
| | % of county | | 11.4% |

### CHANGES IN THE DISTRIBUTION OF LANDHOLDINGS BY SIZE 1970 - 1995

| | 1970 | | | 1995 | | |
|---|---|---|---|---|---|---|
| Acreage threshold | Acres | % of county | No. of owners | Acres | % of county | No. of owners |
| > 100 000 | 130000 | 8.1% | 1 | 148000 | 9.3% | 1 |
| > 75 000 | 130000 | 8.1% | 1 | 148000 | 9.3% | 1 |
| > 50 000 | 252900 | 15.8% | 3 | 211200 | 13.2% | 2 |
| > 40 000 | 297900 | 18.7% | 4 | 211200 | 13.2% | 2 |
| > 30 000 | 365500 | 22.9% | 6 | 281500 | 17.6% | 4 |
| > 20 000 | 450900 | 28.3% | 10 | 368100 | 23.1% | 8 |
| > 10 000 | 795900 | 49.9% | 36 | 617332 | 38.7% | 27 |
| > 5 000 | 980566 | 61.4% | 63 | 866239 | 54.3% | 64 |
| > 1000 | 1404366 | 88.0% | 249 | 1127878 | 70.7% | 185 |

# Renfrew

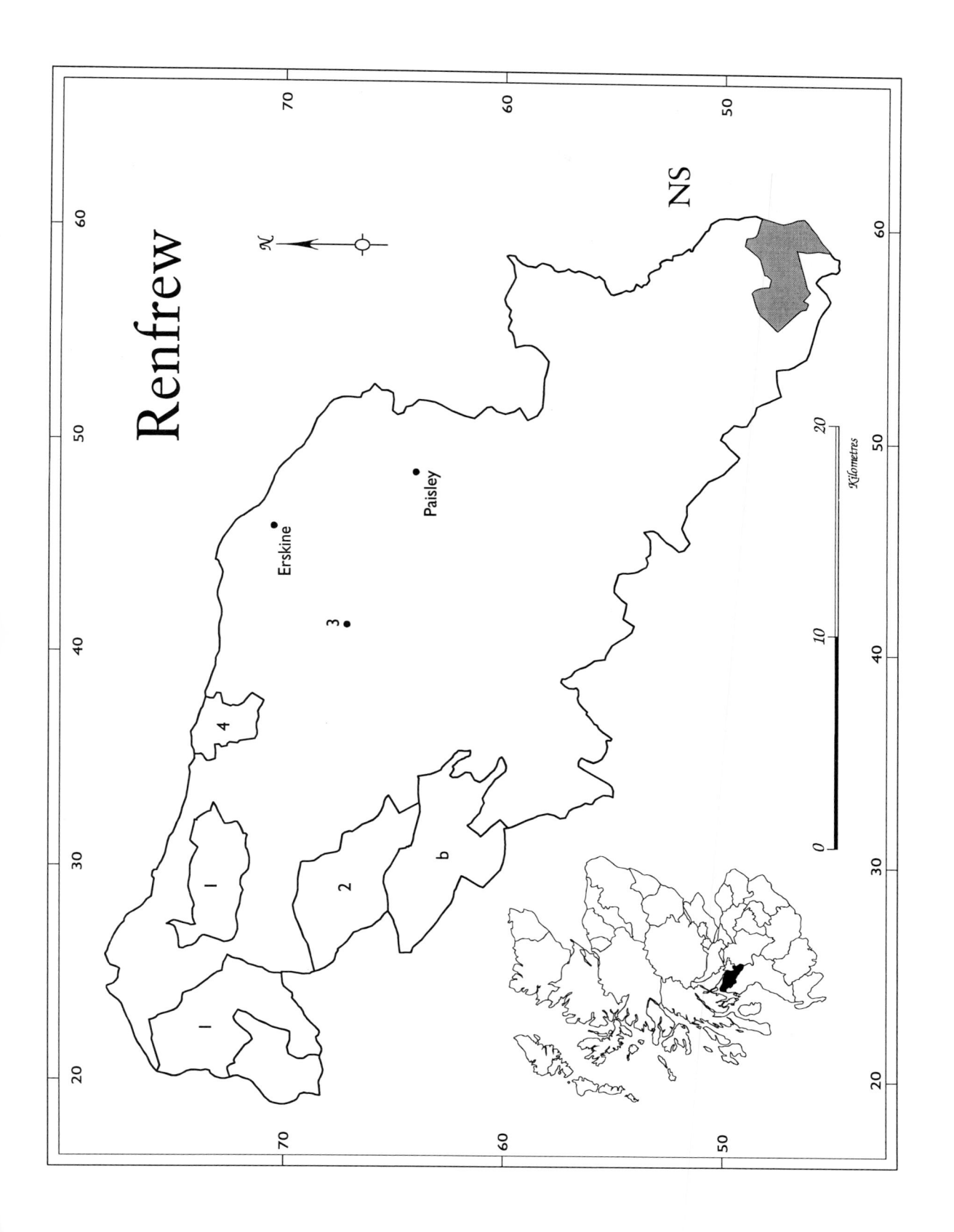

# Renfrewshire
# 143,829 acres

It takes some time to become familiar with a county, after which it becomes easier to decipher the pattern of landownership. Renfrew, being another small county, had less priority attached to it, given that larger counties produced more rewards in terms of time invested and ownerships revealed. This is a pity, since the landownership pattern in counties like Renfrew is liable to be every bit as interesting as that in the bigger counties. Certainly the whole question of land speculation in urban fringes and the needs of urban areas to have an attractive and accessible countryside on their doorstep is becoming a major issue.

| NO. | PROPRIETOR | PROPERTY | PRINCIPAL INTEREST | ACREAGE | GRID REF. |
|---|---|---|---|---|---|
| 1 | H. Shaw-Stewart | Ardgowan | | 9200 | NS 2072 |
| 2 | | Duchal Muir | | 5700 | NS 2867 |
| 3 | Mark A.M. Crichton Maitland | Elderslie | | 5000 | NS 4167 |
| 4 | | Finlaystone | | 1500 | NS 3673 |
| | Total | | | 21400 | |
| | Renfrewshire land area | | | 143829 | |
| | % of county accounted for | | | 14.9% | |

**PUBLIC LANDHOLDINGS**

| | | | |
|---|---|---|---|
| Forestry Commission | Various properties | | 2131 |
| b. Strathclyde Regional Council | Clyde Muirshiel & Eaglesham | | 19000 |
| TOTAL | | | 21131 |
| % of county | | | 14.7% |

**CHANGES IN THE DISTRIBUTION OF LANDHOLDINGS BY SIZE 1970 - 1995**

| | 1970 | | | 1995 | | |
|---|---|---|---|---|---|---|
| Acreage threshold | Acres | % of county | No. of owners | Acres | % of county | No. of owners |
| > 100 000 | 0 | 0% | 0 | 0 | 0% | 0 |
| > 75 000 | 0 | 0% | 0 | 0 | 0% | 0 |
| > 50 000 | 0 | 0% | 0 | 0 | 0% | 0 |
| > 40 000 | 0 | 0% | 0 | 0 | 0% | 0 |
| > 30 000 | 0 | 0% | 0 | 0 | 0% | 0 |
| > 20 000 | 0 | 0% | 0 | 0 | 0% | 0 |
| > 10 000 | 10800 | 7.5% | 1 | 0 | 0% | 0 |
| > 5 000 | 22800 | 15.9% | 3 | 19900 | 13.8% | 3 |
| > 1000 | 59100 | 41.1% | 20 | 21400 | 14.9% | 4 |

## Ross & Cromarty
## 1,977,254 acres

This is the county of the sporting estate. From east coast to west coast, the straths are empty and most of the owners are absentee. In Wester Ross alone, of a total population of around 4000 in 550,000 acres, only between 250 and 300 people live more than one kilometre from the coast. No more than 300 people therefore live in 536,000 acres of land.

Landownership in the county has changed markedly over the past 25 years. Of the 76 estates in 1970, half have changed ownership. The distribution of estates in terms of size has changed little and few have been broken up. The few that have have been distributed between neighbours to create larger holdings. These include the Letterewe Estate which is now larger than the original estate owned by Colonel Whitbread which in 1970 was the largest holding in Ross & Cromarty. At 81,000 acres, it has grown by the steady addition of land culminating in the addition of half of the Kinlochewe Estate which was split between Letterewe and Loch Rosque. Paul van Vlissingen himself owns only the 6270-acre Little Gruinard Estate, the rest being owned by Clyde Properties NV and Utrechtse Beheer Maatschappij Catharijne BV, two of his companies. Pat Wilson, who bought the other half of the Kinlochewe Estate now owns 30,000 acres.

Other holdings that have been built up include the 63,000 acres comprising Killilan, Inverinate, West Benula and Glomach in Kintail which are now owned by Smech Properties Ltd., the offshore company controlled by Sheik Mohammed bin Rashid al Maktoum, one of three brothers who rule Dubai. Controversy has surrounded their activities, which have included the demolition of buildings and blocking of public access. Their factor, Niall Graham Campbell, observed on a recent television programme that 'In my view the best conservationist that you're likely to have is a good old-fashioned Victorian landlord who keeps all the people away because the worst thing for conservation is disturbance from human beings.'[3] Arabian sheiks may turn out to be not so bad after all!

Ross & Cromarty could be one of the most vibrant and dynamic of Highland counties. It has wild and dramatic scenery, interesting wildlife and tremendous outdoor recreational opportunities. All it lacks is people to live and work there and take advantage of it. Comparable areas in Norway are packed full of villages and small farm forestry holdings. There is not one good reason why Ross & Cromarty should not develop in this way. Indeed, if the first Chairman of the local enterprise company had his way it would. John Shepherd-Barron looked at the economy of Ross & Cromarty and concluded that the only way of ensuring a sustainable future was for a restructuring of the sporting estates together with the resettlement of people in the glens on land they have a stake in.

If chairmen of local enterprise companies are having such thoughts there is some hope for the future. Ross & Cromarty has also seen much activity in its last year from the District Council which has sponsored a series of seminars and projects on land reform. These are all are encouraging signs that from a practical economic and political position a better future can be built from the social and environmental wreckage that is much of the Highlands today.

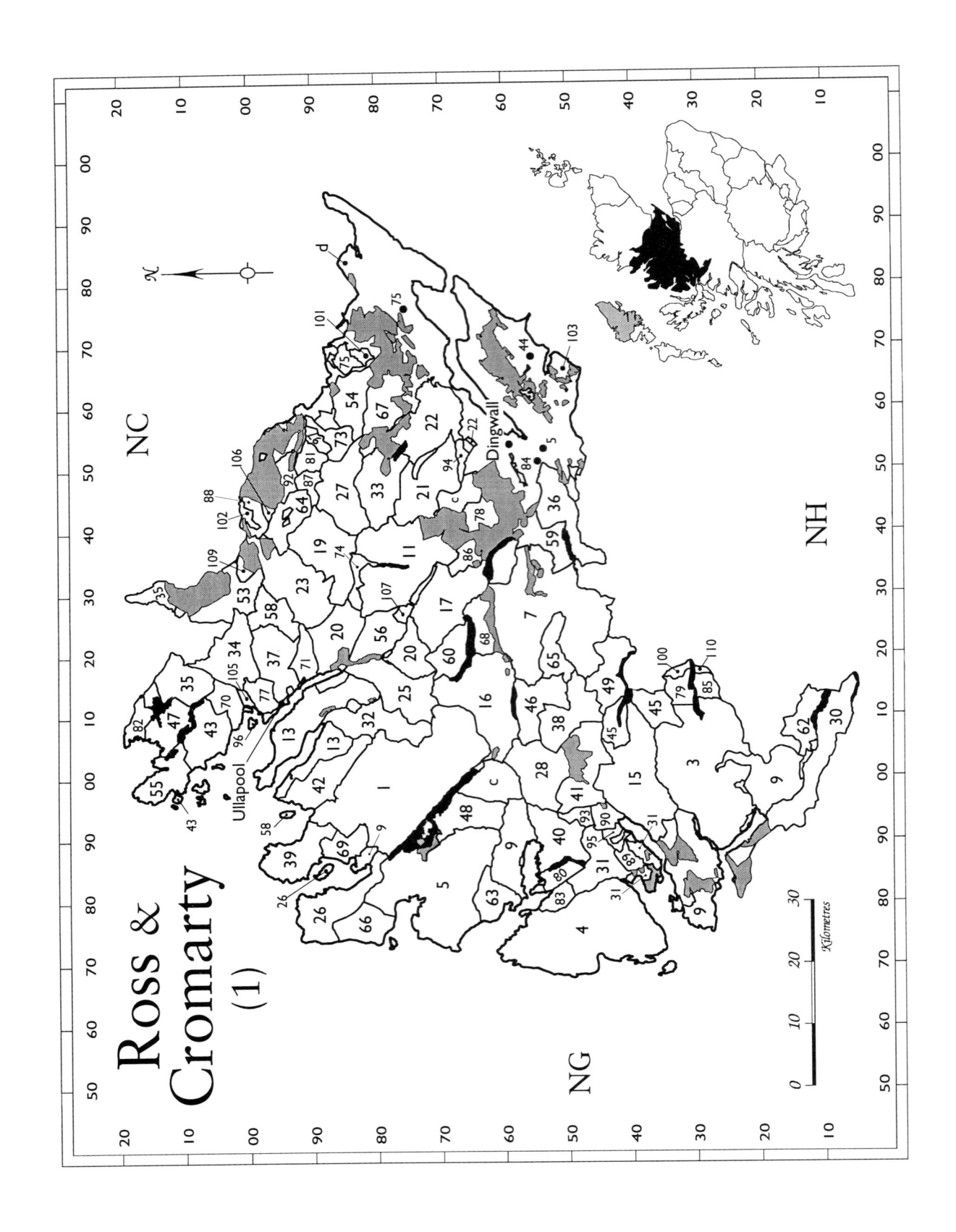

# Ross & Cromarty (1)

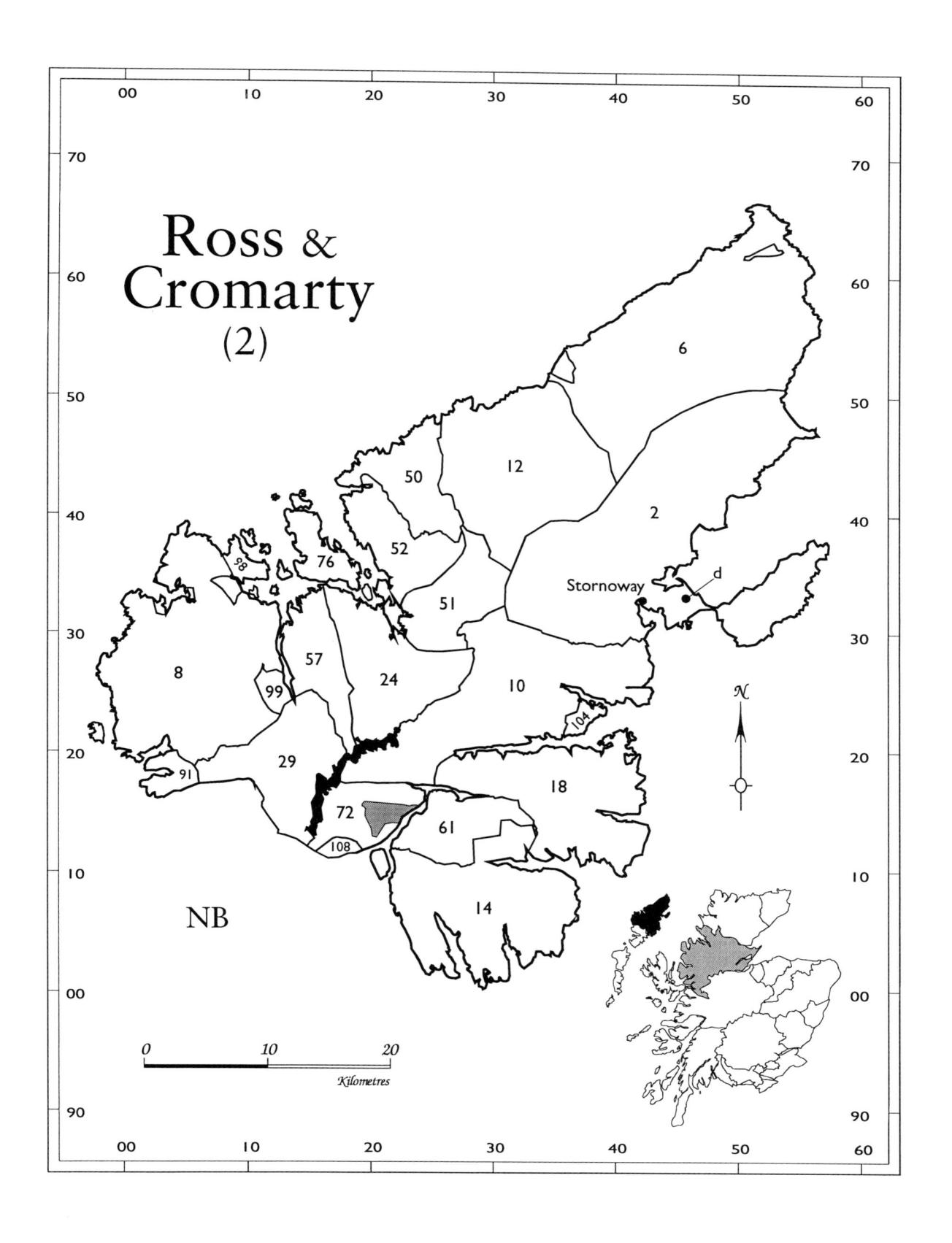

# Ross & Cromarty (2)

NB

## Ross & Cromarty

| NO. | PROPRIETOR | PROPERTY | PRINCIPAL INTEREST | ACREAGE | GRID REF. |
|---|---|---|---|---|---|
| 1 | Clyde Properties NV & U.B. Maatschappij Catharijne BV | Letterewe & Kinlochewe | Paul Fentener van Vlissingen | 81000 | NH 9776 |
| 2 | Stornoway Trust | Stornoway Trust Estate | | 69400 | NB 4037 |
| 3 | Smech Properties Ltd. | Killilan & others | Sheik Mohammed bin Rashid al Maktoum | 63140 | NH 0131 |
| 4 | Applecross Estate Trust | Applecross | Captain Fred. H. Wills | 62000 | NG 7245 |
| 5 | John A. Mackenzie | Gairloch & Conon Estates | | 56900 | NG 8076 |
| 6 | Galson Estates Ltd. | Galson Lodge | See Appendix 3 | 56300 | NB 5055 |
| 7 | Kirkbi Estates Ltd. | Strathconon (part) | Kjeld Kirk Christiansen | 55000 | NH 2656 |
| 8 | Uig & Hamanavay Estate Ltd. | Uig & Hamnaway | Jonathan Bulmer & syndicate | 45000 | NB 0426 |
| 9 | National Trust for Scotland | Kintail, Torridon & others | | 41311 | NH 9716 |
| 10 | Richard P. Kershaw | Soval | | 39000 | NB 3424 |
| 11 | Dickinson Trust | Strathvaich & Strathrannoch | | 37030 | NH 3474 |
| 12 | Barvas Estates Ltd. | Barvas | See Appendix 3 | 34600 | NB 3144 |
| 13 | Alan S.A.F. Roger & N.M. Roger | Dundonnell | | 33600 | NH 1090 |
| 14 | J.N. Oppenehim Eishken 1989 Partnership | Eishken | | 32000 | NB 2707 |
| 15 | Ewen A. Macpherson | Attadale | | 32000 | NG 9238 |
| 16 | Patrick C.G. Wilson * | Kinlochewe & Loch Rosque | | 30000 | NH 1562 |
| 17 | Lochluichart Estate Co. | Kinlochluichart | I. Hamish Leslie Melville | 27400 | NH 2569 |
| 18 | Parc Crofters Ltd. | Parc | Lomas family | 26800 | NB 3617 |
| 19 | Mrs Macaire | Alladale & Deanich | | 26600 | NH 4389 |
| 20 | Beleggingsmaatschappij Festeyn BV | Inverlael & Foich | H.J.E. van Beuningen & others | 23600 | NH 2186 |
| 21 | John Lloyd Co. | Wyvis | Viscount Mountgarret | 23000 | NH 4873 |
| 22 | Richard R.L. Munro Ferguson * | Novar | | 20000 | NH 6167 |
| 23 | Trustees of Corriemulzie Trust | Corriemulzie | Patrick Colvin | 19500 | NH 3295 |
| 24 | Grimersta Estates Ltd. | Grimersta | | 19200 | NB 2130 |
| 25 | Hon. E. Maurice W. Robson * | Inverbroom | | 19000 | NH 1780 |
| 26 | J.I.H. Macdonald-Buchanan | Inveran | | 18500 | NG 8086 |
| 27 | Peter Fowler | Glencalvie | | 18500 | NH 4689 |
| 28 | Philip Smith | Coulin | | 18300 | NH 0154 |
| 29 | Alasdair R. Davidson | Morsgail | | 17800 | NB 1017 |
| 30 | Burton Property Trust * | Glenshiel & Cluanie (part) | Lord Burton | 17000 | NG 9314 |
| 31 | Kinloch Damph Ltd. & Strath Discretionary Trust | Couldoran | Mark & Gillian Pattinson | 16900 | NG 8444 |
| 32 | Execs. of Mrs M.G.S. Dunphie | Eilean Darach | | 16500 | NH 1087 |
| 33 | Mr & Mrs Duncan | Kildermorie | | 16000 | NH 5081 |
| 34 | A.W. Fenwick & Mark J. Fenwick | Langwell Lodge | | 15800 | NC 1702 |
| 35 | Glencanisp & Drumrunie Deer Forest Trust * | Assynt & Benmore | Edmond Vestey | 15800 | NC 1605 |
| 36 | Captain Roderick W.K. Stirling | Fairburn & Corriehallie | | 15300 | NH 4552 |
| 37 | Ewen Scobie | Rhiddoroch West | | 15100 | NH 1795 |
| 38 | Angus M. Sladen | Glencarron | | 15000 | NH 1049 |
| 39 | Aultbea Estates | Aultbea | Jill Dorothy Hardy | 15000 | NG 8788 |
| 40 | Trustees of Ben Damph Estate | Ben Damph | T.D. Gray & D.N. Carr-Smith | 14820 | NG 8753 |
| 41 | Major Michael T.N.H. Wills | Achnashellach | | 14800 | NG 9747 |
| 42 | Gruinard Estate | Gruinard | Hon. Mrs A.G. Maclay | 14800 | NH 9691 |
| 43 | Scottish Wildlife Trust | Ben More Coigach & Isle Ristol | | 14606 | NC 0904 |
| 44 | Broadland Properties Estates Ltd. * | Rosehaugh & Kilcoy | John M. Guthrie | 14500 | NH 6855 |
| 45 | C.S.R. Stroyan | West Monar & Pait | | 13500 | NH 0742 |
| 46 | James R. Ruggles-Brise | Ledgowan | | 13300 | NH 1355 |
| 47 | Polly Estates Ltd. | Inverpolly | | 12515 | NC 1011 |
| 48 | P. John H. Wills | Grudie & Talladale | | 12300 | NG 9170 |
| 49 | Mr & Mrs David C.R. Allen | East Monar | | 12100 | NH 1642 |
| 50 | Lewis Island Crofters Ltd. | Dalmore | See Appendix 3 | 11600 | NB 2244 |
| 51 | Christopher R. Buxton | Garynahine | | 11450 | NB 2331 |

## Ross & Cromarty

| | | | | | |
|---|---|---|---|---|---|
| 52 | Carloway Estate Ltd. | Carloway | See Appendix 3 | 11400 | NB 2042 |
| 53 | Patrick F.J. Colvin | Loubcroy (part) | | 11300 | NC 3501 |
| 54 | Charles W. Brooke | Midfearn | | 11100 | NH 6283 |
| 55 | Execs. of the late Mrs C.D.I. Longstaff | Badentarbat | | 10800 | NB 0110 |
| 56 | Diana Dowdeswell | Braemore | | 10500 | NH 2378 |
| 57 | John H.M. Mackenzie | Scaliscro | | 10100 | NB 1327 |
| 58 | Highland Coastal Trading Co. | E. Rhiddoroch & Gruinard I. | Neil & Maddie Scobie | 10100 | NH 2393 |
| 59 | Packington Estate Enterprises Ltd. | Scatwell & Cabaan | Lord & Lady Guernsey | 9192 | NH 4055 |
| 60 | Malie Goed BV | Fannich | Baron W. van Dedem | 9100 | NH 2266 |
| 61 | Hebridean Fishery Partnership | North Eishken | | 9100 | NB 2613 |
| 62 | I. & H. Brown * | Corrielair | | 8600 | NH 0613 |
| 63 | Sir Paul Nicholson | Diabeg | | 8600 | NG 8062 |
| 64 | The Forest Farm Partnership | Forest Farm | Julian Smith and syndicate | 8400 | NH 4392 |
| 65 | Burnden Park Investments Ltd. (Bermuda) | Scardroy | G. Howard & W. Maycock | 8100 | NH 2151 |
| 66 | William & Moira Cameron | Big Sands | | 7900 | NG 7578 |
| 67 | Baldoon Farms | Strathrusdale | R.D.J. Harington | 7500 | NH 5777 |
| 68 | Mark D. & Mrs L. Seligman | Strathbran | | 6400 | NH 2463 |
| 69 | Sir John Horlick Bt. | Tournaig | | 6400 | NG 8783 |
| 70 | Jean & Col. Lionel Bramall | Runie or Keanchulish | | 6200 | NC 1203 |
| 71 | Charles N. Beattie | Leckmelm | | 6000 | NH 1690 |
| 72 | Aline Estate Ltd. | Aline | See Appendix 3 | 6000 | NB 1912 |
| 73 | Investments Bermuda Ltd. | Gledfield | Rupert Haig-Thomas | 5650 | NH 5790 |
| 74 | Trustees of the late Dr S.M. Whitteridge | Glenbeg | | 5000 | NH 3183 |
| 75 | Ross Estates Co. * | Balnagown Estate | | 5000 | NH 6785 |
| 76 | Comte Robin de la Lanne Mirrlees | Great Bernera | | 5000 | NB 1535 |
| 77 | Dr D. Dumughn | Morefield | | 4850 | NH 1297 |
| 78 | Andrew Allan | Strathgarve | | 4700 | NH 4263 |
| 79 | Carl & M. Lawaetz | East Benula | | 4500 | NH 1331 |
| 80 | M.A.R. Cayzer Will Trust (Rossanes Fund) | Ben Shieldaig | Hugh Tollemache | 4400 | NG8352 |
| 81 | Jean G.K. Matterson | Gruinards | | 4400 | NH 5292 |
| 82 | Graffham Court Estate Ltd. | Eisg-Brachaidh | | 4400 | NC 0718 |
| 83 | Richard & Claire Munday | Kinloch | | 4000 | NG 8052 |
| 84 | Brahan Farms Ltd. & Andrew H.M. Matheson | Brahan | | 4000 | NH 5054 |
| 85 | R.S. Turcan & others | Cozac | | 3979 | NH 1429 |
| 86 | Fridays Cranbrook Ltd. | Corriemoillie | | 3860 | NH 3665 |
| 87 | Mrs Shaw | Amat | | 3200 | NH 4790 |
| 88 | Fountain Forestry Ltd. | Langwell Forest | | 3000 | NH 4298 |
| 89 | Frederick Booker | Glenmhor | | 3000 | NG 8540 |
| 90 | Angus Macdonald | New Kelso | | 3000 | NG 9342 |
| 91 | Andrew G. Millar-Munday | Ard Bheag & Ard Mhor | | 3000 | NB 0318 |
| 92 | Mrs A. Griffiths & Mrs R. Bardswell | Braelangwell Lodge | | 2700 | NH 5192 |
| 93 | Messrs J. Fooks & S. Block | Fionnaraich | | 2700 | NG 9347 |
| 94 | The Milton Trust | Swordale | | 2200 | NH 5466 |
| 95 | Lord Scarsdale | Tullich | | 2050 | NG 9142 |
| 96 | Royal Society for the Protection of Birds | Isle Martin & others | | 2023 | NH 0999 |
| 97 | Trustees of the J.A. Hunter Dounie Settlement | Dounie | | 2000 | NH 5690 |
| 98 | | Valtos | | 1800 | NB 0935 |
| 99 | D.M. MacDonald | Gisla | | 1700 | NB 1225 |
| 100 | Glen Cannich Estate | Glencannich (part) | Sir John & Mr Anthony Fuller | 1500 | NH 1632 |
| 101 | Nick Faldo & others | Balnagowan Woodlands | | 1500 | NH 6882 |
| 102 | Anthony A.C. Hampton | Langwell Lodge | | 1500 | NC 4100 |
| 103 | Hamilton Grierson | Drynie | | 1331 | NH 6751 |
| 104 | Murdo Morrison | Keose Glebe | | 1200 | NB 3621 |
| 105 | David E. Bulmer * | Keanchulish House | | 1200 | NH 1299 |

*The Tables and Maps*

## Ross & Cromarty

| | | | | |
|---|---|---|---|---|
| 106 | Brodie & Co. (Trustees) Ltd. | Strathoykel Hill Ground | 1097 | NH 4396 |
| 107 | | Loch Droma | 1050 | NH 2675 |
| 108 | North Harris Estate Ltd. | Amhuinnsuidhe (part) | 1000 | NB 1712 |
| 109 | Fountain Forestry clients | Loubcroy Plantations | 1000 | NC 3300 |
| 110 | Mr Hay | Mullardoch (part) | 500 | NH 1729 |
| | Total | | 1656954 | |
| | Ross & Cromarty land area | | 1977254 | |
| | % of county accounted for | | 83.8% | |

### PUBLIC LANDHOLDINGS

| | | |
|---|---|---|
| Forestry Commission | Various properties | 98825 |
| a. SOAEFD | See Appendix 4 | 1196 |
| c. SNH | See Appendix 5 | 16076 |
| d. MoD | See Appendix 6 | 3385 |
| TOTAL | | 119482 |
| % of county | | 6.0% |

### CHANGES IN THE DISTRIBUTION OF LANDHOLDINGS BY SIZE 1970 - 1995

| | 1970 | | | 1995 | | |
|---|---|---|---|---|---|---|
| Acreage threshold | Acres | % of county | No. of owners | Acres | % of county | No. of owners |
| > 100 000 | 0 | 0% | 0 | 0 | 0% | 0 |
| > 75 000 | 0 | 0% | 0 | 81000 | 4.1% | 1 |
| > 50 000 | 379400 | 19.2% | 6 | 443740 | 22.4% | 7 |
| > 40 000 | 557200 | 28.2% | 10 | 530051 | 26.8% | 9 |
| > 30 000 | 796784 | 40.3% | 17 | 768281 | 38.9% | 16 |
| > 20 000 | 1041084 | 52.7% | 27 | 915681 | 46.3% | 22 |
| > 10 000 | 1468984 | 74.3% | 55 | 1440472 | 72.9% | 58 |
| > 5 000 | 1610484 | 81.5% | 74 | 1568614 | 79.3% | 76 |
| > 1000 | 1697084 | 85.8% | 114 | 1656454 | 83.8% | 109 |

## Roxburghshire
## 425,564 acres

Like many a border county, the biggest landowners continue to be the Dukes (Abercorn, Buccleuch and Roxburghe), Earls (Haddington) and Marquesses (Lothian). These Borders families never experienced quite the same trauma as did the Highland aristocracy and the main landholdings have been able to survive the centuries relatively unscathed. Roxburgh is the quintessential border county, and the one with the longest border with England.

Whereas Roxburghe Estates were secretive about their landholdings, Buccleuch Estates were extremely helpful. Lothian Estates even invited me to spend the day with them to 'see the Landlord and Tenant System at work; a system that provides employment in the countryside, that provides continuity and that meets the needs of present day political thinking as to conservation of our natural heritage and conservation of buildings and even villages.'

Roxburgh's new landowners consist predominantly of local forestry interests and include British Insulated Callendar Cables, the Northern Ireland Government Superannuation Scheme Trustees, the Halifax Building Society Pension Nominees Ltd., the Midland Bank Pension Trust Ltd. and the WH Smith Pension Trust Ltd.

Someone has yet to explain to me why it is better to have pension funds owning forests than farmers' cooperatives and local communities. The same amount of wood would be available for the processing factories but the forests would create useful employment and contribute to the local economy. The truth is that just as we were masters of the plantation economy during the days of empire, we are slaves of it today and seem incapable of imagining any other way of organising the production of commodities.

# Roxburgh

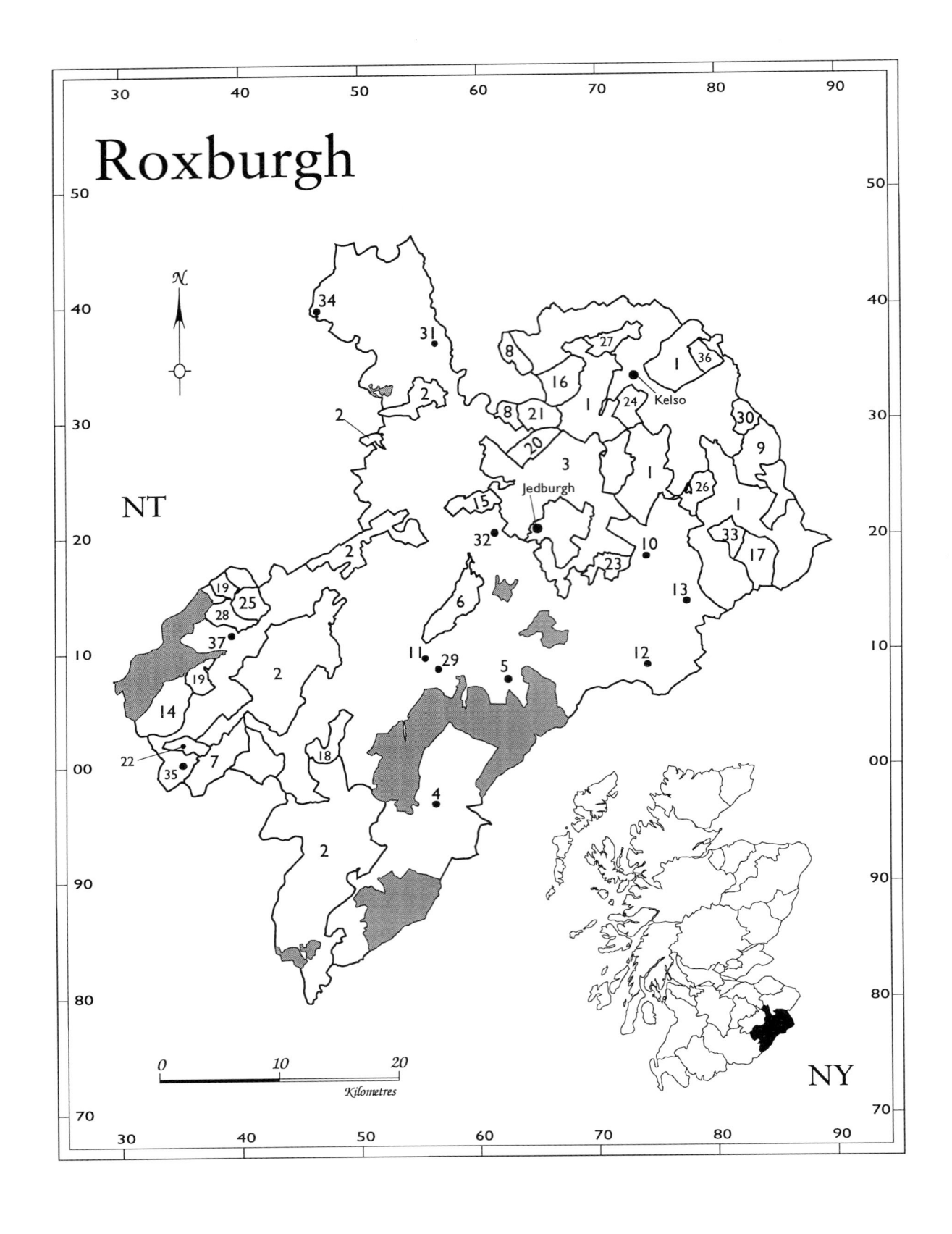

NT

NY

# Roxburghshire

*The Tables and Maps*

| NO. | PROPRIETOR | PROPERTY | PRINCIPAL INTEREST | ACREAGE | GRID REF. |
|---|---|---|---|---|---|
| 1 | Roxburghe Trusts & CIC (Guernsey) Ltd. * | Roxburghe Estates | Duke of Roxburghe | 55500 | NT 7034 |
| 2 | Buccleuch Estates Ltd. * | Liddesdale & others | | 49200 | NY 4286 |
| 3 | Marquess of Lothian, Earl of Ancram & Trusts | Lothian Estates | | 18000 | NT 6424 |
| 4 | Andrew Douglas | Saughtree & Thorlieshope | | 4812 | NY 5696 |
| 5 | PB Forestry Lands Ltd. * | Dykeraw & Westshiels | See Appendix 3 | 4363 | NT 6207 |
| 6 | ON MARKET | Wells | | 3301 | NT 5914 |
| 7 | Philiphaugh Trust * | Lymiecleuch | Sir Michael Strang Steel | 3200 | NT 3802 |
| 8 | Trustees of Ellesmere 1939 Settlement | Mertoun | Duke of Sutherland | 3000 | NT 6131 |
| 9 | Abercorn Estates * | Halterburn & others | Duchess of Abercorn | 3000 | NT 8327 |
| 10 | Douglas | Cunzierton | | 3000 | NT 7418 |
| 11 | B.I.C.C. Group Pension Trust Ltd. * | Stonedge and others | | 2797 | NT 5509 |
| 12 | CERN (European Org. for Nuclear Research) * | Leithope | | 2497 | NT 7408 |
| 13 | Robert J. Tweedie & Co. | Buchtrig | | 2320 | NT 7714 |
| 14 | N. Ireland Local Govt. Superannuation Committee * | Howpasley (Laird's Hill) | | 2305 | NT 3405 |
| 15 | Helen F. Usher & Elizabeth M. Ogilvie | Chesters | | 2000 | NT 6022 |
| 16 | Trustees of late Viscount Ivor C.J. Maitland | Makerstoun | | 2000 | NT 6631 |
| 17 | George Davidson | Calroust | | 1956 | NT 8219 |
| 18 | ON MARKET | Priesthaugh Forest | | 1945 | NT4601 |
| 19 | Kronospan * | Eildrig & West Alemoor | | 1932 | NT 3607 |
| 20 | Post Office Staff Superannuation Scheme * | Fairnington & Upper Blainslie | | 1918 | NT 6427 |
| 21 | John M.C. Rutherford | Rutherford Burnside | | 1800 | NT 6430 |
| 22 | Halifax Building Society Pension Nominees Ltd. * | Ramseygrain & Commonbrae | | 1724 | NT 3502 |
| 23 | Oxnam Row Estates Ltd. | Oxnam Row | | 1570 | NT 7117 |
| 24 | Michael, John & A.M. Salvesen | Spylaw, Ladyrig & Craigrig | | 1500 | NT 7332 |
| 25 | A.W.R. Scott-Noble | Borthwickbrae | | 1500 | NT 4013 |
| 26 | J.W. Girvan & Sons | Gateshaw | | 1500 | NT 7722 |
| 27 | Balgonie Estate Ltd. | Newton Don | | 1500 | NT 7137 |
| 28 | Charles Scott | Milsington | | 1200 | NT 4012 |
| 29 | Andrew Lubbock | Harwood | | 1192 | NT 5608 |
| 30 | David C. Robson | Venchen | | 1100 | NT 8229 |
| 31 | A. & R. Brownlee (Holdings) & Arb Woodlands | Craigsford & Sorrowlessfield | | 1038 | NT 5638 |
| 32 | Timothy P. Finch | Ruecastle | | 1000 | NT 6120 |
| 33 | Peter D. Mather | Belford | | 1000 | NT 8120 |
| 34 | Bowland Estates Ltd. * | Whitelee | Leon G. Litchfield | 1000 | NT 4639 |
| 35 | The W.H. Smith Pension Trust * | Rashiegrain Woodlands | | 900 | NT 3500 |
| 36 | Midland Bank Pension Trust Ltd. * | Hadden | | 894 | NT 7935 |
| 37 | Dalgety Pension Trust * | Maryswood Hoscote Woods | | 739 | NT 3911 |
| | Total | | | 190203 | |
| | Roxburghshire land area | | | 425564 | |
| | % of county accounted for | | | 44.7% | |

## PUBLIC LANDHOLDINGS

| | | |
|---|---|---|
| Forestry Commission | Various properties | 33297 |
| b. Borders Regional Council | Alemoor | 316 |
| TOTAL | | 33613 |
| % of county | | 7.9% |

## CHANGES IN THE DISTRIBUTION OF LANDHOLDINGS BY SIZE 1970 - 1995

| | 1970 | | | 1995 | | |
|---|---|---|---|---|---|---|
| Acreage threshold | Acres | % of county | No. of owners | Acres | % of county | No. of owners |
| > 100 000 | 0 | 0% | 0 | 0 | 0% | 0 |
| > 75 000 | 0 | 0% | 0 | 0 | 0% | 0 |
| > 50 000 | 115600 | 27.2% | 2 | 55500 | 13.0% | 1 |
| > 40 000 | 115600 | 27.2% | 2 | 104700 | 24.6% | 2 |
| > 30 000 | 115600 | 27.2% | 2 | 104700 | 24.6% | 2 |
| > 20 000 | 115600 | 27.2% | 2 | 104700 | 24.6% | 2 |
| > 10 000 | 143500 | 33.7% | 4 | 122700 | 28.8% | 3 |
| > 5 000 | 175900 | 41.3% | 9 | 122700 | 28.8% | 3 |
| > 1000 | 248700 | 58.4% | 47 | 187670 | 44.1% | 34 |

# Selkirk

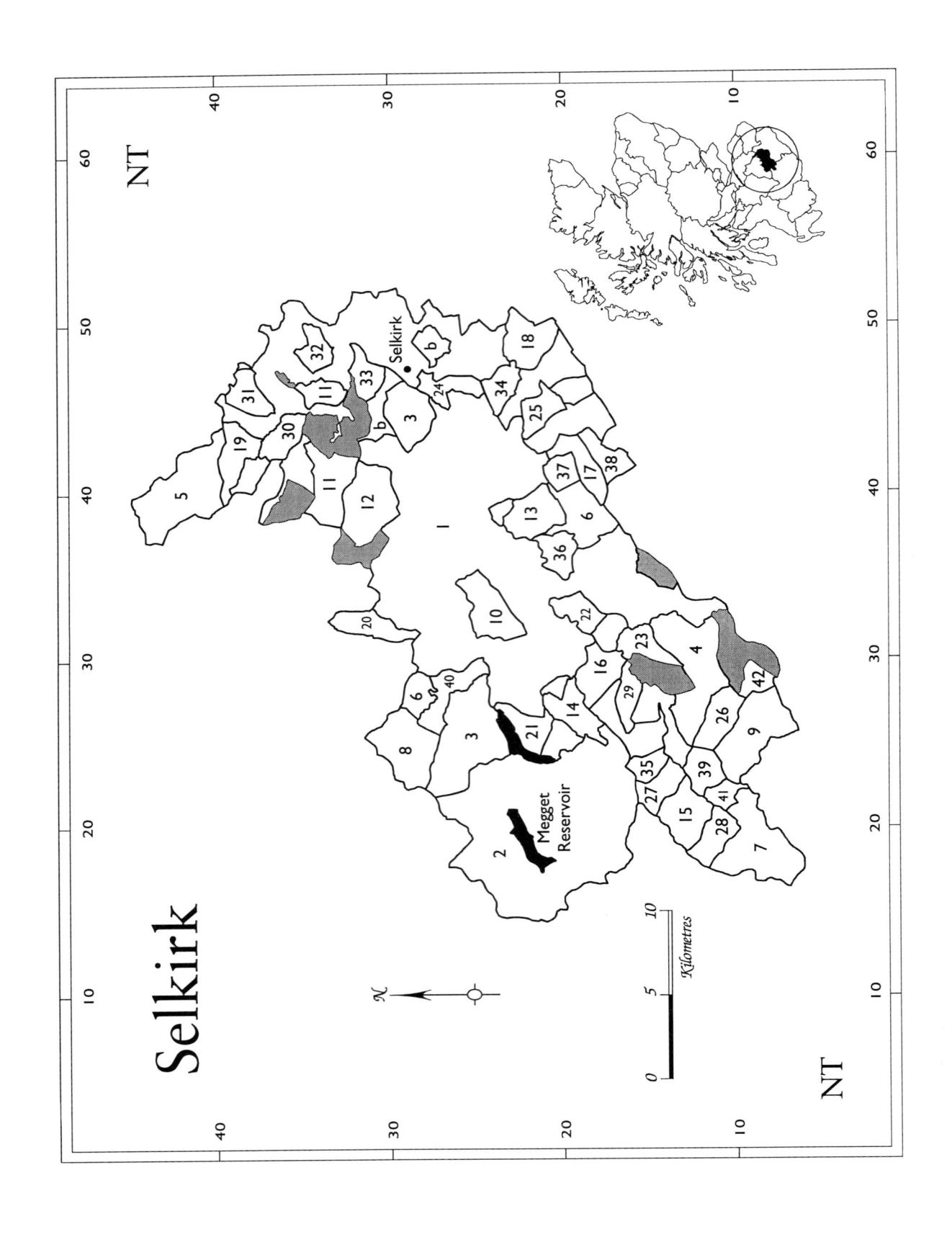

# Selkirkshire
## 171,209 acres

In only four counties in Scotland have I been able to account for the ownership of more than 75% of the county solely by private interests. Three of these were Ross & Cromarty, Sutherland and Nairn and the fourth was Selkirkshire. Roger Millman made as thorough a job of mapping the Borders and Galloway as he did of the Highlands. With the stability in landownership which is generally a feature of the Borders, it proved fairly straightforward, with the aid of some extremely helpful local contacts, to cover virtually all of Selkirkshire.

The heart of Selkirkshire is dominated by the Bowhill Estate, part of the Buccleuch Estates which, at 37,500 acres, is by far the largest holding in the county. Together with the Wemyss estates, they account for over a third of all the land in Selkirkshire.

The rest of the county is in holdings of a few thousand acres, mainly traditional hill farms, but with a growing number of forestry holdings. Overseas interest in Selkirkshire is growing as it is elsewhere with Austrians, Danes and Germans buying up land.

McEwen referred to Selkirkshire as a small, quiet county. This is still the case.

| NO. | PROPRIETOR | PROPERTY | PRINCIPAL INTEREST | ACREAGE | GRID REF. |
|---|---|---|---|---|---|
| 1 | Buccleuch Estates Ltd. * | Bowhill | | 37500 | NT 4227 |
| 2 | E. Benson's & Wemyss 2nd Grandchildrens Trust * | Chapelhope & Meggethead | | 21000 | NT 2219 |
| 3 | Philiphaugh Trust * | Philiphaugh & Dryhope | Sir Michael Strang Steel | 6200 | NT 2624 |
| 4 | PB Forestry Lands Ltd. * | Various forests | See Appendix 3 | 5894 | NT 3114 |
| 5 | Bowland Estates Ltd. * | Bowland & Caddonhead | Leon G. Litchfield | 4450 | NT 4041 |
| 6 | Kronospan * | Hyndhope & Ettrickshaws | | 3412 | NT 3818 |
| 7 | H. Fairhurst & George S. Little-Cook | Over Phawhope & Potburn | | 3035 | NT 1808 |
| 8 | David H Beevers & others | Muttonhall | | 2950 | NT 2528 |
| 9 | Owl Forest Ltd. * | Over Dalgliesh Forest | | 2535 | NT 2508 |
| 10 | John Hume & Sons | Sundhope Farm | | 2450 | NT 3325 |
| 11 | Stephen Dean | Fairnilee & Williamhope | | 2200 | NT 4033 |
| 12 | Alexander J. Telfer | Broadmeadows | | 2000 | NT 4130 |
| 13 | Sir M. Harper Gow | Ettrickshaws Farm | | 1800 | NT 3720 |
| 14 | Jorgen Smidt & Daytoll | Berrybush | | 1537 | NT 2719 |
| 15 | Gordon H. Gray | Overkirkhope & Brockhoperig | | 1500 | NT 2111 |
| 16 | Trustees of William L. Stewart | Tushielaw Farm | | 1500 | NT 2917 |
| 17 | George Easton | Todrig Farm | | 1500 | NT 4219 |
| 18 | Synton Farms | Synton Parkhead | | 1500 | NT 4821 |
| 19 | Thomas & Andrew Elliot * | Blackhaugh & Newhall Farm | | 1450 | NT 4238 |
| 20 | B.N. Howell, E. Eyre & others | Kirkhouse | | 1371 | NT 3231 |
| 21 | Count Alfred Solms | Bowerhope | | 1250 | NT 2522 |
| 22 | John Bernard | Wester Deloraine | | 1250 | NT 3320 |
| 23 | The Duke of Sutherland * | Annelshope Farm | | 1250 | NT 3016 |
| 24 | | The Haining House | | 1250 | NT 4627 |
| 25 | | Castleside | | 1250 | NT 4421 |
| 26 | | Dunhope Rig Forest | | 1250 | NT 2611 |
| 27 | Ogilvie Jackson | Cossarshill Farm | | 1200 | NT 2313 |
| 28 | David Hutton | Broadgairhill Farm | | 1200 | NT 2010 |
| 29 | Lord Napier & Ettrick KCVO | Wardlaw Farm | | 1100 | NT 2916 |
| 30 | J.B. Pate & Son | Caddonlee Farm | | 1050 | NT 4435 |
| 31 | Torwoodlee & Buckholm Estates Co. Ltd. | Torwoodlee | | 1000 | NT 4638 |
| 32 | John Scott | Gala Estate | | 1000 | NT 4834 |
| 33 | Robert D. Smyly | Sunderland Hall | | 1000 | NT 4731 |

## Selkirkshire

| | | | | |
|---|---|---|---|---|
| 34 | Nancy Hunter | Headshaw Farm | 1000 | NT 4622 |
| 35 | Peter Hartley & Mark Willmot | Ettickhill Farm | 1000 | NT 2515 |
| 36 | Robert F.H. Jackson | Old Hyndhope | 1000 | NT 3620 |
| 37 | W.S. & G.S. Easton | Langhope Farm | 1000 | NT 4120 |
| 38 | Patrick A. Campbell Fraser | Whitslade | 1000 | NT 4218 |
| 39 | Miss Naomi A. Simon & others | Shorthope | 1000 | NT 2212 |
| 40 | Thomas Renwick | Craig Douglas | 1000 | NT 2924 |
| 41 | Gallacher Pensions Ltd. * | Nether Phawhope | 881 | NT 2111 |
| 42 | Scottish Amicable Life Assurance Society * | Gair | 804 | NT 2709 |

| | |
|---|---|
| Total | 129519 |
| Selkirkshire land area | 171209 |
| % of county accounted for | 75.6% |

### PUBLIC LANDHOLDINGS

| | | |
|---|---|---|
| Forestry Commission | Various properties | 7991 |
| b. Ettrick & Lauderdale D.C. | Selkirk Common & Linglie | 1300 |
| TOTAL | | 9291 |
| % of county | | 5.4% |

### CHANGES IN THE DISTRIBUTION OF LANDHOLDINGS BY SIZE 1970 - 1995

| | 1970 | | | 1995 | | |
|---|---|---|---|---|---|---|
| Acreage threshold | Acres | % of county | No. of owners | Acres | % of county | No. of owners |
| > 100 000 | 0 | 0% | 0 | 0 | 0% | 0 |
| > 75 000 | 0 | 0% | 0 | 0 | 0% | 0 |
| > 50 000 | 0 | 0% | 0 | 0 | 0% | 0 |
| > 40 000 | 0 | 0% | 0 | 0 | 0% | 0 |
| > 30 000 | 0 | 0% | 0 | 37500 | 21.9% | 1 |
| > 20 000 | 50500 | 29.5% | 2 | 58500 | 34.2% | 2 |
| > 10 000 | 50500 | 29.5% | 2 | 58500 | 34.2% | 2 |
| > 5 000 | 57000 | 33.3% | 3 | 70594 | 41.2% | 4 |
| > 1000 | 97900 | 57.2% | 24 | 127834 | 74.7% | 40 |

# Shetland

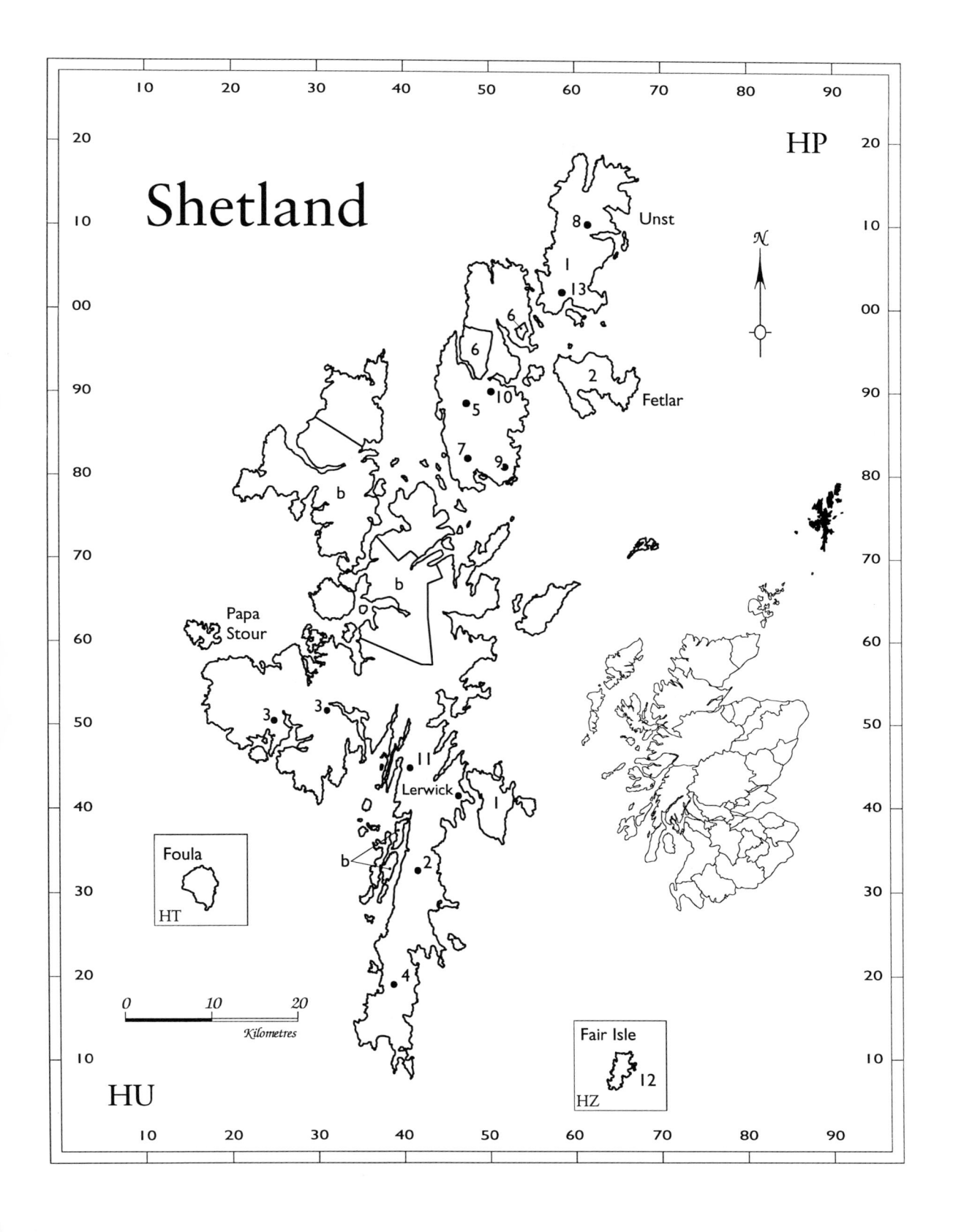

HP

Unst

Fetlar

Papa Stour

Foula
HT

Lerwick

Fair Isle
HZ

HU

0  10  20
Kilometres

# Shetland
## 352,337 acres

Shetland, like Orkney, was not covered by Millman's survey and hence not reported by McEwen. With help from Brian Smith, the Shetland Islands Council archivist, I have managed to pull together some information. So much of Shetland is under crofting tenure of course that a simple look at the landownership situation may not reveal much. Shetland too has udal law which causes further complications, many of which even legal minds have difficulty grappling with. The most pronounced impact of this form of tenure has been on the role which, under feudalism, is accorded to the Crown and from which all feudal authority derives but which has no parallel in udal law. The main controversy this has thrown up has been over the control of the seabed, in particular licensing for moorings and fish farms and the legal status of treasure trove. The St Ninian's Isle treasure described as 'the most important single discovery in Scottish archaeology' was the subject of long legal wrangles.

| NO. | PROPRIETOR | PROPERTY | PRINCIPAL INTEREST | ACREAGE | GRID REF. |
|---|---|---|---|---|---|
| 1 | John & Wendy Scott | Garth | | 14000 | HU 4842 |
| 2 | Mrs O. Borland | Nicolson Estate | | 10000 | |
| 3 | Henry Anderton | Vaila & Burrastow | | 10000 | HU 2247 |
| 4 | George Bell | Sumburgh | | 9000 | HU 4324 |
| 5 | A. Cunningham-Brown | Gossabrough | | 5000 | HU 4488 |
| 6 | Royal Society for the Protection of Birds | Lumbister & others | | 4885 | HU 4897 |
| 7 | John Ballantyne | Ulsta | | 4500 | HU 4680 |
| 8 | D.C. Edmondston | Buness | | 4000 | HP 6209 |
| 9 | Wilson | Burravoe | | 4000 | HU 5279 |
| 10 | L.H. Johnson | Setter | | 3000 | HU 4991 |
| 11 | Captain John Hay of Delgatie * | Hayfield Estate | | 2000 | HU 4145 |
| 12 | National Trust for Scotland | Fair Isle | | 1933 | HZ 2172 |
| 13 | Marquis of Zetland | Zetland Estate | | 1000 | |
| | Total | | | 73318 | |
| | Shetland land area | | | 352337 | |
| | % of county accounted for | | | 20.8% | |

**PUBLIC LANDHOLDINGS**

| | | | | |
|---|---|---|---|---|
| b. Shetland Islands Council | | Burra & Trondra | | 65400 |
| TOTAL | | | | 65400 |
| % of county | | | | 18.6% |

**CHANGES IN THE DISTRIBUTION OF LANDHOLDINGS BY SIZE 1970 - 1995**

| | 1970 | | | 1995 | | |
|---|---|---|---|---|---|---|
| Acreage threshold | Acres | % of county | No. of owners | Acres | % of county | No. of owners |
| > 100 000 | 0 | 0% | 0 | 0 | 0% | 0 |
| > 75 000 | 0 | 0% | 0 | 0 | 0% | 0 |
| > 50 000 | 0 | 0% | 0 | 0 | 0% | 0 |
| > 40 000 | 0 | 0% | 0 | 0 | 0% | 0 |
| > 30 000 | 0 | 0% | 0 | 0 | 0% | 0 |
| > 20 000 | 0 | 0% | 0 | 0 | 0% | 0 |
| > 10 000 | 0 | 0% | 0 | 34000 | 9.6% | 3 |
| > 5 000 | 0 | 0% | 0 | 48000 | 13.6% | 5 |
| > 1000 | 0 | 0% | 0 | 73318 | 20.8% | 13 |

## Stirlingshire
## 288,345 acres

Stirlingshire stretches from the low-lying areas around the Forth at Falkirk and Stirling, over the Campsie, Kilsyth and Fintry Hills with the River Forth the northern boundary, to the banks of Loch Lomond up beyond Inversnaid. The Forestry Commission is a big landowner and others such as the National Trust for Scotland at Ben Lomond and Strathclyde Regional Council at Loch Katrine hold a few thousand acres apiece.

I remain uncertain about landownership in the Fintry and Gargunnock Hills area and what information I have is probably slightly out of date. Not being a large area, I could never justify spending much time sorting it all out but would be delighted to hear from someone who can.

I encountered some helpful owners like Sir Archibald Edmonstone at Duntreath but heard nothing from the Duke of Montrose. Greentops Lands and Estates Ltd, the Danish consortium, appear here again at Comer with 7101 acres and more Danes are around at Auchineden.

Sir George Younger, former Secretary of State for Scotland and now Chairman of the Royal Bank of Scotland, has his family seat here which is now in trust for his grandchildren.

# Stirling

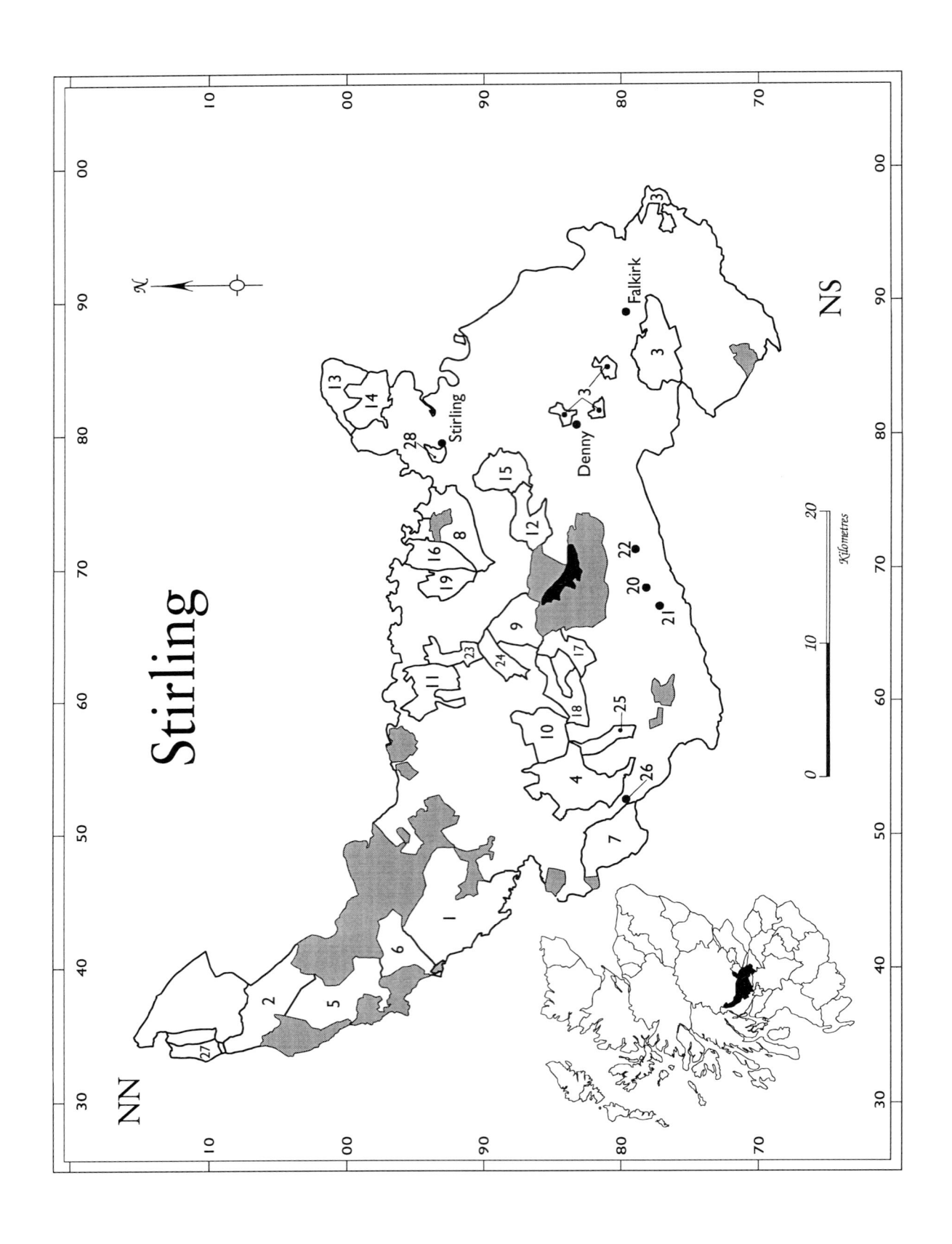

# Stirlingshire

| NO. | PROPRIETOR | PROPERTY | PRINCIPAL INTEREST | ACREAGE | GRID REF. |
|---|---|---|---|---|---|
| 1 | Auchmar Estates Ltd. | Montrose Estates | Duke of Montrose | 8800 | NS 4491 |
| 2 | Greentop Lands and Estates Ltd. * | Comer & Blairhullichan | | 7101 | NN 3804 |
| 3 | Captain W.F.E. Forbes | Callandar Estates | | 7000 | NS 8577 |
| 4 | Duntreath Estate Trust (1978) | Duntreath | Sir Archibald B.C. Edmonstone Bt. | 5600 | NS 5381 |
| 5 | National Trust for Scotland | Ben Lomond | | 5369 | NN 3602 |
| 6 | Mr Maxwell | Cashel Farm | | 3000 | NS 4094 |
| 7 | Auchineden Ltd. | Auchineden | See Appendix 3 | 3000 | NS 5080 |
| 8 | Patrick Buchanan | Touch | | 2700 | NS 7592 |
| 9 | H.S. Chambers & Son. | Todholes | | 2675 | NS 6786 |
| 10 | John McEwen | Mount Farm | | 2500 | NS 5886 |
| 11 | Mr James Stirling of Garden | Garden | | 2500 | NS 5994 |
| 12 | ON MARKET | Craigengelt & Muirpark | | 2115 | NS 7485 |
| 13 | Kippendavie Estate Trust 1988 | Kippendavie | | 2000 | NN 8401 |
| 14 | | Blairlogie | | 2000 | NS 8397 |
| 15 | Sir Ian F.C. Bolton Bt. | Sauchieburn | | 2000 | NS 7789 |
| 16 | Trustees of Gargunnock Estate | Gargunnock | | 1700 | NS 7194 |
| 17 | Joseph Czernin | Lurg & Townhead Farms | | 1665 | NS 6485 |
| 18 | ON MARKET | Jaw Farm | | 1569 | NS 6285 |
| 19 | Rt. Hon. G.K.H. Younger Grandchildren's Trust | Leckie | | 1500 | NS 6894 |
| 20 | D. MacGregor | Burnhead | | 1400 | NS 6878 |
| 21 | J. MacGregor | Dyke | | 1400 | NS 6777 |
| 22 | Archie MacGregor | Allanfauld | | 1400 | NS 7178 |
| 23 | John Struthers | Gribloch | | 1379 | NS 6392 |
| 24 | Andrew Haslam of Culreuch | Culreuch | | 1200 | NS 6287 |
| 25 | Charles R. Connell & Co. * | Ballagan | | 1100 | NS 5779 |
| 26 | Allan M. Barns Graham | Carbeth | | 1000 | NS 5287 |
| 27 | Royal Society for the Protection of Birds | Inversnaid | | 924 | NN 3310 |
| 28 | Crown Estate Commissioners | Stirling | | 431 | NS 7893 |
| | Total | | | 75028 | |
| | Stirlingshire land area | | | 288345 | |
| | % of county accounted for | | | 26.0% | |

## PUBLIC LANDHOLDINGS

| | | |
|---|---|---|
| Forestry Commission | Various properties | 23707 |
| b. Strathclyde Regional Council | Loch Katrine | 7700 |
| TOTAL | | 31407 |
| % of county | | 10.9% |

## CHANGES IN THE DISTRIBUTION OF LANDHOLDINGS BY SIZE 1970 - 1995

| | 1970 | | | 1995 | | |
|---|---|---|---|---|---|---|
| Acreage threshold | Acres | % of county | No. of owners | Acres | % of county | No. of owners |
| > 100 000 | 0 | 0% | 0 | 0 | 0% | 0 |
| > 75 000 | 0 | 0% | 0 | 0 | 0% | 0 |
| > 50 000 | 0 | 0% | 0 | 0 | 0% | 0 |
| > 40 000 | 0 | 0% | 0 | 0 | 0% | 0 |
| > 30 000 | 0 | 0% | 0 | 0 | 0% | 0 |
| > 20 000 | 0 | 0% | 0 | 0 | 0% | 0 |
| > 10 000 | 10200 | 3.5% | 1 | 0 | 0% | 0 |
| > 5 000 | 38800 | 13.5% | 5 | 33870 | 11.7% | 5 |
| > 1000 | 143700 | 49.8% | 60 | 73873 | 25.6% | 26 |

*The Tables and Maps*

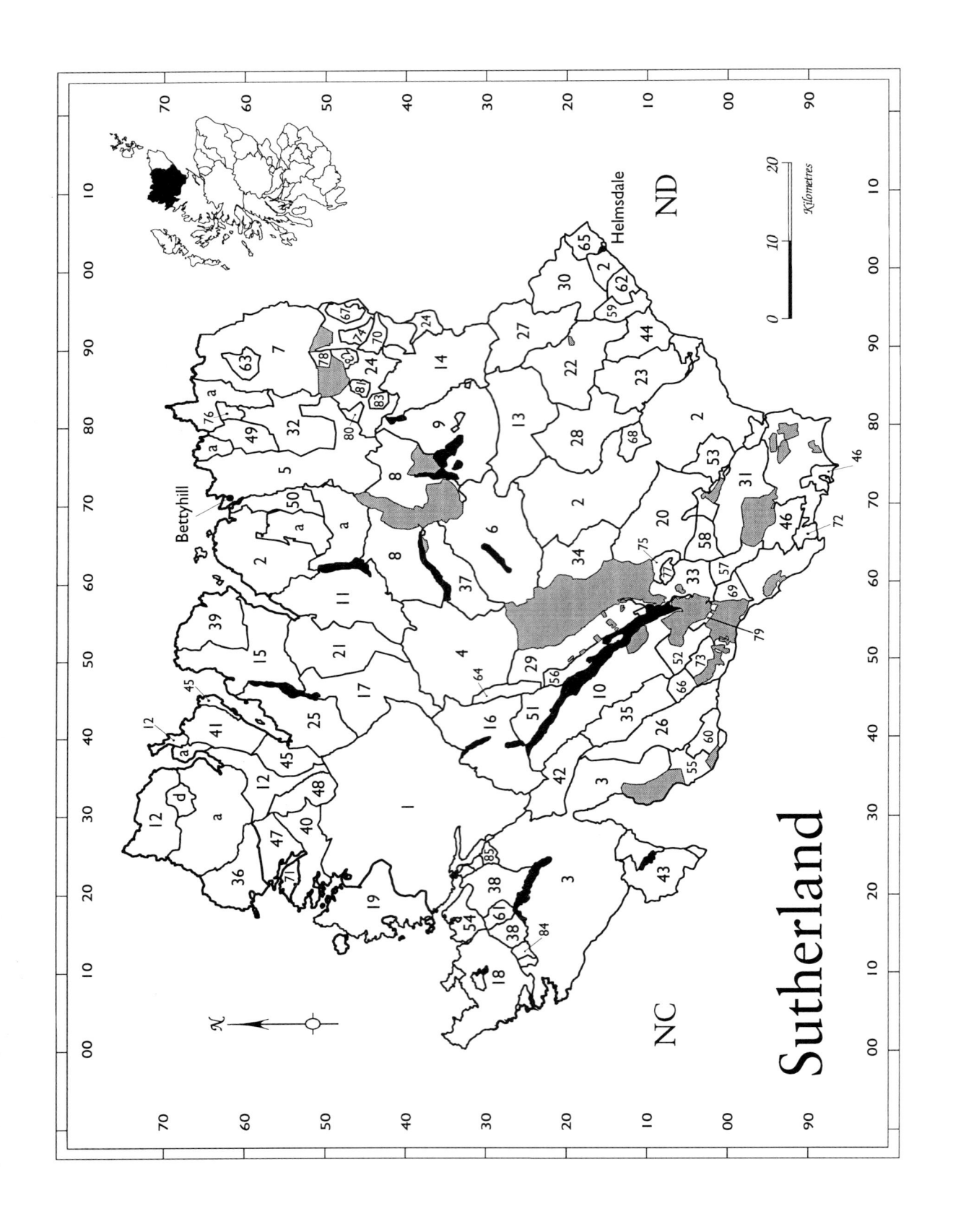

# Sutherland

## Sutherland
## 1,297,803 acres

In 1872 the Duke of Sutherland owned virtually the whole county with the exception of a few glebes and 77 acres in the possession of the Northern Lighthouse Commissioners. By 1970, ownership had fragmented with the sale of the bulk of the estate which now accounts for only 83,239 acres, big enough by any standards but nowhere near the 1,176,454 acres which made it easily the largest private landholding in Scotland, if not in Europe, at the time.

Fragmentation has continued, but looking simply at the number of owners masks some interesting changes. Private forestry companies, principally Fountain Forestry who bought around 100,000 acres here and in Caithness in the 1980s, have sold off parcels to a number of investors. For the purposes of this study they are treated as single ownerships, being in effect syndicates whose principal interest was tax avoidance. But legally, they are separate owners. The Assynt Crofters Trust Ltd., whose success in buying the North Lochinver Estate was a critical turning point in land reform aspirations, has over 100 members. At a stroke, there are 100 more stakeholders than there were before. Such a ratio, applied across Sutherland and Scotland through the taking over of estates by Community Trusts, whilst not changing the number of legal owners, would increase the numbers with a stake in the land from 1500 owning 60% to 150,000 owning 60%.

Sutherland has been the subject of a number of detailed studies into land-occupancy and owner motivation by Professor Bryan MacGregor from the Department of Land Economy at Aberdeen University.[4] MacGregor's work, which has monitored various aspects of ownership motivation over the 1980s, found that the average ownership period of land in north-west Sutherland is 16 years, that the owners of estates can be characterised as elderly absentees who have their origins and their normal residence outwith Scotland, and that the dominant reason for holding land is private enjoyment with the pattern becoming more pronounced since 1980. On employment and investment patterns he concludes, 'In these areas the estate owners are the effective rural planners'. Certainly turnover of land is high. Sandy Mather noted that since 1980 37% of the area has changed hands, involving no less than 70% of the ownership units.[5]

Sutherland remains an empty and lonely county where the road from Helmsdale to Kinbrace up the Strath of Kildonan and on over to Strathnaver is about as bleak and depressing as it is possible to imagine. It was here in 1971 that the HIDB under Sir Robert Grieve presented their proposals for development to Willie Ross, the Secretary of State for Scotland who had been responsible for the setting up of the Board. The proposals failed to make headway due to lack of political will. As the 1970s came to an end, landowners sighed with relief. In 1979 all such thinking was swept aside and a new body, Highlands and Islands Enterprise, eventually took over. The land question has been discreetly dropped with barely a member of staff working on the subject.

A tremendous psychological boost was provided to hopes of better ways of managing the land when in 1993 the Assynt Crofters under their charismatic Chairman, Alan Macrae, took over the 21,000 acre North Lochinver Estate. Their inspirational campaign and eventual success have played no small part in the revival of hopes for far-reaching land reform in Scotland. Where better to start than in Sutherland, a county which, if we had managed things better, would be a much more productive and populated place than it is today.

## Sutherland

| NO. | PROPRIETOR | PROPERTY | PRINCIPAL INTEREST | ACREAGE | GRID REF. |
|---|---|---|---|---|---|
| 1 | Trustees of the 2nd Duke of Westminster | Westminster Estates | Duke of Westminster | 95100 | NC 2938 |
| 2 | Trusts & Countess of Sutherland | Sutherland Estates | | 83239 | NC 7019 |
| 3 | Glencanisp & Drumrunie Deer Forest Trust * | Glencanisp & Inchnadamph | Edmund Vestey | 70500 | NC 2020 |
| 4 | Gray & Adams Ltd. | Altnaharra | | 36603 | NC 5335 |
| 5 | Skelpick Partnership | Skelpick & Rhifail | Lopes family | 34500 | NC 7255 |
| 6 | D. Knowles, D. Melville Leslie, A. & J. Joicey | Loch a Choire | | 32500 | NC 6530 |
| 7 | Fountain International Ltd. | Bighouse | | 28500 | NC 8758 |
| 8 | Yattendon Estates Ltd. & Mynthurst Estates | Lochnaver, Syre & Rhifail | Lord Robert Iliffe & Stone family | 25853 | NC 6239 |
| 9 | Viscount Leverhulme | Badanloch | | 24700 | NC 7933 |
| 10 | H.H. Roesner Land & Forestry (Scotland) Ltd. * | Sallachy & Creanich | | 24000 | NC 5010 |
| 11 | Count Adam W.J. Knuth | Ben Loyal | | 24000 | NC 5854 |
| 12 | Messrs Elliot * | Balnakeil | | 23700 | NC 3968 |
| 13 | Michael I. Wigan | Borrobol | | 23000 | NC 8726 |
| 14 | Achantoul Estate Co. | Achantoul | Sir Anthony Nutting | 22700 | NC 8733 |
| 15 | Michael Foljambe | Hope and Melness | | 22600 | NC 4761 |
| 16 | Robert B. Woods | Merkland & Ben Hee | | 22000 | NC 4029 |
| 17 | Mrs D.H.G. Gow | Strathmore | | 21700 | NC 4743 |
| 18 | Assynt Crofters Trust Ltd. | North Assynt | | 21132 | NC 0828 |
| 19 | Jean Balfour * | Scourie | | 19000 | NC 1644 |
| 20 | Tressady Estates Ltd. | Tressady | See Appendix 3 | 18000 | NC 6904 |
| 21 | Adrian Sykes & Childrens Trust | Kinloch | | 18000 | NC 5552 |
| 22 | Trustees of Mary E.A. Clay | Kildonan | | 18000 | NC 9017 |
| 23 | Richard J. Tyser | Gordonbush | | 18000 | NC 8409 |
| 24 | Royal Society for the Protection of Birds | Forsinard | | 17611 | NC 8843 |
| 25 | James Clark & Alan Clark MP | Eriboll | | 17500 | NC 4356 |
| 26 | Shop & Store Investments Ltd. | Invercassley | See Appendix 3 | 17000 | NC 4107 |
| 27 | The L. & N. Estates Co. Ltd. | Suisgill | E.M. Reeves | 16300 | NC 9023 |
| 28 | James Tyser | Balnacoil | | 14100 | NC 8011 |
| 29 | Christopher Fletcher | Shinness | | 14000 | NC 5314 |
| 30 | Torrish Estates Co. Ltd. | Torrish | See Appendix 3 | 13100 | NC 9718 |
| 31 | Ralph M. Abel Smith | Cambusmore | | 13000 | NH 7697 |
| 32 | Fountain Forestry clients | Strathy | See Appendix 2 | 12600 | NC 8157 |
| 33 | Mrs J.R. Greenwood | Lairg | | 12300 | NC 5723 |
| 34 | Ericht Farming Co. | Dalnessie | Professor Smillie | 12100 | NC 6215 |
| 35 | Lt. Col. R.S. Longsdon | Glen Cassley | | 11850 | NC 4407 |
| 36 | The John Muir Trust | Sandwood | | 11367 | NC 2264 |
| 37 | Mrs P.F. Nicholson, | Clebrig | | 11100 | NC 5932 |
| 38 | Patrick H. Filmer-Sankey | Loch Assynt & Little Assynt | | 10800 | NC 2128 |
| 39 | Melness Crofter Estate Ltd. | Hope and Melness | | 10700 | NC 5763 |
| 40 | Richard Osborne | Rhiconich | | 9600 | NC 2552 |
| 41 | Vibel SA | Durness | | 9400 | NC 4164 |
| 42 | Bocardo Societe Anonyme * | Duchally | | 9400 | NC 3817 |
| 43 | David E. Bulmer * | Ledmore | | 9000 | NC 2207 |
| 44 | ON MARKET | Kintradwell | | 7904 | NC 9107 |
| 45 | Mr & Mrs Charles J.L.B. Marsham | Rispond Lodge & Polla | | 7500 | NC 4565 |
| 46 | Skibo Ltd. | Skibo | Peter de Savary | 7500 | NH 6593 |
| 47 | Robin Barr | Kinlochbervie | | 7200 | NC 2656 |
| 48 | Rarick Ltd. | Gualin | The Hon. David Nall-Cain & others | 6600 | NC 3056 |
| 49 | Joyce Campbell | Armadale Farm | | 5700 | NC 7860 |
| 50 | John T. & Heather Owen | Achnabourin | | 5600 | NC 7054 |

| | | | | | |
|---|---|---|---|---|---|
| 51 | John Hazeleger, Willem van Baalen & others | Overscaig | | 5273 | NC 4223 |
| 52 | | Strath Grudie | | 5000 | NC 5205 |
| 53 | Mr & Mrs William Thomson | Morvich | | 5000 | NC 7500 |
| 54 | Mr & Mrs J. Payne | Ardbhair | | 4700 | NC 1733 |
| 55 | Patrick F.J. Colvin | Caplich & Loubcroy (part) | | 4200 | NC 3705 |
| 56 | Mrs A.L. Parrott | West Shinness | | 4000 | NC 5215 |
| 57 | Patrick & Patrick Macnamara | Garvary Moor | | 3925 | NC 6160 |
| 58 | Oliver Wells | Pittentrail | | 3900 | NC 6402 |
| 59 | Mary G. Dudgeon | Crakaig | | 3500 | NC 9510 |
| 60 | Fountain Forestry clients | Clais Mor | See Appendix 2 | 3303 | NC 3903 |
| 61 | Mrs T. Filmer-Sankey | Loch Assynt Lodge | | 3000 | NC 1728 |
| 62 | Mr & Mrs John A. MacKenzie | Culgower (West Garty) | | 3000 | NC 9912 |
| 63 | William Webster Finlay | Kirkton Farm | | 2979 | NC 8862 |
| 64 | Michael Worsley | Fiag | | 2427 | NC 4626 |
| 65 | Mr & Mrs John T. Bray | Navidale | | 2400 | ND 0316 |
| 66 | Casquets Ltd. | Glen Rossal | Mr Green | 2200 | NC 4604 |
| 67 | Airdrie Property Developments Co. & others | Forsinard ( Fasach etc.) | | 2200 | NC 9446 |
| 68 | | Point | | 2200 | NC 8011 |
| 69 | | Auchinduich | | 2100 | NC 5800 |
| 70 | Christie O'Brien | Forsinard | | 2000 | NC 9043 |
| 71 | Sir Christopher Bland | Kinsaile | | 1960 | NC 2054 |
| 72 | The Woodland Trust | Ledmore & Migdale | | 1756 | NH 6690 |
| 73 | Benito Colarossi & others | Rosehall Forestry | | 1700 | NC 5102 |
| 74 | Fountain Forestry Ltd. clients | North & South Forsinain | | 1700 | NC 9146 |
| 75 | Fountain Forestry Ltd. clients | Craggie & Dola | | 1500 | NC 6208 |
| 76 | ON MARKET | Achrugan (Strathy Forest) | | 1381 | NC 8262 |
| 77 | Andrew Vinen | Challenger Estate | | 1106 | NC 6107 |
| 78 | Janette Angela Morrison | Craggie | | 1018 | NC 8951 |
| 79 | TAP AG | Achany | | 1000 | NC 5502 |
| 80 | Fountain Forestry Ltd. clients | Forsinard (Crocaich etc.) | | 1000 | NC 8146 |
| 81 | Fountain Forestry Ltd. clients | Forsinard (Rashy Burn etc.) | | 1000 | NC 8546 |
| 82 | Fountain Forestry Ltd. clients | Forsinard (The Brig & Dale) | | 1000 | NC 8847 |
| 83 | Fountain Forestry Ltd. clients | Forsinard (The Gunn etc.) | | 1000 | NC 8343 |
| 84 | Lady Hall | Brackloch | | 1000 | NC 1325 |
| 85 | Patrick C.G. Wilson * | Coire a Bhaic | | 800 | NC 2429 |
| | Total | | | 1114387 | |
| | Sutherland land area | | | 1297803 | |
| | % of county accounted for | | | 85.9% | |

## PUBLIC LANDHOLDINGS

| | | | |
|---|---|---|---|
| Forestry Commission | Various properties | 57004 | |
| a. SOAEFD | See Appendix 4 | 58269 | |
| d. MoD | See Appendix 6 | 2700 | |
| TOTAL | | 117973 | |
| % of county | | 9.1% | |

## CHANGES IN THE DISTRIBUTION OF LANDHOLDINGS BY SIZE 1970 - 1995

| | 1970 | | | 1995 | | |
|---|---|---|---|---|---|---|
| Acreage threshold | Acres | % of county | No. of owners | Acres | % of county | No. of owners |
| > 100 000 | 236200 | 18.2% | 2 | 0 | 0% | 0 |
| > 75 000 | 317600 | 24.5% | 3 | 178339 | 13.7% | 2 |
| > 50 000 | 439900 | 33.9% | 5 | 248839 | 19.2% | 3 |
| > 40 000 | 564000 | 43.5% | 8 | 248839 | 19.2% | 3 |
| > 30 000 | 709100 | 54.6% | 12 | 352442 | 27.2% | 6 |
| > 20 000 | 855000 | 65.9% | 18 | 636327 | 49.0% | 18 |
| > 10 000 | 1021000 | 78.7% | 28 | 942755 | 72.6% | 39 |
| > 5 000 | 1094100 | 84.3% | 38 | 1043432 | 80.4% | 53 |
| > 1000 | 1139500 | 87.8% | 53 | 1113587 | 85.8% | 84 |

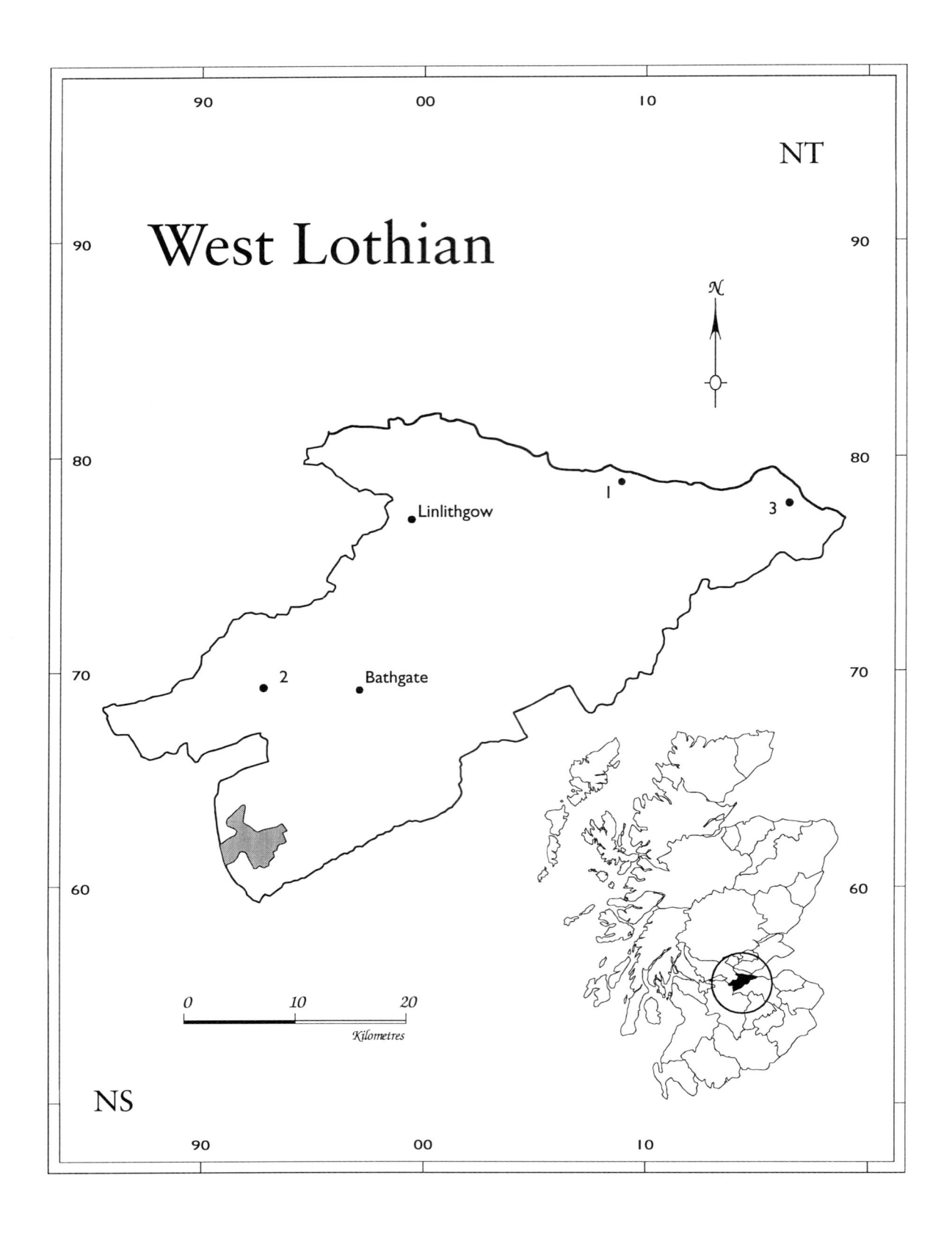

# West Lothian

## West Lothian
## 76,855 acres

Together with Kinross-shire, West Lothian was the only county where McEwen reported no landholdings over 5000 acres. Like other small counties, access to information held by the SOAEFD would have yielded a clearer picture of the pattern of landownership.

| NO. | PROPRIETOR | PROPERTY | PRINCIPAL INTEREST | ACREAGE | GRID REF. |
|---|---|---|---|---|---|
| 1 | Hopetoun Estate Development Co. * | Hopetoun Estate | Marquess of Linlithgow | 3000 | NT 0878 |
| 2 | Roy McNee | Woodend Farm | | 2300 | NS 9269 |
| 3 | Earl of Rosebery | Dalmeny Estates | | 1500 | NT 1677 |
| | Total | | | 6800 | |
| | West Lothian land area | | | 76855 | |
| | % of county accounted for | | | 8.8% | |

**PUBLIC LANDHOLDINGS**

| | | |
|---|---|---|
| Forestry Commission | Various properties | 808 |
| b. Lothian Regional Council | Various properties | 488 |
| TOTAL | | 1296 |
| % of county | | 1.7% |

**CHANGES IN THE DISTRIBUTION OF LANDHOLDINGS BY SIZE 1970 - 1995**

| | 1970 | | | 1995 | | |
|---|---|---|---|---|---|---|
| Acreage threshold | Acres | % of county | No. of owners | Acres | % of county | No. of owners |
| > 100 000 | 0 | 0% | 0 | 0 | 0% | 0 |
| > 75 000 | 0 | 0% | 0 | 0 | 0% | 0 |
| > 50 000 | 0 | 0% | 0 | 0 | 0% | 0 |
| > 40 000 | 0 | 0% | 0 | 0 | 0% | 0 |
| > 30 000 | 0 | 0% | 0 | 0 | 0% | 0 |
| > 20 000 | 0 | 0% | 0 | 0 | 0% | 0 |
| > 10 000 | 0 | 0% | 0 | 0 | 0% | 0 |
| > 5 000 | 0 | 0% | 0 | 0 | 0% | 0 |
| > 1000 | 37900 | 49.3% | 17 | 6800 | 8.8% | 3 |

# Wigtown

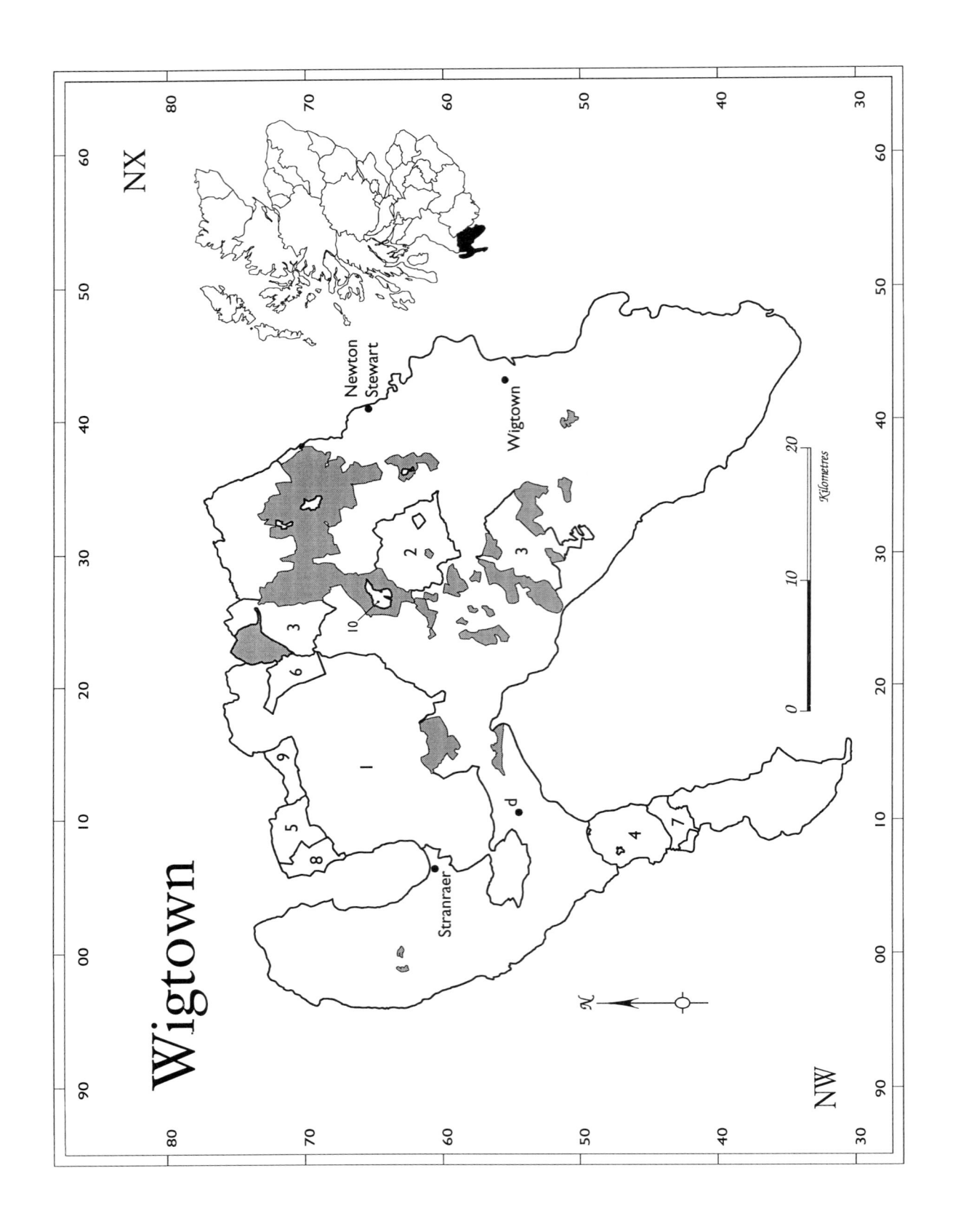

# Wigtownshire
## 311,984 acres

Wigtownshire remains dominated by the Stair Estate. McEwen reported this to cover 105,000 acres. Research for this study leads me to question whether this was accurate and McEwen's figure is thus revised down to 50,000 acres for the purposes of analysing his data. Stair Estates sold their Drummore section on the Mull of Galloway to the Wemyss Development Company (who subsequently sold all the farms 10 years later) in 1973 thus reducing the extent further.

| NO. | PROPRIETOR | PROPERTY | PRINCIPAL INTEREST | ACREAGE | GRID REF. |
|---|---|---|---|---|---|
| 1 | Earl of Stair | Stair Estates | | 43674 | NX 1061 |
| 2 | Craighlaw Estate Trust | Craighlaw | Andrew Gladstone | 7362 | NX 3061 |
| 3 | The Hon. Miss Flora Stuart | Mochrum & High Eldrig | | 5501 | NX 3054 |
| 4 | Ardwell Estates | Ardwell Estates | H.J. Brewis | 5500 | NX 1045 |
| 5 | | Loch Ree | | 2780 | NX 0970 |
| 6 | British Telecom Pension Fund | Purgatory Plantation | | 2056 | NX 2171 |
| 7 | ON MARKET | Logan | | 1819 | NX 0942 |
| 8 | John M.A. Wallace | Lochryan | | 1683 | NX 0668 |
| 9 | | Dalnigap (part) | | 1300 | NX 1371 |
| 10 | Holker Estate Trust | Mark of Lochronald | | 1083 | NX 2664 |
| | Total | | | 72758 | |
| | Wigtownshire land area | | | 311984 | |
| | % of county accounted for | | | 23.3% | |

**PUBLIC LANDHOLDINGS**

| | | |
|---|---|---|
| Forestry Commission | Various properties | 22375 |
| d. MoD | see Appendix 6 | 4569 |
| TOTAL | | 26944 |
| % of county | | 8.6% |

**CHANGES IN THE DISTRIBUTION OF LANDHOLDINGS BY SIZE 1970 - 1995**

| | 1970 | | | 1995 | | |
|---|---|---|---|---|---|---|
| Acreage threshold | Acres | % of county | No. of owners | Acres | % of county | No. of owners |
| > 100 000 | 0 | 0% | 0 | 0 | 0% | 0 |
| > 75 000 | 0 | 0% | 0 | 0 | 0% | 0 |
| > 50 000 | 50000 | 16.0% | 1 | 0 | 0% | 0 |
| > 40 000 | 50000 | 16.0% | 1 | 43674 | 14.0% | 1 |
| > 30 000 | 50000 | 16.0% | 1 | 43674 | 14.0% | 1 |
| > 20 000 | 50000 | 16.0% | 1 | 43674 | 14.0% | 1 |
| > 10 000 | 88500 | 28.4% | 4 | 43674 | 14.0% | 1 |
| > 5 000 | 130300 | 41.8% | 10 | 62037 | 19.9% | 4 |
| > 1 000 | 213200 | 68.3% | 46 | 72758 | 23.2% | 10 |

# Chapter 7

# *The Pattern and the People*

## The Broad Pattern

AN OVERALL SUMMARY of landownership in Scotland is given in Table 1 and the pattern of landownership that emerges from this study is little different to that presented by McEwen.[1] The basic statistics are that:

**In 1970** 1720 owners owned 12,267,226 acres
**In 1995** 1411 owners owned 11,015,405 acres     (Table 2)

The difference of 1,251,821 acres could easily be accounted for by 309 owners owning an average of 4051 acres each. It is quite likely, therefore, that little has changed in terms of the concentrated pattern of private ownership reported by McEwen, although any conclusions from this study should be restricted to landholdings of 5000 acres and above due to the increasing probability of poorer coverage as holding size drops below this. Above 5000 acres, an analysis can be carried out with at least as much, if not greater, accuracy as any carried out using McEwen's figures.

The contemporary pattern of large scale (greater than 5000 acres) private landownership can be summarised as follows.

1. An increase in the number of owners covering 50% of the country (Table 3):

    **1970** 515 owners owned 9,534,316 acres
    **1995** 608 owners owned 9,534,316 acres

2. A decrease in the numbers of owners holding estates of greater than 5000 acres (Table 2):

    **1970** 525 owners owned 9,586,926 acres or 50.3% of Scotland (av. 18,261 acres)
    **1995** 484 owners owned 8,991,368 acres or 47.2% of Scotland (av. 18,577 acres)

These figures show an increase in the number of owners owning 50% of the country held in the largest holdings (an 18% increase) whilst the proportion of the country covered by large (5000 acres and above) estates has reduced (from 50.3% to 47.2%). Ownership of such estates is now in the hands of fewer people but this is not simply due to the reduced acreage. There is a slightly increased concentration *within* this group. The average estate size within the group has increased from 18,261 acres to 18,577 acres. Above 5000 acres in 1995 there are fewer and slightly larger estates.

In other words, half of the country was owned by estates of 5000 acres and above in 1970. By 1995 half of the country is owned by estates larger than 3800 acres. The dilution that has taken place over 50% of the country is accounted for exclusively therefore by an expansion in the number of estates between 3800 and 5000 acres. Below 3800 acres it could be assumed that dilution continues. But at some point it is likely that concentration will reoccur due to the continued trend towards larger farms through the amalgamation of smaller ones.

Looking in greater detail at the figures on a county basis the pattern is slightly different (Table 4). Of the twelve largest counties in Scotland (covering over 75% of Scotland), all but one feature a reduced percentage area covered by estates of 5000 acres and above. But this reduction, together with changes in the number of estates, has led to *smaller* average estate sizes in seven out of the twelve counties. At the county level, therefore, the declining percentage area covered by large estates is consistent with the national picture, but the average size of estates has decreased rather than increased.

The national picture therefore suggests a declining area of large estates with a more concentrated ownership pattern whilst the county picture reveals a declining area of large estates with a dilution of ownership. The difference is explained by an increasing concentration of ownership across Scotland with owners holding land in several counties. Not only has the expansion of organisations such as the Royal Society for the Protection of Birds and the National Trust for Scotland been responsible for this but individual private landowners are building up larger holdings through aggregation of smaller ones in different parts of the country. Examples include Andras Ltd. in Inverness and Banff, Broadland Properties in Argyll, Ross & Cromarty and Moray, and I.&H. Brown in Inverness and Ross & Cromarty. This trend appears sufficient to offset the net disaggregation taking place in most counties although such indications as there are should not perhaps be accorded too much significance. One owner adding 50,000 acres to existing holdings through a single purchase will decrease the numbers of large owners by one. With so few large owners in the first place this would result in a 100-acre increase in average holding size among 500 owners. It doesn't take too many changes to increase the average holding size by 316 acres as has happened here.

## Who Are The Landowners?

Changes in who owns Scotland have obviously taken place over the past 25 years but detailed analysis is difficult. An indication of the kinds of changes that have taken place can be seen by looking at the top 100 landowners in 1970 and 1995 (Table 5). Because of the large acreages often involved in landownership in Scotland, dramatic changes can take place. The Enessey Company from Switzerland, for example, bought Mar Lodge Estate in 1963. During the 70s, they acquired Amhuinnsuidhe Estate in Harris and the Tulchan Estate in Moray – a total landholding of 150,000 acres, making them the second largest private landowner in Scotland (their purchase of Tulchan from Seafield Estates reducing Seafield to third place). Enessey Company Ltd. (now Svenno SA) at present only owns 7000 acres in Harris. Such fluctuations took place *within* the period 1970–1995.

Comparing the top 100 landowners in 1995 with those in 1970, those disappearing include:

| | |
|---|---|
| Lord Lovat (15) | down to number 382 |
| Col. H. Whitbread (18) | sold to Clyde Properties etc. and Patrick G. Wilson |
| A.J. MacDonald Buchanan (19) | sold to Kirkbi Estates Ltd. |
| Sir Hereward Wake (22) | sold to Jonathan Bulmer |
| Harlay & Jones and Enessey Co. (32) | sold to John Kluge then to NTS |
| Benmore Estates Ltd. (42) | split up into Invercassley, Caplich, Loubcroy, Forest Farm and others |
| Sir Oliver Crosswaithe-Eyre (45) | split up and sold |

Most disappearances are due to change in ownership. Only a handful are due to break up or substantial reductions in size.

Newcomers to the top 100 include:

| | | |
|---|---|---|
| Royal Society for the Protection of Birds | in at 11 | amalgamation |
| Clyde Properties etc. | in at 14 | new owner and amalgamation |
| Andras Ltd. | in at 17 | new owners and amalgamation |
| Smech Properties Ltd. | in at 22 | new owner and amalgamation |
| Kirkbi Estates Ltd. | in at 26 | new owner |
| Golden Lane Securities | in at 43 | new owner and amalgamation |
| The John Muir Trust | in at 56 | new owner and amalgamation |
| Greentop Lands and Estates Ltd. | in at 67 | new owner and amalgamation |
| H.H. Roesner Land & Forestry | in at 77 | new owner and amalgamation |

Most newcomers are not the new owners of the same estates that appeared in the top 100 in 1970 but represent new landowners with larger landholdings through the amalgamation of previously separate estates.

Dropping within the top 100 are:

| | |
|---|---|
| Seafield Estates | 2 to 6 |
| Sutherland Estates | 4 to 13 |
| Roxburghe Estates | 9 to 20 |
| Altnaharra Estate | 23 to 52 due to split |

These represent real reductions in acreage. Some holdings appear smaller but this is almost certainly due to inaccuracies in McEwen's figures.

Rising in the top 100 are:

| | | |
|---|---|---|
| Robert Fleming | 33 to 10 | expanded holdings |
| John Guthrie (Broadland Properties) | 78 to 19 | expanded holdings |
| The Queen & Trustees of Balmoral | 68 to 30 | expanded holdings |

Whilst it is beyond the scope of this book to undertake a detailed analysis (as opposed to a straightforward documentation) of who actually owns Scotland, some questions can be addressed. First of all it might be useful to characterise Scottish landownership. This can be done by type of person, land use and legal status. A broad characterisation is outlined in Box 1. It is worth making some comment on a number of these categories.

> **Box 1  A Characterisation of Scottish Landownership**
> This is a broad characterisation of Scottish landownership analysed by the landowner background, the type of holding and the status of the owner. It is only one way of looking at Scottish landownership but should help in obtaining a picture of the different forms in existence.
>
> | **By Landowner Background** | **By Land Use** | **By Status** |
> |---|---|---|
> | The Aristocracy | The Mixed Estate | Companies |
> | Old Money | Forestry | Trusts |
> | New Money | Farms | Individuals |
> | Not for profit Organisations | The Highland Sporting Estate | Partnerships |
> | The State | The Lowland Sporting Estate | |
> | Overseas interests | The Crofting Estate | |
> | The Investment Owners | | |
> | The Working Farmers | | |

## Landowner Background

### The Aristocracy

The aristocracy still owns a lot of land in Scotland. Some of the owners represent long established landed families who have held lands for generations whilst others represent newcomers to both the aristocracy and Scotland. Analysis shows (Table 6) that of the estates over 5000 acres, 2,554,399 acres are held by titled interests. This represents 28.4% of the area held by large estates or 13.4% of Scotland.

The aristocracy is well represented across the country although in greater numbers in the south and east. The Highland aristocracy, having been at the centre of the huge social changes which took place in the 18th and 19th centuries, has more or less disappeared as an element in Highland landownership. The few that remain include Seafield, Cameron of Locheil, Mackenzie of Gairloch, Argyll, MacLeod of MacLeod and various cadet branches of other families who now own tiny rumps of once vast holdings. Huge losses of land by the Highland aristocracy had already occurred by the end of the 19th century. The Mckenzie of Seaforth lands in Lewis, Kintail and Glenshiel were virtually gone by 1844. Walter Campbell of Islay, once the owner of the entire island, was bankrupt by 1848 and sold up in 1853. The MacNeil of Barra, MacLeod of Harris, MacDonald of Bornish and MacDonald of Boisdale had all lost their hereditary estates in the three decades after the end of the Napoleonic wars. One estimate puts the acreage of the Highlands in new ownership by the last quarter of the 19th century as at least 70% of the mainland and insular parishes of western Argyll, Inverness and Ross.[2]

The lowland aristocracy fared substantially better and indeed consolidated their position in the years leading up to the end of the 19th century. Most of the large landed estates of north-east, south-west and south-east Scotland entered the 20th century virtually intact. The big changes came in the years following the First World War when, for example, landownership in Galloway was transformed out of all recognition from the position before 1900.

Today, the houses of Buccleuch, Home, Roxburghe, Stair, Airlie, Lothian, Montrose, Hamilton and Moray still own substantial acreages. Newcomers such as Westminster, Burton, Cowdray and Dulverton ensure that the association between land and class continues.

This percentage of land held by the aristocracy is not surprising given the historic association between land and the power of the aristocracy. Over the last 100 years this association has weakened, as David Cannadine observed in his study *The Decline and Fall of the British Aristocracy*: 'The fact remains that the traditional landed class has ceased to exist as the unchallenged and supreme elite in which wealth, status and power are highly correlated, and are underpinned by territorial preeminence.'[3]

This has been challenged, however, by Edinburgh sociologist David McCrone who claims that, whilst they have inevitably declined in political terms, much of their status has been transformed by the rise of the 'heritage industry'. He concludes that,

'In a country where the lairds and the land question have a salience in politics of some significance, and in the context of Scotland's place in the British state being questioned as never before, Scotland's lairds appear to have succeeded in converting their own and the nation's history into commodities whereby they can save themselves.'.[4]

## The Not for Profit Organisations

Bodies which come under the broad heading of not for profit organisations represent a significant new element in Scottish landownership (Table 7). Not for profit landowners are essentially organisations whose constitutions stipulate that profits or surpluses cannot be distributed to members either on an ongoing basis or upon winding up. In addition, the executive board or council of such bodies are elected by a membership and are therefore accountable to a wider social grouping. Despite efforts in the 19th century to set up such bodies which would buy land for social reasons, principally as a response to land reform agitation, it was not until Lord Leverhulme gifted the Parish of Stornoway to the Stornoway Trust in 1923 that community ownership became a reality. Since then, a number of other bodies including the National Trust for Scotland, the Royal Society for the Protection of Birds and the Assynt Crofters Trust have been created with social purposes. They vary enormously in structure, objectives, motivation and style and can be broadly categorised into three types.

Firstly, there are bodies such as the Stornoway Trust whose membership represents a community of geography – all voters on the electoral roll in the Parish of Stornoway can vote in elections and all those who own or occupy land can stand for election. This little-documented or publicised example of community ownership has been in existence for over 70 years.

Secondly, there are bodies who represent a community of interest such as the RSPB and others whose membership share common interests.

Thirdly are those bodies whose membership share a community of attachment to a place or to values embodied in a place. It is wild land for members of the John Muir Trust and Assynt for members of the Assynt Crofters Trust.

There are of course overlaps and different ways of structuring such interests. Membership of the Assynt Crofters Trust for example is open to and restricted to crofters on the estate. On the other hand, membership of Borve and Annishader Township Ltd. is open to all residents on the estate.

The not for profit sector is not only a growing, albeit still small, force in landownership. It is in many ways the sector which will increasingly provide many of the answers to the problems that landownership in Scotland has thrown up over the years and is an essential part of a move towards forms of ownership which occupy the middle ground between outright state ownership on the one hand and strictly private on the other.

## The State

The state has had an expanding role in landownership in the 20th century. State ownership represents the ultimate in public control over land use and, whether at local or national level, government has clearly indicated that for specific purposes, state ownership is necessary. Just as private ownership of land is politically sensitive, so is public ownership. Historically, left-wing opinion has held public ownership to be the ultimate goal of the socialist project but in Scotland public ownership has seldom been pursued with a view to advancing essentially ideological objectives. Instead, the development of a public estate has been pursued for pragmatic reasons ranging from the establishment of a strategic reserve of timber by the Forestry Commission, to securing vital defence requirements by the Ministry of Defence, and settlement of landless ex-servicemen by the then Department of Agriculture.

The Secretary of State for Scotland is Scotland's largest landowner, owning both the lands of SOAEFD and the FC, a total of 1,942,278 acres, just over 10% of Scotland. Land in public ownership in Scotland today stands at 2,275,768 acres (Table 1). Little has changed in overall terms since 1970 but this masks the important turning point that was the 1979 General Election. The public estate had been steadily expanding to this point since shortly after the First World War. The election of a Conservative government, however, led to a very different political agenda which stressed the role of the private sector. This change has been manifested by sales of FC, SOAEFD, and HIDB land in the 1980s and 90s. The general trend is well illustrated by the changes which have taken place in the largest public sector body, the Forestry Commission (Table 8). From a holding of 1,783,800 acres in 1970, it rose to 1,976,928 acres in 1981 and has subsequently fallen to 1,699,949 acres as of 31 March 1995, a level it was last at in 1968.

Detailed trends in public landownership are frustrated by the lack of good historical records. Gordon Clarke, a geographer from the University of Lancaster, examined the extent of public ownership of land in Scotland in 1981.[5] Among his conclusions were that we remain better informed about the extent of public ownership in 1872 than we do today. A full breakdown of land owned by the Secretary of State for Scotland (SOAEFD), SNH and the MoD is contained in Appendices 4, 5 and 6.

## Overseas Interests

Overseas ownership of land has been a frequent subject of debate in Scotland and has been responsible perhaps more than any other topic for ensuring that the question of landownership receives a regular if somewhat spasmodic and ill-informed airing in the

## Box 2   Danish Interest in Scottish Land

'Danes lead Highland land-grab invasion' was how the *Press and Journal* led a story on 3 March 1987. It reported how a 'Scandinavian spending spree' was being predicted by land agents particularly in the wake of the introduction of a Wealth Tax in Denmark. Andrew Rettie of land agents Strutt & Parker predicted a new wave of 'absentee landlords': 'A very considerable number of Danish clients have retained us to find them an estate in Scotland', he is quoted as claiming. 'It appears that the coming of a Wealth Tax in their own country is the main motivation.'

And so it turned out. Not only were financial advisors advising wealthy Danes to invest in Scottish land, but Scottish companies were developing close links with Danish interests. Scottish Woodlands Ltd., a land and forestry management company, and a Hans Jorgensen appear to have worked closely together in attracting Danish investors to

| PROPRIETOR | PROPERTY | COUNTY | ACREAGE |
|---|---|---|---|
| Kirkbi Estates Ltd. | Strathconon | ROSS & CROMARTY | 60,000 |
| Greentop Lands and Estates Ltd | Various properties | | 29,643 |
| Count Adam W.J. Knuth | Ben Loyal | SUTHERLAND | 24,000 |
| Wefri A/S & Lurga Ltd. | Laudale | ARGYLL | 12,500 |
| Lucas Aardenburg | Pitmain | INVERNESS | 10,800 |
| Poul Johansen | Glenmoriston | INVERNESS | 9250 |
| Neils Tandrup & Viggo & Helle Sorensen | Glencripesdale | ARGYLL | 4500 |
| Carl & M. Lawaetz | East Benula | ROSS & CROMARTY | 4500 |
| Horsens Folkeblad Foundation | Conval & Revack Forests | INVERNESS & BANFF | 4236 |
| Søren Engaard | Moorbrock & Strahanna | KIRKCUDBRIGHT | 3500 |
| Auchineden Ltd. | Auchineden | STIRLING | 3000 |
| Jorgen Smidt & Daytoll | Berrybush | SELKIRK | 1537 |
| TOTAL DANISH INTEREST | | | 167,446 |

Scotland. The results of such activity soon became obvious.

All but one of the owners identified in the table bought land in the late 1980s or early 1990s. An interesting example of the trend is illustrated by Greentop Lands and Estates Ltd. This company is a Scottish registered branch of a Liechtenstein company, Greentop Lands and Estates AG which was set up in 1989 with a Board of three directors: Mette Skov, Lars Møller Nielsen and Guido Meier. It currently owns 12 properties in Scotland (see Appendix 2) ranging from the 9650 acre Claonaig estate in Argyll to smaller estates of a few hundred acres. The Liechtenstein parent company appears to be a channel through which funds can be invested in Scotland from the Aage V Jensens Fonde (the Jensen Foundation), a Danish charitable organisation with broad conservation aims whose principal beneficiary is a Mrs Dorte Aamann-Christensen. The total funds loaned to the company stood at £6,231,745 as at 31 December 1992.

Mrs Aamann-Christensen's late father made his fortune in the construction industry in post-war Denmark and made provision for the Foundation in his will. She bought the 2345-acre island of Rona in January 1993 and also owns commercial forestry in Inverness-shire. The properties, which are all the responsibility of Lars Møller Nielsen, the Chief Forester of the Foundation, fall into three types. Rona represents a holiday retreat for Mrs Aamann-Christensen. Comer, in Stirlingshire, is being managed for conservation and is a net recipient of Jensen funds whilst others, principally Claonaig, are viewed as investments which will yield a return to the Foundation. Funds appear to be coming both from a private trust for Mrs Aamann-Christensen and the charitable Jensen Foundation.

Scottish Woodlands Ltd. provide the management of all the properties in Scotland and have developed a close relationship with the fund through their manager in Lochgilphead, Mr Robin Dixon. His involvement goes beyond straightforward management services as he is also a Director of Lurga Ltd., another Danish landowning company mentioned in the table on p. 164.

Another Director of Lurga Ltd. is Leif Skov, a lawyer who is involved in many of Greentop's transactions. In 1991/92, for example, he bought 185 acres of farmland in Stirlingshire for £77,022. In 1994 he sold it to Greentops for £425,000. Further farmland at Glenny, Mondowie and Over Glenny were sold to a company called Glenrock Ltd. for £173,850 in December 1989, then to Leif Skov (c/o Scottish Woodlands in Lochgilphead) in September 1991 for £185,059 before being sold to Greentops for £425,000 in 1994. Nether Glenny appears in Greentops' balance sheet for 1994, valued at £430,447. Greentop Lands and Estates Ltd reported a loss of £1,612,599 in 1994.

Danish interest in Scottish land is part of a wider interest by Scandinavians whose activities are restricted by landownership legislation in their home countries but who can buy as much land as they wish in Scotland.

Wider connections between the various Danish interests are apparent. One of the Directors of Auchineden Ltd., which owns land in Stirlingshire, is Hans Jorgensen who also manages Strathconon Estate on behalf of Kirkbi Estates Ltd and is believed to be the same Hans Jorgensen who is involved with Scottish Woodland Ltd. Lars Møller Nielsen, of the Jensen Foundation, also appears to be involved in the management of Glencripesdale in Argyll.

media. The 1970s saw a rash of land speculation mainly by Dutch nationals such as Johannes Hellinga but also the beginnings of substantial Middle Eastern interest in Scottish land. McEwen noted this trend in his book but did not quantify it. For what it is worth, the current extent of land held by overseas interests is outlined in Table 9. It indicates a growing interest from Danish nationals in landownership in Scotland, a fuller exploration of which is made in Box 2.

Depending on how one defines overseas interest, one can produce varying statistics. For the purposes of Table 9, I have abstracted all land whose legal owner is an overseas interest (outwith UK), whether they be an individual or a company. Offshore companies, whether their beneficial owners are UK nationals or not (which is often impossible to determine) are therefore included. Companies such as Alcan Highland Estates Ltd., which is a wholly owned subsidiary of British Alcan Aluminium plc., which in turn is wholly owned by the Canadian based Alcan Aluminium Ltd., are also included as overseas since the beneficial owners are the parent company and its shareholders.

There is no doubt that there has been an increase in the amount of land held by overseas interests but quantifying it is difficult. One investigation into overseas activity in the Scottish land market accounted for around 300,000 acres in Caithness, Banff, Aberdeen, Kincardine, Moray, Inverness, and Ross & Cromarty alone in 1978.[6] It is noticeable from that study that much of the land which was bought by overseas interests in the 1970s has remained in overseas hands even upon a change of ownership. The current figure of 1,104,223 acres represents 5.8% of Scotland. Overseas ownership has probably increased around fourfold since 1970 with the first wave taking place in the 1970s and a second wave in the late 1980s and early 90s.

## The Investment Owners

As one land agent is reported to have said, 'the thing about land is that they don't make it any more'. Land has always been a reasonably secure long term investment. Many people have also seen the short-term gains to be had from property speculation. Within landownership in Scotland there is a small but significant sector of landowners to whom land is first and foremost an investment. Some key players are listed in Table 10. It is difficult to determine without detailed knowledge which landowners look primarily to the long term investment represented by growth in capital values. Although some, such as the pension funds and the Crown Estate Commissioners, are explicit about this, others are less certain. For example, the exact motivation of the Danish consortium, Greentop Lands and Estates, would appear from their accounts to be about investment but they decline to be drawn on the subject.

Investment interests build up and disappear. General Accident, for example, appear to be moving out of landownership whereas Eagle Star are consolidating around slightly different types of investment.

## Land Use

It is beyond the scope of this book to take a detailed look at how land is used in Scotland. To understand how landownership interacts with land use in a broad sense, however, it is useful to consider the kind of landholdings outlined in Box 1.

## The Mixed Estate

Mixed estates are typically owned by well-established Scottish landed families such as Buccleuch, Dalhousie, Seafield and Roxburghe. They have developed as mixed estates due to the extensive nature of the holdings and the continuity of ownership. In some cases this has been disrupted where, for example, upland parts of an estate are sold as was the case with the Lovat estate before its virtually complete breakup in 1995.

## Forestry

Forestry ownerships have developed particularly during the 1980s with the growing emphasis placed on the private sector. Much private forestry is still included in mixed estates but there is now a substantial forest investment sector which is a specialised owner of forestry land.

## Farms

Farms are the dominant feature of the lowlands and around 65% of holdings are owner-occupied. Research into changing patterns of agricultural ownership was the central concern of the Northfield Committee set up in 1977 to study particularly the growth of financial institutions in farm ownership.[7] Greater freedom of access to SOAEFD information would allow a better understanding of the changing pattern of farm ownership.

## The Highland Sporting Estate

The Highland Sporting Estate looms large in any analysis of landownership in the Highlands of Scotland. Suffice it to say that the idea of the sporting estate in social and economic terms as a place in which private indulgence continues to take precedence over social and economic development is the key reason why so much of the debate on landownership has focussed on this particular type of landholding. Whilst other types of holdings such as working farms may be placed on the land market with as much regularity as sporting estates tend to be, no other holding consistently attracts land prices which bear so little relationship to the productive capacity of the land. Their role as a status symbol which is capable of attracting worldwide attention in the property market is another reason why they provide something of a touchstone for ideas on landownership and use.

## The Crofting Estate

The crofting estate is a creation of the 1886 Crofters Act which introduced a radical change in land tenure through the provision of statutory protection to crofters' agricultural tenancies. In recent years crofting has re-emerged politically to assert itself as a system of land tenure with much to commend it. The events of Assynt further emphasised that within crofting there is still the hunger for land reform that led to its development in the first place. The crofting estate therefore is another important type of landholding with respect to landownership in Scotland and one where, although the crofting element is increasingly confident about the future, there is a very real question mark over the future role of the landowner.

Further exploration of the relationship between various land uses and landownership is provided in the chapters which follow.

## Status

Regardless of the character of landowners or their particular interests as far as type of land are concerned, every owner of heritable property in Scotland has a legal identity. Both natural and legal persons are recognised as legitimate owners even under some unlikely names (such as Footloose and Fancy Free Investments Ltd.). Depending on the motivations, origins, background and objectives of landowners it may suit them to hold land in a variety of different ways. The most common are as individual natural persons, companies and private or public trusts. Others such as partnerships are also found but are less common in the holdings analysed in this survey. Table 11 outlines the role played by companies and trusts. It should be emphasised that the term trust is widely used where it does not strictly apply. Private and public trusts are defined by a clear body of Scots law. Companies which call themselves trusts may be doing it to convey the impression of benevolence and worthiness. In some cases the distinction is finer. The John Muir Trust, for example, is a company limited by guarantee with no share capital and has charitable status with the Inland Revenue. Clearly the word trust conveys an accurate impression of the general purpose of the organisation even if it is not legally accurate.

The taxation regime is the most common reason for individuals choosing to own their land through a company or trust. Companies operate under company taxation rules and it may be convenient for a loss-making sporting estate, for example, to be operated as a company whose losses can be offset against other income. Trusts are legal entities which as has been indicated already are often used to allow for the continued possession of land by certain beneficiaries without the problems posed by Inheritance taxes. They are used in the same way as entailment was used in the past to prevent creditors staking a claim on land in lieu of debts. They are a device for entrusting land to future generations in a secure and private way. Their growth represents one of the biggest changes in landownership since 1970 with fully 2,372,733 acres now owned by private trusts, representing over 12% of Scotland. This is likely to be a substantial underestimate since this figure represents only those holdings that could be identified as trusts within the constraints of the survey. If one determined how all land was legally held the figure would certainly be much higher. It compares with a figure of 8.4% for 1970.[8]

## Turnover in Ownership

The rate of turnover of land is beyond the scope of this book although it is an important component in understanding the changing patterns of landownership. The only information that is available is some limited survey data and anecdotal evidence.[9]

## What is Scottish Landownership?

Beyond the straightforward pattern of landownership that emerges from this study, it is interesting to look at the institution of Scottish landownership and at how landowners have organised themselves, since this has played no small part in the continuing relative political security which is a characteristic of landownership in Scotland. Up until the beginning of the 20th century, landowners were in little need of any structured organisation. Their status as an elite grouping with existing networks was sufficient to secure their power. But as the 20th century opened, new institutions became urgently required to counter perceived threats to private landownership.

## The Scottish Landowners' Federation

The Scottish Landowners' Federation (SLF) is the only government-recognised voice of landowning in Scotland. It was founded in November 1906 (as the Scottish Land & Property Federation) to protect landowners' interests and oppose the proposed provisions of the Small Landholders (Scotland) Bill, which extended crofting tenure to the whole of Scotland. From its early concerns with protecting landowning interests in the face of land-reforming governments in the 20s and 30s, its objectives have changed little and today it describes itself as 'the only organisation which represents and acts to protect the rights of private ownership of rural land'. Its aims include 'promoting high standards of management and use of land' and 'ensuring that legislation is prepared with proper consideration for the responsibilities and rights of landowners, in addition to the well-being of rural communities, the environment, and the wider public interest.'[10]

SLF membership is split into Ordinary, which is for those holding 10 acres of land or more; Associate, for those with less than 10 acres or others simply interested in land; and Business (land agents, solicitors etc.) who wish to promote their services to other members. Ordinary members' subscriptions are based upon acreage owned and they pay according to this figure weighted by the type of land.

SLF literature claims that the organisation has 4000 members owning seven million acres or '80% of Scotland's land in private ownership'. Closer analysis reveals a slightly different picture. In 1994 the SLF had 3690 members of which 2922 were Ordinary, 615 were Associate and 201 were Business. Assuming that all Associate members own land, this gives a landholding membership at 1994 of 3537. A 1994 analysis published by the SLF in its Annual Report reported the following breakdown.

Of the Ordinary membership
366 members or 12% own 125 acres or less
935 members or 32% own 250 acres or less
1607 members or 55% own 500 acres or less

Five hundred acres represents an important threshold for the SLF since it makes great play in its literature of the fact that the 55% of 'farmers and owner-occupiers' who own less than this 'form the base of the Federation'.

Given the lack of information on the current ownership pattern of SLF members it is interesting to note that figures do exist for 1975.[11] These are reproduced in Table 12 which can be compared with the current situation in so far as data allows, in Table 13.

In 1975 fully 80% of its members (2957 people) owned less than 1233 acres representing 16% of the total land held by SLF members. In 1994 something between 55% and 63% of members (1607–2222 people) own land in holdings of less than 500 acres. In 1975 20% of members (755 people) owned holdings larger than 1233 acres. In 1995 45% of members (1315 people) owned holdings larger than 500 acres.

Direct comparison is impossible due to the lack of comparable data but there is no evidence that SLF membership has changed dramatically in the past 20 years. What is evident is a declining membership which, rather that representing 4000 landowners owning seven million acres or 80% of private land, represents possibly as few as 2922 people who between them own not 80%, but less than 42%, of private rural land in Scotland.

Numerically, the membership is concentrated in the wealthier farming counties of Aberdeenshire, Ayrshire and Perthshire as illustrated in Table 14. Interestingly, English addresses account for 6.7% of the SLF's membership putting England fourth in terms of place of origin. Following England are Angus, Dumfries, Fife, Lanark and Roxburgh.

The SLF is not the only organisation representing landowners. Both the National Farmers Union of Scotland (NFUS) and the Timber Growers Association (TGA) represent private farming and forestry interests although, since trees can only legally be owned by landowners, the TGA is exclusive to landowners whilst the NFUS also includes tenant farmers.

**Wider Networks**

Beyond the SLF are wider connections which are relevant to any understanding of landownership in Scotland today. Marriage and business connections have served to cement much of the landownership institution in place. The kinds of relationships are well illustrated by the following examples.

The late Duke of Atholl's mother, Angela, who died in 1981 was the third daughter of the second Viscount Cowdray (Dunecht Estates). She married for a second time Robert Campbell-Preston and had a daughter Sarah Troughton who owns Ardchattan and substantial parts of Atholl Estates. The Atholl Estates factor Andrew Gordon owns land at Wester Glenquoich in Inverness-shire and Lude in Perthshire (neighbouring Atholl estates) as does his father at Barrisdale in Inverness-shire. He is also the factor for Robert Fleming of the Scottish merchant banking family who owns the Blackmount, Glen Etive and Dalness estates in Argyll. His cousin, Mrs Fleming (who married his brother, Major Richard Fleming) owns Glenkinglass together with her sister Mrs Schuster who is married to Mr Schuster who owns Duilleter. Robert is chairman of Robert Fleming Holdings of which Henry Keswick (Hunthill in Angus and Glenkiln in Kirkcudbrightshire) is also a director. He and his youngest brother are Chairman and Director of Jardine Matheson whose founder, James Matheson, at one time owned the Island of Lewis. At least six other Dumfriesshire landowners have close connections with Jardine Matheson. Henry's other brother, Sir John 'Chips' Keswick owns Auchendolly estate in Kirkcudbrightshire and Henry himself is married to Tessa, Lady Reay, younger daughter of the late Lord Lovat. Sir John 'Chips' Keswick is married to Lady Sarah Ramsay, daughter of the 16th Earl of Dalhousie (Dalhousie Estates in Angus) who in turn is also related to the Lovats through his mother-in-law who was the daughter of the 13th Lord Lovat. The Earl of Dalhousie's cousin is Captain Ramsay of Mar (Mar Estate in Aberdeenshire) and his late mother was Lady Mary Heathcote-Drummond-Willoughby, daughter of the first earl of Ancaster. Her great-niece is Baroness Jane Heathcote-Drummond-Willoughby de Eresby (Drummond Estate in Perthshire) whose grandfather on her mother's side was the second Viscount Astor. The fourth Viscount Astor owns Tarbert Estate on Jura. The second son of the first Viscount Astor was the first Baron Astor of Hever whose grandson is Philip Astor (Tillypronie Estate in Aberdeenshire). Philip's sister, the

Honourable Sarah Violet Astor is married to George Lopes (Skelpick and Rhifail Estate in Sutherland).

One can go on. The owners outlined above (leaving out the late James Matheson) between them own over 625,000 acres or 3.3% of Scotland.

Another more blue-blooded relationship centres around the Queen herself.

The Queen Mother is the daughter of the 14th Earl of Strathmore (Glamis in Angus). The Queen (land in Angus and Aberdeenshire) herself has a cousin, the fifth Earl of Granville (North Uist Estate) whose daughter is married to Jonathan Bulmer (Amhuinnsuidhe Estate in Inverness-shire) whose brother David also owns Ledmore Estate in Sutherland. The second Earl of Granville's daughter was the mother of John Granville Morrison, Lord Margadale (Islay Estate). The Queen is also related to the Earl of Airlie (Airlie Estates) through his brother, Sir Angus Ogilvy who is married to Princess Alexandra of Kent. The Countess of Airlie is also a Lady to the Bedchamber of the Queen. The Earl of Airlie was Chairman of Schroders, the merchant bank, from 1977 to 1984 whilst Bruno Schroder himself owns Dunlossit Estate on Islay next door to Lord Margadale. The Earl of Airlie's daughter, Lady Doune Ogilvy, is married to Sir Hereward Wake, a previous owner of Amhuinnsuidhe Estate. The private secretary to the Queen from 1972 to 1977 and still one of her Lords in Waiting is Lord Charteris of Amisfield, the brother of the Earl of Wemyss and March (Wemyss Estates in the Borders). Lord Charteris's daughter is married to Lord Pearson of Rannoch (Cruach in Perthshire). The Queen's aunt, the Duchess of Gloucester, is the third daughter of the seventh Duke of Buccleuch whose widow is the daughter of the 13th Earl of Home. The current Duke of Buccleuch's sister is the Duchess of Northumberland (Burncastle in Berwickshire).

Total acreage for this group is 648,470 acres or 3.4% of Scotland.

Such connections are not ad hoc. They provide an insight into the very heart of the British Establishment.[12] The British Establishment is emphasised in this context not because Scottish counterparts are unimportant but because, in the absence of any political autonomy in Scotland, it is to a British context that Scottish landowners have looked for influence. Scottish institutions such as the Royal Company of Archers, the Queen's Body Guard in Scotland, do exist of course and facilitate easy connections with the wider Scottish establishment.

Such networks play a key role in supporting the 'landowning interest'. Reference to such an interest is worth qualifying in order to remove any misunderstandings. It is clearly evident that there is a core body of beliefs, a value system, incorporated within the term which is to do with the sanctity of private property rights, an often barely disguised distaste for any notion of the public interest and a recognition that land is still at the heart of the status which members of the Establishment enjoy and want to hold onto. These core beliefs are promoted by a small number of landowners whose networks are sufficiently wide for others to be drawn into them. The vast majority of landowners in Scotland may not indeed be aware of the politics of such a network and may indeed be much more liberal and progressive in their outlook. It is, however, the views of the 'landowning interest' which are often seen to prevail in cases where their wider interests are deemed to be threatened. The case of Mar Lodge will be looked at later as recent evidence of the role of such networks.

Land agents too are worth looking at since they form an even more concentrated group whose outlook and views are perhaps more important in some instances than landowners in determining how land is used and managed. Many landowners are also land agents and many land agents come from landowning families. Their involvement with landownership was highlighted by the claim by one leading land agent that 'there are ten land agents, ten individuals, in Britain who could tell you who owns every acre in the country'.[13]

Finally, the connections between wealth and landownership are by no means reduced by the decline of feudal authority (Table 15). Newcomers to Scottish landownership from finance and industry ensure that today no less than 46 of Britain's richest 500 people, representing around £10 billion according to the *The Sunday Times* 1996 survey, own over 1.25 million acres of land in Scotland. Of these only about a quarter are from traditional landed families although the aristocracy often have access to wealth far and beyond what their landholding represents. Buccleuch Estates for example represent a mere 5% of the Buccleuch family assets according to one recent analysis.[14] The wealth represented by Scottish landowners is of course far in excess of £10 billion if one includes the various Middle Eastern Sheiks and other overseas owners whose wealth is certainly greater than this figure, probably by at least an order of magnitude.

## Conclusions

It remains remarkable that the private ownership of over half of Scotland can be so easily contained within a few pages of a modest book. That the institution of landownership in Scotland is so tightly controlled by so few people remains its greatest strength and its greatest weakness. At the end of the day, landownership as a system of property rights cannot exist separate from the wider public interest. How this wider public interest could be expressed and embodied in new arrangements for the distribution of rights to land will be explored in the closing chapter of this book. Meanwhile, to further illustrate the impacts of changing patterns of ownership, we now turn in the next five chapters of Section II to look at the key areas of agriculture, the sporting estate, forestry, crofting and the conservation landowners.

TABLE 1
# How Scotland is Owned 1995

|  | Acres | % |  |
|---|---|---|---|
| **TOTAL LAND AREA OF SCOTLAND** | 19068631 | 100.00% | 1 |
| Urban Scotland | 585627 | 3.07% |  |
| Rural Scotland | 18483004 | 96.93% |  |
| **PUBLICLY OWNED LAND** |  |  | 2 |
| Secretary of State for Scotland – Forestry Commission | 1660923 | 8.71% | 3 |
| Secretary of State for Scotland – SOAEFD | 281355 | 1.48% | 4 |
| Local Authorities | 152771 | 0.80% | 5 |
| Scottish Natural Heritage | 84488 | 0.44% | 6 |
| Secretary of State for Defence (MoD) | 50429 | 0.26% | 7 |
| British Coal | 40000 | 0.21% | 8 |
| Highlands & Islands Enterprise | 5802 | 0.03% | 9 |
| **TOTAL PUBLICLY OWNED** | 2275768 | 11.93% |  |
| **NON-PUBLICLY OWNED** | 16792863 | 88.07% |  |
| **ACCOUNTED FOR IN THIS BOOK** | 13291173 | 69.70% |  |
| consisting of: |  |  |  |
| PUBLIC OWNERSHIP | 2275768 | 11.93% |  |
| PRIVATE OWNERSHIP | 10559641 | 55.38% |  |
| NOT-FOR PROFIT OWNERSHIP | 455764 | 2.39% | 10 |

1. For the purposes of this book, the total land area of Scotland (19,068,631 acres) is the figure used to represent 100% of Scotland. The area of inland water almost entirely consists of large lochs which form the boundaries between landholdings and which in law are recognised as being held in common by all adjacent proprietors.
2. Publicly owned land includes all land held by government ministers, departments, agencies and local authorities where the owner is accountable to the electorate.
3. This figure represents the total area of land in the ownership of the Secretary of State for Scotland as Forestry Minister. It is derived from the figure reported in the 75th Forestry Commission Annual Report 1994-1995 (1,699,949 acres) less 23,456 acres which are leased and a further 15,570 acres which are included in the County Tables as being land on the market in 1995.
4. Source: SOAEFD Personal communication 30 October 1995 (see Appendix 4 for further details).
5. Source: Personal communications from various local authorities.
6. Source: SNH Personal communication 27 October 1995 (see Appendix 5 for further details).
7. Source: MoD Personal communication 11 October 1995 (see Appendix 6 for further details).
8. The British Coal estate is in the process of being sold. This figure is an estimate of the extent of their holdings as at 31 December 1995.
9. This figure represents the Highlands & Islands Enterprise Cairngorm estate.
10. See page 146 and Table 7 for definition and further details.

TABLE 2
## Distribution of Landholdings by Size Class: Comparisons between 1970 & 1995

**1970** (1)

| SIZE CLASS | NO. | % NO. | ACRES | % ACRES | CUM. NO. | CUM. % | CUM. ACRES | CUM. % ACRES (2) |
|---|---|---|---|---|---|---|---|---|
| >100,000 | 7 | 0.4% | 1038100 | 5.4% | 7 | 0.4% | 1038100 | 5.4% |
| 75000 - 99 999 | 8 | 0.5% | 720485 | 3.8% | 15 | 0.9% | 1758585 | 9.2% |
| 50 000 - 74 999 | 20 | 1.2% | 1195900 | 6.3% | 35 | 2.0% | 2954485 | 15.5% |
| 40 000 - 49 999 | 19 | 1.1% | 825900 | 4.3% | 54 | 3.1% | 3780385 | 19.8% |
| 30 000 - 39 999 | 25 | 1.5% | 867800 | 4.6% | 79 | 4.6% | 4648185 | 24.4% |
| 20 000 - 29 999 | 43 | 2.5% | 1020400 | 5.4% | 122 | 7.1% | 5668585 | 29.7% |
| 10 000 - 19 999 | 163 | 9.5% | 2293241 | 12.0% | 285 | 16.6% | 7961826 | 41.8% |
| 5 000 - 9 999 | 240 | 14.0% | 1625100 | 8.5% | 525 | 30.5% | 9586926 | 50.3% |
| 4 000 - 4 999 | 98 | 5.7% | 430800 | 2.3% | 623 | 36.2% | 10017726 | 52.5% |
| 3 000 - 3 9999 | 194 | 11.3% | 662100 | 3.5% | 817 | 47.5% | 10679826 | 56.0% |
| 2 000 - 2 999 | 351 | 20.4% | 842100 | 4.4% | 1168 | 67.9% | 11521926 | 60.4% |
| 1 000 - 1 999 | 552 | 32.1% | 745300 | 3.9% | 1720 | 100.0% | 12267226 | 64.3% |
| Total | 1720 | | 12267226 | | | | | |

**1995**

| SIZE CLASS | NO. | % NO. | ACRES | % ACRES | CUM. NO. | CUM. % | CUM. ACRES | CUM. % ACRES (2) |
|---|---|---|---|---|---|---|---|---|
| >100 000 | 6 | 0.4% | 924727 | 4.8% | 6 | 0.4% | 924727 | 4.8% |
| 75000 - 99 999 | 10 | 0.7% | 860643 | 4.5% | 16 | 1.1% | 1785370 | 9.4% |
| 50 000 - 74 999 | 17 | 1.2% | 1025661 | 5.4% | 33 | 2.3% | 2811031 | 14.7% |
| 40 000 - 49 999 | 10 | 0.7% | 457784 | 2.4% | 43 | 3.0% | 3268815 | 17.1% |
| 30 000 - 39 999 | 23 | 1.6% | 811298 | 4.3% | 66 | 4.7% | 4080113 | 21.4% |
| 20 000 - 29 999 | 57 | 4.0% | 1384269 | 7.3% | 123 | 8.7% | 5464382 | 28.7% |
| 10 000 - 19 999 | 145 | 10.3% | 2017173 | 10.6% | 268 | 19.0% | 7481555 | 39.2% |
| 5 000 - 9 999 | 216 | 15.3% | 1509813 | 7.9% | 484 | 34.3% | 8991368 | 47.2% |
| 4 000 - 4 999 | 114 | 8.1% | 495114 | 2.6% | 598 | 42.4% | 9486482 | 49.7% |
| 3 000 - 3 9999 | 118 | 8.4% | 392881 | 2.1% | 716 | 50.7% | 9879363 | 51.8% |
| 2 000 - 2 999 | 230 | 16.3% | 526773 | 2.8% | 946 | 67.0% | 10406136 | 54.6% |
| 1 000 - 1 999 | 465 | 33.0% | 609269 | 3.2% | 1411 | 100.0% | 11015405 | 57.8% |
| Total | 1411 | | 11015405 | | | | | |

(1) See Table 3 for explanation of the source for 1970 figures.
(2) The acreage in this column is calculated as a percentage of Scotland's total land area

TABLE 3
## The Concentration of Land Ownership in Scotland: Comparisons between 1970 & 1995

| % LAND | ACRES | 1970 NO. OWNERS (1) | 1995 NO. OWNERS |
|---|---|---|---|
| 10 | 1906863 | 17 | 18 |
| 20 | 3813726 | 55 | 58 |
| 30 | 5720589 | 125 | 136 |
| 40 | 7627452 | 253 | 283 |
| 50 | 9534316 | 515 | 608 |
| 57.8 | 11021669 | 985 | 1411 |
| 60 | 11441179 | 1136 | |
| 64.3 | 12280198 | 1720 | |

(1) These figures are derived from McEwen's data (2nd edition 1981). There are five important differences however in comparison to other interpretations of his data.
First of all, I have added information on the National Trust for Scotland, the Crown Estate Commissioners and the Church of Scotland to his figures. With the exception of 6500 acres of NTS land at Brodick on Arran, McEwen made no mention of these bodies. Figures have been added to reflect their landholding as of 1970.
Secondly, the lands of the Wills family, which in his Scottish summary McEwen treated as a single ownership (covering 263,000 acres, the second largest landowner in his analysis), have been split to reflect the separate landholdings of different members of the family. A further edit was made to the Earl of Stair's holding in Wigtownshire which was never anywhere near the 110,000 attributed to it by McEwen. I have entered it as 50,000 acres.
Thirdly, it should be pointed out that McEwen's information excluded Orkney and Shetland. This study includes them.
Fourthly, properties in separate counties held by the same owner have been amalgamated. This allows a comparison to be made with the 1995 data.
Finally, some arithmetic errors made in McEwen's tables have been corrected. Taken together, these edits improve the quality of McEwen's data.

TABLE 4
## Analysis of Acreage Covered by Estates Larger Than 5000 Acres in 12 Largest Counties 1995

| | TOTAL ACREAGE | ACRES >5000 1970 | ACRES >5000 1995 | % of County 1970 | % of County 1995 | No. of owners 1970 | No. of owners 1995 | Average acreage 1970 | Average acreage 1995 |
|---|---|---|---|---|---|---|---|---|---|
| Inverness | 2695094 | 1594161 | 1781481 | 59.2% | 66.1% | 81 | 100 | 19681 | 17815 |
| Argyll | 1990522 | 983767 | 884684 | 49.4% | 44.4% | 68 | 59 | 14467 | 14995 |
| Ross & Cromarty | 1977254 | 1610484 | 1568614 | 81.5% | 79.3% | 74 | 76 | 21763 | 20640 |
| Perth | 1595804 | 980566 | 866239 | 61.4% | 54.3% | 63 | 65 | 15565 | 13327 |
| Sutherland | 1297803 | 1094100 | 1043432 | 84.3% | 80.4% | 38 | 53 | 28792 | 19687 |
| Aberdeen | 1261333 | 639300 | 526240 | 50.7% | 41.7% | 44 | 28 | 14530 | 18794 |
| Ayr | 724234 | 127300 | 100479 | 17.6% | 13.9% | 12 | 11 | 10608 | 9134 |
| Dumfries | 688112 | 372893 | 247232 | 54.2% | 35.9% | 24 | 8 | 15537 | 30904 |
| Lanark | 574473 | 114700 | 82569 | 20.0% | 14.4% | 6 | 6 | 19117 | 13762 |
| Kirkcudbright | 574024 | 58700 | 45264 | 10.2% | 7.9% | 8 | 6 | 7338 | 7544 |
| Angus | 559090 | 265400 | 253600 | 47.5% | 45.4% | 18 | 18 | 14744 | 14089 |
| Caithness | 438943 | 304100 | 199970 | 69.3% | 45.6% | 17 | 11 | 17888 | 18179 |
| Total | 14376686 | 8145471 | 7599804 | 56.7% | 52.9% | 453 | 441 | 17981 | 17233 |
| SCOTLAND | 19068631 | 9586926 | 8991368 | 50.3% | 47.2% | 525 | 484 | 18261 | 18577 |

TABLE 5
# Top 100 Non-Public Landowners in Scotland

1970 (1)

| | | | ACRES |
|---|---|---|---|
| 1 | Buccleuch Estates Ltd | Buccleuch Estates | 272900 |
| 2 | Earl of Seafield | Seafield Estates | 185200 |
| 3 | Duke of Atholl | Atholl Estates | 130000 |
| 4 | Countess of Sutherland | Sutherland Estates | 123500 |
| 5 | Duke of Westminster | Westminster Estates | 112700 |
| 6 | British Aluminium Ltd. | British Aluminium Estates | 109500 |
| 7 | Captain A.A.C. Farquharson | Invercauld & Torloisk | 104300 |
| 8 | Sir Donald Cameron of Locheil | Locheil Estates | 97600 |
| 9 | Duke of Roxburghe | Roxburghe Estates | 95500 |
| 10 | Crown Estate Commissioners | Crown Estates | 94015 |
| 11 | E.H. Vestey | Vestey Estates | 93100 |
| 12 | South Uist Estates Ltd. | South Uist Estates | 92200 |
| 13 | Viscount Cowdray | Cowdray Estates | 87200 |
| 14 | National Trust for Scotland | Various properties | 84870 |
| 15 | Lord Lovat | Lovat Estates | 76000 |
| 16 | Morrison family | Islay Estates | 74400 |
| 17 | Duke of Argyll | Argyll Estates | 73400 |
| 18 | Colonel W.H. Whitbread | Letterewe | 73100 |
| 19 | A.J. MacDonald-Buchanan | Strathconon | 71100 |
| 20 | Earl of Ancaster | Drummond Estates | 65000 |
| 21 | Stornoway Trust | Stornoway Trust Estate | 64300 |
| 22 | Sir Hereward Wake | Ammhuinnsuidhe | 62500 |
| 23 | Michael Berry | Altnaharra | 62300 |
| 24 | Ross Estates Ltd. | Balnagowan | 61100 |
| 25 | Major T.G. Moncreiff | Strathmore Estates | 60000 |
| 26 | Sir Edward Wills | Meggernie | 57900 |
| 27 | Sir H.P. MacKenzie | Gairloch & Conon Estates | 57600 |
| 28 | Lord Home | Douglas and Angus | 53500 |
| 29 | Lord Dulverton | Glenfeshie & Fassifern | 52700 |
| 30 | Sinclair Family Trust | Ulbster Estates | 52600 |
| 31 | Galson Estates Ltd. | Galton Lodge | 52200 |
| 32 | Harlay & Jones (Investors) Ltd. | Mar Lodge | 51200 |
| 33 | Robert Fleming | Blackmount | 51000 |
| 34 | Earl of Granville | North Uist Estates | 50000 |
| 35 | Earl of Stair | Stair Estates | 50000 |
| 36 | Duke of Portland | Langwell | 48000 |
| 37 | Sir E.W. Gladstone | Fasque | 47700 |
| 38 | Uig Crofters Ltd. | Uig Crofters Estate | 46300 |
| 39 | Major John & Captain A. Wills | Applecross | 45700 |
| 40 | Earl of Moray | Moray Estates | 45600 |
| 41 | Brigadier Colvin | Camusericht | 45000 |
| 42 | Benmore Estates Ltd. | Benmore | 44100 |
| 43 | Lord Thorneycroft | Eishkin | 43900 |
| 44 | Earl of Dalhousie | Dalhousie Estates | 43800 |
| 45 | Sir Oliver Crosswaithe-Eyre | Knoydart | 43000 |
| 46 | Sir W. Pennington-Ramsden | Ardverikie | 42900 |
| 47 | Sir Ivar Colquhoun of Luss | Luss Estates | 42700 |
| 48 | Barvas Estates Ltd. | Barvas Estates | 41900 |
| 49 | Clan Donald Lands Trust | Sleat Estates | 41700 |
| 50 | Earl of Mansfield | Scone | 41300 |

1995

| | | | ACRES |
|---|---|---|---|
| 1 | Buccleuch Estates Ltd | Buccleuch Estates | 261600 |
| 2 | National Trust for Scotland | Various properties | 176827 |
| 3 | S. Troughton & Blair Trust | Atholl Estates | 148000 |
| 4 | Invercauld & Torloisk Trusts | Invercauld & Torloisk | 120500 |
| 5 | Alcan Highland Estates Ltd. | Mamore & Glenshero | 116800 |
| 6 | Earl of Seafield | Seafield Estates | 101000 |
| 7 | Duke of Westminster | Westminster Estates | 95100 |
| 8 | Crown Estate Commissioners | Crown Estates | 94015 |
| 9 | South Uist Estates Ltd. | South Uist & Islands | 92000 |
| 10 | Robert Fleming & Trusts | Blackmount and others | 88900 |
| 11 | RSPB | Various properties | 87489 |
| 12 | Glencanisp Deer Forest Trust | Assynt & Benmore | 86300 |
| 13 | Countess of Sutherland | Sutherland Estates | 83239 |
| 14 | Clyde Properties & UBMC BV | Letterewe | 81000 |
| 15 | Viscount Cowdray & Trusts | Dunecht Estates | 76600 |
| 16 | Lochiel Estates | Achnacarry | 76000 |
| 17 | Andras Ltd. | Braulen & Glenavon | 70800 |
| 18 | Stornoway Trust | Stornoway Trust Estate | 69400 |
| 19 | Broadland Properties | Conaglen & others | 68361 |
| 20 | Duke of Roxburghe | Roxburghe Estates | 65600 |
| 21 | Baroness Willoughby de Eresby | Drummond Estates | 63200 |
| 22 | Smech Properties Ltd. | Killilan & others | 63140 |
| 23 | North Uist Estate Trust 1990 | North Uist & Islands | 62200 |
| 24 | Applecross Estate Trust | Applecross | 62000 |
| 25 | Trustees of 10th Duke of Argyll | Argyll Estates | 60800 |
| 26 | Kirkbi Estates Ltd. | Strathconon | 60000 |
| 27 | John A. Mackenzie | Gairloch & Conon Estates | 56900 |
| 28 | Cawdor Trusts | Cawdor Estates | 56800 |
| 29 | Galson Estates Ltd. | Galson Lodge Estate | 56300 |
| 30 | H.M. the Queen | Balmoral Estates | 55270 |
| 31 | Bute Estate Ltd. | Bute Estates | 53990 |
| 32 | North Harris Estate Ltd. | Amhuinnsuidhe | 50900 |
| 33 | Luss Estates Company | Luss Estate | 50000 |
| 34 | Islay Estates Company | Islay Estate | 49500 |
| 35 | Joseph & Lisbet Koerner | Corrour | 48210 |
| 36 | Burton Property Trust | Dochfour & Glenshiel | 48000 |
| 37 | C.A. Gladstone Property | Glendye & Fasque | 47700 |
| 38 | Dalhousie 1964/1971 Trust | Dalhousie Estates | 47200 |
| 39 | Uig & Hamanavay Estate Ltd. | Uig & Hamnaway | 45000 |
| 40 | Wellbeck Estates Company Ltd. | Langwell & Braemore | 45000 |
| 41 | Earl of Stair | Stair Estates | 43674 |
| 42 | Will Woodlands | Glen Feshie | 42000 |
| 43 | Golden Lane Securities Ltd. | Glenfiddich & Cabrach | 41500 |
| 44 | Richard P Kershaw | Soval | 39000 |
| 45 | Lady P. Ogilvie Grant Nicholson | Revack & Dorbrack | 38700 |
| 46 | Coignafearn Estate Co. Ltd. | Coignafearn | 38000 |
| 47 | Ardverikie Estate Ltd. | Ardverikie | 37800 |
| 48 | ON MARKET | Dunbeath & Glutt | 37400 |
| 49 | Earl of Airlie & Lord Ogilvie | Airlie Estates | 37300 |
| 50 | Dickinson Trust | Strathvaich | 37030 |

| | | | |
|---|---|---|---|
| 51 | Lady Wyfold | Glenkinglass | 41200 |
| 52 | Jura Ltd. (Astor) | Tarbert | 41100 |
| 53 | R.J. Tyser | Gordonbush | 40000 |
| 54 | J.E. Elliot | Dunfelling Estates | 40000 |
| 55 | W. Gordon | Lude & Barrisdale | 38400 |
| 56 | Earl of Cawdor | Cawdor Estates | 38300 |
| 57 | Lord Burton | Dochfour Estates | 38300 |
| 58 | Liberton Properties Ltd. | Bighouse | 38300 |
| 59 | V.G. Balan | Forsinard | 37800 |
| 60 | M.H., F.H. & D.H. Wills | Torran Estate | 37400 |
| 61 | Earl of Wemyss & March | Wemyss Estates | 36700 |
| 62 | I. MacPherson | Attadale | 35700 |
| 63 | Major Buchanan-Jardine | Castlemilk Estates | 35700 |
| 64 | Benmore Estates Ltd. | Benmore | 35200 |
| 65 | J. MacLeod of MacLeod | MacLeod Estates | 34500 |
| 66 | Mrs E.M. Janson | Dalnessie | 34500 |
| 67 | R.F.T. Foljambe | Hope and Melness | 34500 |
| 68 | H.M. the Queen | Balmoral Estates | 34400 |
| 69 | Ardtornish Estate Ltd. | Ardtornish | 34400 |
| 70 | David S. Wills | Glen Avon | 33900 |
| 71 | M.S.M. Threipland | Wass Dale, Toftingall | 33800 |
| 72 | D. Steuart Fothringham | Fothringham Estates | 33800 |
| 73 | A.B.L. Munro-Ferguson | Novar Estates | 33700 |
| 74 | A.S., A.F. & M.M. Roger | Dundonnell | 32700 |
| 75 | E.J.M. Douglas | Killilan | 31500 |
| 76 | J.F. Robinson | Morsgail | 31400 |
| 77 | Earl of Airrlie | Airlie Estates | 31400 |
| 78 | J.M. Guthrie | Conaglen | 31000 |
| 79 | Noble family | Ardkinglass | 30500 |
| 80 | Lady Jean Fforde | Arran Estates | 29000 |
| 81 | Lochluichart Estate Co. | Kinlochluichart | 28700 |
| 82 | Eagle Star Insurance Co. Ltd. | Eagle Star Estates | 28400 |
| 83 | H. & H. Blythe | Dunbeath | 27500 |
| 84 | Lady Boscawen | Dougarie | 27000 |
| 85 | Captain Sandison | Glentromie | 27000 |
| 86 | The late Lord Glentanar | Glen Tanar | 26900 |
| 87 | E.E. Bonnington Wood | Sallachy | 26700 |
| 88 | Carloway Estates Ltd. | Carloway | 26600 |
| 89 | Trustees of R. Midwood | Syre | 25400 |
| 90 | Marquess of Bute | Bute Estates | 25100 |
| 91 | Earl of Rosebery | Dalmeny Estates | 24500 |
| 92 | Fyvie Settlement Trust | Fyvie | 24400 |
| 93 | Lady McCorquodale | Gruinard | 24300 |
| 94 | R.M. Abel-Smith | Cambusmore & Laudale | 24300 |
| 95 | Rattray Discretionary Trust | Haddo-Rattray | 24200 |
| 96 | Major I.M. Scobie | Rhiddoroch | 24200 |
| 97 | Auchentoul Estates Co. | Auchentoul | 24100 |
| 98 | Sir Alan Wigan | Borrobol | 23700 |
| 99 | Mrs M. Garton | Merkland | 23200 |
| 100 | Mr & Mrs Balfour | Balbirnie & Scourie | 23100 |
| Total | | | 5186485 |

| | | | |
|---|---|---|---|
| 51 | Viscount Thurso of Ulbster | Dalnawillan & Thurso | 36800 |
| 52 | Gray & Adams Ltd. | Altnaharra | 36603 |
| 53 | Beverley Jane Malim | Meggernie & Lochs | 36500 |
| 54 | Patrick C.G. Wilson | Loch Rosque and others | 35350 |
| 55 | Earl of Wemyss & March | Wemyss Estates | 35100 |
| 56 | The John Muir Trust | Various properties | 35015 |
| 57 | Barvas Estates Ltd. | Barvas | 34600 |
| 58 | Skelpick Partnership | Skelpick & Rhifail | 34500 |
| 59 | Ardtornish Estate Co. Ltd. | Ardtornish | 34100 |
| 60 | Earl of Mansfield | Scone & Logiealmond | 33800 |
| 61 | Alan S.A.F. & N.M. Roger | Dundonnell | 33600 |
| 62 | Douglas & Angus Estates | Douglas & the Hirsel | 33000 |
| 63 | David R. Knowles & others | Loch a Choire | 32500 |
| 64 | Ewen A. Macpherson | Attadale | 32000 |
| 65 | J.N. Oppenehim Partnership | Eishken Estate | 32000 |
| 66 | John Macleod of Macleod | Dunvegan & Glen Brittle | 30600 |
| 67 | Greentop Lands & Estates Ltd. | Various Properties | 29643 |
| 68 | Moray Estates Development Co. | Moray Estates | 29400 |
| 69 | Glentanar Trusts | Glen Tanar | 29150 |
| 70 | Andrew D. Gordon | Glenquoich & Lude | 29100 |
| 71 | Hon. E. Maurice W. Robson | Inverbroom & Erchless | 29000 |
| 72 | Scottish Wildlife Trust | Various properties | 28620 |
| 73 | Fountain International Ltd. | Bighouse | 28500 |
| 74 | R.M.M. Maclean of Ardgour | Ardgour | 27900 |
| 75 | Charles R. Connell & Co. Ltd. | Colquhaalzie & Garragie | 27800 |
| 76 | Lochluichart Estate Co. | Kinlochluichart | 27400 |
| 77 | H.H. Roesner Land & Forestry | Lanfine & Sallachy | 27200 |
| 78 | Leon G. Litchfield | Bowland & Tulchan | 26950 |
| 79 | Parc Crofters Ltd. | Parc | 26800 |
| 80 | Mrs Macaire | Alladale & Deanich | 26600 |
| 81 | John B. Cameron | Glen Lochay & Finglas | 26400 |
| 82 | Rodney M. Hitchcock | Bays of Harris | 26400 |
| 83 | Agro Invest Overseas Ltd. | Ben Alder & Dalwhinnie | 26000 |
| 84 | Electricity Supply Nominees | Various properties | 25950 |
| 85 | Yattendon Estates Ltd. | Syre & Rhifail | 25853 |
| 86 | I. & H. Brown | Glen Kingie & Corrielair | 25450 |
| 87 | Jean Balfour | Scourie & Balbirnie | 25321 |
| 88 | Messrs. Elliot | Balnakeil & Blackhaugh | 25150 |
| 89 | Capt. A.A.A.D.M. Ramsay | Mar | 25143 |
| 90 | Stephen Gibbs | Dougarie | 24908 |
| 91 | Viscount Leverhulme | Badanloch | 24700 |
| 92 | Sir William J. Lithgow | Inver & Ormsary | 24700 |
| 93 | J.W. Buchanan-Jardine's Trust | Castlemilk Estates | 24500 |
| 94 | Rothiemurchus Estate Trust | Rothiemurchus | 24000 |
| 95 | Count Adam W.J. Knuth | Ben Loyal | 24000 |
| 96 | Edward Humphrey | Dinnet & Wester Coull | 23800 |
| 97 | Eagle Star Insurance Co. Ltd. | Various properties | 23518 |
| 98 | D.K.D. & G.M.L. Buckle | Braeroy | 23500 |
| 99 | Eira Drysdale | Drumochter & Ralia | 23400 |
| 100 | D.C. Fleming & L.F. Schuster | Glenkinglass | 23200 |
| | | | 4970069 |

See Table 3 for explanation of the source for 1970 figures.

TABLE 6
# Top 20 Aristocratic Landowners in Scotland 1995

| OWNER | ACRES |
|---|---|
| Duke of Buccleuch & Queensberry | 261600 |
| Capt. A.A.C. Farquharson of Invercauld | 120500 |
| Earl of Seafield | 101000 |
| Duke of Westminster | 95100 |
| Crown Estate Commissioners | 94015 |
| Countess of Sutherland | 83239 |
| Viscount Cowdray | 76600 |
| Sir Donald Cameron of Locheil | 76000 |
| Duke of Roxburghe | 65600 |
| Baroness Willoughby de Eresby | 63200 |
| Duke of Argyll | 60800 |
| John A. Mackenzie of Gairloch | 56900 |
| Earl of Cawdor | 56800 |
| H.M. the Queen | 55270 |
| Marquess of Bute | 53990 |
| Sir Ivar Colquhoun of Luss | 50000 |
| Lord Burton | 48000 |
| Earl of Dalhousie | 47200 |
| Lady Anne Bentinck | 45000 |
| Earl of Stair | 43674 |
| TOTAL | 1554488 |
| Total acreage > 5000 acres owned by aristocracy | 2554399 |
| % of Scotland | 13.4% |
| % of estates > 5000 acres | 28.4% |

TABLE 7
# Principal Not For Profit Landowners in Scotland

| OWNER | PROPERTY | ACRES |
|---|---|---|
| National Trust for Scotland | Various properties | 176827 |
| Royal Society for the Protection of Birds | Various properties | 87489 |
| Stornoway Trust | Parish of Stornoway | 69400 |
| The John Muir Trust | Sandwood, Torrin, Strathaird etc. | 35015 |
| Scottish Wildlife Trust | Various properties | 28620 |
| Assynt Crofters Trust Ltd. | North Assynt Estate | 21132 |
| The Church of Scotland General Trustees | Glebes | 14841 |
| Melness Crofter Estate Ltd. | Melness | 10700 |
| The Woodland Trust | Various properties | 5000 |
| Borve and Annishader Township Ltd. | Borve and Annishader | 4500 |
| Co-operative Wholesale Society | Various properties | 2240 |
| TOTAL | | 455764 |
| % of Scotland | | 2.4% |

TABLE 8
## Extent of Forestry Commission Estate in Scotland 1970–1995

| YEAR | TOTAL ESTATE (ACRES) | ANNUAL CHANGE |
|---|---|---|
| 1970 | 1783800 | |
| 1971 | 1843600 | + 59800 |
| 1972 | 1849049 | + 5449 |
| 1973 | 1839907 | - 9142 |
| 1974 | 1829281 | - 10626 |
| 1975 | 1845096 | + 15815 |
| 1976 | 1895504 | + 50408 |
| 1977 | 1940723 | + 45219 |
| 1978 | 1949619 | + 8896 |
| 1979 | 1957279 | + 7660 |
| 1980 | 1976059 | + 18780 |
| 1981 | 1976928 | + 869 |
| 1982 | 1970650 | - 6278 |
| 1983 | 1960837 | - 9813 |
| 1984 | 1877362 | - 83475 |
| 1985 | 1833465 | - 43897 |
| 1986 | 1809152 | - 24313 |
| 1987 | 1801895 | - 7257 |
| 1988 | 1798072 | - 3823 |
| 1989 | 1792898 | - 5174 |
| 1990 | 1787761 | - 5137 |
| 1991 | 1780274 | - 7487 |
| 1992 | 1775218 | - 5056 |
| 1993 | 1751346 | - 23872 |
| 1994 | 1717896 | - 33450 |
| 1995 | 1699949 | - 17947 |

Source: Forestry Commission Annual Reports.
The figures include land leased from other owners and land on the market in 1995.
See Table 1 for explanation.

## TABLE 9
## The 25 Largest Overseas Landowners in Scotland 1995

| OWNER | COUNTRY OF ORIGIN | PROPERTY | ACRES |
|---|---|---|---|
| Alcan Highland Estates Ltd | Canada | Mamore and Glenshero | 116800 |
| Clyde Properties NV & Utrechtse Beheer Maatschappij Catharijne BV | Netherlands | Letterewe & Heights of Kinlochewe | 81000 |
| Andras Ltd. | Malaysia | Braulen & Glenavon | 70800 |
| Smech Properties Ltd. | Dubai, UAE | Killilan, Inverinate, West Benula & Glomach | 63140 |
| Kirkbi Estates Ltd. | Denmark | Strathconon | 60000 |
| Joseph & Lisbet Koerner | USA | Corrour | 48210 |
| Coignafearn Estate Company Ltd. | Liechenstein & Belgium | Coignafearn | 38000 |
| Stanton Avery | USA | Dunbeath & Glutt | 37400 |
| Greentop Lands & Estates Ltd. & Mrs Dorte Aamann-Christensen | Denmark & Liechtenstein | Various Properties | 29643 |
| H.H. Roesner Land & Forestry Management (Scotland) Ltd. | Germany | Lanfine & Sallachy & Creanich | 27200 |
| Agro Invest Overseas Ltd. & Hanbury family | Switzerland | Ben Alder & Dalwhinnie | 26000 |
| Count Adam W.J. Knuth | Denmark | Ben Loyal | 24000 |
| Beleggingsmaatschappij Festeyn BV | Netherlands | Inverlael & Foich | 23600 |
| Rodolphe R.B. & Miss Diane M. de Spoelbergh | Belgium | Altnafeadh (Black Corries) | 21000 |
| Blackford Farms Ltd. | Dubai, UAE | Blackford Farms | 20000 |
| Balmac Forest Ltd. | Unknown | Balmacaan | 19300 |
| Gaick Estate Ltd. | Switzerland | Gaick | 18500 |
| Invermearan Estates Ltd. | Germany | Invermearan | 16500 |
| Bocardo Societe Anonyme & Ross Estates | Egypt & Liechtenstein | Duchally & Balnagown | 14400 |
| Kilchoan Estate Ltd. | Belgium | Kilchoan | 12800 |
| Cinco Ltd., Forrest Estate Ltd. & Fred Olsen Ltd. | Norway | Forrest Estate & Dalreoch | 12786 |
| Tulchan of Glenisla Forest Ltd. | Germany | Tulchan Estate | 12500 |
| Wefri A/S & Lurga Ltd. | Denmark | Laudale | 12500 |
| Establissement Entraide et Solidaritie | Belgium | Glenure & Glencreran | 12300 |
| Avion Holdings SPA | Italy | Glen Banchor & Strone | 12200 |
| Total | | | 830579 |
| Total overseas ownership > 5000 acres in Scotland | | | 1036732 |
| Total overseas ownership > 1000 acres in Scotland | | | 1104223 |
| Overseas ownership > 5000 acres as % of estates > 5000 acres | | | 11.5% |
| Overseas ownership > 1000 acres as % of estates > 1000 acres | | | 10.0% |
| Overseas ownership > 1000 acres as % of Scotland | | | 5.8% |

## TABLE 10
## 10 Top Investment Landowners in Scotland 1995

| OWNER | PROPERTY | ACRES |
|---|---|---|
| Crown Estate Commissioners | Various properties | 94015 |
| Greentop Lands and Estates Ltd. | Various properties | 29643 |
| Electricity Supply Nominees | Various properties | 25200 |
| Eagle Star Insurance Company Ltd. | Various properties | 25150 |
| Midland Bank Pension Trust Ltd. | Various properties | 14695 |
| Commercial Union Assurance Company Ltd. | Panmure Estate | 13600 |
| Prudential Assurance Company Ltd. | Southesk & Rossie School | 8000 |
| Scottish Amicable Life Assurance Society | Various properties | 6591 |
| British Insulated Callendar Cables | Various forests | 6142 |
| Refuge Farms Ltd. | Various properties | 5789 |
| CERN (European Organisation for Nuclear Research) | Various forests | 5461 |
| TOTAL | | 234286 |
| % of Scotland | | 1.2% |

## TABLE 11
## Company and Trust Ownership (Estates larger than 5000 acres)

| OWNER STATUS | ACRES | NUMBER | ACREAGE % OF ESTATES >5000 ACRES | ACREAGE % OF SCOTLAND |
|---|---|---|---|---|
| Companies | 2796247 | 127 | 31.1% | 14.7% |
| Trusts | 2372733 | 90 | 26.4% | 12.4% |

## TABLE 12
## Scottish Landowners' Federation Membership 1975

| ACRE CLASS | 0-1233 | 1234-2468 | 2469-12353 | 12354-24708 | 24709+ | TOTAL |
|---|---|---|---|---|---|---|
| Total acres | 1135714 | 450205 | 2019892 | 1242328 | 2234670 | 7082809 |
| No. of members | 2957 | 262 | 374 | 71 | 48 | 3712 |
| Mean acreage | 384 | 1718 | 5401 | 17498 | 46556 | 1908 |
| % of members | 79.7% | 7.1% | 10.1% | 1.9% | 1.3% | 100.0% |
| % of acreage | 16.0% | 6.4% | 28.5% | 17.5% | 31.6% | 100.0% |

Source: Royal Institution of Chartered Surveyors, 1977. The Agricultural Resources of the United Kingdom. The Future of Land Ownership and Occupancy. RICS.

TABLE 13
# Scottish Landowners' Federation Membership 1994

**OPTION 1**

| ACRE CLASS | 0-499 | 500+ | TOTAL |
|---|---|---|---|
| Total acres | 853248 | 6146752 | 7000000 |
| No. of members | 2222 | 1315 | 3537 |
| Mean acreage | 384 | 4674 | 1979 |
| % of members | 62.8% | 37.2% | 100.0% |
| % of acreage | 12.2% | 87.8% | 100.0% |

**OPTION 2**

| | 0-499 | 500+ | TOTAL |
|---|---|---|---|
| Total acres | 734976 | 6265024 | 7000000 |
| No. of members | 1914 | 1315 | 3229 |
| Mean acreage | 384 | 4764 | 2168 |
| % of members | 59.3% | 40.7% | 100.0% |
| % of acreage | 10.5% | 89.5% | 100.0% |

**OPTION 3**

| | 0-499 | 500+ | TOTAL |
|---|---|---|---|
| Total acres | 617088 | 6382912 | 7000000 |
| No. of members | 1607 | 1315 | 2922 |
| Mean acreage | 384 | 4854 | 2396 |
| % of members | 55.0% | 45.0% | 100.0% |
| % of acreage | 8.8% | 91.2% | 100.0% |

Note: Analysis of 1994 landowning membership depends on assumptions about how many Associate members own land (see text for explanation).

Option 1 assumes that all do.

Option 2 asumes that 50% do.

Option 3 assumes that none do.

Mean acreage of holdings < 500 acres based on mean of 1975 (See Table 12).

TABLE 14
## Scottish Landowners' Federation membership by County 1994

| COUNTY | NO. | % | CUMULATIVE % |
|---|---|---|---|
| Aberdeen | 331 | 11.3% | 11.3% |
| Ayr | 240 | 8.2% | 19.5% |
| Perth | 238 | 8.1% | 27.6% |
| ENGLAND | 196 | 6.7% | 34.3% |
| Angus | 162 | 5.5% | 39.9% |
| Dumfries | 146 | 5.0% | 44.9% |
| Fife | 144 | 4.9% | 49.8% |
| Lanark | 125 | 4.3% | 54.0% |
| Roxburgh | 125 | 4.3% | 58.3% |
| Inverness | 117 | 4.0% | 62.3% |
| Kirkcudbright | 89 | 3.0% | 65.4% |
| Argyll | 88 | 3.0% | 68.4% |
| Berwick | 86 | 2.9% | 71.3% |
| Ross & Cromarty | 81 | 2.8% | 74.1% |
| Wigtown | 66 | 2.3% | 76.3% |
| Banff | 63 | 2.2% | 78.5% |
| East Lothian | 63 | 2.2% | 80.6% |
| Moray | 59 | 2.0% | 82.6% |
| Kincardine | 56 | 1.9% | 84.6% |
| Midlothian | 55 | 1.9% | 86.4% |
| Stirling | 47 | 1.6% | 88.0% |
| Renfrew | 45 | 1.5% | 89.6% |
| Selkirk | 33 | 1.1% | 90.7% |
| Edinburgh | 32 | 1.1% | 91.8% |
| West Lothian | 30 | 1.0% | 92.8% |
| Peebles | 28 | 1.0% | 93.8% |
| Sutherland | 28 | 1.0% | 94.7% |
| Caithness | 26 | 0.9% | 95.6% |
| Kinross | 22 | 0.8% | 96.4% |
| Glasgow | 21 | 0.7% | 97.1% |
| Dunbarton | 16 | 0.5% | 97.6% |
| Clackmannan | 15 | 0.5% | 98.2% |
| Nairn | 15 | 0.5% | 98.7% |
| Orkney | 15 | 0.5% | 99.2% |
| OUTWITH SCOTLAND | 14 | 0.5% | 99.7% |
| Bute | 7 | 0.2% | 99.9% |
| Shetland | 3 | 0.1% | 100.0% |
| TOTAL | 2927 | | |

Source:   Scottish Landowners' Federation membership list 1994. Member origin is by home address.

TABLE 15
# THE 30 WEALTHIEST LANDOWNERS IN SCOTLAND 1996

| OWNER | PROPERTY | SOURCE OF WEALTH | ACRES | WEALTH (£MILL) |
|---|---|---|---|---|
| Duke of Westminster | Westminster Estates | Land | 95100 | 1650 |
| Lisbet Koerner (1) | Corrour | Food packaging | 48210 | 1000 |
| Bruno Schroder | Dunlossit | Banking | 16500 | 950 |
| Edmund Vestey | Assynt & Benmore | Food, shipping & finance | 86300 | 650 |
| Robert Fleming | Blackmount & Dalness | Banking | 88900 | 560 |
| Earl Cadogan | Snaigow | Land | 4000 | 450 |
| H.M. the Queen | Balmoral and Delnadamph | Inheritance | 55270 | 450 |
| Viscount Cowdray | Cowdray Estates | Media | 76600 | 400 |
| Simon & Henry Keswick | Glenkiln & Hunthill | Commerce | 22481 | 380 |
| Cayzer family | Kinpurnie and others | Caledonia Investments | 9500 | 325 |
| Cameron Mackintosh | North Morar | Entertainment | 12000 | 250 |
| Duke of Northumberland | Burncastle | Land and art | 9000 | 250 |
| Ann Gloag | Beaufort Castle | Buses | 128 | 220 |
| Bulmer family | Ammhunsuidhe | Cider | 50900 | 170 |
| John Menzies | Kames | Newsagent | 1390 | 150 |
| Sir Jack Hayward | Dunmaglass | Finance - Grand Bahamas | 13000 | 140 |
| Duke of Sutherland | Mertoun | Land and art | 4750 | 140 |
| Marquess of Bute | Bute Estates | Land | 53990 | 130 |
| Phil Collins | Pennyghael | Pop music | 7900 | 115 |
| Lord Laing and family | Land in Moray and Argyll | Food manufacturing | 27100 | 81 |
| Lady Anne Cavendish-Bentinck | Langwell & Braemore | Land | 45000 | 80 |
| Salvesen family | Various properties | Food distribution | 13295 | 75 |
| J. Crosthwaite-Eyre | Camusrory | Publishing | 8129 | 70 |
| Earl of Rosebery | Dalmeny Estates | Land | 22400 | 70 |
| Duke of Roxburghe | Roxburghe Estates | Land | 65600 | 70 |
| Lord Robert Iliffe | Syre & Rhifail | Marinas and property | 25853 | 69 |
| Leon Litchfield | Tulchan and Bowland | Plastics | 26950 | 68 |
| Christopher Moran | Glenfiddich and Cabrach | Finance and property | 41500 | 65 |
| Earl of Inchcape | Glenapp & Dryfehead | Trade & finance | 14085 | 44 |
| Duke of Buccleuch | Buccleuch Estates | Land and art | 261600 | 40 |

TOTAL 1207431

TOTAL £ 9112

Source: Sunday Times Britain's Richest 500, 1996.
(1) Lisbet Koerner is the daughter of Hans Rausing who together with his brother Gad are estimated to be worth £4000 million. Quite how much of this will be inherited by Lisbet is uncertain. A notional figure of £1000 million is used.

# Chapter 8

# Agriculture

RURAL SOCIETY HAS traditionally been underpinned by the agricultural economy. Today, however, with agriculture providing less than 2% of Scotland's gross domestic output and a little over 2% of employment, it is no longer in the powerful position it once was. Agricultural land use covers around 14 million acres (73%) of Scotland, however, and is therefore a critical influence on how land is managed. The occupation and landholding pattern within it is also crucial in determining the social and economic structure of the countryside.

The ownership structure of agricultural holdings across Scotland is both a response to the geography and productivity of land and to the historical development of landownership. Specific trends in ownership of farms are outwith the scope of this book but the factors which might determine these trends are not. As agriculture has intensified and outputs have increased, labour has been shed and structural changes have taken place in the rural economy and patterns of settlement.

The changes are influenced by two important factors, namely agricultural support policy and land tenure. The dominant policy framework for Scottish agriculture is the Common Agricultural Policy or CAP. Set up under Article 39 of the Treaty of Rome, the CAP has transformed European agriculture. It is also expensive, accounting for around 50% of EU spending. The CAP has been remarkably successful in its objective of boosting food supplies but spectacularly unsuccessful in terms of its contribution to wider rural development. Since support is tied to production levels, farmers on better ground with more flexibility and fewer constraints have benefited most. Those in poorer areas, further from markets, have gained least.

In 1993, a specialised sheep farm in the Less Favoured Area which covers most of Scotland was in receipt of £23,000 in agricultural subsidy whilst having an income of £11,345. Such farms have lost out in a more important respect also. Being so critically dependent on subsidy, they enjoy virtually no latitude for diversifying. In the UK as a whole it has been estimated that 80% of agricultural support is received by 20% of farmers. In Scotland, the county receiving the highest level of support per head is Berwickshire, hardly an area in desperate need of public subsidy.

The legacy of the CAP is therefore a small and very wealthy proportion of landowners enjoying high levels of income and land value which have been dramatically enhanced by the CAP regime. At the other end of the scale is the farmer on poorer ground totally dependent on a subsidy regime and with little choice over future management. Increasingly, farmers in the hills and uplands are leaving the industry and selling their farms. Incoming owners are typically forestry investors, wealthy individuals seeking to create a sporting estate, or neighbouring farmers, expanding their holdings to maintain the viability of their farming business.

Landownership is thus heavily influenced both through the increasing wealth accruing in income and land values to large farmers and landowners and through the instability in the land market at the other end of the scale. Other countries, as will be outlined later, have typically taken a very different approach to their agricultural policy. They have generally sought to regulate land markets to retain viable rural communities, to ensure a reasonably equitable distribution of available agricultural support, to prevent the conversion of agricultural land to other uses (in particular private recreation and 'hobby farming') and to facilitate the entry of newcomers to agriculture through maintaining low land values and equitable patterns of landownership.

There is now an active and widespread debate taking place almost daily over the future of agricultural policy. What is clear is that the substantial financial support provided by the EU in the form of subsidies is unsustainable in the medium to long term. The expansion of the EU to include the countries of Eastern Europe will ensure that this is so. Agricultural support will be reduced and the challenge is to determine how best to target what remains. Critical also is to question whether the future of the countryside is best served by a free market in land whereby fairly crude economic signals emanating from remote political institutions determine investment levels, settlement patterns, social structure and cultural survival through the impact they have on landownership.

One form of land tenure which is of particular relevance to agriculture is tenant farming which accounts for around 35% of Scottish farms. There has been a vigorous and at times acrimonious debate underway for some time as to the reform of agricultural tenancy laws. The Agricultural Tenancies Act 1995 radically altered the law in England and Wales by allowing new tenancy arrangements to be entered under the principle of freedom of contract. Up until this time, agricultural tenancies were difficult to create outwith the protective framework of the Agricultural Holdings Act which provides security of tenure for farming tenants.

In Scotland, farmers have resisted such reforms even though existing tenancies would not be affected. In a situation where landowners have admitted to owning 'surplus land' and there is an unsatisfied demand from young farmers wishing to start out in farming, their reluctance may appear strange. At heart, however, it is a political struggle which engages tenant farmers keen to retain the protection which the law provides them as tenants, and landowners who wish more flexibility in letting arrangements.

The possible resolution of this dilemma goes to the heart of the issues this book is concerned with, namely the appropriate framework within which private property rights should be exercised. As will be argued later, if a landowner is sitting on surplus land and there is a demand for that land, important questions should be asked about the land tenure laws. Should they be relaxed to favour the further consolidation of private property rights, with the attendant benefits which flow by way of rents and capital values from public subsidies to the existing landowner? Or should they be reformed to effect the redistribution of 'surplus' land to those with the desire, need, ability and enthusiasm to make use of it?

Experience in countries such as Denmark shows how real land reform can produce results which provide more people with a stake in the land, which ensure the availability of land at modest prices to newcomers and which ensure that Danish agriculture remains amongst the most competitive in the world. Denmark turned its back on the landowner-tenant model in the late 18th century and has seen no reason to return to it.

# Chapter 9

# The Sporting Estate

IN THE SCOTTISH Highlands, large areas of land from the grouse moors of the eastern Highlands to the deerstalking estates of the western and northern Highlands are currently managed for shooting and stalking. They have attracted particular attention in the landownership debate and have frequently been the subject of some controversy.

There is a long tradition of hunting in Scotland, going back to the very first arrivals of people in the area after the ice retreated. As the Scottish nation developed, hunting was widely enjoyed both as an everyday activity in pursuit of food and as a recreational activity by the nobility. Many of the forest laws that were enacted in mediaeval times were designed to protect and conserve game species. Prior to the 17th century, however, there was no relationship between game and landownership. Everyone was free to hunt game and to claim the fruits of their endeavours. Subsequently, however, and culminating in an Act of 1621, game was converted into an exclusive right of property, not by claiming ownership of wild animals which are still legally 'res nullis' or belonging to no-one, but by effectively excluding all but landowners from the right to kill them. This remains the legal position today. Landowners have the rights to game not by any specific rights to the quarry but through the power to prevent anyone else from hunting it. Rights to game have thus become a valuable incident of landownership and as a result cannot be separated from the land. Salmon, being part of the regalia majora, or Crown rights, are a real exception as these can be held independently of the land.

Not only are exclusive rights to game of relatively recent origin but the exclusive dedication of large areas of ground to their pursuit is even more recent. Whilst the earliest Scottish monarchs enjoyed the pursuit of game in royal hunting forests, many other people used the same areas of ground for farming. By 1811, however, there were only six or seven such areas left in the Highlands. The modern sporting estate did not exist. By 1873, however, the number had risen to 79. With increasing wealth in the south and the Victorian passion for all things Highland, the end of the 19th century saw a rapid increase in the number of deer forests which were rented out to wealthy aristocrats and industrialists. By the end of the 19th century, there were between 130 and 150 deer forests covering 2.5 million acres. By 1906, the total area had climbed to an all-time peak of around 3.5 million acres. By 1957, the last date for which accurate figures are available, there were 183 deer forests covering some 2.8 million acres.[1]

Sporting estates are thus a relatively modern phenomenon and a direct response to the economic and social changes which took place during the 19th century. They were not short of their critics at that time. Particular debate at the turn of the century centred round the respective merits of the sheep and the deer economy. J.M. MacDiarmid, the Labour candidate for Perth and Kinross wrote a particularly critical pamphlet which, as a foreword, quoted Sir John Stirling-Maxwell, the Chairman of the Departmental Committee on Deer Forests in 1919:

'It may be true, I believe it often is, that a deer forest employs more people than the same area under sheep. It certainly brings in a larger rent. From a purely parochial point of view it may therefore claim to be economically sound; but from no other. It provides a healthy existence for a small group of people, but it produces nothing except a small quantity of venison, for which there is no demand. It causes money to change hands. A pack of cards can do that. I doubt whether it could be said of a single deer forest, however barren and remote, that it could serve no better purpose.'[2]

The ownership of Highland sporting estates has provided fuel for the debate about landownership in Scotland for many years.[3] Their somewhat equivocal presence today is no doubt due to the rapidity with which they developed and the role they played in converting sheep farms, themselves created by clearance of people, into a land use which to most Highlanders was at best peripheral to their interests and at worst a brutal reminder of who was in charge in Highland affairs.

But there are more profound reasons why they remain a problematic issue. Sporting estates tend to undergo changes in ownership on a frequent basis. They attract, just as their creation attracted, a wealthy elite whose priorities have never been ones of rural development. Indeed, they have frequently been quite to the contrary. The system of valuation for sale, which is based on the numbers of game shot or caught, together with their transfer in an international free market, has pushed land values to astronomical heights which are way beyond the level at which an economic return can be made. Most sporting estate businesses also run at a loss since their economy is based upon a recreational activity which continues to form a main element of an elite lifestyle. Many people, including ostensibly establishment figures, have continued to criticise a land use which, to many, appears to be a gross under-utilisation of valuable land.[4] Recent controversy raged over the successful attempts by the SLF to abolish the rates paid by sporting estates. The move was portrayed by government as bringing Scotland into line with England but enraged not only critics of sporting estates but also the independent chairmen of Scotland's rating valuation tribunals who, in a report to the Scottish Office, made no secret of their anger.

'Sporting estates', the document explained, 'like to describe themselves, when it suits them, as being part of a sporting industry. In fact they are part of an inefficient trade which pays inadequate attention to marketing their product, largely because profit is not the prime objective.' It continued, 'These sporting estates change hands for capital sums which far exceed their letting value and which are of no benefit to the area, and are often bought because there are tax advantages to the purchaser, not necessarily in the UK.' Dismissing the argument that sporting estates provide employment and should therefore be freed of the rates burden, the chairmen's report points out that 'The local staff are poorly paid, their wages bearing no relation to the capital invested in the purchase price, and it is not unusual to find a man responsible for an investment in millions being paid a basic agricultural wage. Many of the estates use short-term labour during the sporting season, leaving the taxpayer to pay their staff from the dole for the rest of the year. Estates can in many cases be deliberately run at a loss, thereby reducing their owner's tax liability to central funds elsewhere in the UK.'[5]

The fact that such places cost so much to run is undoubtedly true. Informed commentators such as Michael Wigan, an impassioned advocate of the Highland sporting estate, claim that there are no pure deer forest properties which turn in a regular profit. Estimates of the private subsidy required range from £4 per acre for disadvantaged west coast estates to £2 for land in the eastern and central Highlands which have additional income from grouse shooting.[6]

What bewilders many people is why such obviously loss-making ventures should be the cause of any complaint on the grounds of cost from owners who seem perfectly happy to pay such inflated prices for them. The sporting estates, due to the characteristics and motivations of their owners, do not in any way observe the rational economic decision-making that normally informs land markets, and represent a good example of how dysfunctional such markets have become.

Not only do they fail to make economic sense but the 100 years of their existence have perpetuated a state of affairs whereby no real investment has been made which by now might be expected to have secured some more economic return. Such money that has been poured in is better categorised as conspicuous consumption which has little local multiplier effect and is entirely dependent for its generation on a continuing stream of wealthy external interests.

Just as starvation in Africa will not be sorted out by pumping aid relief money in, neither will the structural problems of the sporting estate economy be overcome by an equally misguided policy of relying on a stream of external subsidies from the various maverick characters who regularly find themselves the proud owners of a Highland sporting estate.

The sporting estate in reality is an indulgence by wealthy people who like hunting. They are uneconomic because they were never designed to be economic. No rural development programme anywhere in the world advocates the sale of land to a few wealthy individuals who will then support the rural economy by injecting cash from outside which will in turn support a few jobs. Nobody in any serious development agency if given a blank sheet of paper would design such an economy for the Highlands. As James Hunter recently observed when it was suggested that landowners might feel threatened by the developing debate about landownership, 'The more they feel threatened in my view the better. They need to feel threatened and they should feel threatened because there can be no future in Britain in the 21st century for a rural economy dependent on tweedy gentlemen coming from the south to slaughter our wildlife. That is not the way to run the Highlands and Islands.'[7]

# Chapter 10

# *Forestry*

SCOTLAND IS A deforested country and is much the poorer for it. Many of the large landed estates recognised the desirability, if only from an economic point of view, of doing something about this in the 19th century and the extensive forested areas on large estates such as Buccleuch and Atholl are a result of this forward-thinking policy. It is worth highlighting again in this context that trees can only legally belong to landowners. A tenant who plants a tree and a turnip can harvest and eat the turnip but the tree belongs to the landowner. This, together with the concentrated pattern of private ownership, is one reason why no tradition of farm forestry exists in Scotland.

In 1919 the Forestry Commission was set up, charged with the job of establishing forests for the nation as well as encouraging private landowners to replant wartime fellings and expand their wooded areas. Its development has resulted in the single greatest transformation of the Scottish countryside in the 20th century.

The Forestry Commission has built up an impressive landholding in Scotland and now professes to multi-purpose forestry, managing its land for a wide range of environmental, economic and recreational purposes. Its continued existence in the form of a state-owned and run body has repeatedly been called into question however. The Thatcher and Major governments have both at varying times looked into the prospect of privatising the FC and one of the first things the Conservative government did in 1981 was to initiate a process of partial privatisation through the sale of FC land to the private sector. In 1989, this process was reaffirmed with government setting a target of 250,000 acres to be disposed of by the end of the century. The FC estate extended to 1,660,923 acres in 1995, with an additional 23,456 acres held on long leases and 15,570 acres on the open market.

Until the 1960s planting by private interests was mainly on traditional landed estates. Identification of significant tax advantages in that decade, however, led to the recent phenomenon of investment forestry whereby people and institutions buy land specifically to afforest it. Such owners almost invariably have little interest beyond the financial and are almost exclusively absentee landowners. The Conservative government has encouraged the expansion of private forestry to complement their scaling down of state forestry, and the expansion of private forest land together with the decline of the FC estate has been one of the most significant features of the changing pattern of landownership in Scotland in the 1980s and 90s. In 1995 the area of forest land in Scotland stood at 2,883,657 acres or 15% of the land surface. Private ownership accounted for 55.9% of the total.

The precise ownership structure of private forestry remains something of a mystery. Unlike most other European countries, which not only consider the ownership of forests to matter a great deal but collect and publish extensive data on the subject, the Forestry Commission collects minimal information on forest holdings and publishes nothing.

There is no forestry equivalent to the agricultural census and therefore no information on the current pattern of private ownership of woodlands and forests in Scotland despite the important influence government incentives have had on ownership patterns. Until 1988 the availability of tax incentives meant that a high proportion of forest owners were high-rate taxpayers who invested in forestry in order to be able to offset such expenditure against other sources of income. This led to rapid changes in landownership. Since the abolition of such incentives and their replacement by direct grants, existing landowners, many of whom are not high-rate taxpayers, are benefiting to a greater degree although there is still a significant involvement from external investors.

A first attempt to analyse forest ownership was made by Sandy Mather in 1987.[1] The extent of new investor forestry was underlined by the finding that traditional landed estates accounted for less than half of the private forest area compared with over 90% in the 1960s. Corporate interests accounted for 20.5% of private forest holdings with pension, insurance and other financial institutions such as Electricity Supply Nominees and the Midland Bank accounting for 44% of such corporate lands. Mather observed that 'there has been no stated policy towards ownership structure. Whether by design or by default, the state has exerted an influence of fundamental significance for the structure of forest ownership through its choice of policy instruments. Whether by design or default, the state has facilitated the expansion of financial ownership of forests in Scotland.'

Whilst the state therefore has never consciously sought through forestry policy to encourage, for example, community forestry or farm forest cooperatives which are so common in many other countries, it has nevertheless substantially influenced landownership patterns. Not only have new private owners appeared but they have displaced in turn a variety of previous owners and occupiers. Whether this has been a beneficial change or not is a moot point since, whilst forestry has the potential to play a constructive role in rural development, it can also be hugely destructive of rural economies and communities if badly handled, a charge which is all too frequently levelled at both private and public forestry.[2]

The present study has not had the resources to look into the current position regarding private forest ownership but has yielded some information as part of the wider investigation (Table 16). Pension funds and financial institutions are still well represented but the bodies concerned have changed over the years. The Michelin Pension Fund and the Rolls Royce Pension Fund, for example, have both sold their land. Newcomers include a growing number of timber-processing companies who appear to be going in for 'vertical integration' as a security against future uncertainty in timber supply. Kronospan, a producer of wood-based panels, based in North Wales, now own at least 7,425 acres of forest. New forms of ownership are also being introduced with syndication now being developed which, in the case of Appin Forest in Dumfriesshire, involves shares being sold by auction. There is a fundamental difference in origin, outlook, motivation, and investment patterns between such investment forestry owners and more traditional landowners, many of whom are engaged in multiple land uses.

Since forestry policy has, in the private sector, sought to persuade landowners to plant and manage woodland and forests, it follows that it is landowners who have benefited from the incentives that have been available from the FC. These benefits can be substantial and for new planting are granted on an area basis. Although very small schemes receive higher payments, above 25 acres a flat rate is payable. This has meant that for particularly large schemes of new planting it is possible to end up making a surplus on the expensive process of afforestation. This has been turned to advantage by a number of schemes in the past five years.

Historically, it has been impossible to obtain any information on how much grant aid was paid to whom. As recently as May 1994, the FC responded to queries about grant payments by claiming that such matters were confidential.[3] In response to a parliamentary question in 1995, however, the FC published for the first time a list of recipients for 1993.[4] This list includes all payments made in 1993 in excess of £1000. Since grant schemes typically stagger payments over a number of years, it is difficult to associate the payments directly with work on the ground but they do offer some interesting insights (Table 17).

Of the top 20 payments, a number are of particular interest. J.&A. Galloway Ltd. were in receipt of the highest amount for a tree planting scheme at Lochlyoch in Lanarkshire. At the time this was the largest project ever carried under the Farm Woodland Scheme, an incentive designed to encourage farmers to plant trees and which, in addition to grant aid, provides up to 15 annual payments. In this case, the landowners had originally been forced to put the farm on the market as a result of financial difficulties but on learning that a prospective purchaser had been identified by a private forestry company who intended to implement such a scheme, decided that this would be just the project to pull them out of trouble. They withdrew the farm from the market and engaged the company on their own behalf. The Farm Woodland Scheme in particular appears to be an attractive prospect for external investors. Intended as a means by which farmers can diversify from farming, it places no restrictions on who precisely can benefit. There are a growing number of cases where farmers are selling up due to financial pressure only to be succeeded by a new breed of absentee investors who scale down farming operations to the very minimum consistent with retaining an agricultural business, very often letting the land to a neighbouring farmer. The new owners are attracted by the returns on offer which can be up to 14% on capital. Whilst most owners are understandably reluctant to divulge details of such arrangements, one scheme by Mr and Mrs Hall of Cathpair near Lauder in the Borders was advertised as an example of how on 420 acres of land a profit of £353,813 could be made after 15 years.[5]

Also represented among the top 20 payments is the Forest Farm scheme in Sutherland that is reported to have netted a £350,000 profit for the syndicate involved. This project attracted considerable controversy in 1992 due to its environmental and social impacts following the eviction of six families from the glen where it took place. The Danish consortium Greentop Lands and Estates Ltd. (see Box 2) are fourth. Fifth is a partnership of two couples who have developed various Community Forestry schemes including the largest one in Britain at Balkello near Dundee which was launched by Ian Lang, the then Secretary of State for Scotland in September 1993. These community forestry schemes are strange in that vast sums of money are available to private landowners who need not even live in the locality where they are established. The sixth largest recipient is Booker, which is the parent company for Tilhill Economic Forestry, a private forestry management company, and represents an unknown number of individual schemes conducted on behalf of clients. Two of the other owners mentioned are offshore companies, Andras Ltd. and Gong Hill Ltd. whose beneficial owners are unknown.

Public policy ignores as a variable the question of who owns the land. Instruments of policy appear to be uninterested in the question and lacking in vision about how people and forests should relate. As will be argued later, this is a misguided and politically vulnerable way in which to promote forestry in Scotland.

TABLE 16
## Top Forestry Investors in Scotland 1995

| OWNER | PROPERTY | ACREAGE |
|---|---|---|
| Greentop Lands & Estates Ltd. & Mrs Dorte Aamann-Christensen | Various Properties | 29643 |
| Electricity Supply Nominees | Various properties | 25200 |
| Eagle Star Insurance Co. Ltd. | Various properties | 25150 |
| Midland Bank Pension Trust Ltd. | Various properties | 14695 |
| Cinco Ltd., Forrest Estate Ltd. & Fred Olsen Ltd. | Forrest Estate | 12786 |
| Adam Wilson & Sons Ltd. | Avondale Estate | 10400 |
| PB Forestry Lands Ltd. | Various forests | 10257 |
| The Forest Farm Partnership | Forest Farm | 8400 |
| Pennyghael Estates Ltd. | Pennyghael Estate | 7900 |
| Post Office Staff Superannuation Scheme | Various properties | 7769 |
| Kronospan | Various properties | 7425 |
| Senor Raphael Cruz Conde | Glenample | 6950 |
| Securum | Knockdow | 6726 |
| Neils Tandrup & Viggo & Helle Sorensen | Glencripesdale | 6650 |
| Scottish Amicable Life Assurance Co. | Glenmuck & Brownhill | 6591 |
| British Insulated Callendar Cables | Various properties | 6142 |
| Refuge Farms Ltd. | Various properties | 5789 |
| CERN (European Organisation for Nuclear Research) | Leithope | 5461 |
| Multioptique International Ltd. & EGW (UK) Ltd. | Hearthstanes & others | 5400 |
| Willem B. van Baalen, Stephanus H. Oosterbeek & others | Overscaig | 5273 |
| Gallacher Pension Trust Ltd. | Resipole & others | 5135 |
| Glenmassan Ltd. | Glen Massan | 4900 |
| Halifax Building Society Pension Nominees | Various properties | 4299 |
| Horsens Folkeblad Foundation | Conval & Revack | 4236 |
| Dr Frischmann | Garabal Estate | 4118 |
| Keith Duckworth | Tungadal Forest | 4090 |
| N. Ireland Local Government Officers Superannuation Fund | Bidhouse & Howpasley | 4047 |
| TOTAL acreage | | 245432 |

TABLE 17
# Top 20 Forestry Grant Recipients 1993

| RECIPIENT | COUNTY | AMOUNT (£) |
|---|---|---|
| J. & A. Galloway Ltd. | Lanark | 815114.11 |
| The Forest Farms Partnership | Ross & Cromarty | 369949.12 |
| Ballindalloch Trust | Banff & Moray | 293803.39 |
| Greentop/Christensen/Glenrock | Various | 252646.41 |
| Sutherland Parke Partnership | Angus | 221238.81 |
| Booker | Various | 206641.50 |
| Rothiemurchus Estate | Inverness | 159461.25 |
| Glenmore Properties Ltd. | Moray | 158287.37 |
| Dowson | Argyll | 149672.25 |
| A.H. Graham & Co. | Fife | 138754.08 |
| Gong Hill Ltd. | Argyll | 128071.76 |
| The Countess of Seafield | Inverness | 126750.00 |
| Meladave Property Ltd. | Dumfries | 116161.97 |
| Pottinger | Caithness | 95734.25 |
| Andras Ltd. | Inverness | 85410.00 |
| Polly Estate Limited | Ross & Cromarty | 85039.50 |
| Scobie | Ross & Cromarty | 77532.00 |
| The Hon A. Fraser | Inverness | 76537.50 |
| Searle | Perth | 76232.76 |
| Glasgow City Council | Glasgow | 71205.84 |
| | TOTAL | £3704243.87 |

Source: Written parliamentary answer to Calum Macdonald MP 10th July 1995

Of a total sum of £10,385,260.25 paid out in payments over £1000 to 1045 landowners in 1993, the distribution was as follows:

| % of funds | No. of recipients |
|---|---|
| 20 | 6 |
| 40 | 28 |
| 60 | 80 |
| 80 | 219 |
| 100 | 1045 |

# Chapter 11

# *Crofting*

CROFTING TENURE WAS introduced in 1886 through the Crofters Holdings (Scotland) Act. It gave security of tenure, rights to judicially reviewed rents, the right to bequeath tenancy and the right to compensation for permanent improvements, to all crofters in the seven crofting counties of Argyll, Inverness, Ross & Cromarty, Sutherland, Caithness, Orkney and Shetland. It was a radical piece of land reform legislation pushed through in extraordinary political circumstances, the impacts of which have been profound for many areas in the Highlands and Islands.[1]

Essentially, however, it was an ad hoc piece of legislation which was criticised at the time for making no provision for the landless cottars and subsequently for having retarded the development of a more economic and efficient agricultural economy. The security it offered to agricultural tenants however has proved ultimately to have ensured its one great contribution to the rural economy, namely that it has retained populations in some of the most inhospitable regions of Scotland.

Crofting developed as a system of land tenure inside the existing system of Highland estates and croft land covers around one fifth of the total land area of the Highlands and Islands. The crofting community today therefore consists of crofters with their individual crofts held on an annual tenancy from their landowner together with an area of common grazings. Whilst crofting defined the crofter as an agricultural tenant with statutory rights, it did nothing to redefine the role of landowners other than to constrain their rights. The tension that persisted between crofter and landlord together with the developing confidence of the crofting community was to eventually inspire the event which as much as anything catapulted landownership back onto the political agenda in the 1990s.

On the 1st February 1993 the Assynt Crofters Trust took possession of the 21,000 acre North Lochinver Estate from the receivers of a bankrupt Swedish property company and wrote themselves into the history books. It was not the first time crofters had had the opportunity to become landowners. The Stornoway Trust was 70 years old by this time and the crofters on the Glendale Estate on Skye had owned their estate since 1956. What marked the Assynt case out, however, was that for the first time since the late 19th-century land agitations, ordinary people had organised a political campaign to take over land and won. No government scheme or philanthropic landlord was involved: indeed government was at best neutral to the initiative and the landlord had disappeared and was represented by determined receivers.

The Assynt case also took place against the background of a resurgence of confidence in crofting which the formation of the Scottish Crofters Union (SCU) in 1985 had done much to engender. It served to increase this confidence and drew the attention of the outside world to a system of land tenure which, although it had much to commend it, was still very much in need of reform.

In the 1980s and 90s, crofting was being advocated with new vigour as a form of land tenure which, it was argued, had not only been successful in retaining people in regions which otherwise would probably be sparsely populated but, by being associated with part-time low intensity agriculture, has encouraged a diverse economy and a less damaged environment than that associated with mainstream farming.[2] This was recognised by environmental organisations such as the RSPB which produced reports jointly with the SCU arguing the benefits of crofting to the environment.[3]

But the crofting system, which has much to commend it, needs to face up to internal problems related to the complexity of crofting legislation. Many of these problems stem from the 1976 Crofting Reform Act which, amongst other things, allowed crofters to purchase their individual crofts from their landlord. This Act enabled crofters who exercised such rights to subsequently apply for permission to remove the land from crofting tenure and sell it on the open market. Crofts were soon being 'decrofted' at an average rate of one a week.[4] Crofters who bought their croft under the 1976 Act and then sold it after the statutory five years for a sizable sum were arguably making no greater contribution to rural development than the land speculators who, solely by virtue of being wealthier, deal in larger sum over larger areas. An extreme example involved a particularly large 4090-acre croft on Skye which had been bought by its crofting tenant for £1,855 in June 1977 to be sold in 1982 for £300,000 to the Duckworth family for private forestry. It rapidly became obvious that such legislation together with other emerging problems such as absentee crofters could destabilise the entire system.

In 1995, the annual meeting of the SCU committed itself to the setting up of a Crofting Trust which would be available to take over the ownership of estates on behalf of their crofting tenants. Such a move was made all the more relevant in the light of the announcement by the then Secretary of State for Scotland, Michael Forsyth, that he was prepared to consider the transfer of the SOAEFD's estates into crofter-controlled community trusts. These two announcements played an important part in bringing landownership and reform back onto the political agenda in the mid 1990s.

The establishment of Crofting Trusts is a useful move forward as far as it goes but fails to address two important issues of a more general significance to land reform in crofting. First, such trusts merely take the place of existing landowners. Under the Scots law of property they enjoy precisely the same rights as any other landowner whether it be the Secretary of State for Scotland or an Arabian sheik. In so far as it will be argued that this law needs reform, crofting trusts will be affected as much as any other proprietor.

Secondly, the proposal does nothing to reform crofting tenure itself which many have argued needs reformed. Not only is it now difficult to create new crofts under existing crofting legislation but the existing structure is seen by many as cumbersome, over-bureaucratic and open to abuse.

The principles of crofting tenure and the expansion of community landownership though Crofting Trusts, however, remain sound. Crofting tenants enjoy security and independence. As tenants of a landlord body which they themselves have a share in, they can furthermore take responsibility for planning their own future.

These principles are critical. The Glendale estate on Skye, having been bought by the crofters under arrangements introduced in 1897, now has amongst the most expensive housing on Skye since the occupiers elected to become owners rather than remain as tenants, and Glendale Crofters Ltd is a company with share capital, allowing members to dispose of their share individually. Many of the crofts have now been sold on the open market. The communal framework for decision making has been virtually destroyed. The Assynt Crofters Trust on the other hand has retained the crofting tenure system, (although individual crofters still retain the option to purchase their crofts under the 1976 Act), and is constituted as a company with no share capital. Land held by the Trust can only be disposed of on a collective basis.

Crofting is capable of addressing these problems only if strong leadership is shown. Crofters have been successful in raising the profile of crofting and those at Assynt and Borve on Skye have demonstrated that it is a system capable of some imaginative adaptation to modern day needs. The wider challenge is to tackle crofting's internal problems and build a new legal structure for crofting which is simpler, more logical and stable and which can be expanded to other parts of the country. Such reforms will also need to enfranchise others in the community who have no access to natural resources beyond a house and garden, if they are to meet the wider ideals of land reform.

# Chapter 12

# *The Conservation Landowners*

THE CONSERVATION OF wildlife and landscape in Scotland has been of growing significance in the 20th century. As early as 1931, with the founding of The National Trust for Scotland, the commitment of individual voluntary organisations to countryside protection was established. Within four years the NTS had made a start towards purchasing Glencoe (13,962 acres). In 1944 Kintail and Morvich were added (17,422 acres) and in 1950 Ben Lawers (8,266 acres). All these purchases had been made possible by the generosity and effort of Percy Unna, a mountaineer and President of the Scottish Mountaineering Club, who along with others established the Mountainous Country Fund.

These land acquisitions marked the beginning of a process of increased involvement in landownership by voluntary bodies interested in the protection of the countryside for wildlife, amenity and wild landscapes to the point where they now own over 330,000 acres of land (Table 18). In addition, the government through first of all the Nature Conservancy Council and, since 1992, Scottish Natural Heritage (SNH), now owns 84,488 acres, making a total of over 400,000 acres in the ownership of organisations dedicated to some form of countryside conservation.

The period 1980 to 1995 alone saw the acreage owned by the voluntary sector increase by 197,460 acres, a 146% increase in only 15 years. Over 70% of this increase was in the 1990s. At this rate of increase, such organisations will own around 10% of Scotland by 2010.

Driving such expansion has been an explosion in environmental awareness and a failure of public policy measures designed to protect the environment. Many conservation organisations believe that the only certain way to secure wildlife and wild land conservation is through direct ownership. This has been the particular motivation of the RSPB and the John Muir Trust (JMT). Both recognise, however, that it would be impossible to buy all land of conservation value in the country. Alternatives to purchase include developing partnerships with private landowners and leasing land of high conservation value. The Scottish Wildlife Trust (SWT) has been particularly active in both leasing nature reserves and managing others by agreement. In addition to the 28,620 acres it owns, it leases 1533 acres and has agreements over a further 15,600 acres. The RSPB, in addition to the 87,491 acres it owns, leases 14,396 acres and has agreements over a further 4393 acres.

Such a rapid increase, however, has brought to the surface fears that many of these organisations are concerned more with wildlife than with people. Such fears are not without foundation but it is noteworthy that bodies such as the JMT include in their objectives the need to work in partnership with communities in securing their aims. Nevertheless, it remains to be seen whether the expansion of such organisations with, in some cases, rapidly growing memberships in faraway places, can complement the equally dynamic process of increased efforts by local communities to own land and control their own destinies. The danger is that competing agendas will frustrate efforts at sustainable development. At the back of many minds is the hope that the need for such groups will be shortlived and that they can play a constructive role in enabling local people to be, at the end of the day, protectors and managers of wildlife and wild land.

Neither have such changes been received well by some other landowning interests, who have frequently been suspicious if not explicitly hostile. This was dramatically illustrated by the efforts of three conservation organisations, the JMT, RSPB and World Wide Fund for Nature (WWF) to purchase the Mar Lodge Estate in the early 90s. As related in Box 3, the case highlighted the highly charged and politicised issue that landownership continues to be. In 1994, another row erupted over the sale of the Glen Feshie Estate which was eventually sold for £4,713,600 to a private charitable trust from England, the Will Woodlands Trust.

Relationships between conservation bodies and the landowning interest have been strained at times not least because of the involvement of prominent landowners themselves with such bodies. Their private views may at times conflict with the policies of the organisation. In most cases this appears not to matter although it can influence the position taken by the organisation concerned.

Examples of landowning involvement include the Duke of Edinburgh who is the International President of WWF, whilst the President is HRH Princess Alexandra, whose husband is Angus Ogilvy, the brother of the Earl of Airlie. The Honorary President of the Scottish Wildlife Trust was until February 1995 the Duke of Atholl and its honorary Vice-Presidents include Jean Balfour and the Duke of Roxburghe. No organisation, however, can compare with the landowning pedigree of the National Trust for Scotland whose Patron, President Emeritus and four Vice Presidents are all landowners. Of the 50 members of Council, no less than 13 are large landowners. Of the Executive Committee, which is where the real power lies, of 31 members, 12 are major landowners. Its Chairman in addition to being a landowner is also Chairman of Scottish Woodlands Ltd., a private forestry company.

Looking to the future, it is an open question whether conservation organisations will continue to expand their estates. Already tensions are emerging both internally and externally as to the appropriate role of these bodies as landowners. These tensions reflect a fundamental unease with the idea that the only way to protect wildlife and landscapes is through ownership by dedicated conservation bodies. Such bodies can often alienate local opinion through their strength of purpose and resolve which often assumes that only they are in a position to care for the countryside. They are essentially first aid organisations and although there is undoubtedly a continued role for them, there is no good reason why local communities, crofters, farmers and local authorities amongst others should not ultimately play an equal or greater role in the management of Scotland's natural heritage.

The rapid rise of conservation landowning in Scotland is, in the final analysis, a statement of failure not success. Those involved should be asking themselves not how much more land they can buy but how soon they can get rid of it.

## Box 3   The Strange Case of Mar Lodge

The 72,561-acre Mar Lodge estate is located in the Cairngorm mountains in north-east Scotland. The Cairngorms are internationally recognised for their outstanding nature conservation and wild landscape values. In 1987 the estate was bought by American billionaire John Kluge and in 1991, he was ready to put it on the market. The prospective sale triggered one of the most intensive efforts ever to bring a privately owned estate into conservation ownership.

Due to its outstanding importance for conservation, a consortium of the John Muir Trust, the Royal Society for the Protection of Birds and the World Wide Fund for Nature launched a bid to purchase the estate in June 1991. The whole question of the future management of the Cairngorms had been the subject of intense controversy for many years and during 1991 and 1992 was the subject of a government-appointed working party headed by Magnus Magnusson to recommend a strategy for future management. Conservation was at the heart of their work. The drama played out over the next four years is yet to be fully explained but at the time support for the consortium was widespread and prominent. By August 1991, the Secretary of State for Scotland, Ian Lang, accompanied by the Earl of Mansfield, had himself visited Mar Lodge amidst growing criticism of government for not acting to assist the proposed purchase. The Scottish Office subsequently expressed firm support publicly for the consortium's bid. A crucial turning point in the fortunes of the bid came in late September 1991.

On Friday and Saturday, 27th and 28th September 1991, the National Heritage Memorial Fund visited Mar Lodge to assess an application for £5 million towards purchase costs to match £5 million already pledged by the conservation consortium. Lord Charteris, former private secretary to the Queen and who remains close to her, was the Chairman. He had tea at Balmoral after the visit. By the end of October, however, the consortium was reported to fear that their bid had been damaged by behind-the-scenes lobbying by major Scottish landowners. Landowners were reported to have been stung by suggestions that an estate such as Mar Lodge was not safe in private ownership. The fact that figures such as Ian Lang had been supportive of a purchase for conservation could only serve to heighten their fears that the landowning establishment was losing control.

By November, a neighbouring landowner, the Duke of Atholl, went public. Purchase of Mar Lodge by conservation bodies would be 'an absolute disaster', he claimed. 'I very much hope it will be bought by a private person who will continue to run it as a deer forest', he continued. Such views had been passed on to Ian Lang.

On 1 April 1992, Scottish Natural Heritage, the government's newly created conservation advisor, came into existence. One of its main aims was to rebuild good relations with landowners after a series of controversies surrounding the way in which the previous GB agency, the Nature Conservancy Council, had gone about its business. Landowners were generally feeling bruised by an agency which had traditionally taken a fairly hard line over a range of nature conservation controversies. One of the main priorities of the new Chairman, Magnus Magnusson, who had just submitted the final report of the Cairngorms Working Party to the Scottish Office, was to build a new relationship based on partnership and dialogue. The heated debate which had taken place over the previous year had hardly helped to create such a climate.

By this time, the main stumbling block to further progress by the consortium was agreement with the emerging new agency for long-term financial support tied to a management plan which by this time was a common way of securing conservation management by private landowners. By now, however, SNH had become distinctly cool in its relationship with the consortium. Constant negotiations over the management package became entangled as more and more detailed demands were made by the agency to clarify details of the management plan. By May 1992, an impasse was reached and the consortium announced its withdrawal from any further efforts to purchase Mar Lodge Estate.

From a position where senior figures from the Scottish Office had backed the consortium's bid, final agreement on a management plan proved impossible to reach. What had gone wrong was never revealed but it seems clear that at a critical stage in late 1991, landowning interests had successfully persuaded Magnus Magnusson directly or indirectly that the newly set-up SNH would be in no position to build any credibility with landowners if it persisted in supporting the conservation consortium. Sources close to the negotiations have since confirmed that pressure came from the highest levels of British society. The fact that the Duke of Edinburgh was the International President of WWF and has strong views on the management of highland sporting estates would suggest that he at the very least had been aware of the situation. Lord Charteris, of whom it has been claimed it would be hard to think of anyone closer to the heart of the British Establishment, was intimately aware of the negotiations and had visited Balmoral the day after his visit to Mar Lodge. Five weeks later the Duke of Atholl was speaking to the press to voice his concerns in no uncertain terms. Soon afterwards the consortium found itself embroiled in a painstaking and frustrating series of negotiations with SNH before giving up in despair the following spring.

If round one smacked of an establishment backlash, round two was to prove equally intriguing. By the summer of 1994 it had been announced that Mar Lodge had been taken off the market. John Kluge planned to keep the estate 'for the foreseeable future'. But by August 1994 it was public knowledge that the National Trust for Scotland was engaged in intensive negotiations. On 26 April 1995 the NTS announced they had secured £10.2 million from the National Heritage Memorial Fund supported by £4 million from a private and anonymous source, the Easter Charitable Trust. Behind the scenes NTS had been hard at work. But it was top secret work involving, to the virtual exclusion of all other staff, the Chairman-designate, Hamish Leslie Melville.

Members of the NTS council and senior staff were kept in the dark about the details and the final deal remains shrouded in mystery. The original plan was for John Kluge to lease the Estate to NTS but this was unacceptable. Instead, the NTS purchased it and paid the money into a bank account from which Mr Kluge is drawing annual payments via his private trust, the Morven Trust, named after his house in Virginia. This appears to be a device enabling him to offset the sale proceeds against tax.

At the time of sale the estate was owned by John Kluge's company Mar Lodge Inc. It was sold to the NTS by feu disposition, the lodge itself being sold separately for $1. Mar Lodge Inc. therefore is the feudal superior of the NTS. John Kluge's consent is required for any developments within a 500-metre radius of Claybokie, a property to the west of Mar Lodge which he has retained. His consent is also required for any mortgage the NTS may wish to take out over the property. Any contravention of the feudal burdens allows Mr Kluge to repossess the estate. Even the primary management objective of the NTS is included as a burden, enabling Mr Kluge to challenge activities which, in his interpretation, do not accord with 'management of the feu in a sustainable manner for the benefit of the nation, ensuring the continuing conservation and restoration of its internationally important geology, flora, fauna, wild land quality and archaeological value.'

Not only has the NTS had to accept being a vassal of John Kluge but it has had to observe the confidential terms of the Easter Trust which are believed to require the continued management of Mar Lodge as a highland sporting estate. Such an objective indeed is embodied in the management plan agreed with SNH.

The Mar Lodge story is yet to be fully told. Certainly the conservation consortium's efforts were firmly sabotaged by the pressure from landowning interests. The NTS, on the other hand, had impeccable credentials in the landowning world and was seen as much less of a threat to landowning interests. None of the problems (which were experienced by the conservation consortium) in reaching a management agreement with SNH seemed insurmountable in round two.

The government had every opportunity to secure the purchase in round one and, with the launch of SNH and John Major's attendance at the 1992 Rio Earth Summit, bringing Mar Lodge Estate into competent conservation ownership would have provided a tremendous boost to the government's environmental reputation.

That the consortium was unsuccessful says as much about the politics of landownership, however, as it does about conservation policy. In the end it is hard to escape the conclusion that the former won over the latter. The strange case of Mar Lodge is a microcosm of the politics of Scottish landownership.

TABLE 18
**Conservation Landowners in Scotland**

| OWNER | ACRES |
|---|---|
| **NOT FOR PROFIT** | |
| National Trust for Scotland | 176827 |
| Royal Society for the Protection of Birds | 87489 |
| The John Muir Trust | 35015 |
| Scottish Wildlife Trust | 28620 |
| The Woodland Trust | 5000 |
| **PUBLIC** | |
| Scottish Natural Heritage | 84488 |
| TOTAL NOT FOR PROFIT | 332951 |
| TOTAL PUBLIC | 84488 |
| SCOTLAND TOTAL | 417439 |
| % of Scotland | 2.2% |

# Conclusions

THIS STUDY HAS revealed a pattern of landownership in Scotland not substantially different to that revealed by Roger Millman and John McEwen. It reflects the latest point in the long continuum of feudal landownership and as Robin Callander observed,

> One of the most conspicuous features of this continuity has been the small number of large estates that have always dominated the pattern. Fewer than 1500 private estates have owned the majority of Scotland's land throughout the last nine centuries. It has been around this core that the overall numbers of landowners have fluctuated.[1]

Not only does the pattern remain concentrated in few hands but these hands are in themselves substantially and closely related to one another.

Whether this matters is of course an important question and one to which we now turn. Landownership has been the subject of debate for many years not least in response to the concentrated pattern revealed here. How has that debate been framed, what values have informed it and what impact has it had? How does the Scottish situation compare with other countries? What if anything should we do about it? These are questions which are addressed in the final section.

# Section III

# Chapter 13

# *International Comparisons*

IF LITTLE IS known about land tenure and landownership patterns in Scotland, even less is understood about how the situation here differs from that in other countries. There is a broad awareness that private landownership is more concentrated in Scotland than in the rest of Europe, that other countries have tighter controls over landownership and land sales, and that information on such matters is more readily and publicly available. But there have only been limited efforts to study these issues systematically in the context of Scottish landownership.

The experience of working and studying overseas has, however, frequently informed views on the subject. In 1978 one leading political activist who now farms in Fife observed:

'It once befell me, while working in East Africa, to read widely concerning land tenure in Africa and its relation to problems of social and economic development. These days I often find myself stressing two items of African experience that seem to bear more than passing relevance to Scotland. First, no country with so inequitable a land distribution as Scotland would ever receive a jot or tittle of overseas aid in the rural sector. Second, any country with such a land distribution and with much of the landownership in alien hands would, anywhere but Scotland, be facing a revolutionary phase. Why should what is unacceptable in Rhodesia [Zimbabwe] or imperial Ethiopia be of no consequence in Ross-shire?'[1]

Scotland, of course, has never been in open revolt about anything and this is significant. Land tenure systems all over the world are the product of historical events and political forces. This is as true of Scotland as it is of Zimbabwe or Ethiopia. Differences in land tenure systems and landownership patterns are usually understood best by studying the history and politics of the place.

One study, carried out in 1980, looked specifically at the Norwegian and Danish situation.[2] In Norway, for example, in the 1814 Constitutional Assembly farmers negotiated the 'peasant clause' which gave them substantial political power. The Assembly also agreed to abolish tenancies so that by 1907 only 6.2% of all farms were tenanted. Farmers, who were politically enfranchised and powerful, were well prepared for the economic crisis which hit Norwegian agriculture in the 1870s. In 1825, for example, legislation was enacted which ensured a favourable banking regime for agriculture. By 1900, of 413 banks in Norway, 350 were rural savings banks. The Co-operative Movement was established which today has an annual turnover of £3.5 billion. Norwegian farmers continue to enjoy political power and political support.

In Denmark, from the late 18th century, landowners themselves launched land reform movements. About 800 estates covered three quarters of Denmark at this time. Landlords were short of capital and the more progressive of them concluded that an independent peasantry on owner-occupied holdings was the surest way of improving agricultural productivity. English agrarian developments were studied but the model of large landowners and small dependent tenants which it presented was rejected in favour of reforms which would create an independent farming community. That Danish landowners were not only supportive of such reforms but took an active part in developing them may seem surprising. Critically, however, the landed classes at the time enjoyed no political power under an absolute monarchy. This was, of course, in stark contrast to the situation in Scotland.

In both Norway and Denmark the legal framework has developed to support an independent owner-occupied pattern of landownership. Land sales are regulated and potential owners are required, among other things, to reside on their holdings. As a result, Denmark currently enjoys some of the lowest prices of agricultural land in Europe and one of the most efficient and profitable agricultural industries. Both countries have sizable rural populations and a pluralistic pattern of landownership.

In other Scandinavian countries, such as Sweden, the Land Purchase Act 1965 gives County Agricultural Boards the authority through prohibition on sales and the power of preemption to ensure that purchasers will use the productive potential of the land. Companies are not allowed to buy land unless their capital is essential to some agricultural or forestry operation.

Even some of the most free market economies impose limitations on who can buy land. In New Zealand, for example, overseas interests are prohibited from purchasing certain categories of land such as 'reserve land' which is designated for its ecological, cultural or scenic qualities. Legislation also covers holdings larger than five acres where approval may be given subject to agreement that specified conditions relating to beneficial use of the land from a national viewpoint are observed. New Zealand is also developing are of the most comprehensive computer-based land information systems anywhere in the world.

Virtually all European countries have taken the opportunity to regulate and reform their land laws in response to political revolutions, economic pressure and national liberation movements. Usually these controls have consisted of limitations to the amount of land which can be owned by foreign nationals, controls designed to support agrarian populations and more sophisticated systems of land-use controls and support packages. Some element of land taxation is not uncommon either.

Such comparisons have not gone unnoticed in Scotland. Professor Tony Carty, an international legal specialist, has undertaken most of the available analyses of west European land tenure. In a major study of the international implications of an independent Scotland, he and the late J. Ferguson analysed the pattern of land sales in Scotland by foreign nationals and compared the situation with that of other countries:

'In most Western European countries', they wrote, 'controls are placed on the purchase of land for speculative or other purposes which are not conducive to the survival of agriculture and the agrarian community. The North of Scotland and particularly the Highlands are almost unique in Western Europe in a number of ways. Perhaps the most significant is the peculiar legal framework prevailing. The complete absence of legal control of rural land inevitably attracts foreign purchasers who are constrained by their own national laws. It is quite unusual to be able to dispose of land suitable for, or at least traditionally employed in, agriculture, forestry or other primary land uses, without any guarantees at all as to the future uses to which the land might be put. However, equally remarkable is the unique character of the Scottish Highlands, the only region in Europe in which no measure of land reform has ever been attempted, save for legislation affecting crofting tenure. The sheer size of many estates makes individual purchases significant in themselves because of the vast acreages which change hands. The political, social and economic consequences of such purchases have major implications both at local and national level and yet they depend upon the personal choice of a very small number of individuals who are very often ill-informed even as to their own best economic interests let alone that of local communities.'[3]

Overseas specialists such as Jan van der Ploeg from the Agricultural University at Wageningen often make much the same observations when visiting Scotland:

'In Europe, several peripheral areas are now being repopulated. The Barosa area in north Portugal is one example of excellent smallholdings where the smallholders are returning. Areas like this [Scotland] have space, they are hardly affected by pollution and they have enormous potential for rural development. New services and products can be produced here. Such areas have huge potential as long as land is made available to farmers, crofters and rural communities.'

'It is very curious how people treat land [in Scotland]. Land is simply a commodity. This is wild-west capitalism. One of the most valuable assets for the future, the land, can be bought and sold at will. Elsewhere in Europe this is not the case. It makes Scotland a truly unique case.'[4]

It is remarkable that the system of land tenure and ownership in Scotland has not been more critically reviewed in the light of the obvious influence it has on rural development. It has been suggested, for example, that Scotland would not receive development grants from the World Bank or other multilateral aid funds without a major programme of land reform.[5]

Ironically the UK has some of the world's foremost experts in land reform and rural development. The UK government spends millions of pounds in its overseas aid budget to reform land tenure as part of wider development programmes. In Scotland, however, land reform is regarded as an irrelevance, and feudal land tenure and the most concentrated pattern of private ownership in Europe is deemed to have no bearing on rural development policies and outcomes.

Increasingly such a position is leading to growing embarrassment within overseas development circles. It does not add to the credibility of an Overseas Development Administration official on a posting to West Africa to implement a rural development programme and then have local people turn around and ask about the Scottish experience.

The study of land tenure and ownership is normal in most of the rest of the world. Its relationship with economic development and environmental protection is also well understood. In its land laws and its pattern of landownership, Scotland already meets many of the criteria of under-development which the UK government is very active in tackling overseas. Scotland needs land reform just as much as Nepal, South Africa and Eastern Europe.

Chapter 14

# Land Reform and the Landownership Debate

## The Development of the Debate

LANDOWNERSHIP IS AN issue which surfaces from time to time in public debate. Media attention is often attracted when a particular estate comes up for sale or when the activities of a particular landowner are exposed. Such periodic debate reflects and reinforces a deep-seated feeling that landownership in Scotland remains an item of unfinished business.

The debate about who should own the land has rarely been conducted within the framework of any serious political commitment to land reform. The late 19th to the early 20th century is the only period when serious and far-reaching land reform legislation reached the statute book, in the form of the 1886 Crofters Act, the 1911 Small Landholders Act and the 1919 Land Settlement Act. These measures protected and expanded the rights of small tenants and included provisions which eventually saw substantial areas of land taken into public ownership.[1] Subsequent legislation in 1949 gave security of tenure to all tenant farmers.

More recent legislation has concerned itself with the further consolidation and reform of these earlier measures. Such reforms, however, were by their very nature concessions, and little has been done to reform fundamentally Scotland's land laws, far less the wider pattern of ownership, beyond specific tenurial and conveyancing reforms.

The debate that has taken place about landownership, therefore, has essentially been one where reformers have focused their attention on the most obvious manifestation of their grievance, namely landowners. This took its most dramatic form in Tom Johnston's *Our Scots Noble Families*, his trenchant polemical attack on the Scottish aristocracy, published in 1909.

'Show the people', he wrote, 'that our Old Nobility is not noble, that its lands are stolen lands – stolen either by force or fraud; show people that the title-deeds are rapine, murder, massacre, cheating, or Court harlotry; dissolve the halo of divinity that surrounds the hereditary title; let the people clearly understand that our present House of Lords is composed largely of descendants of successful pirates and rogues; do these things and you shatter the Romance that keeps the nation numb and spellbound while privilege picks its pocket.'[2]

This was by way of a general indictment! His subsequent exposure of how 35 of the Scottish noble families originally came by their titles was no less damning. Of the Primrose family, to which the Earl of Rosebery belongs, he wryly observed: 'So that although he killed the Scots Small Holdings Bill, he himself has taken care to see that he has room to plant a few cabbages'. Or of the Boyles (Earls of Glasgow):

'They do not, any of them, appear to have been engaged in notorious theft or scandalous murder, and, indeed, with the exception of the first Earl, who got his titles for his labours in promoting the union of the Crowns, the Boyles have done little but quietly breed successors to the privilege of drawing rents. The family motto is 'Dominus Providebit' – The Lord will provide. So far the task has been undertaken by the working classes of the West of Scotland.'

Rural Scotland was never going to rise up in agrarian revolt however and an urban working class constituency failed to be convinced that their troubles could be laid solely at the door of the Scottish aristocracy.

Tom Johnston was later to become Secretary of State for Scotland during the Second World War and leave as his legacy the North of Scotland Hydro-Electric Board. The post-war years saw increased public sector involvement in land matters. The Highlands and Islands Development Board was set up and tried unsuccessfully to tackle the problem of underdeveloped land in the Highlands and Islands. The corporatist governments of the 60s and 70s were no great friends of private landownership and landowning interests lived on occasions in real fear of land nationalisation. Although landowners still had substantial influence in the political affairs of the country, they had little presence in public debate.

In the mid to late 1970s there was a dramatic upsurge of interest in the subject. The nationalist revival of the early 70s and the exposure of growing involvement by offshore foreign companies speculating in Scottish land both raised the political temperature. The continuing but ultimately frustrated attempts by the HIDB to tackle the land question had led them to develop proposals for new legislation to allow more effective powers over rural land use.[3] The Northfield Committee was set up in 1977 to enquire into the acquisition and occupancy of agricultural land, and in the same year John McEwen's *Who Owns Scotland* appeared, the first attempt in over 100 years to account for how Scotland was owned.

The 1970s were also an important period in the evolution of political ideas about landownership. John McEwen's book advocated the complete nationalisation of rural land in Scotland and this statist approach was very much in tune with thinking in the British Labour Party at the time. This period also witnessed, however, the rise of the Scottish National Party and the creation of the Scottish Labour Party, both of whose work on the land question broke new ground in their rejection of the nationalisation approach. In a discussion paper prepared for the SLP, the contrasts with traditional nationalisation approaches were made clear: 'Public ownership of land is not the same as nationalisation of agriculture. There is no constructive purpose in nationalising the actual agricultural process. The SLP is in no way interested in building a system of bureaucratic and alienating collective farms.'[4]

Further arguments by the author of this paper emphasise the more liberal approach taken to public landownership: 'Drumnadrochit is no Dnepropetrovsk! You have seen the Forestry Commission, now we bring you the Agriculture Commission!'[5]

By the end of the 70s, although even McEwen and many others still advocated outright nationalisation, most radical opinion was beginning to move towards ideas of community ownership and more pluralist private ownership in association with an enhanced role for public ownership. John McEwen had produced the facts, the nationalist left had developed the ideas and writers such as James Hunter, John Prebble and Ian Carter had published a substantial body of historical information and analysis which challenged more conservative interpretations of Scottish history.

This activity all contributed to a growing expectation that, in 1979, a devolved Scottish parliament would tackle the subject. In the event the parliament didn't arrive and 1979 ushered in a Conservative government which is still in power as this book is being written.

The 1980s were a very different decade from the 70s. The corporate state agenda was swept away in favour of a private sector, free-market philosophy in which the role of the state was to be reduced. Although the question of landownership did not disappear, anyone with land reforming aspirations quickly gave up any hope that the government would help. Each successive term of Conservative government, however, boosted the confidence of landowning interests. The Scottish Office was filled with Ministers who were innately supportive of private ownership and who developed policies which stressed their abhorrence of compulsion or state intervention. They supported instead the 'voluntary principle', whereby the persuasion and cooperation of landowners was sought in preference to a more interventionist role by the public sector.

By the 1990s, people had got used to developing strategies which accommodated the prevailing political philosophy. This was to prove critical in the success of the Assynt crofters. By 1994, the debate about landownership had moved from a sharply divided public versus private discourse to one which stressed the role of communities and people. The Conservatives, however, continued to pay more attention to a tiny constituency of landowning and business interests than they did to the wider constituency of people who were interested in various aspects of land reform, whether they be ramblers campaigning for public access or conservationists demanding public intervention to buy land such as Mar Lodge Estate.

By 1990 landowners were feeling secure about their role again and the landowning establishment was enjoying a level of confidence not experienced for decades. Their influence was felt whenever a sensitive issue such as red deer or salmon came up for detailed public scrutiny.

The debacle over Mar Lodge has already been described and continuing frustrations over such cases and many more which were to hit the headlines in the 1990s led to the position by 1995 where landownership was once more on the political agenda. Renewed media interest had been aroused not only by the sagas of Assynt, Mar Lodge, the Isle of Eigg, Knoydart and renewed overseas interest in the Scottish land market but by the activities of the Conservative administration itself.

The arrival of Michael Forsyth at the Scottish Office in the summer of 1995 marked a change in style and attitude in comparison with previous incumbents. Forsyth was a younger politician whose roots were not with the traditional landed interests of the Tory party and as part of an energetic bid to recover Conservative popularity in the country he set out to portray himself as a land reformer. In response to representations made to him by a number of individuals with land reform ambitions, he opened up a debate on the future ownership of crofting estates and made what may yet turn out to be his most significant intervention by signalling his approval of attempts by the local community in Laggan, Inverness-shire, to take over the management of a 3000-acre Forestry Commission plantation, Strathmashie Forest. Whatever his motives and ultimate achievements may have been, if nothing else he certainly focused the minds of opposition parties who, whilst they all took an interest in the land debate from time to time had not, with the exception of the SNP and Scottish Green Party, produced any coherent agenda for change. Forsyth won support in principle for his intervention particularly from those who in the 1970s had been critical of both outright nationalisation of the land and the unregulated free market.

These events, together with some high-profile land sales and ongoing initiatives by crofting interests to develop crofting land trusts, led to heightened media interest in landownership. With a General Election less than 18 months away, landowners suddenly began to feel nervous again.

## Key Features of the Debate

Whatever the origins and motives of the debate that has arisen at various times about landownership, one thing has remained constant: landowners seldom get a good press. This is not simply due to the monotonous frequency with which some individual owner is the target of criticism, whether justifiable or not, but to the ease with which the press and public focus on individuals rather than on the underlying issues.

In recent years much of the debate has focused on the colourful and bizarre characters that are sadly in plentiful supply in Scottish landowning circles. That such individuals exist is undoubtedly of legitimate interest and worthy of comment, but it does little to further constructive land reform beyond prompting anguish and indignation in the letters columns of the national newspapers. Conspicuous by its absence has been any attempt to investigate, analyse and present the economic, social, cultural and environmental issues which landownership is so central to. The result has been a rather ill-informed debate about landownership which has merely succeeded in marginalising the participants. Between the politics of envy and outrage, and the ideological battlefield of private versus public, little has emerged.

Landowners themselves have usually taken up rather defensive and reactive positions to debates about landownership. This is partly because much of the popular debate has been implicitly or explicitly anti-landlord. Given that landowners are thin on the ground in any case, it is not surprising that they have found it difficult to project anything other than a defensive and at times reactionary attitude.

Their case is not helped either by people like Max Hastings, the former editor of the *Daily Telegraph*, who in one particularly insulting comment claimed that 'The delusion is widely held in Scotland, for instance, that the Highlands are a paradise in a state of natural grace, which might more properly be held in public ownership. The Scots must be told again and again until they start to believe it, that their hills are in reality intensively and expensively managed by private landowners, almost all of whom incur huge financial cost in doing so, which would have to be made good from the public purse if they were not there.'[6]

Such views are not entirely helpful to anybody's case, least of all that of private landowners. Such attitudes aside, it remains a mystery why bodies such as the SLF are not capable of articulating a sensible critique of the current tenure system and ownership pattern without necessarily prejudicing the interests of their own membership. They have, for example, publicly congratulated the Assynt crofters on their achievements but have not come forward with ideas as to how sensible reforms may make such developments easier in the future. Other opportunities have been ignored for constructive engagement in debate.

Press coverage of the extent of overseas interest, for example, raises important questions not only about the desirability of foreign nationals owning land, but about the free market in land, the impacts on land prices and the political rationale for spending public money supporting foreign nationals' investment portfolios. The SLF, however, instead of redirecting press anxieties into these more productive areas, consistently defends the open market and has even suggested that such purchases represent inward investment.

Even the frequent criticism that opportunities for access to land are no more than a lottery is accepted with peculiar and worrying sanguinity. As SLF Convener, Graeme Gordon recently observed when challenged on the issue: 'Well it is a lottery. Life is. I would hate to see it [the land market] so regulated that you didn't have a bit of a lottery which makes Great Britain one of those wonderful places to live.'[7]

Those whose lives are caught up in this lottery, however, have a rather different view. As Alan Macrae of the Assynt Crofters observed of their success in purchasing the North Lochinver Estate, 'For my mind, for a community like this to own the land and resources should be the most natural thing in the world. Indeed the only unnatural thing that happened in Assynt was that we had to pay £300,000 for land that really should have belonged to us.'

Meanwhile, the lottery continues with one islander on Eigg recently pointing out that more checks and controls are exercised over the creditworthiness of the purchaser of a washing machine than of anyone from anywhere in the world buying an island like Eigg.

The debate remains lively but the polarisation between private and public which was so much a feature of earlier times has been replaced by a more subtle and complex set of arguments which began to emerge in the 1970s and which stresses the role of local communities, the enterprise of individuals, common responsibilities and public accountability. The argument, in short, is that private land ownership per se is perhaps not the problem but that the opportunities should be expanded, the responsibilities made more accountable and the freedom to buy and sell land at a whim dramatically restricted. A new set of rules should be introduced which encourage the responsible players and bar the unfit and unsuitable.

For the first time in a decade and a half, the debate on landownership is on a much firmer political footing with wide support and some practical proposals for reform. Before developing such arguments, however, it is worth having a look at some of the myths that have entered the debate. They raise their heads occasionally and can be a distraction.

# Chapter 15

# *Debunking the Myths*

**It's not who owns the land that's important. It's how it's managed that matters.**
THIS HAS BECOME the mantra of defenders of the status quo when faced with questions of landownership. By choosing to change the focus of attention onto land management it suggests that landownership is entirely unimportant. The comment therefore serves to deflect attention from important questions about who owns the land and about the system of land tenure onto territory which is often more palatable to discuss. It is disingenuous for two reasons.

Depending on the context such deflection may or may not be relevant. Who owns the land and the system under which land is held directly influence land management. Whilst it would be possible to find a whole spectrum of standards of management, in general terms each type of owner and tenure system provides differing motivations toward different land uses and this is reflected in management regimes. It is facile to suggest that ownership has nothing to do with it. Management is almost always a product of the tenurial status, owner motivation and status together with public policy. It does not exist in isolation from the question of landownership.

Furthermore, landownership is important for reasons which have nothing to do with land management. In theory, the highest standards of land management can be achieved within widely varying landownership systems. Standards of management tend not to be of great significance in discussions about how such a regime should operate. What is of more concern tends to be issues of democracy, opportunity, accountability, access to capital, freedom and public interest. A benign ecological dictatorship can produce high standards of management. Of course management matters, but so does ownership.

**Scottish estates need wealthy owners who are prepared to subsidise them with wealth earned elsewhere.**
This point is often made in response to criticism of the sporting estate in particular. The argument is made that much of rural Scotland is not economically viable without external input to maintain it. Private patronage is essential to the future of such areas.

Firstly, in the case of the sporting estate, this is merely stating the obvious. Such holdings were never designed to make money or even be self-financing in the first place. They were established as recreational retreats for wealthy industrialists in the 19th century. Vast sums of money were spent on building lodges, roads and other infrastructure to support deer-stalking and other forms of hunting and shooting. They have been sustained in this fashion by successive generations of recreational owners who are content to bear this cost in return for the recreation and, in many cases, prestige that this affords them. To argue therefore that this is the best way of managing such areas presumes a continuation of a form of land management which was devised under very different circumstances.

Such an argument is also somewhat paradoxical when the value of sporting estates is way above what can reasonable be expected to provide a return. If they are so uneconomical why do they command such high values? The answer is of course that they are not economic enterprises in the first place. They are bought and sold as assets of an elite leisure industry whose owners do not depend on them for their livelihoods. This, together with a free market in land, serves to keep prices artificially high and thus beyond what persons with modest means could afford.

Many Scottish estates are unprofitable. But this is entirely down to the lack of investment in productive land uses and enterprises. This tends to have been compounded by the narrow outlook of successive proprietors. Land is unprofitable because it has been managed unprofitably. In many cases the only way to return land to profitable use is through investment.

Patterns of land use evolve due to a complexity of factors including public policy, owner motivation, market conditions, indigenous knowledge and skills, land capability and the form of land tenure. The most dynamic and stable economies tend to be those where there are many occupants, pursuing a diversity of activities, creating a diverse economy, making maximum use of indigenous knowledge, investing in land capability and businesses and with a stake in the land. Sporting estates do not generally conform to this pattern. Most people associated with them do not have a proprietorial stake but tend to be tenants or employees. The few who do have a stake come from a very narrow background, often regard the land as an asset which can be treated as an investment, and have few family or wider links with the rest of the rural economy. Consequently, innovation and diversity tend to be in short supply.

Such arguments also suggest that the only option for such estates is to have them run as loss-making concerns. Such arguments fail to distinguish between land and capital. One of the most successful ways of facilitating greater investment by local people with the help of banks and enterprise companies would be if the price of land were cheaper. This is one argument for restrictions on land sales. High capital values discourage investment. Land priced in the millions and run at a loss is economic madness.

### The access myth

A noticeable feature of the landownership debate has been the perpetuation of a number of myths about access in Scotland. Among them are the notions that access is a land use and that 'freedom to roam' is an extreme and irresponsible demand to make.

Access is not a land use and should not be considered as synonymous with hillwalking or any other form of recreation. Access is a question of rights. Just as the right to free speech is regarded as a fundamental right, so should access. Legitimate questions arise over when, how and where such rights are exercised but that is a separate debate. Whether we have the right to be in our own country is therefore a fairly fundamental political question for society as a whole to determine.

At the root of the problem is the draconian nature of the Scots law of property which under common law defines anyone interfering with the rights to exclusive possession of property (except where such rights have been legally defined) as a trespasser. If the legal right of access is to be established we either need to redefine the Scots law of property or enshrine such rights in legislation. The current situation is unacceptable since it contains the explicit assumption that landowners have exclusive rights except where these have been removed. The rest of the population of Scotland enjoys no rights. Indeed in many cases what were de facto rights are not only being removed but criminalised. The Criminal Justice and Public Order (Scotland) Act of 1994 and the Freshwater and Salmon Fisheries (Scotland) Act of 1976 both for the first time in Scottish legal history erode de facto rights by making certain activities criminal offences.

Arguments about freedom to roam having been a historic right are difficult to establish since the doctrine of exclusive possession denies any legal protection for rights no matter how well established in practice, unless they are enshrined in statute. The act of trespass is to be where one has no right to be and, whilst not an offence in itself in Scotland (unlike England), is still regarded as the legal position of anyone on somebody else's ground. This raises the interesting question of whether, in the absence of legally enshrined rights to be on another person's land, trespass can have any real legal effect. Trespass takes as its premise the notion that just because access rights have never been legally enshrined landowners have the right to define others as trespassers. Yet the fact that I have no legal right to drink the rain that falls from the sky should not make me a thief if I do so. It is self evident that we must all be somewhere at some time. The laws of gravity alone dictate this.

Trespass, therefore, is a nonsense concept which should not enjoy legal protection simply through defining by default the legal status of everyone not in possession of land which they are occupying. This is not merely a matter of legal semantics. The notion that anyone can be defined as a trespasser is the moral authority which opponents of freedom to roam claim in order to sustain arguments to restrict access. The notion of trespass assumes that in the absence of any other right to the contrary, one section of society has the authority to enshrine this position in law. It has no more authority to do this than it would have to say that everyone has the right to roam. Authority to pass such fundamental judgments on our rights can only be taken with the consent of society as a whole.

Access is a political issue to be decided by 5 million Scottish citizens as it has been decided by the citizens of Norway and Sweden, for example, who enjoy a universal freedom to walk unhindered over uncultivated ground provided they cause no damage and no nuisance. Freedom to roam is the natural condition of humanity. Like many other freedoms it has been sacrificed on the altar of exclusive property rights.

**There is nothing strange about so few people owning so much of Scotland. So much land is poor and mountainous that one would expect a large number of large estates simply due to the poor land.**

The pattern and distribution of large estates in Scotland does correlate in substantial areas with areas of low land quality. Land quality of itself, however, cannot explain or justify the large-scale pattern of landownership. Low land quality, for example, can result in the necessity for large scale ownership due to low financial returns. Even where it does, however, such returns are seldom linked to land use potential alone but more often to agricultural support policies. Furthermore, much of the low quality land in large-scale ownership is not used as the basis for profitable enterprises and hence its quality is irrelevant to the size of the property. Large-scale ownership is also prevalent on good ground. The Buccleuch, Douglas and Angus, Roxburghe, Bute, Lothian and Seafield Estates all contain sizable proportions of good land.

The description of land as good or poor is also subject to interpretation. Much of the poor land in Scotland is poor not solely through inherent constraints such as soil quality and climate but as a result of abuse and failure to exploit its full potential. Sir Frank Fraser Darling, in his West Highland Survey, encountered an apricot tree flourishing on the west coast. The shelter afforded by a neighbouring forestry plantation was removed when the plantation was felled and the apricot tree died. It is easy therefore to see vast areas of 'poor land'. With some effort and input, however, such land can be improved substantially at least on a local scale.

Furthermore, even land which on the face of it is poor can turn out to be of immense value. Oil-related developments around the coast of Scotland have boosted land values where onshore developments have been permitted. The quality of the land is irrelevant. Public policy can boost land values as the rapid expansion of tax-avoidance forestry in the 1980s proved. Minerals can also transform the definition of poor land as the Lingerabay Quarry proposals on Harris demonstrate.

The pattern of landownership in reality has much more to do with economic, social and political developments than simply land quality. Norway, for example, has only 3% of its land capable of cultivation. Compared to Scotland it has vast areas of 'poor' land yet it has nothing like the concentrated pattern of large-scale private ownership that exists in Scotland.

**The typical landowner is either a crusty aristocrat in tweeds or a filthy-rich Arab who has paid vast sums of money for an estate and keeps the people out.**

One problem with the debate on landownership as has already been highlighted is that it has tended to focus both on landowners as individuals and on certain stereotypes of landowners. Quite apart from the fact that much of this criticism should be directed at problems of the landownership and tenure system, such critiques have often tended to convey the impression that Scotland is owned by certain types of owner. With little information as to who does actually own Scotland, it is easy for certain impressions to gain credibility. This study has attempted to shed some light on how Scotland actually is owned but has obvious limitations. Until information can be more easily gathered, abstracted, analysed and presented, no-one should be surprised how easily certain ideas can gain currency. Speculation can only be encouraged in the absence of hard information.

**Private property rights are sacrosanct and should not be interfered with**

This is an observation often made in response to perceived threats to private property interests. As long ago as 1886, the *Scotsman* condemned the Crofters Act as 'a great infringement of the rights of property'. In 1995, following Michael Forsyth's announcement of plans to set up Crofting Trusts to take over the SOAEFD estates, Simon Fraser of the SLF commented, 'The most appropriate thing is that it is voluntary. I would not want to be part of a society that went in for compulsory appropriation of legally held land.' Such comments are made with regularity by landowning interests who frequently ominously refer to the various articles of European Treaties and Conventions.

Land reformers, however, should be familiar with the accepted legal framework in which private property rights can be interfered with.

Right at the outset it should be stressed that all land in Scotland is legally held by the Scottish people. This is because Feudal tenure derives its authority from the Crown and in Scottish constitutional theory dating back to the Declaration of Arbroath the Crown itself is a subordinate authority to the sovereignty of the people. It follows that all rights in property are held not only under the authority of the Crown but, in turn, under the authority of the people. Private property rights have not only been extensively interfered with in the past but perfect authority exists to redefine them in the future.

Perhaps the next most important consideration is the Treaty of Rome, in particular Article 52, which guarantees a right of establishment in any European Union country to all EU citizens. It has variously been invoked to argue against the possibility of any controls being placed on foreign nationals buying land. Importantly, however, the guarantee only applies within the conditions established by the law of the host state for its own nationals. Hence any restrictions which are applied need to ensure that they are not discriminatory, i.e. that an EU national is not treated any differently from a UK national. The Danish Agricultural Act of 1973, for example, was approved by the EU despite the restrictions it placed on purchasers because the restrictions equally applied to Danes themselves.

Further consideration should also be given to Article 1 of the European Convention on Human Rights, which states that,

'Every natural or legal person is entitled to the peaceful enjoyment of his possessions. No-one shall be deprived of his possessions except in the public interest and subject to the conditions provided for by law and by the general principles of international law. The preceding provisions shall not, however, in any way impair the right of a State to enforce such laws as it deems necessary to control the use of property in accordance with the general interest or to secure the payment of taxes or other contributions or penalties.'

This has already been tested in the English Courts. In 1986 the Trustees of the Second Duke of Westminster argued that the Leasehold Reform Act of 1967, which enabled tenants under long leases to purchase their freehold interest at what were regarded as favourable rates, breached this Article. Although the court recognised that the Act did indeed deprive the applicants of their possessions, it also recognised that 'the compulsory transfer of property from one individual to another may, in principle, be considered to be 'in the public interest', if the taking is effected in pursuance of legitimate social policies'.

No less a body than the Scottish Law Commission have cited this case as support for their contention that the abolition of the feudal system in Scotland, 'long after it has been abolished in other European countries is, in our view, a legitimate policy'. They further state that, 'We do not consider that the abolition of the superiority interest in itself should give rise to entitlement to compensation'.[1]

In practice the history of land reform is littered with examples of the redefinition of property rights, from the Crofting Act of 1886 to the Town and Country Planning Act of 1947 and the Land Tenure Reform (Scotland) Act of 1974. Since the restriction of individual private property rights usually involves the expansion of everyone else's, land reform measures will justifiably continue to redefine property rights in the wider public interest.

# Chapter 16

# *Opportunities for Change*

THERE HAVE BEEN numerous controversies surrounding the question of landownership in Scotland. The immediate concerns aroused by such controversies seldom, however, come to rest on the question of landownership. Its influence is deep-seated and its effects are often too subtle. Understanding and analysis of how landownership influences such issues are seldom adequate to permit anything to be done about it. But a strong empirical basis exists to tackle such concerns at their root.

Criticism of Scotland's land tenure regime has been well rehearsed and ranges from the flaws in feudalism, the free market in land, lack of accountability, privatisation of public land to the inequitable pattern of landownership itself. Numerous local difficulties have demonstrated time and time again the problems inherent in a system which allows entire regions to be placed at the whim of international land markets and the various fanciful vanities of existing and aspiring lairds. The pattern of landownership revealed in this book merely reinforces such concerns.

Scotland faces the next millennium with the same legal framework for land tenure that it began this one with. In 1814, Sir John Sinclair, the Caithness improver and author of the first Statistical Account of Scotland was moved to observe that, 'In no country in Europe are the rights of proprietors so well defined and so carefully protected'.[1] The reforms that were commonplace in Europe by the end of the 19th century never took place in Scotland.

Professor Bryan MacGregor observed in 1993:

'The present structure of tenure in Scotland is the interaction of complex historical and economic forces overlaid with government intervention on a large scale and influenced by the varying power of the different interest groups over time. There is no reason to assume that it is the best for contemporary society or even that it is able to deliver desired policy objectives. Indeed, many of the residual aspects of feudalism might suggest urgent change is required.'[2]

Landownership, whilst it may at any one time appear to be amongst the most robust of political and legal institutions, is in practice a mechanism for achieving social objectives and as such is capable of adaptation and change to meet the changing needs of society. The only real question is what kinds of adaptations, for what reasons, on what terms and to whose benefit.

At the heart of any case for change in landownership in Scotland is the simple fact that power to influence how land is used remains hugely concentrated and frequently abused. Indeed any study of virtually any aspect of landownership and use in Scotland can with relative ease be turned into a study of power relations. How such power is derived, distributed and exercised determines what options are available, the kinds of decisions that are made, the viability of rural economies and the fate of entire communities. It determines how the land is used. As the RICS concluded in 1977 in their study of landownership and occupation:

'Rights in land are rights of power. To grant rights grants power. To remove rights removes power. A discussion about the ownership of agricultural and forestry land is therefore about power. Since rights in land give power of some kind, ownership of those rights does matter in terms of the use of the resource for food and timber production – if only because the power may be employed not to use the land for food and timber production.'[3]

It is the contention of many people who have been involved in land issues in Scotland that a dramatic transfer of power from the few to the many is required if we are to aspire to any influence over our own destiny. The power and influence which go with landownership not only include that which has been built up over the past 900 years but the wider political power which was highlighted in Chapter 7. This power, however, is almost totally ignored as an influence in how the country is run.

It is ignored partly because we know so little about how it operates. We know so little about how it operates because we know so little about who is involved. In agriculture, for example, the Northfield Committee argued that more knowledge is needed 'on almost every aspect of landownership, acquisition and occupancy if Government policy is to be formulated on an adequately informed basis'.[4]

In industry, government has at its disposal a raft of information on everything from factory gate prices to capital investment levels. This information informs industrial policy. In contrast, government can tell us nothing about levels of investment in land or patterns of occupancy.

This is important because the current concentrated pattern of private ownership is only one option. It stands in stark contrast to much of the rest of Europe where, for example, small farmers are organised into powerful cooperative movements which are capable of competing in global markets. In Norway, for example, there are 55,000 members of the Norwegian Forest Owners' Federation. They control 75% of the timber market in Norway and together they built up Norske Skog, Norway's biggest forest products company, in which the Federation still has a 36% state. Across the border in Sweden, Södra, a market leader in chlorine-free pulp, is owned by 27,000 forest farmers.

In Scotland, we don't even know how many forest owners there are. Farm forestry schemes have found more favour with city investors than with farmers, and vast numbers of farmers have no legal rights to plant or manage woodlands because they are tenants. In important respects, the land-based rural economy of Scotland is something like 150 years behind that of most west European countries. Central to such differences is the pattern of landownership and the system of land tenure.

Tremendous opportunities could open up for the economy and people of Scotland if landownership and tenure were to be the subject of the same kind of critical appraisal that industrial, social, health and education policy is exposed to. The challenge for Scotland as it moves into the 21st century is to recognise this and develop a system of land tenure and ownership which is flexible, democratic and accountable. Such a challenge is as much about determining and meeting the needs of the landless as it is about understanding and analysing the landed.

The kind of approach required to bring this about is outlined in the following chapter.

# Chapter 17

# *Towards a Land Reform Agenda*

## The Need For Information

AN ESSENTIAL PREREQUISITE to developing any new system of land tenure and ownership in Scotland is the need for publicly available, comprehensive, and detailed information on a wide range of issues. This is no more than a reiteration of calls which have been made by many agencies and enquiries over many decades.

A much more consistent approach is also needed towards the availability of such information. We need to clearly review and define the status of information gathered for public policy purposes and agree that it is legitimate, for example, to know who receives what in public financial support. Above all, greater openness and transparency is needed on who has interests in land and who owns it.

Most other European countries have cadastres and registers of landownership, for example, which go beyond strictly legal functions. Numerous academics and government enquiries have lamented the fact that the 1872 survey and McEwen's interpretation of Millman's maps remain the only sources of information available. The Registers of Scotland remain one of the most comprehensive registers of property in the world and the new Land Register is an important development since it is a computerised, map-based register. It is still, however, and quite appropriately, structured and run as a register of legal interest. What is needed to satisfy a wide range of public needs is a simple cadastral map available in every local authority office which shows clearly defined boundaries of different proprietors together with a comprehensive database. Such a register would have no legal function but be purely geographical and political. Such a system could easily be developed to meet well-defined needs and some proposals for establishing it are presented in Appendix 1.

The desire to know who owns the country is not restricted to a small number of land reform activists or even frustrated government officials wasting time and money in discharging routine responsibilities. The private sector is sufficiently motivated by the need to know that the Royal Institution of Chartered Surveyors recently launched the Domesday 2000 initiative with the aim of working towards the free flow of information about all land and property in Britain. The idea is to develop a communications network connecting all suppliers of land and property data. Of itself it will not yield any information that is not already being collected but it is intended to integrate the information into a National Land Information System so that users may have access to 'high quality, comprehensive and continually updated data'.

- A wide range of information and data should be assembled to enable a better understanding of the operation of the land tenure system and current pattern of landownership.
- A cadastral, map-based register of landownership should be developed and made available in every local authority office.

With accessible and reliable information, a programme of land reform can begin to be developed.

## A Structured Approach To Land Reform

Land reform is a comprehensive package of legal, administrative and fiscal measures designed to redefine and redistribute property rights. It contains many potential elements which in the Scottish situation could range from the reform or abolition of feudal tenure to the reform of the Common Agricultural Policy. These elements are often confused in discussions about landownership but are essential to identify since they are applicable both in isolation and in totality to resolving the land question.

But land reform needs to go beyond property rights to tackle other social, economic and institutional issues. The behaviour and culture of institutions and bureaucracies need to be considered. Laws on taxation and inheritance are important. Programmes of rural development including support systems and advisory services need to be reformed since they will be structured according to the old pattern of landownership. If, for example, it is felt desirable to maintain small and family farms, it is no good limiting farm size without reforming agricultural support policies which continue to favour larger farms.

It is also important to recognise the distinction between reforming land tenure and a wider programme of land reform. It is perfectly possible to reform feudal tenure but do nothing to regulate who then operates within the system. Given the fact that feudal tenure has been a central influence in the current pattern of ownership, however, it would be sensible to tackle both since the current pattern of ownership is substantially the product of feudal tenure and the mere abolition of feudalism is unlikely to achieve much if it leaves this pattern unaltered.

Land reform needs to create an environment where the worst of current problems are less likely to occur and to proactively encourage those things which are positively desirable. Key to any reforms needs to be a set of agreed political principles.

Fundamental principles to underpin a programme of reform are that:

1. Land is both legally and morally the common property of all the people of Scotland.
2. Private landholding, appropriately defined, is in the public interest.
3. A more equitable distribution of property rights and a more accountable framework of such rights are in the public interest and should be pursued.

The aims of a Scottish programme of land reform should be to conserve, utilise and develop the land of Scotland in an accountable and democratic manner whilst protecting, sustaining and enhancing the resource base. It should be to create an enabling and flexible system which seeks to expand individual freedoms and rights within a collective framework of responsibility. The remainder of this chapter outlines a structured agenda for land reform consistent with the above principles and aims.

## The Derivation of Property Rights

An apocryphal story is told of a Fife miner walking home one evening with a brace of pheasants in his pockets. He meets the landowner unexpectedly who informs him that this is his land and he had better hand over the pheasants.

'Your land eh,' asks the miner.

'Yes,' replies the laird, 'and my pheasants.'

'And who did you get this land from?'

'Well, I inherited it from my father.'

'And who did he get it from?' the miner insists.

'His father of course. The land has been in my family for over 400 years,' the laird splutters.

'OK, so how did your family come to own this land 400 years ago?' the miner asks.

'Well . . . well . . . they fought for it!'

'Fine,' replies the miner. 'Take your jacket off and I'll fight you for it now.'

What such a story suggests is not that all land is illegally held or that there should be any justification for seizing land by force, but that historically, legal and political systems have acknowledged rights to land on the basis that the ownership is already properly established. Historically, such claims can be relatively easily disputed and it is only the existence of an agreed code of law that prevents rival claims being entertained. Laws are, however, social constructs. Rights in land have no absolute sanctity and are entirely dependent on the sanction of the wider society within which they are granted.

In Scotland, the system of feudal law, together with the laws of prescription whereby land held without challenge becomes owned by whoever is first to stake a recognised legal claim, has been a major factor in the persistent concentrated pattern of private ownership. Nine hundred years of feudalism have been highly successful in effecting the transformation of common property into private property.

As a system of land tenure feudalism has little to commend it in terms of the principles outlined above. It was designed as a system of central authority over territory but many of the elements which made it such an effective system of government have long since disappeared. Indeed for many reasons what remains is entirely inappropriate. Conveyancing is complex, the distribution of rights are poorly understood, it stifles enterprise through the burdens and restrictions that can be placed by superiors and it is undemocratic since it introduces into the property system private interests whose authority can override public interests. The obligation for vassals to obtain permission, often at substantial cost, for permission to do anything from putting in new windows to opening up a business has been appropriately described by one commentator as 'lucrative legalised blackmail'.[1]

Feudalism should be abolished in its entirety as the basis for Scotland's land tenure law. Its abolition, however, raises the question of what to do with the Crown. Currently all authority under feudalism is derived by the Crown from God. Given that it is beyond the scope or authority of this author to open up theological questions, God should certainly remain. It is, however, legitimate to question the role of the Crown. Under the current system, the Crown is the effective guarantor of the public interest. It was through the Crown that feudalism evolved from a system of government to a system of property rights and in Scottish constitutional theory, the people, rather than parliament or the Crown, are sovereign.

It would seem appropriate therefore that in abolishing feudalism, the authority of the Crown should be made the subject of a contemporary interpretation such as that provided by the traditional 'Community of the Realm' with other Crown rights such as those of minerals, salmon and the seabed being held in some form of trust under the authority of a Scottish parliament.[2]

It is also suggested that since the Crown (and Ministers of the Crown) has reclaimed certain rights such as coal and reserved others such as salmon, oil and gas, its successors could equally extend this process by, for example, reserving certain rights which could be held in perpetual public trust even if leased or granted to local or other forms of management.

The Scottish Law Commission is currently reviewing proposals to abolish the feudal system. Many questions remain to be resolved, however, not least the role of the Crown which is barely addressed in its proposals. Legal reforms must not simply be drawn up for the convenience of the conveyancing profession but must also address the wider social and political objective of abolishing feudalism in its entirety.

- Feudalism should be abolished as the basis for the Scots law of land tenure.
- In the process the authority of the Crown should be re-enacted as part of a modern democratic institution such as the Community of the Realm.

## A Redefinition of Ownership

Any new system of land tenure needs to strike a clear balance between the private and the public interest. Currently, the legal doctrine of exclusive possession underlies the Scots law of property. This doctrine of exclusive possession and, in turn, enjoyment (through preventing others from interfering with such rights) has evolved from the assumption that, save where otherwise legislated, a landowner owns all rights. This has led to an unsatisfactory state of affairs whereby, for example, the de facto freedom to roam enjoys no legal protection whilst those who exercise it are by law defined as trespassers. It is inappropriate that proprietorial rights should be framed in such an essentially exclusive fashion.

Private landownership has for a long time been subject to numerous restrictions on the exclusive right to enjoy in any case and a redefinition of ownership would provide a clearer and more democratic framework for the exercise of the freedoms which it brings. Central to such a redefinition must be that it encompasses only those rights which it is in the public interest to have held privately. Under a simplified system of land tenure, private ownership will be restricted to such rights.

In the context of the need to redefine private property rights it is worth noting that a distinction needs to be made between the ownership of property rights and rights to use. Virtually all game, for example, belongs to no-one, and the legislation which matters is that governing the rights to hunt and take animals such as fish and deer. It follows, therefore, that regulations covering rights to use, also need to be considered in any redefinition of ownership.

Related to a redefinition of ownership is the question of what types of impersonal legal arrangements should be competent to own land. At present, in addition to real persons, any number of legal arrangements from trusts to companies to partnerships may be employed to hold land. Two issues are relevant to the question. The first relates to accountability and the second to motivation.

Trusts and companies are often used as devices to conceal the identity of beneficial owners. For this reason alone the law governing them should be amended to incorporate a requirement to disclose beneficial owners. Such arrangements are also often used to perpetuate ownership indefinitely and thus avoid, for example, exposure to inheritance tax. A trust or company can live forever even whilst the beneficiaries and trustees (in the case of trusts) or directors and members (in the case of companies) may change at any time. It is not in the public interest that land should effectively be sterilised for future generations whose aspirations and needs may be very different to those of today. Whilst reforming the laws governing trusts and companies may go some way in addressing some of the issues, it would be much simpler to exclude them altogether from ownership of land. This would, in addition, ensure that the wider measures designed to reform landownership are not rendered ineffective. This reform would not be unusual in a European context. Many countries constrain or even prohibit certain activities by trusts and companies.

In a Scottish context, companies whose prime objective (or whose parent company's prime objective) is not the occupation and use of land, should be prohibited from owning land. This would include pension funds and investment concerns as well as companies which own land in order to write off losses against other taxable income. Also prohibited as a matter of principle would be all offshore companies and branches of foreign companies.

Where landownership is central to the activities of a business such as a shop or factory, however, corporate landownership would be allowed provided that such a business constituted the prime objective. Companies, co-operatives, and public trusts would also have a role in providing vehicles for community ownership of land.

- Private rights of ownership should be redefined to provide a proper balance between the public and private interest.
- Private trusts and companies whose prime concern or those of its beneficiaries or parent company is not the occupation and use of land should be prohibited from holding title to land.
- Regardless of purpose, all offshore companies and Scottish branches of overseas companies should be prohibited from holding land.

## The Distribution of Authority

Central to any reform of the most concentrated pattern of private ownership in Europe must be measures to redistribute land and rights in land. The abolition of feudalism and redefinition of ownership as already outlined will go some way to achieving this but if a serious effort is to be made to expand private ownership many more measures should be considered.

The most obvious and straightforward measure to effect a redistribution of land would be to limit individual ownership to single landholdings with upper size limits based on land quality. Such measures are common in countries such as Denmark. Forms of community ownership should also be developed which extend the opportunities for a stake in landholding beyond individual landholders. Any prospects of promoting more equitable opportunities for gaining access to land must embrace such measures.

Another tool for redistribution is to extend and amend where necessary the rights of tenants to purchase their land. At the moment this is restricted to council housing and crofts. It should be extended to tenant farmers and smallholders. In the case of tenant farmers, we have a situation where landowners have surplus land which they are reluctant to let under existing tenancy legislation since this confers security of tenure for the tenant. Instead of reforming the tenancy laws, existing tenants should be given the right to buy their farms. Surplus land, currently held by the landowner, would be thus transferred to new entrants to agriculture under the reforms dealing with limits to landholding. This should be allied to measures which allow more flexible arrangements for letting land in certain circumstances.

There must also be a strengthened role for public bodies to intervene in the land market. In this respect, reconsideration should be given to the kinds of proposals outlined by the HIDB in 1978[3] which, although they will undoubtedly require revision, represent the most recent attempt by a public body with experience in rural development to develop new powers. At the very least, certain public bodies should, for clearly defined purposes, have powers to intervene over land which is for sale. Such powers would be nothing new and to some extent are already contained in the Agriculture Act of 1967 which was used successfully by the North Pennines Rural Development Board during its short life from 1969 to 1970.[4] Land settlement could also be extended through the statutory powers introduced earlier this century and which remain on the statute book.

But redistribution should not be restricted to private land. A new understanding of the potential role of public ownership of land is desperately needed in order to get away from old ideas of public versus private. The assumption is often made that public ownership somehow brings in its wake the dead hand of bureaucracy and management by committee. Certainly, the particular notion of public ownership developed in the UK has involved this since public ownership by central government has usually been vested in British cabinet ministers. Opportunities for genuine public participation have been limited and accountability at a local level has been notoriously lacking. It does not follow that just because land is held by a public body that it is necessarily best managed by that same public body, especially if the owner is (as in the case of FC and SOAEFD land) the Secretary of State for Scotland.

Public ownership of land could also be pursued with a view to making resources available to willing, creative and enterprising people whether they be farmers cooperatives, crofters or local community organisations. Free from the uncertainty of titles changing hands, investment can be attracted and built up by those with the greatest needs, abilities and enthusiasm. An argument can be made for a substantial programme of 'land nationalisation' without it being ideologically driven by statist principles which necessitate state management. It can equally be driven by capitalist principles. Adam Smith and the founding fathers of modern capitalism never dreamt that the basic resource, land, would be treated as just another form of capital. To them the role of the state was to make available the means by which people could release their full potential. One of these means is access to land and the democratic power to influence its use.

The Forestry Commission, which has been described by one commentator as 'a centrally organised bureaucracy which is to Scottish forestry what collectivisation was to Soviet agriculture'[5] is perhaps most ripe for such moves. Not only has it had in the past a social remit which involved the development of forest villages and forest worker holdings, but the UK government is currently spending millions of pounds of overseas aid money in promoting the transfer or sharing of power by communities and state forest authorities in countries such as Nepal and India. If it is good enough for these sister countries of the Commonwealth, it is good enough for Scotland.

Finally, the inheritance tax regime and other measures targeted at more equitable distribution of wealth should be harmonised with the objectives of redistributing land and should, where supportive, be strengthened.

Approaches to the redistribution of property rights are many and varied and it is important that as wide as possible a range of options are developed to suit widely varying circumstances. The key to successful redistribution is a range of flexible options.

- Landownership by individuals should be limited to single holdings with upper size limits based on land quality.
- Existing and new forms of common and community ownership should be developed and expanded.
- All agricultural tenants should be extended the right to purchase their land on appropriate terms allied to the introduction of more flexible tenancy arrangements.
- Strengthened powers should be provided to specified statutory agencies for specified purposes to intervene in the land market.
- A new approach should be developed towards the management of existing public land together with its possible expansion.
- The land held by the Secretary of State for Scotland (or successor under a Scottish Parliament) should as a matter of priority be the subject of detailed proposals to bring substantial areas under local management through farmers cooperatives and community associations.
- The taxation regime governing inheritance should be consistent and harmonious with the above measures.

## Methods of Obtaining and Disposing of Land

The regulation of land transfers is one of the commonest features of landownership systems in other countries. The lack of any regulation is one reason why Scotland remains very different from its European neighbours. Land can come into the ownership of persons through inheritance or sale.

The laws governing inheritance of property have been one of the key elements leading to the present concentration of private ownership. It is important that any law on inheritance should be consistent with the reforms outlined so far. There is little point in restricting the size of holdings for example if the existing pattern can simply be inherited by the next generation. The role of inheritance tax has already been mentioned. There is, however, a clear and logical argument which suggests that everyone should be treated equally with respect to land holding. Whilst other arrangements or indeed no change at all may be made for the inheritance of other forms of property and assets such as money, shares, movable property, titles etc., land should be treated separately in view of its special nature. Inheritance in these circumstances should be restricted to dwellings and land consistent with the upper size limits already proposed.

A secure basis for family inheritance is an important component of most stable land tenure regimes and has many advantages in terms of long-term planning and investment. It should be encouraged and protected under any land reform programme although it is not unusual for inheritance to be severely restricted and for heritors to be treated in just the same way as other aspiring landowners.

The second method of land disposal is sale. The market in land is one of the most important areas in which change can be effected and there have been regular calls for sales to be regulated in one way or another. As with other types of transfer, land sales should be consistent with the reforms already outlined so that, for example, no-one could buy land above the permitted size ceiling. Many countries, however, also impose other restrictions. These typically seek to allow neighbouring farmers, local people and members of the existing owner's family to have some form of priority when land is for sale. Regulations also frequently require owners to be resident and to meet certain standards of husbandry.

In a Scottish context it is proposed that land sales are regulated with a view to securing the objectives of the wider land reform programme. All planned sales should be notified to local authorities or a similar body set up for the purpose such as a Land Commission. All owners should be required to take up permanent residence on land within a fixed period of time. Where planning or physical restrictions make this impossible, owners should be required to take up residence within a fixed distance from the land.

With regard to foreign nationals, it is proposed to follow the practice of other European countries and, notwithstanding priorities which may be given to neighbours etc, restrict purchase to individuals over 16 years old who are citizens of a member state of the EU.

The question of land sales also raises the question of prices. Whilst governments regularly enact measures which have substantial impacts on labour and capital markets, the idea that such measures are equally appropriate for land tends to be regarded as some kind of communist plot. It is not proposed that the free market be done away with but some restrictions in addition to those already mentioned would help to bring prices within the reach of many more people. Prices for farmland, for example, should not exceed the capacity of the land to yield a return.

In addition, land prices should also be regulated to exclude the influence of public subsidies such as the agriculture support which was largely responsible for the 25–30% rise in Scottish land prices between 1993 and 1995. The capitalisation of public subsidies in enhanced land values has been one of the most obvious effects of the CAP and has ended up benefiting existing owners through no effort on their part whilst making it difficult for new entrants to farming.

- All land transfers through inheritance should be consistent with other elements of the land reform programme, in particular the limitation of holding size.
- All land sales should be notified to an appropriate public body prior to the land being put on the market.
- All purchasers of land should be required to take up residence on their property.
- Land purchase should be open to all EU citizens over 16 years old.
- Where appropriate land prices should be regulated to prevent them exceeding the productive capacity of the land.

## Obligations of Ownership

Landownership confers rights and obligations. Reasonable obligations should include the requirement to maintain certain standards of land management, but one of the principal obligations arises out of the very nature of land as a private monopoly. Since bare land is created by no-one and is restricted in supply, its ownership confers economic power in so far as all economic activity relies on land and land can be withheld from use. Land value taxation (LVT) is a form of public revenue which is levied on land values which in turn are determined on the basis of bare land value (excluding all improvements) at current permitted uses. A high value parcel of land in the city centre therefore would attract a high valuation by virtue of its valuable permitted use. This value is entirely due to its fortuitous location and the wider efforts of society in developing the surrounding area.

Land value taxation is not so much a tax as a fee paid by landowners in recognition of the exclusive rights which accompany such ownership. LVT can contribute substantially to public revenues and has been introduced in countries such as Denmark and New Zealand. In Britain it has been calculated that such measures could contribute as much as 44% of all central and local government revenue and exceed the income tax paid by people.[6] Its introduction would therefore allow the total elimination of taxes on income. The exact levy can initially be low but ultimately the purpose is to eliminate any financial benefit accruing to landowners by virtue of property rights alone. It is designed to ease he burden of taxation on those things that create wealth such as labour and capital and increase it on land whose supply is fixed and held by private monopoly.

It is worth noting that, with the abolition of sporting rates on April 1 1995, land in Scotland now attracts no tax burden at all for the first time in over 500 years. A precedent has already been set in the application of the principle of LVT. Crofting rents are invariably low, something in the order of £10–£30 per year. The Crofting Act of 1976, which allowed crofters to purchase their crofts at prices roughly equal to 15 times the annual rent, enabled crofts to be bought for very low prices. These rents which, since the Crofting Act of 1886, have been the subject of adjudication by the Scottish Land Court, are low because they represent the bare land value of the croft. All the agricultural and infrastructural improvements that have been carried out are the work of successive generations of crofting tenants and as such are clearly recognised by the Land Court and others as outwith the scope of crofting rents. The rent payable to the landlord should never therefore change unless the bare land value itself changes. This is the principle of Land Value Taxation in operation. The only difference of course is that under LVT the rent would be paid into public revenues since the landlord has no authority other than a paper title to intercept it.

LVT would obviously have beneficial effects on land prices which would facilitate the wider reform programme. Unless one abolishes totally the market in land, property rights will always be valued and rightly so. The relevant question is how this value is arrived at and what obligations are placed on those who enjoy such rights.

- Land should be used as the basis for raising a proportion of public revenues through Land Value Taxation based on its bare land value and current permitted uses.

## Land Use Support

Under current arrangements for the support and regulation of key land uses, landowners play a pivotal role in both choosing whether to take advantage of such support and in benefiting from it. The agricultural, forestry and environmental support systems however tend to be grossly deficient in achieving anything other than the relatively straightforward task of making sure that food is grown and timber is produced (environmental protection has been rather more problematic). Beyond this, they have achieved little by way of a contribution to wider rural development. Indeed they have done precisely the opposite in many cases. Agricultural support geared to production output has resulted in massively distorted incomes. Overproduction is being tackled by paying the beneficiaries of such measures further sums to produce nothing! Forestry support has equally been available only to those who have or are capable of obtaining property rights and has led to gross abuses. Vast sums in environmental support have been paid to landowners to desist from undertaking environmentally damaging activities which many of them had no intention of undertaking in the first place. To cap it all, all such payments have been regarded as confidential and information denied to the public despite it being public money!

Land use support is therefore critical to any land reform programme. Not only does it have a substantial impact on the pattern of landownership, but the manner in which it has been developed in the UK has played a decisively negative role in promoting a more equitable pattern of ownership whereby more people could benefit from such support.

Given the need to harmonise the various policy objectives with an impact on land reform it is necessary to reform land use support policies. The kinds of reforms already outlined would go some way to achieving this by altering the pattern of landownership but land use policy itself must play a supportive role.

Scotland needs an integrated land use policy and strategies to deliver it. This reflects a concern going back as far as the postwar years which has still not yet been addressed. Forestry and agriculture, so well integrated in other countries, continue to be pursued in a competitive and mutually exclusive manner. Such strategies should be developed not as some blanket prescription but through participatory methods working at local level. This is especially important in a Scottish context since environmental conditions change dramatically over very short distances. Strategies which have been partially developed in the past fail to take account of the need to work on a local scale.

All land use support measures should be targeted specifically and exclusively at resident landowners. This condition may be redundant in view of the existing proposal to insist on residency as a condition of owning land but since there will in practice be a transition period it is vital that it is introduced with immediate effect.

Finally, all payments associated with land use support should not only include social and environmental conditions but should be subject to cash limits per holding. This would ensure a dramatically more equitable distribution of public funds, the availability of which may very well be reduced in response to wider European political developments.

Such measures will help to stimulate local economies, encourage settlement, support family businesses and direct support to maximum economic benefit.

- Locally based land use strategies should be developed.
- Land use support measures should be restricted to resident landowners.
- All public support payments should be subject to upper limits per holding.

## Administrative Framework

An administrative system which is designed to deliver policies geared to the existing pattern of ownership is in no condition to deliver to a reformed pattern and will need to adapt. These adaptations need to include the working culture and practices, organisational structures, lines of accountability, skills and delivery mechanisms. Above all, bureaucracies must adapt to embrace the broad aims of land reform. Too often, in spite of political will, land reform has failed due to the inertia and indeed outright hostility of the various organs of permanent government. The current composition and structure of government agencies, local government and quangos in Scotland will require review in terms of their capacity to support such land reforms.

There are good arguments also for turning much of the current administrative framework on its head. At present, land occupiers are at the receiving end of centrally constructed and centrally regulated support frameworks. There is no reason why such support frameworks should not be devised on a local or regional basis to meet the diverse range of conditions across the country. It is common in Norway, for example, for farmers to construct and propose their own financial support packages to Parliament which then debates and votes on the issue. Farmers' producer organisations are then left with the responsibility of administering and regulating the package even to the extent of deciding for themselves how to deal with surplus agricultural production.

Not only must the administrative framework adapt but new institutions may be required. The concept of a permanent Land Commission which would oversee such a long-term programme has been proposed by many people. Financial support may also require adjusting. It is notable in recent years that the Scottish banks for example seem to have lost interest in investing in real people in the real Scottish economy. As John Goodlad, who wears many hats connected with the Shetland fishing industry, pointed out recently,

'It is both an indictment of the Scottish banking system and a reflection of the professionalism of the Scandinavian banking system that most of the modern Shetland purse seine fleet have been financed by Norwegian banks. Perhaps the long term solution to this problem lies in a Highland based bank dedicated to serving the economy of the area within which it is based.'[7]

New arrangements along such lines will be needed as will new forms of credit and cooperative institutions. Land reform will not only promote important political changes, it should also promote important economic changes. The growth of the social economy, which commonly consists of voluntary organisations, cooperatives and mutual and friendly societies, is an important supporting framework for land reform and one which is already present in many parts of rural Scotland. With appropriate support and assistance the sector could grow rapidly and play an enhanced role in the rural economy.

- Existing government departments and agencies will need to adapt their structure, role, procedures and internal culture to support land reform.
- New institutions such as a Land Commission may be required to complement or replace existing bodies.
- New private and public financial support measures and structures are necessary to stimulate and develop the social economy.

## Implementation of Land Reform

Many of the above proposals are by no means original. In Scotland, various land reform proposals have been developed in recent years and should be studied as a complement to the above.[8]

Neither is there anything in these proposals which does not already have a precedent either in other countries or indeed in Scotland. It is worth highlighting, for example, how the myriad regulations of crofting tenancies contain many if not all of the elements of this land reform programme.

Crofting regulations cover, among other things, assignation (transfer to other parties), succession, absenteeism, decrofting (removal from crofting tenure) and the maintenance of a register of crofts. These are all areas which have perfectly properly been considered to be in the public interest. Whilst crofting law is in as much need of tightening up and simplifying as feudal tenure law, its basic principles are equally applicable to all forms of landholding. Just as the Crofters Commission regulates crofting, so a Land Commission would regulate landholding. Even within the body of Scots land law therefore there is nothing particularly novel about these land reform measures except to propose that what is good enough for crofters is good enough for landowners. It seems perfectly logical and natural that all holders of land regardless of the form of tenure should be subject to the same controls.

There are some strictly political questions raised by such a land reform programme however. For example, should owners enjoy their current rights unaffected until death or transfer? Given that an appointed date will be set by which all reforms will come fully into effect, should a transitional period be introduced? How should large landowners divest themselves of land to meet size limitations? These questions need to be carefully explored so as to ensure justice and fairness in their application and to avoid any attempts to frustrate both the spirit and the letter of reform.

Land reform will lead to a redistribution of power from the few to the many. It is critical that this is carried out in such a way as to prevent any notion of compulsion and force. It will involve an expansion of private ownership and should therefore enjoy political support from those who support the principle of private ownership. The only point of difference arises when one begins to decide how widely such private interests should be spread. Most of the reforms outlined are capable of adaptation to meet varying degrees of balance between the private and the public interest.

Finally, if there are any problems in developing, legislating and implementing such reforms, there exists a substantial body of expertise in organisations such as the Overseas Development Institute, and in the government's Overseas Development Administration. There are major programmes, policies and research findings devoted to land reform to which Scottish expertise has in many cases contributed.[9]

Land reform need not be a problem.

# Conclusions

IT IS AN indictment of the current political settlement that such a book as this needs to be written. What this book has revealed is a system and pattern of private landownership without parallel anywhere in the world. Not only is it merely the contemporary expression of 900 years of feudal land law, it is also the most concentrated and secretive in Europe.

It is no coincidence that Scotland should be the last outpost of feudal land law and the country with the most concentrated patterns of private landownership in Europe. For the last 300 years it has had little effective say in its own domestic affairs, being virtually the only country in the world with its own legal system but with no legislature to enact and amend such laws. Such a situation is, in the final analysis, the responsibility of the people of Scotland to resolve.

A number of political, as distinct from technical, questions are therefore raised by any land reform programme. Foremost among these is the need for the political will to carry them out. Historically Westminster has proved incapable of addressing a progressive programme of land reform. Indeed due to its structure and the existence of a hereditary second chamber with direct interests in land it has frequently frustrated such attempts. To build a modern legal system of property rights and carry out a meaningful programme of land reform, a sovereign Scottish parliament is required. Scotland cannot be properly governed by a parliamentary timetable which allows for a handful of Scottish Bills and which is dominated by elected representatives whose constituents are, with some exceptions among the ranks of those who own land in Scotland, totally unaffected by any of the changes proposed.

Scotland needs a parliament which has the time and the political will to devote to land reform.

It needs a parliament with full control over land law, tenure, occupancy and use in both the private and the public sector. It needs to have a direct role in European affairs which are critical to agriculture, fisheries, rural development and environmental policies, and in taxation matters which, as highlighted by inheritance tax provisions, are an important tool in wealth redistribution.

Land reform is normal, it is practical and it is achievable. The archaic, secretive, anti-democratic, feudal and exclusive system that constitutes Scottish landownership in the late 20th century needs to be finally consigned to the history books. In its place needs to be constructed an open, accountable, equitable and flexible system of distributing land rights which provides opportunities for entrepreneurial flair, for environmental protection and restoration and for the development of a vibrant and healthy economy. There is nothing wrong in principle with the notion of private landownership. We just need to redefine and expand it.

Scotland needs land reform for spiritual, cultural, moral and economic reasons. Land reform could be the engine of a wider process of spiritual and cultural renewal to prepare the people of Scotland and the wider world for the challenges of the 21st century.

This book is no more than a small contribution in an enormous vacuum. It is time for politicians, academics and others to rise to the challenge of achieving a better understanding of landownership in Scotland, of assembling more information and stimulating a more informed debate about how to regulate the relationship between the two things that make Scotland: its people and its land.

# *References*

## Introduction
1 Such ignorance is frequently no more than the normal uncertainties about Scottish issues displayed by the London media and others. But often it is more deep rooted and even affects serious academic work on landownership. See for example Cox et al. 1988, 'Private Rights and Public responsibilities: the Prospects for Agricultural and Environmental Controls', *Journal of Rural Studies* 4 (4) pp. 323–337. It includes an analysis of the policies of the National Farmers Union and the Country Landowners Association, both English organisations, and yet purports to be a paper about the British countryside. It also claims that game rights in Britain are separable from landownership unlike 'elsewhere in Europe' where the 'right to sport has gone with the ownership of land'. Elsewhere in Europe includes Scotland.

## SECTION I

### Chapter 1: The Development of Feudalism
1 For comprehensive and detailed accounts of feudal land law see:
Sir J. Rankine, 1986. *Laws of Landownership in Scotland*. W. Green, Edinburgh.
For a wider picture of laws relating to land see:
W.M. Gordon, 1989. *Scottish Land Law*. W. Green, Edinburgh.
For a more concise guide to property law see:
R. Robson and K. Miller, 1991. *Property Law*. W. Green/Sweet & Maxwell, Edinburgh
2 The most comprehensive, succinct and authoritative recent study of the development of feudalism in Scotland is that provided by:
Robin Callander, 1987. *A Pattern of Landownership in Scotland*. Haughend Publications, Finzean. Most of this chapter is derived from this work.
For more details on land tenure in early Scotland see:
R.A. Dodgshon, 1981. *Land and Society in Early Scotland*. Clarendon Press, Oxford.
3 These figures are derived from Callander, 1987 op. cit.
4 Cmnd 4099 'Land Tenure in Scotland – A Plan for Reform', House of Commons, London.

### Chapter 2: Landownership in Scotland Today
1 The ideas of Jean-Jacques Rousseau which were so influential in the French Revolution are typical of how land and its ownership were so often inseparable from wider critiques of how society should order itself. Twentieth century examples include the Chinese and Russian revolutions, the Cuban revolution, the Sandanista revolution in Nicaragua and the Zapatista revolution in Mexico.
2 Some studies which look critically at the role of landownership as part of wider social changes include:
James Hunter, 1976. *The Making of the Crofting Community*. John Donald, Edinburgh.
R.H. Campbell, 1991. *Owners and Occupiers: Changes in Rural Society in South-West Scotland before 1914*. Aberdeen University Press.
T.M. Devine, 1994. *Clanship to Crofters' War. The social transformation of the Scottish Highlands*. Manchester University Press.
Ian Carter, 1979. *Farm Life in North-East Scotland 1840–1914*. John Donald, Edinburgh.
J.M. Bryden and G. Houston, 1976. *Agrarian Change in the Scottish Highlands*. Martin Robertson/HIDB, London.

Ian Carter, 1992. (ed.) *Rural life in Victorian Aberdeenshire by William Alexander.* An edited version published by Mercat Press, Edinburgh.

James Hunter, 1986. (ed.) *For the People's Cause. From the Writings of John Murdoch – Highland and Irish Land Reformer.* HMSO, Edinburgh.

3 Callander, 1987 op. cit.
4 For a concise review of the importance of the land tenure system see:
Bryan MacGregor, 1993. *Land Tenure in Scotland: The John McEwen Memorial Lecture.* Rural Forum, Perth.
5 For the cultural significance of land see:
George Bruce and Frank Rennie, 1991. *The Land Out There: A Scottish Land Anthology.* Mercat Press, Aberdeen.
Malcolm MacLean and Christopher Carrell (eds.), 1986. *As an Fhearran: From the Land. Clearance, Conflict and Crofting. A Century of Images of the Scottish Highlands.*
James Hunter, 1995. *On the Other Side of Sorrow. Nature and People in the Scottish Highlands.* Mainstream, Edinburgh.
6 Auslan Cramb, 1996. *Who Owns Scotland Now? The use and abuse of private land.* Mainstream, Edinburgh
7 See for example Working Party for the Science, Religion and Technology Project, 1986. *While the Earth Endures.* SRT Project, Edinburgh.
8 Two studies begin to uncover the importance of owner motivation:
Bryan D. MacGregor, 1994. 'Owner Motivation and Land Use Change in North West Sutherland.' Research report for WWF Scotland. Department of Land Economy, University of Aberdeen.
A.M. Armstrong and A.S. Mather, 1983. 'Land Ownership and Land Use in the Scottish Highlands.' O'Dell Memorial Monograph No. 13. Department of Geography, University of Aberdeen.
9 Bryan D. MacGregor, 1993, op. cit.

## SECTION II

### Chapter 3: Who Owns Scotland

1 A.S. Mather, 1995. 'Rural Land Occupancy in Scotland: resources for research.' *Scottish Geographical Magazine* vol 111, no. 2 pp. 127–131.
2 John McEwen, 1977. *Who Owns Scotland.* E.U.S.P.B. Edinburgh. A second edition was published by Polygon in 1981 which contained updated information.

### Chapter 4: Availability of Information

1 A.S. Mather, 1995, op. cit.
2 J. Bateman, 1883. *The Great Landowners of Great Britain and Ireland.* 4th edition. Harrison, London. This was reprinted by Leicester University Press in 1971 with a commentary from D. Spring.
3 R. Millman, 1969. 'The marches of the Highland estates.' *Scottish Geographical Magazine* 85, pp. 172–181.
R. Millman, 1970. 'The landed estates of northern Scotland'. *Scottish Geographical Magazine* 86, pp. 186–203.
R. Millman, 1972. 'The landed estates of southern Scotland.' *Scottish Geographical Magazine* 88, 125–133.
4 See for example:
A. Harrison, R.B. Tranter & R.S. Gibbs, 1977. 'Landownership by public and semi-public institutions in the UK.' CAS Paper 3. Centre for Agricultural Strategy, University of Reading.
5 Alasdair Steven, James Ferguson and John McEwen, 1971. *The Acreocracy of Perthshire.* Perth and Kinross Fabian Society, Blairgowrie.
6 McEwen, 1977 op. cit.
7 Scottish Forestry 32, p. 67 1978.
8 Scottish Record Office, RHP 20 000.

9  See for example:
   Gordon Clark, 1981. 'Some secular changes in landownership in Scotland.' *Scottish Geographical Magazine* 97: 27–36.
   This paper examines the national and regional trends in concentration of landownership from 1872/3 to 1970 and provides some interesting insights into the statistical interpretation of such trends.
10 Armstong & Mather op. cit.
   MacGregor op. cit.
   Bryden and Houston op. cit.
11 A.S. Mather & E.M. Soulsby, 1991. 'Land Tenure Review.' Report for Countryside Commission for Scotland.
12 Callander op. cit.
   Skye Forum, 1993. *The Isle of Skye Data Atlas*, Skye Forum, Portree.
   Mountaineering Council of Scotland and The Scottish Landowners' Federation, 1993 (3rd impression with revisions). *Heading for the Scottish Hills*. Scottish Mountaineering Trust, Edinburgh.
13 For a detailed research guide to the Register of Sasines and the Land Register see:
   N.J. Williams and F.E. Twine, 1991. 'A Research Guide to the Register of Sasines and the Land Register in Scotland.' Report to Scottish Homes, Technical Information Paper 3. Scottish Homes, Edinburgh.

## Chapter 6: The Tables and Maps

1 R.H. Campbell op. cit.
2 W.G. Cumming, 1994. 'Scotland's Uplands – The Future.' *Scottish Forestry* Vol 48. No. 2.
3 Quoted from Grampian Television's *An e Farmad a ni Treabhadh*. 13 December 1993.
4 MacGregor, 1994 op. cit.
5 Mather & Soulsby op. cit.

## Chapter 7: The Pattern and the People

1 John McEwen, 1981 (2nd ed.), *Who Owns Scotland*. Polygon, Edinburgh.
2 Devine op. cit.
3 D. Cannadine, 1990. *The Decline and Fall of the British Aristocracy*. Yale University Press, London.
4 D. McCrone, A. Morris & R. Kelly. *Scotland the Brand. The making of Scottish Heritage*. E.U.P., Edinburgh.
   See also:
   D. McCrone & A. Morris. 'Lords & Heritages: the Transformation of the Great Lairds of Scotland.' in: T.M. Devine (ed.), 1994. *Scottish Elites*. John Donald, Edinburgh
5 Gordon Clark, 1981. 'Public Ownership of Land in Scotland.' *Scottish Geographical Magazine*. 97: 140–46.
6 T. Carty & J. Ferguson, 1978. 'Land.' In: T. Carty & A. McCall Smith (eds.), *Power and Manoeuvrability. The international implications of an independent Scotland*. Q Press.
7 HMSO, 1979. 'Report into the Acquisition and Occupancy of Agricultural Land.' Northfield Committee, Cmnd 7599.
8 Armstrong & Mather op. cit.
9 Ibid.
10 Disney Barlow, 1993. *Landowning in Scotland Summer Special*. SLF, Edinburgh and 'Aims and Objectives' leaflet.
11 Royal Institution of Chartered Surveyors, 1977. *The Agricultural Resources of the United Kingdom. The Future Pattern of Land Ownership and Occupation*. RICS.
12 For an insight into the nature and operation of the British Establishment see:
   Jeremy Paxman, 1990. *Friends in High Places*. Michael Joseph, London.
13 George Inge, Director of Savills, quoted in R. Norton-Taylor, 1982. *Whose Land is it Anyway?* Turnstone Press Ltd., Wellingborough. p.28.
14 McCrone & Morris op. cit.

## Chapter 9: The Sporting Estate

1. For a thorough account of the development of deer forests see:
   Willie Orr, 1982. *Deer Forests, Landlords and Crofters.* John Donald, Edinburgh.
2. J.M. McDiarmid, 1926 (2nd ed.). 'The deer forests and how they are bleeding Scotland white.' Scottish Home Rule Association, Glasgow.
3. For the perspective of a sporting estate owner see:
   Michael Wigan, 1991. *The Scottish Highland Estate: Preserving an Environment.* Swan Hill Press, Shrewsbury.
   His more recent publication, 1993. *Stag at Bay. The red deer crisis.* Swan Hill, Shrewsbury marks an unfortunate departure from his previous writing standards.
4. See for example:
   John Lister-Kaye, 1994. *Ill Fares the Land: a sustainable land ethic for the sporting estates of the Highlands and Islands of Scotland.* Barail, Isle of Skye.
5. Quoted in *West Highland Free Press*, 10 June 1994.
6. Michael Wigan, 1993 op. cit.
7. James Hunter speaking on *Eorpa*, BBC Scotland TV, 19 October 1995.

## Chapter 10: Forestry

1. A.S. Mather, 1987. 'The Structure of Forest Ownership in Scotland: a First Approximation.' *Journal of Rural Studies*, Vol. 3 (2) pp.175–182.
2. See for example:
   Reforesting Scotland, 1993. 'Norway and Scotland. A Study in Land Use.' Reforesting Scotland, Ullapool.
   R. Callander, 1995. 'Forests and People in Rural Scotland. A Discussion Paper prepared for the Forests and People in Rural Areas Initiative.' Scottish Office Environment Department, Edinburgh.
3. See for example *Scottish Sunday Express*, 8 May 1994, in which a Forestry Commission spokesman is quoted as saying in response to controversy over grant payments to the Countess of Seafield, 'The amount of the grant is confidential.'
4. Written Parliamentary answer to Calum Macdonald, MP, 10 July 1995. Figures are contained in: 'Forestry Commission, July 1995. Recipients of Payments over £1000 made under the Woodland Grant Scheme in Scotland in 1993–94.' A copy is in the House of Commons library.
5. Figures prepared by Border Consultants to demonstrate the implications of a large Farm Woodland Premium scheme.

## Chapter 11: Crofting

1. For a detailed history of the development of crofting, the classic work is:
   James Hunter, 1976. *The Making of the Crofting Community.* op. cit.
   For recent developments (up to 1991) see:
   James Hunter, 1991. *The Claim of Crofting.* Mainstream, Edinburgh.
2. For an example of how perceptions of crofting were changing see articles by Allan Macinnes and James Hunter in *Radical Scotland* Nos. 25 and 26, 1987.
3. SCU and RSPB, 1992. 'Crofting and the Environment: a new approach.' SCU/RSPB, Broadford/Edinburgh.
4. Hunter, *The Claim of Crofting.* op. cit. page 145.

## Conclusions

1. Callander, *A Pattern of Landownership.* op. cit.

## SECTION III

## Chapter 13: International Comparisons

1. Danus Skene, 1978. 'Am I a chauvinist paranoid?' *Crann Tara*, No.2. Spring 1978.
2. Tony Carty, 1980. 'Danish and Norwegian Land Ownership and Land Use,' in: C. Archer

& S. Maxwell (eds), 1980. *The Nordic Model. Studies in Public Policy Innovation.* Gower, Farnborough.
3 T. Carty and J. Ferguson, *Power and Manoeuvrability.* op. cit.
4 Jan van der Ploeg speaking on *Eorpa*, BBC Scotland TV, 19 October 1995.
5 Callander, 1986. 'The Law of the Land,' in J. Hulbert (ed.) *Land, Ownership and Use.* Andrew Fletcher Society, Edinburgh.

## Chapter 14: Land Reform and the Landownership Debate
1 For more details on land settlement by the state see:
Leah Leneman, 1989. *Fit for Heroes? Land Settlement in Scotland after World War 1.* A.U.P., Aberdeen.
A.S. Mather, 1978. 'State-aided Land Settlement in Scotland.' O'Dell Memorial Monograph No. 6, Department of Geography, University of Aberdeen.
2 Thomas Johnston, 1909. *Our Scots Noble Families.* Forward Publishing, Glasgow 1909.
3 HIDB, 1978. 'Proposals for changes in the Highlands and Islands Development (Scotland) Act 1965 to allow more effective powers over rural land use.' HIDB, Inverness.
4 Danus Skene, 1976. 'Rural Land Policy.' A discussion paper prepared for the Scottish Labour Party.
5 Danus Skene, ibid.
6 Max Hastings, 1995. 'Animal Rights and Wrongs.' *The Field*, June 1995.
7 Quoted from interview on BBC Scotland, *Whose Land is it Anyway.* Part III 26 October 1994.

## Chapter 15: Debunking the Myths
1 Quoted in Scottish Law Commission, 1991. *Property Law. Abolition of the Feudal System.* SLC, Edinburgh. pages 136–137.

## Chapter 16: Opportunities for Change
1 Sir John Sinclair, 1814. Quoted in Callander, 1986 op. cit.
2 MacGregor, John McEwen Lecture. op. cit.
3 RICS op. cit.
4 HMSO op. cit.

## Chapter 17: Towards a Land Reform Agenda
1 Ruaridh Nicoll, 1995. 'Feudal system given notice'. *Scotland on Sunday*, 9 July 1995.
2 Ideas about the transformation of the role of the Crown have been developed by Robin Callander. An early outline of such ideas is outlined in: Callander, 1986 op. cit.
3 HIDB, 1978 op. cit.
4 See Armstrong and Mather, 1983, op. cit for a brief discussion of such matters in the context of the Scottish Highlands.
5 James Hunter, 1992. Guest Editorial in *Reforesting Scotland* Issue No. 7 Autumn 1992.
6 For an analysis of the value of land in Britain see:
Ronald Banks (ed.), 1989. *Costing the Earth.* Shepheard-Walwyn, London.
7 John Goodlad, 1992. 'Shaping the Future. A Shetland perspective.' The Sabhal Mor Lecture. Acair, Stornoway.
8 See for example:
Frank Rennie, 1995. 'The Dingwall Agenda.' Ross & Cromarty District Council, Dingwall.
James Hunter, 1995. 'Towards a Land Reform Agenda for a Scots Parliament.' The 2nd John McEwen Memorial Lecture. Rural Forum Scotland, Perth.
9 For a recent review of experience around the world with land reform programmes see:
Martin Adams, 1995. 'Land Reform: New seeds on old ground?' *Natural Resources Perspectives* No. 6, October 1995. Overseas Development Institute, London.

# Appendix 1

## A Cadastral Land Register

As outlined in Chapter 4, existing sources of information on landownership in Scotland are variable in quality, accessibility, status and usefulness. Persistent demands for the creation of a land register have most frequently been made in response to the lack of accessible information on who exactly owns what. The fact that an official Register already exists is usually acknowledged but since its exact nature and purpose are poorly understood, there has been little done to clarify exactly what it is that would satisfy such demands.

Research for this book clearly backed up the view held by many academics and policy makers that a simple and accessible map-based register of landownership is both necessary and practicable. Much of the information necessary to compile such a cadastre is already in the public domain. The SOAEFD have IACS forms. The FC have maps containing details of forestry grants. SNH have proprietary maps covering SSSIs and the RDC have maps showing the main estates in Red Deer Range. District Valuers have information on property transactions and of course the Land Register contains maps for all properties registered. In addition, information on public holdings is readily available from the relevant organisations.

What is clearly needed is the political will to develop a cadastral register consisting of map-based plans of landownership boundaries together with an accessible database containing information on ownership and value. Such a register would represent a straightforward *application* of existing information rather than a new system altogether. It would provide the public with an easily accessible source of information on individual landholdings, would provide essential preparatory information for surveys of all kinds and would enable many agencies with statutory functions which rely on information about landholdings to access such information easily and cheaply.

The SCOTLIS project of the Royal Institution of Chartered Surveyors has already stimulated moves to integrate various sources of public information. What is still required is the political will to make it happen. Most other countries in the world have high quality integrated information systems about land, its nature, ownership and use. It is normal to be collating, integrating and publishing such information in various forms. A critical aspect of this political will is the need to define which kinds of information are justifiably private and which are public. The lack of consistency about this question was one of the most striking features of research for this book.

There are two options for pursuing the creation of a cadastral register. The first is to rely on the integration of existing sources of information and the abstraction of the relevant details. This might take some time but is worth exploring. One move which could be made without delay is the speeding up of the introduction of the Land Register which, because the Land Registration (Scotland) Act 1979 was introduced principally as a conveyancing reform, has started with the counties with the greatest number of property transactions. It will be 2003 before counties such as Sutherland, Ross & Cromarty, Inverness, Caithness and Moray are brought into it. Even then, registration will only take place when a property is transferred. Given the extent of land currently held by trusts, for example, which may not change hands for decades, it will be many years before the majority of properties are included.

The speeding up of the introduction of the Land Register is one necessary measure but one which is dependent on extra resources being provided. Another measure which could be taken is to require all remaining unregistered interests to be registered. Provision exists in the Act for the Secretary of State for Scotland to do this by means of a statutory instrument. All land could therefore be registered in a modern computerised mapping system by, say, 2005.

Further legislation would be required, however, if the Land Register is to provide all the information which a cadastral register would need. Currently, for example, there is no obligation to provide any details of the beneficiaries of companies or trusts, nor the full addresses of proprietors.

The second option is to proceed with the immediate setting up of a cadastral register which, although it initially would require some extra effort, would eventually simply abstract the relevant details from existing public sources such as the Land Register.

A simple system would be as follows.

Maps would be prepared at 1:25,000 scale annotated by codes and related to a database containing full details of the proprietor. This would be done on a county basis by a nominated local authority to a common standard and the information would be made available to anyone wishing to use it.

This information could be collated from existing sources and opportunity given for confirmation by proprietors. Alternatively, following the example of the 1872 survey, statutory powers could be given to relevant authorities to require an annual submission of information by proprietors. This would include the following.

Name of property.

Map at 1:10,000 or 1:25,000 scale showing boundaries of legal ownerships.

Names of legal owners together with addresses of directors of companies and trustees, trusters and beneficiaries of private trusts.

Tenurial status of holdings (whether tenanted, under crofting tenure, whether held by feu disposition, etc.)

This is the most attractive option since it would put the onus on landowners to provide the information rather than public officials working from imperfect sources.

This information would be updated on a rolling basis. Eventually, of course, the Land Register would be adapted so as to enable its use as the principal source of the information.

Whatever efforts are eventually made to improve the quality and accessibility of information on landownership, it is important that speedy moves are taken to identify the specific needs of various parties and to bring forward recommendations as to how they can be met.

# Appendix 2

## Multiple Proprietors

Where a proprietor owns land in more than one county of Scotland, their individual landholdings are listed here for ease of reference. The holdings are referred to by their place in the county tables (e.g. AB1 refers to holding number 1 in Aberdeen). Where holdings are held contiguously across county boundaries, this is indicated by (part) appearing after the property in the county tables. Such holdings do not appear in this Appendix.

Also listed are holdings which have been treated as one holding for the purposes of analysis but which in fact are owned by several people. In practice the latter category is restricted to a few private forestry holdings in the north of Scotland.

## Multiple Proprietors

| | |
|---|---|
| Abercorn & Mount Castle Trusts | AR120, RX9 |
| Andras Ltd. | BA3, IN15 |
| Jean Balfour | FI1, KK42, SU19 |
| Lady Benson & Earl of Wemyss | EL3, PB2, SE2 |
| Domenico Berardelli | AR100, IN95 |
| BICC | AR169, PR108, RX11 |
| BMF Group | AB11, BA13 |
| Bocardo Societe Anonyme & Ross Estates Co. | RO75, SU42 |
| Bowland Estates & Leon Litchfield | MI14, SE5, MO1, RX34 |
| I.H. Brown | IN36, PR137, RO62 |
| Buccleuch Estates Ltd. | DM1, LA6, MI9, RX2, SE1 |
| David E. Bulmer | RO105, SU43 |
| Lord Burton | IN12, RO30 |
| Bute Estates | AR102, AY1, BU1 |
| CERN | PB19, RX12 |
| Charles R. Connell | IN18, PR145, ST25 |
| Co-op Wholesale Society Ltd. | AB109, AY70, PR159 |
| Viscount Cowdray | AB3, KC2 |
| Dalgety Pension Trust | PR156, RX37 |
| Douglas & Angus | BE11, LA1 |
| Dunlin Ltd. & J.H. Richmond Watson | AY8, IN75 |
| Eagle Star | AR30, AY23, KR5, KK20, PR38 |
| Electricity Supply Nominees | AB96, AN46, AR128, KK2, LA4, PB20 |
| Thomas Elliot & Elliot Bros | SE19, SU12 |

| Owner | Holdings |
|---|---|
| Faccombe Estates Ltd. | BE4, EL5 |
| Richard Munro Ferguson | FI5, RO22 |
| Robert Steuart Fothringham | AN15, PR13 |
| Gallacher Pensions Trust Ltd. | AR75, SE41 |
| General Accident | KK51, MO21, PR183 |
| Glencanisp & Drumrunie Deer Forest Trust | RO35, SU3 |
| Andrew D. Gordon | IN33, PR24 |
| Gong Hill Ltd. | AR178, AY47 |
| Greentop Lands & Estates & Christensen | AR26, IN123, KK27, LA37, PB43, PR69, ST2 |
| J.M. Guthrie & Broadland Properties | AR4, MO2, RO44 |
| Halifax Building Society Pension Nominees | DM62, LA25, RX22 |
| Captain John Hay of Delgatie | AB110, SH11 |
| Hopetoun Estates | LA2, WL1 |
| Horsens Folkeblad Foundation | BA15, IN147 |
| Earl of Inchcape | AY2, DM60 |
| Invercauld & Torloisk Trusts | AB1, AR20, PR9 |
| Henry Keswick | AN5, KK4 |
| Kronospan | DM26, RX19, SE6 |
| Midland Bank | AR87, PR27, RX36 |
| Moray Estates | MO3, PR17 |
| Northern Ireland Local Government | LA21, RX14 |
| Fred Olsen & Cinco Ltd. | AY48, KK1 |
| Owl Forest | DM38, SE9 |
| John Paterson | KR7, PR171 |
| PB Forestry Lands Ltd. | RX5, SE4 |
| Philiphaugh Trust | RX7, SE3 |
| Post Office Staff Superannuation Scheme | IN134, MO16, RX20 |
| HM Queen & Trustees of Balmoral | AB4, AN19 |
| Refuge Farms Ltd. | AY38, DM71, EL13, KK36 |
| Hon. E. Maurice W. Robson | IN56, RO25 |
| H.H. Roesner Land & Forestry Management | AY18, SU10 |
| Earl of Rosebery | MI1, PB1 |
| Duke of Roxburghe | BE1, RX1 |
| Scottish Amicable | AY35, DM25, KK25, SE42 |
| Earl of Seafield | BA4, IN5, MO5 |
| Andrew G. Simpson | CA22, FI14 |
| Duke of Sutherland | BE8, SE23 |
| W.H. Smith Pension Fund | KK41, RX35 |
| Patrick Wilson | PR67, RO16, SU85 |

## Multiple Holdings

| ALTNABREAC and LOCHDU (Caithness) | | Acres |
|---|---|---|
| Station Hill | Geoffrey Marshall, Godalming | 212 |
| Raphan | Peter Riches, Milton Keynes | 638 |

| | | |
|---|---|---|
| Alltan Dubh 1 | Gladys Jeyes, Northamptonshire | 204 |
| Alltan Dubh 2 | David Jeyes, Northamptonshire | 232 |
| Lonielist | Michael Thompson, Colchester | 729 |
| Caol | B. & M. Booth's Grandchildren's Settlement | 422 |
| Maol Donn | Saul A.S. Djanogly, London | 904 |
| Sleach | Clifford P. Lockyer, Coventry | 368 |
| Catanach | Wynford Dore, Solihull | 519 |
| Lochdhu etc. | Fountain International | 4709 |
| **Total** | | **8937** |

## BROUBSTER & CLAISE BRICE (Caithness)

| | | |
|---|---|---|
| Claise Brice | Michael T. Murray | 326 |
| Saroch | John L. Rowlands, Surrey | 489 |
| Torigil | Shelagh Hunting, Slough | 531 |
| Luachair IV | Kim Lewison, London | 89 |
| Luachair II & III | Jeremy D. Spofforth, London | 235 |
| Lon Breac I | Michael T. Wogan | 109 |
| Lon Breac II | Jo Gurnett Personal Management Ltd. | 539 |
| Luachair I | Paul Bliss and Michale Chrysostomon, Gloucs. | 116 |
| Achaveilan South | Keith Londrop, Watford | 277 |
| Thormaid | David A. Broad, Huntingdon | 665 |
| Achaveilan North | David Roberts, Hertfordshire | 282 |
| Achvarasdal | Forell Forestry Ltd. | 630 |
| Griffin Wood | Peter Jennings, Berkshire | 89 |
| **Total** | | **4377** |

## TULLOCH LET WOODLANDS (Inverness)

Eastaff Estates Ltd.
Bent Also
A.M.G. Pearse
D.B. Knox, London
Mary Tarr
S.L. Tanner, London
C.R.T. Edwards, Ross on Wye
Undalica Investments, Jersey
M.E. Beaumont, London
Mr & Mrs G.F. Bach, Norway

## STRATHY (Sutherland)

| | | |
|---|---|---|
| Strathy East & Strathy Bog | Fountain Forestry Ltd. | 2364 |
| Strathy East | Fountain International Ltd. | 1987 |
| Strathy Wood | Chester J. Kelly, Bristol | 1562 |
| Coille a Chaileach | Brian Lewis, Essex | 596 |
| Coille a Saobhaidhe | Charlotte Forestry | 796 |
| Coille Buidhe | Raymond H. Green, London | 751 |

| | | |
|---|---|---:|
| Coillenan Clach I | Clifford J. Ellis, Tyne & Wear | 306 |
| Coillenan Clach II | Dr Ramesh Manchanda, London | 147 |
| Coille am Sealbach | Shirley Porter, London | 852 |
| Coille Meadhonach | Alasdair C. Fraser, London | 317 |
| Coille an Reidhe | Michael Snell, London | 641 |
| Coille Fhada | Michael R. Cousins, Kent | 421 |
| Bad Coille | Douglas C.A. Bramall | 456 |
| Dalangwell | Jack & Avril Paterson, Edinburgh | 24 |
| Coille a Badach | Derek C. & Beryl Frost, Farnham | 1157 |
| Dubh Chlais | Anthony C. Lowrie, London | 223 |
| **Total** | | **12,600** |

CLAIS MOR (Sutherland)

| | | |
|---|---|---:|
| Brochain | Dr Allan G. Wolstenholme, Sussex | 362 |
| Dhonnadh | Elizabeth Brocklebank, Norfolk | 390 |
| Carn Mor & Tutim | Eardley K. Bourne, Surrey | 968 |
| Thurnaig | Barry E. Austen, Ramsgate | 100 |
| Oisean | Ian Crawford, Ilkley | 121 |
| Buillsgean | John Laxton, Ilkley | 108 |
| Brae | Clifford Minney, Surrey | 373 |
| Innis Beithe | Timothy D. & Judie C.R. Barry | 257 |
| Carn Bheag | Christopher J.N. & Rowlena Weston, Ramsgate | 104 |
| Rosail | Christine Paganelli, Camberley | 370 |
| The Park | Jonathan A. Hampton, Strathoykel | 150 |
| **Total** | | **3303** |

# Appendix 3

## Directors of Companies

This Appendix lists the directors of some of the companies which own land in Scotland and which appear in the County Tables. It is derived from records held by Companies House. Not all landowning companies are listed here since this would have been prohibitively expensive. The companies that are listed are mainly those about whose directors I had little or no information. Even with a list of directors, however, it may still be virtually impossible to determine who exactly is the beneficial owner of a parcel of land. For those wishing to retain anonymity, it is quite simple to set up a company and nominate solicitors as directors who then act on behalf of the beneficial owner.

Companies are listed in alphabetical order. The property and county together with the acreage is indicated in brackets.

### ALINE ESTATE LTD
(*Aline, Ross & Cromarty 6000 acres*)
Christopher T.G. Fish, Guernsey
Christopher R.S. Sheppard, Aline Estate, Lewis
Iain M.C. Maiklejohn, Edinburgh
Shepherd & Wedderburn, Edinburgh
James R. Will, Gifford, E. Lothian

### AUCHINEDEN LTD
(*Auchineden, Stirling 3000 acres*)
Hendry Miller, Perth
Hans H. Jorgensen, Kibek, Denmark
Jens K. Rasmussen, Kolding, Denmark
Ledingham Chalmers, Aberdeen
Durano Ltd., Aberdeen

### BARVAS ESTATE LTD
(*Barvas, Ross & Cromarty 34,600 acres*)
Robert M. Clerk, Edinburgh
Althea B. Armitage, Rushton, Cheshire
Peter J. Armitage, Rushton, Cheshire
Peter W. Trevor, Preston
George P. Gray, Lancashire
Colin D.R. Whittle, Forres
Richard G.C. Duckworth

### BLACKFORD FARMS LTD
(*Blackford, Perth 20,000 acres*)
Geoffrey W.M. Waverley, Haywards Heath, West Sussex
Maher Mahdi Al Tajir, PO Box 1800, Dubai, United Arab Emirates
Mohammed Sadiq Al Tajir, PO Box 1800, Dubai, United Arab Emirates
Ian D. John, Camberley, Surrey
Kenneth E. Aspinall, Surbiton, Surrey
Sydney Boag, Oxford

### CADOGAN ESTATES (AGRICULTURAL HOLDINGS) LTD
(*Glenquaich, Perth 6200 acres*)
Jack L. Treves, Bishops Stortford, Hertfordshire
Charles G.J. Cadogan, Wantage, Oxon
Stuart A. Corbyn, London
Simon D.H.L. Staughton, Chesham, Buckinghamshire

### CARLOWAY ESTATES LTD
(*Carloway, Ross & Cromarty 11,400 acres*)
Simon Fraser, Stornoway
Catherine Aldred, Stornoway
Anne Galloway, Stornoway

### COIGNAFEARN ESTATE COMPANY LTD
(*Coignafearn, Inverness 38,000 acres*)
South Forrest, Macintosh & Merchant, Solicitors, Inverness

Eric T. Allan, Inverness
Bruce A. Merchant, Inverness

### DELNABO ESTATE LTD
(*Delnabo, Banff 2200 acres*)
Vera I. Yeowart, Lewes, E. Sussex
Brian A. Yeowart, Lewes, E. Sussex
Brodies WS, Solicitors, Edinburgh
Alistair C. Campbell, Edinburgh
David W.A. Guild, Edinburgh

### ENGA LTD
(*Hareshawhead, Lanark 1200 acres*)
Reynolds P. Chamberlain, London
Bjorn A. Askert, Berkhamsted, Hertfordshire
Gustav A.C. Koskull, Alvesta, Sweden
Anders J.M. Koskull, Alvesta, Sweden

### FACCOMBE ESTATES LTD
(*Tollishill & The Hope, Berwick and East Lothian, 8233 acres*)
Katherine I.M.I. Nicolson, London
David F. Harbottle, Andover
Rosemary L.H. Raynsford, London

### FROGMORE INVESTMENTS LTD
(*Glenkindie, Aberdeen 7300 acres*)
Trevor M. Birchmore, Welwyn, Hertfordshire
Dennis J. Cope, Bayford, Hertfordshire
Phillip G. Davies, London
Barry G. Kitcherside, Oxted, Surrey
Gerald A. Malton, Chelmford, Essex

### GAICK ESTATES LTD
(*Gaick, Inverness 18500 acres*)
George P. Christie, Kingussie
Vital Hanser, Zurich, Switzerland
Domingo Bezzola, Zollikon, Switzerland

### GALSON ESTATE LTD
(*Galson Lodge, Ross & Cromarty 56,300 acres*)
Alasdair Macrae, Stornoway
Anne Graham, Upper Bayble, Lewis
Jean Macmillan, Stornoway

### GOLDEN LANE SECURITIES LTD
(*Glenfiddich & Cabrach, Banff 41,500 acres*)
Michael E. Cutting, London
Christopher J. Moran, London
Anthony A. Ehrenzweig, London

### INVERMEARAN ESTATES LTD
(*Invermearan, Perth 16,500 acres*)
Henderson Boyd Jackson WS, Edinburgh
Helmut Hoss, Birstein, Germany
Gisela Hoss-Estenfeld, Birstein, Germany

### KEIR & CAWDOR ESTATES LTD
(*Keir & Leny, Perth 3000 acres*)
Shirley M. Mackie, Doune
Douglas W. Armstrong, Bridge of Allan
David M. Dixon, London
Archibald H. Stirling, Stirling
Daniel F. Church, Glasgow
Richard J.B. Blacke, Guildford, Surrey
Archibald D. Stirling, London

### LEWIS ISLAND CROFTERS LTD
(*Dalmore, Ross & Cromarty 11,600 acres*)
Simon Fraser, Stornoway
Andrew I. Bremner, Stevenage, Hertfordshire
Geoffrey S. Ironside, Maidenhead, Berkshire

### LURGA LTD
(*Laudale, Argyll 12,500 acres*)
John R.H. Dixon, Tarbert, Argyll
Leif Skov, Farnham, Surrey
Oswalds of Edinburgh Ltd., Edinburgh
Jordans (Scotland) Ltd., Edinburgh

### LUSS ESTATES COMPANY
(*Luss, Dunbarton 50,000 acres*)
W. & J. Burness, Glasgow
Frances M. Colquhoun
Ivar Colquhoun of Luss Bt., DL, JP
Kathleen N. Colquhoun of Luss, Luss
Robin W.A. Parr, Dundrennan, Kirkcudbrightshire
Michael I. Wigan, Kinbrace, Sutherland
Donald McGrigor, Glasgow

**MILLDEN ESTATES LTD**
(*Millden, Angus 18,700 acres*)
Mark W. Pollard, London
Malcolm J.S. Charleton, Harpenden
Richard J. Golland, Herefordshire
Swift Incorporations Ltd., Bristol
David J.M. Wilson, St Albans

**NEVIS ESTATES LTD**
(*Nevis Estates, Inverness 12,000 acres*)
David M. Rose, London
Cameron Mackintosh, London
Martin McCallum, London
Debbie Moore, London
Kevin T. Brown, London

**PB FORESTRY LANDS LTD**
(*Various properties, Roxburgh and Selkirk 10,257 acres*)
Donald Dooley, Harpenden, Hertfordshire
Michael S. Macgregor, Chislehurst, Kent
Alan & Ian Pangdale-Brown, Beccles, Suffolk

**SHOP & STORE INVESTMENTS LTD**
(*Invercassley, Sutherland 17,000 acres*)
Zdzislaw M. Gruszczynski, Keighley
David B. Greenwood, North Yorkshire
Enid D. Greenwood, West Yorkshire
Geoffrey B. Greenwood, Ilkley, West Yorkshire
Patricia M. Urry, Cranleigh, Surrey
Stewart W. Urry, Craneigh, Surrey
David J. Parker

**SIDEBELL LTD**
(*Fordie, Perth 5307 acres*)
Charles Smith, Esher, Surrey
Emily W. Richards, Wokingham, Berkshire
Michael A. Richards, London
Simon A. Richards, Oxon
Timothy J. Richards, London
Kate E. Taplin, Reading

**SOUTH UIST ESTATES LTD**
(*South Uist, Inverness 92,000 acres*)
Timothy P. Atkinson, Akernish, South Uist

David K.L.R. Keene, Oxford
John S. Burrell, North Berwick
Charles A. Ponsonby, London
Rupert S. Ponsonby, London
Jennifer C. Ponsonby, London
Patrick Smiley, London
Jocelyn F. Walker, London and Edinburgh
Susan M. Wood, Northumberland
Alastair Paterson, Askernish
John A. Simons, Askernish
Peter Voy, Askernish
David C. Greig, Lockerbie
David R. Keene
Rupert O. Steel, Newbury

**TINSLEY (BRANSTON) FARMS LTD**
(*Corrybrough, Inverness 7400 acres*)
Nicholas M. Moor, Lincoln
Jonathan M. Tinsley, Lincoln
Judith E. Tinsley, Lincoln
David J. Hovin, Lincoln
Charles B. Nelstrop, Lincoln

**TORRISH ESTATES CO. LTD**
(*Torrish, Sutherland 13,100 acres*)
Colm M. McCorquodale, London
Alastair McCorquodale, Grantham, Lincolnshire
Ian H. McCorquodale, London
Neil E. McCorquodale, Grantham, Lincolnshire

**TRESSADY ESTATES LTD**
(*Tressady, Sutherland 18,000 acres*)
George G.P. Mason, Golspie
Daniel de Bergeyck, Antwerp, Belgium
Alistair C. St Clair Sutherland (Lord Strathnaver)

**TULCHAN OF GLENISLA FOREST LTD**
(*Tulchan, Angus 12,500 acres*)
Thorntons WS, Solicitors, Dundee
Gunther M.J. Kuhnle, Tulchan of Glenisla
Renate H.M. Kuhnle, Tulchan of Glenisla
Ivan J.G. Carnegie, Dundee

# Appendix 4

## SOAEFD LANDHOLDINGS

This Appendix lists all the landholdings owned by the Secretary of State for Scotland and administered by the Scottish Office Agriculture, Environment and Fisheries Department.

| County | Property | Acres | Total for County |
|---|---|---|---|
| ABERDEEN | Various properties | 33 | 33 |
| ANGUS | Mylnefield & Bullionfield | 242 | |
| | Gourdie Farm | 187 | 429 |
| ARGYLL | Kinkchlaich | 3706 | |
| | Sunart | 3430 | |
| | Other properties | 899 | |
| | Younger Botanic Garden | 109 | 8144 |
| CAITHNESS | Dunn & Scarmclate | 1174 | |
| | Forss | 1320 | |
| | Other properties | 1433 | 3927 |
| DUMFRIES | Crichton Royal Farm | 576 | 576 |
| INVERNESS | Kilmuir | 47,186 | |
| | Bracadale | 42,640 | |
| | Harris | 16311 | |
| | North Uist | 16195 | |
| | Raasay | 14137 | |
| | Kingsburgh | 13158 | |
| | Scorrybreck | 9884 | |
| | Barra & Vatersay | 9459 | |
| | Kilbride | 8527 | |
| | Scallasaig | 4902 | |
| | Claigan | 3086 | |
| | Benbecula | 2580 | |
| | Beolary | 2402 | |
| | Other properties | 242 | 190,709 |
| KINCARDINE | Glensaugh | 3952 | 3952 |
| LANARK | Hartwood Farm | 883 | 883 |
| MIDLOTHIAN | Firth Mains | 300 | |
| | Woodhouselee Farm | 118 | |
| | Royal Botanic Garden | 78 | 496 |
| ORKNEY | Stove | 415 | 415 |
| PEEBLES | Dawyck Botanic Garden | 62 | 62 |

| | | | |
|---|---|---|---|
| PERTH | Kirkton Farm | 5782 | 5782 |
| ROSS & CROMARTY | Various properties | 1196 | 1196 |
| SHETLAND | Westafirth, Ordale & others | 5340 | 5340 |
| SUTHERLAND | Keoldale | 27,260 | |
| | Syre | 11,703 | |
| | Armadale | 11,638 | |
| | Borgie (leased to FC) | 7668 | 58,269 |
| WIGTOWN | Logan Botanic Garden | 25 | 25 |
| SCOTLAND WIDE | Various properties | 1117 | 1117 |
| TOTAL | | 281,355 | 281,355 |

# Appendix 5

## SNH LANDHOLDINGS

This appendix lists all the landholdings owned by Scottish Natural Heritage.

| County | Property | Acres | Total for County |
|---|---|---|---|
| ABERDEEN | Glen Tanar | 450 | 450 |
| ANGUS | Caenlochan | 395 | 395 |
| ARGYLL | Ben Lui | 2380 | |
| | Glencripesdale | 1505 | |
| | Claish Moss | 1391 | |
| | Moine Mhor | 1218 | |
| | Taynish | 872 | |
| | Mealdarroch | 506 | |
| | Glasdrum Wood | 418 | 8290 |
| CAITHNESS | Dunnet Links | 894 | 894 |
| FIFE | Tentsmuir Point | 299 | 299 |
| INVERNESS | Rum | 26,400 | |
| | Creag Meagaidh | 9756 | |
| | Invereshie | 7618 | |
| | Glen Roy | 2886 | |
| | Loch Druidibeg | 2577 | |
| | Abernethy | 657 | 49,894 |
| KIRKCUDBRIGHT | Cairnsmore of Fleet | 3247 | 3247 |
| PERTH | Rannoch Moor | 3704 | 3704 |
| ROSS & CROMARTY | Beinn Eighe | 10,297 | |
| | Ben Wyvis | 5780 | 16,077 |
| SCOTLAND WIDE | Various properties | 1238 | 1238 |
| TOTAL | | 84,488 | 84,488 |

# Appendix 6

## MoD LANDHOLDINGS

This Appendix lists all the landholdings owned by the Secretary of State for Defence and administered by the Ministry of Defence.

| County | Property | Acres | Total for County |
|---|---|---|---|
| ABERDEEN | Crimond | 484 | 484 |
| ANGUS | Barry Buddon | 2909 | |
| | RM Condor | 508 | 3417 |
| ARGYLL | Machrihanish | 987 | 987 |
| AYR | Beith | 1186 | 1186 |
| DUMFRIES | Eastriggs | 2431 | 2431 |
| DUNBARTON | Garelochhead | 8248 | |
| | Coulport | 1798 | |
| | Glen Douglas | 570 | |
| | Faslane | 255 | 10,871 |
| FIFE | Rosyth | 1256 | |
| | Leuchars | 968 | |
| | Crombie | 759 | 2983 |
| INVERNESS | RA Ranges Hebrides | 2219 | |
| | Fort George | 897 | 3116 |
| KINCARDINE | Edzell | 486 | 486 |
| KIRKCUDBRIGHT | Dundrennan | 4716 | 4716 |
| MIDLOTHIAN | Castlelaw Ranges | 1907 | |
| | Kirknewton | 269 | 2176 |
| MORAY | Kinloss | 1753 | |
| | Lossiemouth | 1327 | |
| | Milltown | 490 | 3570 |
| ROSS & CROMARTY | Tain | 2579 | |
| | Melbost | 806 | 3385 |
| SUTHERLAND | An Garbh-Eilean | 2700 | 2700 |
| WIGTOWN | West Freugh | 4569 | 4569 |
| SCOTLAND WIDE | Various properties | 3352 | 3352 |
| TOTAL | | 50,429 | 50,429 |